Henry George and the
Crisis of Inequality

Columbia History of Urban Life

The Columbia History of Urban Life
Kenneth T. Jackson, General Editor

Henry George and the Crisis of Inequality

Progress and Poverty in the Gilded Age

Edward T. O'Donnell

Columbia University Press   New York

Columbia University Press
Publishers Since 1893
New York   Chichester, West Sussex
cup.columbia.edu

Portions of chapter 4 have been reprinted from Edward T. O'Donnell's "Soggarth Aroon: The Rise and Fall of Rev. Edward McGlynn" in *Catholics in New York: Society, Culture, and Politics, 1808–1946,* ed. Terry Golway, 147–61 © 2008. Used by permission of Fordham Univerity Press.

Portions of chapter 6 have been reprinted and adapted from Edward T. O'Donnell's "Striking Scenes: Robert Koehler, *The Strike* (1886), and Competing Visions of Labor-Capital Conflict in the Gilded Age" in *Common-Place* 11, no. 1 (October 2010), http://www.common -place.org/vol-11/no-01/lessons. Used by permission of the publisher.

Library of Congress Cataloging-in-Publication Data

O'Donnell, Edward T., 1963–
   Henry George and the crisis of inequality : progress and poverty in the gilded age / Edward T. O'Donnell.
      pages cm. — (Columbia history of urban life)
   Includes bibliographical references and index.
   ISBN 978-0-231-12000-5 (cloth : alk. paper) — ISBN 978-0-231-53926-5 (e-book)
   1. George, Henry, 1839–1897. 2. Equality—New York (State)—New York. 3. Poverty—New York (State)—New York. 4. Labor movement—New York (State)—New York. 5. New York (N.Y.)—Social conditions—19th century.   I. Title

HM821.0664   2015
330.092—dc23   2014040179

Cover design by Diane Luger

References to websites (URLs) were accurate at the time of writing. Neither the author nor Columbia University Press is responsible for URLs that may have expired or changed since the manuscript was prepared.

For Stephanie
for believing

Everywhere is it evident that the tendency to inequality . . . cannot go much further without carrying our civilization into that downward path which is so easy to enter and so hard to abandon. . . . Though knowledge yet increases and invention marches on . . . and cities still expand, . . . civilization has begun to wane when, in proportion to population, we must build more and more prisons, more and more almshouses, more and more insane asylums.

—Henry George, *Progress and Poverty*, 1879

It came to the weary and heavy laden as the talisman of a lost hope. All their lives long they had been taught that poverty was a "dispensation of Providence" needful to keep them humble and teach them patience, but if cheerfully borne, it would somehow contribute to their happiness in the dim beyond. *Progress and Poverty* reversed all this, teaching that poverty is an artificial condition of man's invention. . . . Workingmen and women, learning all this, . . . commenced to wrestle with their chains.

—Labor activist C. P. Atkinson, on the impact of Henry George and *Progress and Poverty* on American workers, 1886

Contents

PART III. The Great Upheaval, 1886–1887

Acknowledgments

You know it has taken you a *really* long time to finish a book when your oldest daughter, who once used to refer to it as "your book about Curious George," is now twenty-four years old. I will not revisit here the many things that emerged over the years to prevent me from completing this book. Instead, I will use this space to express my heartfelt gratitude to all the people who played a role in the process, some by providing helpful criticism on the manuscript and others for urging me on as I worked to complete it.

I will begin by thanking the extraordinary scholars Elizabeth Blackmar, Alan Brinkley, Richard Bushman, David Cannadine, Daniel Czitrom, Barbara J. Fields, Eric Foner, Joshua Freeman, John A. Garraty, Kenneth T. Jackson, Ira Katznelson, Thomas Kessner, Eric McKitrick, Kerby Miller, James P. Shenton, and Alden Vaughn, all of whom played such an important role my development as a historian and in the shaping of this book. I also need to thank the many historian friends I have made over the years. Walter Friedman, David Gerwin, Terry Golway, Mike Green, Seth Kamil, Kevin Kenny, Peter Maguire, Andy Meyers, Yanek Mieczkowski, Phil Napoli, Max Page, Adam Rothman, Michael Sappol, Jeffrey Sklansky, Vernon Takeshita, Thorin Tritter, Eric Wakin, Michael West, Andrew Wiese, and Craig Wilder provided both friendship and scholarly insight into my work on Henry George. I am likewise indebted to my many fine colleagues at the College of the Holy Cross, especially Stephanie E. Yuhl, for their friendship, support, and inspiration.

Every historian depends on the brilliant and generous people who staff the archives and libraries where we work. I could not have completed this book were it not for the assistance of the great people at the Butler Library at Columbia University, Dinand Library at the College of the Holy Cross (especially Laura Hibbler), the New York History Society, the Museum of the City of New York, and the New York Public Library (especially Warren Platt). Thanks are also due independent researcher April White, who helped me track down genealogical and biographical information on Henry George's parents and grandparents. I am also indebted to the Robert Schalkenbach Foundation for awarding me a grant to help me finish the book.

I am likewise indebted to my editors at Columbia University Press, notably Kate Wittenberg, who originally signed the book, and Philip Leventhal, who in the last three years guided it to publication. I also greatly appreciate the insightful and helpful critiques the anonymous readers secured by the press provided for this book.

Special thanks also goes to the wonderful staff at the Nu Café in Worcester, Massachusetts, for feeding and caffeinating me for hundreds of hours over the past few years as I worked on this book.

I am so grateful for my many enduring friendships with people from my hometown of Gloucester, Massachusetts, as well as those at the College of the Holy Cross, New York City, and more recently Worcester and Holden, Massachusetts. You all have enriched my life in so many ways. The same goes for my six siblings and their spouses, in addition to my wonderful in-laws. And a very special thank you to my four amazing daughters Erin, Kelly, Michelle, and Katherine—they always keep me focused on what really matters in life.

Finally, my deepest gratitude goes, of course, to my wife Stephanie Yeager O'Donnell. We were married just before I began graduate school and through all the ups and downs of life (including many overdrawn checking accounts) in the years that followed she has remained my best friend and staunch supporter, not to mention the wonderful mother of our daughters. Henry George was similarly blessed in marriage. His wife Annie once wrote to him on their anniversary that they had experienced "years of care, trouble, and sorrow, but also hope and love. We can look back and say we have indeed been one, sharing each other's troubles and joys. But few husbands and wives are as nearly one as we." I could not say it any better.

Abbreviations

CLU	Central Labor Union of New York
HGP	Henry George Papers (New York Public Library)
HGSB	Henry George Scrap Books (New York Public Library)
JSP	*John Swinton's Paper*
NYSBLS	New York State Bureau of Labor Statistics
RCSRLC	*Report of the Committee of the Senate upon the Relations Between Labor and Capital*
ULP	United Labor Party

Introduction

More than a million people gathered in New York City on October 28, 1886, to witness the unveiling of the completed Statue of Liberty. Among those present were President Grover Cleveland, various members of Congress, representatives of the French government, and other foreign dignitaries. The theme of this grand civic occasion, as well as of the many speeches and editorials that marked it, was the celebration of *progress* and the health and vitality of the American republic. "We will not forget," proclaimed the president, "that Liberty has here made her home." The editors of the *New York Times* concurred, gushing, "On our shores . . . has been realized . . . with all its imperfections, the most successful and hopeful of all the social systems that have grown up in the history of mankind." Chauncey Depew, a railroad magnate and a powerful figure among the city's elite, seized upon the occasion to deliver his own speech lauding democracy and self-government as the best remedy for the social unrest then rocking the nation. "The problems of labor and capital . . . of property and poverty will work themselves out," he declared, "under the benign influence of enlightened law-making and law-abiding liberty, without the aid of kings and armies, or of anarchists and bombs."[1]

Two days later, in that same great city, a very different set of citizens organized a very different event, the central message of which challenged the
rosy assessments of the few days past. On the evening of Saturday, October
30, 1886, thousands of spectators lined the sidewalks of lower Manhattan to
witness one of the more extraordinary events in the city's history—a "Monster Parade" of some thirty thousand workers of virtually every rank, trade,
and ethnicity marching in support of an insurgent political campaign. Outraged by an unprecedented campaign of repression by business and civic
leaders against organized labor that spring and summer, workers had formed
the United Labor Party (ULP) and selected the reformer Henry George as
their candidate for mayor. The motivation behind both the campaign and
parade was the conviction that the American republic was actually in crisis,
its sacred principles of liberty and equality in jeopardy. Expressing this sentiment, the ULP's announcement of the parade described workers as being
"unjustly deprived of the blessings which should be secured by [republican]
society . . . because avaricious men have possessed themselves by means of
unrepublican laws of the free gifts of nature." This parade, and the larger
political campaign, represented an effort to secure, "equal rights, social
reform, true Republicanism, and universal Democracy." Days later, Henry
George would stun the city and the nation by garnering more than 68,000
votes and finishing second in a three-man contest.[2]

These two starkly contrasting events, separated only by a few days, illu-
minate the dramatically dualistic character of the Gilded Age, a period
defined roughly between the years 1865 and 1900. As the name suggests,
many at the time considered it a *golden age*, one marked by spectacular
advances in industrial output and technological innovation that transformed the United States from a predominantly agricultural nation ranking
well behind England, Germany, and France to the world's most formidable
industrial power by 1900. Americans celebrated one astonishing achievement after another, from the completion of the transcontinental railroad
(1869) to the opening of the Brooklyn Bridge (1883), from the laying of the
Atlantic Cable connecting London and New York by telegraph (1866) to
the unveiling of the Statue of Liberty (1886). Nowhere was this ebullient
spirit more evident than at the World's Fairs held in Philadelphia (1876)
and Chicago (1893), massive events that afforded superb opportunities to

showcase the wonders of American technological genius. On these occasions and seemingly at any opportunity, Americans invoked the optimistic themes of ingenuity, progress, expansion, growth, and success. "Our growth has not been limited to territory, population and aggregate wealth, marvelous as it has been in each of those directions," posited President Benjamin Harrison in a typical address in 1889. "The masses of our people are better fed, clothed, and housed than their fathers were. . . . No other people have a government more worthy of their respect and love or a land so magnificent in extent . . . and so full of generous suggestion to enterprise and labor."[3]

And yet for many other Americans there was abundant evidence that there was more to this upbeat vision of national development than met the eye. Put another way, the name of the era—the Gilded Age—also suggested a disturbing *superficiality* to all this evidence of progress. As with a gilded piece of jewelry, it suggested that one need only to scratch the surface of the thin gold layer to find the baser metal that lay beneath. When Americans peeked beneath the surface of progress, they saw the darker consequences of industrialization, especially the immense power accrued by large corporations and the men who ran them, the growing number of workers living in squalid slums, and the frequent episodes of labor-capital violence (the years 1880–1900 alone witnessed nearly 37,000 strikes). If these were the trends of the future, warned an aging Walt Whitman in 1879, then "our republican experiment, notwithstanding all its surface successes, is at heart an unhealthy failure."[4]

Conservative middle- and upper-class Americans interpreted this increase in social turmoil and poverty in cultural rather than economic terms. Praising and embracing laissez-faire individualism and its offshoot, social Darwinism, as never before, they determined that the greatest threat to the American republic was not the widening gap between the rich and the poor, but rather the possibility that the poor would mobilize *collectively* against their betters, via either the ballot or the bullet, and take what did not belong to them. Accordingly, they demonized the poor as unfit, grasping losers and took steps to sharply curtail charity and other social assistance, which they deemed dangerous to the morals and manners of the needy. This spirit of social Darwinist hostility toward the poor was most famously captured in a widely reprinted sermon by

Rev. Henry Ward Beecher, the nation's most renowned preacher. Dismissing the claims of workers that they could not live on wages as low as a dollar a day, he asserted that too many workingmen "insist on smoking and drinking beer." A frugal workingman could support his family on a simple diet of bread and water, argued Beecher, and "the man who cannot live on bread and water is not fit to live."[5]

Central to these middle- and upper-class dismissals of the plight and protests of workers was the conviction that these agitators had become infected with one or more of the varieties of European radicalism, such as socialism, communism, or anarchism. The United States, they insisted, was a classless society. "We have among us a pernicious communistic spirit," wrote Allan Pinkerton, head of the infamous Pinkerton Detective Agency in the wake of the great 1877 railroad strike, "which is demoralizing workmen, continually creating a deeper and more intense antagonism between labor and capital. . . . It must be crushed out completely, or we shall be compelled to submit to greater excesses and more overwhelming disasters in the near future."[6]

Workers and farmers, however, offered a very different interpretation of the problems besetting the nation. In 1878, for example, the Knights of Labor adopted a constitution, the preamble of which denounced the "recent alarming development and aggression of aggregated wealth" that if left unchecked "will inevitably lead to the pauperization and hopeless degradation of the toiling masses." One of the most pointed and widely read analyses of the Gilded Age's social turmoil was *Progress and Poverty*, published in 1879 by Henry George, the man nominated by the ULP as labor's candidate for mayor of New York in 1886. The book's title itself perfectly captured the vexing duality emerging in late nineteenth-century America: the great progress for some and the increased poverty for many brought about by rapid industrialization. "It is as though an immense wedge were being forced, not underneath society, but through society," wrote George. "Those who are above the point of separation are elevated, but those who are below are crushed down." George warned that the very fate of the republic was at stake. "This association of *poverty with progress*," he asserted, "is the great enigma of our times. . . . It is the riddle which the Sphinx of Fate puts to our civilization, and which not to answer is to be destroyed."[7]

The year 1886, the year which would be long known as the Great Upheaval, marked the highpoint of labor radicalism in nineteenth-century New York City and the nation. How did this remarkable mobilization by labor originate and how did Henry George come to assume so important a place in it? Labor's mobilization began nearly a decade earlier in the aftermath of the economically devastating 1870s. The legacy of the 1870s—depression, wage reductions, unemployment, evictions, devaluation of skills, alienation from employers, and government repression of strikes—forced workers to challenge the veracity of antebellum free labor mantras and embrace new modes of thinking and action. Critical to this development was the rise of a small but influential group of socialists and the Knights of Labor, which provided both organizational and ideological strength to workers.

In New York City, the capital of capitalism in the United States, labor activists faced an enormous challenge. The city's great size, dynamic economy, and diverse ethnic and cultural demography made for difficult conditions in which to encourage working-class solidarity and build a lasting labor movement. Nonetheless, following the depression years of the 1870s, New York City experienced a remarkable resurgence in working-class activism. Workers benefited not only from the energy and leadership provided by the Knights, but also from the creation of the Central Labor Union (1882), an umbrella labor organization dedicated to fostering solidarity among working men and women, organizing new unions, and coordinating strikes and boycotts. By mid-1886, after city and state officials responded to a wave of strikes and boycotts by arresting more than a hundred labor activists, the ranks of the CLU swelled to over two hundred member unions representing more than 150,000 workers from the New York metropolitan area. It was a combination of confidence stemming from four years of successful activism and fury over the recent crackdown that led these workers to launch a full-scale political challenge, one that would culminate in the formation of the ULP. Similar efforts to crush working-class activism across the country led labor activists in nearly two hundred towns and cities to field independent labor parties and candidates in 1886 and 1887.[8]

If these events explain in part the rise of working-class solidarity and mobilization in the 1880s and the Great Upheaval of 1886, how do we explain the rise of Henry George? Or, put another way, how did a middle-class English-American Protestant calling for land reform gain such a widespread following among landless urban wage-earners, especially among Irish Catholics? George's rise to prominence among American workers represents one of the most intriguing—and revealing—stories of late nineteenth-century labor history. He had been born in the Age of Jackson and reared on the principles of antebellum Christian perfectionism and free labor ideology. Yet, in adulthood, he experienced the hard times and frustrations of the hardscrabble 1860s and 1870s. These influences and experiences placed him in a unique position from which to observe and interpret the revolutionary changes in social, economic, and political relations brought on by advanced industrial development.

As a reform-minded California newspaper editor in the 1870s, George had become disturbed by the growing conflict between labor and capital and the increasing gap between the rich and the poor. The resulting book, *Progress and Poverty: An Inquiry into the Cause of Industrial Depressions and of Increase of Want with Increase of Wealth* (1879), went on to become one of the most widely read and compelling works of the latter half of the nineteenth century. Advocating radical land reform (via land-value taxation that came to be called "the single tax") as a means of eliminating the crushing mass poverty, restricted opportunity, and increased inequality that accompanied industrial progress, the book became immensely popular among the urban working class. George's work of radical republicanism hit the presses at precisely the moment that these Americans were struggling to refashion earlier forms of republicanism rendered increasingly hollow in the face of modern industrial capitalism. Written in an engaging, easily understood style and employing traditional American political idioms and concepts infused with new, radical meaning, *Progress and Poverty* provided American workers with an ideological framework with which to analyze their predicament and changing circumstances. It succeeded because it assured workingmen and workingwomen that a new and just republican order was possible, and that they were the key actors in the struggle to attain it.

Central to George's growing popularity and influence on Gilded Age thought was his decision to move from San Francisco to New York City in 1880. Not only did this change of venue allow him to promote the book on a bigger stage, it also brought him into contact with a wide range of radicals, ranging from Irish nationalists who sought to apply his land reform ideas to the situation of the Irish peasantry to socialists and progressive trade unionists. By the mid-1880s, *Progress and Poverty* had become the largest selling book on political economy in American history. In the words of one contemporary economist, "Tens of thousands of laborers read *Progress and Poverty* who have never before looked between the covers of an economics book, and its conclusions are widely accepted articles in the workingmen's creed."[9]

So when New York City workers formed the ULP in the summer of 1886, they chose George as their nominee. George came to lead one of the most energetic and democratic campaigns in the city's history. The ULP lacked the money, experience, and access to institutional power enjoyed by the well-established Republican and Democratic parties, but it nonetheless managed to garner a groundswell of popular support for their candidate, as evidenced by the tens of thousands of workers and spectators who braved the drenching rain on the eve of the election to be part of the Monster Parade.

Three days after the parade, George and the ULP stunned contemporaries by garnering an impressive 68,110 votes (31 percent), finishing second to Democrat Abram Hewitt (41 percent) and ahead of the third-place finisher, Republican Theodore Roosevelt (28 percent). Labor activists believed the results pointed to a dramatic resurgence of working-class political power, one destined to upend the status quo and pave the way for a national labor party. "It was an unprecedented uprising of the working classes which shook this city," declared John Swinton, the influential editor of a weekly labor newspaper. "It was a revolt that signifies the opening of a new political era." Observing events across the Atlantic from London, Frederick Engels concurred: "The Henry George boom . . . was an epoch-making day. . . . The first great step of importance for every country newly entering into the movement is always the constitution of the workers as an independent political party, no matter how, so long as it is a distinct workers' party. And this step has been taken, much more rapidly than we had a right to expect."[10]

However, these optimistic hopes were soon dashed as the ULP collapsed just one year later, riven by ideological factionalism (much of it stoked by George himself). Nationally, the rising tide of worker mobilization foundered in the face of internal dissent, government repression, a more unified front by business interests, and the successful co-optation of selected labor agenda items by the major political parties.

But the story of Henry George and the Great Upheaval did not end in 1886 and 1887. While George the man lost credibility among working-class Americans, his ideas lived on in public discourse. His advocacy of a radical break from the nation's liberal past by abolishing absolute private property rights and empowering the state to secure a just republican society was a significant contribution to the emergence of progressivism in American political culture.

Because the broad details of the life of Henry George are well known, I have chosen not to write yet another traditional biography of the man. As a result, this work combines biography, intellectual history, and social history to examine and make sense of his time and thought as a thinker and activist. It seeks to explain the origins and meanings of his influential writings on social reform, especially *Progress and Poverty*, while also examining how and why they gained such great traction among Gilded Age workers struggling to comprehend the revolutionary changes brought on by industrial capitalism. It is, therefore, what some have called a "social biography," a study concerned as much about the era as the man. As a result, there are times in the course of this book when Henry George is not the main focus. This characteristic reflects the fundamental belief that it is impossible to understand George without fully understanding the political culture into which he was born, to make sense of *Progress and Poverty* without addressing the social context which produced it, or to discover the impact of the author and the book without delving into the world of the workers who found them so compelling.

Like many historians, I always want my research and writing to have some relevance to the age in which I live. And yet it is with profoundly conflicted emotions that I acknowledge the sudden, terrible relevance that Henry George and Gilded Age America have taken on in the wake of the great financial meltdown of late 2008 and the subsequent deep economic recession. There were a good number of scholars, activists, and social critics in the decade prior to 2008 who warned Americans about rising corporate power, wealth inequality, and poverty and the threats they posed to the nation's republican values. Some even invoked the phrase "Second Gilded Age" to describe this current era in an attempt to conjure up images of an age of unrestrained robber baron industrialists and financiers, roiling social conflict, and a widening chasm between rich and poor.[11] But few people seemed to pay them any heed until after the collapse occurred and the ensuing debate over government aid to bailout banks and large corporations such as General Motors commenced. Since that moment, however, the phrases "Second Gilded Age" or "New Gilded Age" have become increasingly popular. Indeed, a rough search of the Lexis-Nexis database for the term "Gilded Age" shows 11 articles employing it in the 1970s, 76 in the 1980s, 184 in the 1990s, and 541 in the 2000s. And the trend shows no sign of abating; the period between the years 2010 and 2014 already has generated well over a thousand articles. Many books since 2008 now bear the phrase "Gilded Age" in their titles, such as Larry M. Bartels's *Unequal Democracy: The Political Economy of the New Gilded Age.*[12]

The sudden return of "Gilded Age" to common American parlance reflects a keen awareness of the eerie similarities between the United States of today and that of the last third of the nineteenth century. The nation then and now was consumed with intense debates over wealth inequality, labor unions, immigration, terrorism, women's rights, family values, money in politics, voter eligibility, Wall Street recklessness, political polarization and paralysis, religion vs. secularism, individualism vs. the common good, free market capitalism vs. regulation, and wars of choice vs. diplomacy. Taking a closer look at just one of these issues, we learn that in 1890 the top 1 percent of Americans owned 51 percent of all wealth, while the lower 44 percent of Americans owned just 1.2 percent.[13] Income taxes, inheritance taxes, and other measures adopted since the early twentieth century reduced the 1 percent's share significantly by 1979 to 20.5 percent. But the trend has shifted dramatically back toward increased wealth and income inequality after 1980. By 2010, the top 1 percent owned 35.4 percent of all wealth, a statistic that helps explain the successful popularization of the pejorative phrase "the 1 percent" by progressive protesters like the Occupy Wall Street movement.[14]

Little wonder then that many observers believe the United States has entered into a second Gilded Age. These are, of course, *similarities* to the

Gilded Age of the late nineteenth century, not identical trends and events. (It should be noted that Americans in the first Gilded Age did not worry about climate change or online privacy, just as Americans in the twenty-first century no longer worry about the Indian Wars or the annual ravages of typhoid fever.) Mark Twain, the man who coined the phrase "gilded age," reminds us that "history doesn't repeat itself, but it does rhyme." It is this rhyming that many Americans who possess a sense of history and political values to the left of center find so disturbing.

History does not offer a specific map, formula, or blueprint for dealing effectively with contemporary social, economic, and political challenges. But we study history in part because we believe it allows us to understand where we as a society have come from and why things—institutions, ideas, practices, customs, and power arrangements—are as they are. We believe these insights have the capacity to guide individuals and societies as they make the choices that will shape the future. "Trying to plan for the future without knowing the past," Daniel Boorstin once quipped, "is like trying to plant cut flowers."[15] In the late nineteenth century, the United States faced a host of vexing challenges regarding policies related to economic opportunity, democracy, citizenship, freedom, and human rights. Ultimately political leaders—prodded by labor unions, farmers' alliances, muckrakers, goo-goos, and visionaries like Henry George—chose to adopt policies that ameliorated many of them, preserving and in many cases expanding the promise of a republic of liberty founded "of the people, by the people, for the people." The United States in the early twenty-first century also faces a great many problems that remind us of that past Gilded Age. What choices the American people and their political leaders make in the coming years will, as they did in the late nineteenth and early twentieth centuries, have a profound impact on the future vitality of their nation and its cherished values.

Henry George and the
Crisis of Inequality

PART I

The Making of a Radical,
1839–1879

This association of poverty with progress, is the great enigma
of our times. . . . It is the riddle which the Sphinx of Fate puts
to our civilization, and which not to answer is to be destroyed.
—Henry George, *Progress and Poverty*

I

"To Be Something and Somebody in the World"

Thou Henry still art young,
And does not see the wonder Thou wilt tread . . .
—from a poem by George's girlfriend at age 16

BORN BETWEEN TWO REVOLUTIONS

Henry George was born in Philadelphia on September 2, 1839. His mother, Catherine Pratt Vallance, came from an old family from that city. His father, Richard Samuel Henry George, published religious books for the Episcopal Church.[1] Henry grew up in a tiny, two-story brick house on Tenth Street located, as George later recalled, "almost within the shadow of Independence Hall." The Georges eventually moved when the house became too small for their ten children.[2]

Philadelphia in the Age of Jackson was second only to New York City in terms of commerce and population. In the early decades of the nineteenth century, the city's economy grew at a phenomenal rate. As the very embodiment of "metropolitan industrialization," the city's hundreds of small workshops produced a huge variety of goods, the value per capita of which rose from $10.00 to $86.00 between 1820 and 1840 alone. Philadelphia's population jumped from 112,000 to 220,000 over the same period. By the late 1830s, when George was born, Philadelphia was a city both steeped in tradition and galvanized by the revolutionary potential of the nascent market economy. Put another way, George was born between two revolutions. In

1839, the republican ideals of the American Revolution remained salient, yet they were fast being transformed by the new demands and opportunities presented by the Industrial Revolution. This duality would shape George's worldview throughout his life.[3]

The very different experiences of George's father and maternal grandfather exemplify this world of rapid change and competing values in which George was raised. His maternal grandfather, John Vallance, came to Philadelphia from Scotland at the age of twenty-one in 1791. Like his American-born contemporaries, he had come of age in a pre-industrial order centered on the artisan. These highly skilled men engaged in scores of craft occupations, producing finished goods ranging from boots to bread to books. Even though signs of commercialism and individualism among some craftsmen had appeared in the eighteenth century, for the most part the economy and society was still dominated by time-honored traditions, obligations, and codes that constituted what E. P. Thompson termed the "moral economy."[4] Although we have no record of John Vallance's early life, it is clear that he received a traditional artisan's training in the "art and mystery" of engraving while a young man in Scotland, a process that embodied the core elements of this pre-modern order, following the traditional path from apprentice, to journeyman, to master craftsman, and, once settled in Philadelphia, to shop owner by the 1790s.[5]

The culture of early nineteenth-century artisans like Vallance celebrated the independent lifestyle and flexible work routine made possible by the possession of special skills rather than the headlong pursuit of wealth. In some trades, spontaneous holidays (such as St. Monday) and ubiquitous drinking were especially revered. Most artisans aspired to acquire a "competence," an income that allowed for modest material comfort, personal independence, social respectability, and an old age free of degrading want. The available evidence of John Vallance's career makes it clear that he achieved these goals.[6]

Like many of his generation, Henry George grew up with both an awareness of and sentimental feelings for this system in which his grandfather had flourished. As he remembered it in an 1883 essay:

> The workman may have toiled hard and long, but in his work he had companionship, variety, the pleasure that comes of the exercise of

creative skill, the sense of seeing things growing under his hand to finished form. He worked in his own home or side by side with his employer. Labor was lightened by emulation, by gossip, by laughter, by discussion. As apprentice, he looked forward to becoming a journeyman; as journeyman, he looked forward to becoming a master and taking an apprentice of his own. With a few tools and a little raw material, he was independent. He dealt directly with those who used the finished articles he produced.[7]

This culture found ideological expression in an artisanal republicanism that drew upon key elements of eighteenth-century classical republicanism to support a belief that craftsmen occupied a special place within the American republican polity. Craft morality, it was argued, positioned artisans as the truest practitioners of republican citizenship. They were, as one put it in an 1809 Fourth of July oration, "the sinews and muscles of our country . . . the very axis of society." When men of Vallance's era gathered on such occasions, they also touted their own status as *independent* producers, free from economic, social, or political coercion in everyday life. Likewise, when artisans spoke of *virtue*—the placing of the common good above private interests—they emphasized a similar sensibility that dominated the master–journeyman–apprentice relationship, namely that virtue restrained the unbridled pursuit of self-interest over the well-being of the trade. Artisans, in other words, were the most authentic republicans.[8]

Yet this centuries-old artisanal world in which John Vallance prospered rapidly disintegrated in the decades following 1815. Evidence of a tendency among some master craftsmen toward profit-seeking, competition, and individualism existed at least as far back as the mid-eighteenth century, but it was not until the resumption of commerce following the War of 1812 that the foundation of this social order of mutuality, tradition, and obligation began to give way. Even as they expressed rhetorical fidelity to their craft, some master craftsmen, enthused and enticed by a growing ethos of individualism and the pursuit of higher profits, began to alter the traditional forms and rules of craft production. These entrepreneurial masters took in more apprentices but taught them only a portion of the craft. They set journeymen to perform only some of the necessary tasks needed to produce a finished product. In both cases, they began to substitute market-rate cash payments for customary obligations like food, board, and education. Gradually, the casual rhythm of the workday was eliminated in favor of longer days regulated by a clock, fewer breaks, and no alcohol.

As they advanced these new values and practices, profit-minded master craftsmen, shopkeepers, professionals, financiers, merchants, and others engaged in the new commercial marketplace began to articulate what might be termed an entrepreneurial republicanism, an ideology that celebrated and sanctified the new capitalist order as thoroughly republican in nature while rejecting the criticisms of radical journeymen. Entrepreneurial republicanism championed absolute private property rights, freedom of contract, and individualism, and it utterly repudiated any suggestion that American society was divided into conflicting social classes. Accordingly, its adherents deemed those who branded competition, individualism, and innovation as incompatible with republican principles as jealous, lazy, dangerously un-American, or a combination of all three. As the *New York Journal of Commerce* argued in 1836, "All combinations to compel others to give a higher price or take a lower one, are not only inexpedient, but at war with the order of things which the Creator has established for the general good, and therefore wicked."[9]

By the late 1820s, these changes in practice and ideology signaled the passing of the traditional artisan's world of small-scale production, craft integrity, mutual obligations, and anticipated advancement before a new reality of segmented work, low wages, and fading hopes among journeymen of ever obtaining a competence.[10] Philadelphia's journeymen organized to resist this revolutionary transformation of their world, but their Workingmen's Party and General Trades Union efforts were no match for the emerging market economy.[11]

Henry George's maternal grandfather escaped the full impact of these changes; he died at the age of fifty-two a prosperous, though not rich, master engraver in 1823.[12] He thus represented a vanishing generation of men who grew up in the final phases of the artisan's pre-commercial world. Had he lived another twenty years, Vallance might have enthusiastically embraced the new logic and rules of the market economy—or been crushed by them. Instead, an early death in 1823 meant his life would stand as the classic fulfillment of the traditional artisanal aspiration—from immigrant, to apprentice, to journeyman, to independent master craftsman. By the time Henry George was born in 1839, many features of this tradition had all but disappeared. However, as shown in later chapters, certain ideological and cultural aspects of the bygone artisan's world would remain vibrant for many decades, wielding a powerful influence on George and many others of his generation.

In contrast to the experience of John Vallance, Henry George's father took a very different career path. The son of a successful Philadelphia sea captain, Richard George did not receive an artisan's apprenticeship. Rather, it appears from the available evidence that he entered the emerging commercial world as a clerk, itself a new form of apprenticeship for a future in capitalist enterprise. Just as Henry George's grandfather embodied the economic traditions of the late eighteenth century, his father's life symbolized the new era of entrepreneurship and individualism.[13]

As late as 1831, when he was thirty-two years old, Richard George worked as a clerk in the U.S. Customs House. Soon, however, he joined with a partner to open a shop that published religious books. Unlike the entrepreneurial master printers and binders that moved into manufactory production, Richard George was what Bruce Laurie has termed an "outsider," someone who entered a modernizing trade without having any formal training in the field.[14] George employed many skilled printers, compositors, and binders to handle the physical process making books, while he performed the functions of investor, manager, and marketer. The fact that his firm stayed in business during the severe depression of 1837–1844 suggests he performed these tasks well. Other evidence supports Richard George being an expectant capitalist. He was a devout evangelical, which, as studies of antebellum workers have shown, more often than not indicated an enthusiastic embrace of "Christian capitalism." His decision to specialize in religious books undoubtedly stemmed in part from a commitment of faith, but it also likely reflected an entrepreneur's awareness of a booming market for such works during the Second Great Awakening.[15]

Born in 1839, Henry George entered a social and economic order undergoing sweeping change. Though fading fast, the ideological legacy of the artisanal world of his grandfather would last well into his adult life and leave a lasting impression on his mind. At the same time, the entrepreneurial world of his father was, quite literally, gathering steam. Its promise of progress, both for individuals and society at large, as a reward for industriousness, perseverance, and risk taking would leave its mark on the worldview of Henry George, who would one day become famous as a radical seeking to save capitalism from itself by insisting upon the necessity of overturning one of its core principles—absolute private property in land.

"NEITHER POVERTY NOR RICHES"

George's concern with poverty did not stem from a penurious childhood; he was raised in modest lower middle-class comfort. His family took small summer vacations and enjoyed a home with all the furnishings and simple decorations of bourgeois respectability. "Neither poverty nor riches," wrote Catherine George to her son in 1858, "that is the happy medium. If only we can live comfortable and make both ends meet that is all I ask for. I hope that we will all possess the true riches, have an inheritance beyond the skies. This alone will bring true happiness."[16]

Catherine George's words illustrate vividly the first of two critical influences in Henry George's early life: his family's strong evangelical Christian faith. The Georges were among countless antebellum city dwellers caught up in the ideological fervor of the Second Great Awakening. The family belonged to nearby St. Paul's Episcopal Church, whose congregation subscribed to a distinctly low-church, evangelical style more closely resembling Methodism than "high"-church Episcopalianism. They attended Sunday worship regularly and recited prayers together every morning and evening. Overall, they created within their home a pervasive atmosphere of faith marked by outward signs of piety—reading and studying the scriptures, supporting church missions, adhering to the Ten Commandments—as well as a vigilant introspection requiring one to consider all decisions and actions in the light of faith and salvation.[17]

Looking back on the life and writings of Henry George, it is easy to see just how extensive the influence of this evangelical upbringing was. All of his writings reveal not simply an intimate familiarity with the Bible, but also a spirituality of mission. Throughout his adult life, he took time to scrutinize his moral state and set about righting his course in pursuit of his goals. This sense of optimism and calling sustained him in his darkest hours of poverty and career failure. Through it all, he held fast to the belief that God had chosen him, much like He would a prophet, as one who would influence his fellow citizens and push humanity toward the realization of the millennium.[18]

The second critical influence in Henry George's early life that shaped his outlook as an adult was the aforementioned emerging culture of entrepreneurial republicanism and its offshoot, the celebrated ideology of "free labor." Although promoted by elite interests through their newspapers and speeches, it enjoyed widespread currency at all levels of antebellum Northern society. Where merchants and employers found their entrepreneurial efforts and commitment to liberal capitalism validated as "republican," farmers, artisans, and laborers drew strength from the elements of free labor ideology that emphasized producerism, opportunity, and wage work as but a temporary stage on the way to economic independence. And in the increasingly contentious atmosphere around the slavery question, free labor offered Americans of all classes in the North a comforting cultural contrast to the South. "We know Southern men declare that their slaves are better off than hired laborers amongst us," wrote Abraham Lincoln in 1854. "How little they know whereof they speak! There is no class of permanent laborers amongst us. Twenty-five years ago I was a hired laborer. The hired laborer of yesterday labors on his own account to-day, and will hire others to labor for him to-morrow." Antebellum free labor ideology offered Northerners in particular a basic set of shared civic values updated to accommodate a burgeoning commercial economy; at the same time, it remained sufficiently ambiguous to perpetuate faith in republican ideals and, more importantly, to discourage class consciousness and a search for alternatives to the market and capitalist production.[19]

Like many Americans of his generation, George absorbed the central mantras of free labor and the influence of these precepts never left him. As a young man in California (his very move out West is revealing enough), George exhibited all the signs of a young man on the make, seeking opportunities for advancement and recognition. Later, as a reformer, his radicalism would retain many of the core beliefs learned in his childhood, including a commitment to democratic politics, a focus on the distribution of wealth (as opposed to simply its production), and a faith in capitalism, though with two vital exceptions: the sanctity of private property and the negative state.

Surprisingly, given his eventual reputation as a scholar, formal education exerted far less an influence on George's mind than evangelicalism or entrepreneurialism. A disinterested and marginal student, he bounced between public and private schools for seven years until June 20, 1853, when he quit his formal studies for good, less than three months shy of his fourteenth birthday. It is at this point that George commenced his real education, one gained through self-study and life experience rather than from formal study.[20] He relied upon local libraries for books and often attended a lecture series offered at the Franklin Institute. Soon he joined the Lawrence Society, a literary club comprised of young men in their mid-teens. Although far less refined than the Franklin Institute, the club did meet regularly to discuss works by Emerson, Aristophanes, and Byron. They also read romantic novels and poetry—works that likely exceeded his conservative family's limits of acceptable literature.[21]

Self-education, however, took second place to securing a career. Immediately after George left school for good in 1853, his father, evincing the entrepreneur's desire to set his son on a course in business, secured for him a series of clerk jobs. None of these stints paid very well, nor did they offer much stimulation for the restless young man.

But a surprising opportunity to both break the monotony of clerking and free himself from the constraints of parental authority presented itself. A family friend and fellow member of St. Paul's, Captain Samuel Miller, invited George to serve aboard his ship. George jumped at the idea. His parents agreed, likely confident of Captain Miller's moral influence and hopeful a year-long voyage of hard work would mold their restless boy into a mature man with purpose and direction. On April 10, 1855, after a layover in New York, George shipped out as a foremast boy aboard the *Hindoo*, bound for Australia and India. At sixteen years of age, the young man faced the coming adventure with a combination of fear and excitement.[22]

During the fourteen-month voyage, George engaged in his first sustained writing in the form of a sea journal. From it, we read of a journey that had its share of remarkable sights, such as the Cape of Good Hope and the exotic cities of Melbourne, Australia, and Calcutta, India, as well as eye-opening experiences like a strike by the crew upon reaching Australia, the death of the ship's cook, and the stunning poverty of India. But mostly the voyage meant monotonous hard work that George appears to have executed to the satisfaction of himself and Captain Miller. For his own part, George found the experience immensely rewarding. Upon returning to New York harbor on June 14, 1856, he wrote that it had been "an eventful year; one that will have a great influence in determining my position in life."[23]

His parents allowed Henry a short time to bask in his local celebrity as a world traveler and then set about arranging for his future. Given his past frustrations in trying to steer young Henry toward commerce, his father made arrangements for him to learn a trade. In September, he began an apprenticeship with the printing firm of King and Baird at $2.00 per week. He proved adept at the trade and within eight months learned to set type at a rate of a competent journeyman. Few decisions in George's early life would prove so important to his future as his becoming a printer. It endowed him with a skill that he constantly fell back upon in tough times. It also provided an avenue into journalism, his first significant career. Later in his life, after numerous publishing houses rejected the manuscript of *Progress and Poverty*, George would set the plates himself—a cost-saving step that convinced D. Appleton to publish the work. And in 1886, when George became the mayoral candidate of the United Labor Party, he answered those who challenged his working-class credentials by reminding them that he was a printer, a member of a typographical union and the Knights of Labor.[24]

His apprenticeship was not the only sign of George, now seventeen, entering full-blown adulthood. His earlier resistance to the constraints of his parents' household now blossomed into open defiance. The Lawrence Society had evolved from literary club to more of a social circle, and George's diary and letters indicate that he did his share of drinking and smoking with friends and kept late hours, habits that led to arguments with his parents. He also argued with his mother, a conservative Democrat like his father, over the issue of slavery.[25]

His subsequent decision to leave the family home came as the result of two unrelated events. First, George was fired from his apprenticeship in

June 1857 after arguing with the foreman (over what we do not know). For a while he took on piecework, but by the late summer of 1857 George was unemployed and frustrated. Then came the recession of 1857—George's first experience with the capriciousness of the emerging industrial economy. By mid-fall of that year, unemployment in Philadelphia soared. "The times are getting hard and practically getting worse every day," wrote George to a friend. "There are thousands of hard-working mechanics now out of employment in this city . . . among them is your humble servant." It was "the pressure of the hard times" that prodded George and hundreds of thousands of his contemporaries to look beyond their community, and even their state, for work.[26]

If George could go anywhere, it could only be California, already fixed in the American imagination as a land of opportunity and personal reinvention. Out west, George was convinced, lay immense opportunities for him to put behind him his shortcomings and finally achieve success. "The chances for a young man of average pluck and energy are unquestionably much better in the West than in the East. He shares the advantages of being among the first to open a fresh storehouse of natural wealth," opined one newspaper editor, expressing a common sentiment of the era. Fired by such an idea, all George needed was to get there. Lacking money for passage, he signed on for one year's work as a steward in the Lighthouse Service (the precursor to the Coast Guard) aboard a ship bound for San Francisco. The contract provided for free passage and pay of $40 per month. On December 22, 1857, with his parents' blessing, George steamed away from Philadelphia aboard the *Shubrick*. He did so, as he wrote to his parents two weeks later, "with scarcely a regret and without a tear," believing "that it was my duty both to myself and to you to go." Although he would visit many times thereafter, George would never again call Philadelphia home.[27]

"THE INTERESTS OF THE STATE ARE THE INTERESTS OF ITS CITIZENS": FINDING HIS WAY IN CALIFORNIA

If George felt a sense of purpose in striking out on his own for California, it was of the vaguest sort. No doubt he hoped to make his mark doing something and, as his mother encouraged him in a departing letter, "to be

Eighteen-year-old Henry George just before he shipped out on the *Shubrick* (1857). Courtesy of the New York Public Library

something and somebody in the world." At the moment, however, his only immediate plan was to look up his cousin James George, who had moved to San Francisco some years before.[28]

The clearest indication of his state of mind comes from a phrenological exam he administered to himself just before departure. It contained a list of thirty-seven categories by which to evaluate his strengths and weaknesses. He judged himself to be very good in matters of love, competition, self-esteem, firmness, hope, and individuality—an assessment borne out as accurate in subsequent years. So, too, was his assessment of his deficiencies—concentration, acquisitiveness, and calculation. Somewhat less keen was his estimation of himself as possessing the qualities of caution, conscientiousness, and punctuality. Following this list, George expanded in prose his self-evaluation:

> Will more likely make a general than a critical scholar . . .
>
> Is qualified to meet difficulties, overcome obstacles, endure hardships, contend for privileges, maintain opinions, resent insults, and defend his rights to the last; generally takes sides on every contested question; naturally hasty in temper. . . .
>
> Desires money more as a means than as an end, more for its uses than to lay up; and pays too little attention to small sums.
>
> Is slow in commencing, yet when once interested in any project pushes it with great spirit. . . .
>
> Is inclined to enter largely into business and to push his projects with so much energy and zeal as to appear rash and nearly destitute of caution; yet will come out right in the end and will seldom fail entirely in his projects, though he may be obliged to retrace his steps.[29]

Apart from illustrating the curious phenomenon of phrenology, George's self-estimation indicates a young man possessing a great but unfocused store of zeal and determination. It shows a confident and emotional adventurer, but one honestly aware of his shortcomings—at least some of them.

The voyage around Cape Horn to San Francisco lasted five months and passed without incident. George arrived on May 27, 1858, and found the city an exciting place, "rather faster than Philadelphia." Almost immediately he showed himself a young man long on ambition, but short on application. Shortly after arriving, he broke his contract with the Lighthouse Service and headed for a gold rush in British Columbia only to return penniless and despondent a few weeks later.[30] When Jo Jeffries, a close friend from Philadelphia, heard of the ill-fated venture, he admonished George about his character flaw "of half-doing things":

You vacillate about the execution of that which alone secures permanent success and lasting fame. . . . Now you are competent for any
labour to which your inclinations may direct you. You are not competent to succeed at a dozen employments, nor can you expect to amass
a fortune by labouring at them alternately.[31]

But a combination of George's restless personality and an unpredictable
economy rendered stable employment a near impossibility. For the next
few years, he tried his hand as a printer, a weigher at a rice mill, and a
nomadic farm laborer. Nothing seemed to suit him, nor did anything make
him much money. Indeed, he often found himself hungry, and on more
than one occasion bedded down in a barn.[32]

By late summer 1860, however, George finally appeared to be settling
down. He returned to printing again, this time at the *California Home
Journal*. On September 2 he turned twenty-one, becoming a journeyman
printer capable of securing the princely wage of $24 per week. Journeyman
status also allowed George to join the local typographical union, which he
did in short order. To the joy of his family back home, he also wrote that he
had found religion and, judging the local Episcopal church too high, joined
a Methodist congregation. George also evidenced at this time a growing
political awareness and social conscience. His letters reveal a keen awareness of national issues like slavery and secession, and contain complaints
of California's provincialism when it came to such things, especially John
Brown's raid on Harpers Ferry. In November he voted for the first time—
for Lincoln—and in the coming year agonized over whether or not to join
the Union Army, eventually deciding against it, he told others, out of fear
that he would draw frontier duty in the West.[33]

The following year found George struggling financially once again. But
this state of affairs was offset by a budding courtship with a woman named
Annie Corsina Fox. By year's end, he overcame his worries about money
and his parents' possible negative reaction to his marrying a Catholic
woman and proposed. They were married at George's Methodist church on
December 3, 1861, and soon thereafter procured a Catholic sanction. By all
accounts their marriage proved a loving and strong one, strengthened, they
believed, by the adversity of their early years together. On their seventh

anniversary, Annie would write to him of their marriage as "seven years of care, trouble, and sorrow, but also hope and love. We can look back and say we have indeed been one, sharing each other's troubles and joys. But few husbands and wives are as nearly one as we."[34]

Within a few months the Georges moved to Sacramento, where Henry joined the state capital's largest paper, the *Sacramento Union*. For the next two years, as the nation plunged into bloody civil war, the couple prospered as George's income rose to $40 per week. Their first son, Henry George Jr., was born on November 3, 1862, and by the summer of 1863 they moved into a rented house. Confident of his success now, George began to act like many young men on the make in California, investing in mining stocks (and losing money in the process) and contemplating speculative printing ventures in Nevada. He also met James McClatchy, editor of the *Sacramento Bee*. As a Radical Republican, Irish nationalist, and ardent champion of land reform, McClatchy became one of the most important influences on the young George as the latter began to ascend the career ladder (from typesetter to journalist to editor) and develop his mind as a progressive reformer.[35]

But just as the restless George seemed to be finding stability in a respectable career, he quickly found himself struggling yet again, only this time with a growing family. After losing his job at the *Union* (the result of a falling out with his boss), George took on a series of temporary typesetting jobs and even tried selling clothes wringers door-to-door. Matters worsened considerably in December when George, recklessly ambitious as ever, moved to San Francisco to start a printing firm. It quickly proved an ill-advised decision as customers failed to materialize.[36]

George's lack of success and distressing propensity to make ill-advised and risky career decisions troubled him. He was now twenty-five years old and soon to be a father for a second time. On Christmas Eve 1864, he resolved in his diary to overcome his faults: "Determined to keep a regular journal, and to cultivate habits of determination, energy, and industry. Feel that I am in a bad situation, and must use my utmost effort to keep afloat and go ahead." One sees in such a passage the anxiety of a young man raised in the confident antebellum mantras of free labor, upward mobility, and independence now confronting the uncertain realities of industrial life. He was young, talented, and ambitious, but unable to grasp success, at least not for very long. For now, reflecting the pervasive notion in mid-nineteenth century American culture that anyone with enough pluck could succeed and that those who failed had only themselves to fault, George blamed himself for his shortcomings. In the coming decade, he would conclude that a much greater force—economic monopoly—was responsible for his financial woes. For the time being, however, it was a question of acquiring a steady income to support his family. "Saw land-lady," the Christmas Eve passage grimly concluded, "and told her I was not able to pay rent."[37]

The hard times intensified with the coming of the new year. The foundering printing business brought the Georges' a paltry 25 cents per day, restricting them to a diet of fish, potatoes, and bread. For milk, George bartered printed business cards with the milkman. Annie, now more than eight months pregnant, pawned all the family jewelry except her wedding band and took in sewing. George reached the height of his desperation on January 27, when his son Richard George was born. As his wife convalesced, a despondent George stepped out into the rain:

> I walked along the street and made up my mind to get money from the first man whose appearance might indicate that he had it to give. I stopped a man—a stranger—and told him I wanted $5. He asked what I wanted it for. I told him that my wife was confined and that I had nothing to give her to eat. He gave me the money. If he had not, I think I was desperate enough to have killed him.[38]

These trying experiences burned an indelible mark on George's psyche. For the rest of his life, he never forgot the haunting character of poverty and want.[39]

Again George resolved to overcome his shortcomings and achieve success. In the opening pages of a new diary for 1865, George wrote: "I am starting out afresh, very much crippled and embarrassed, owing over $200. I have been unsuccessful in everything. I wish to profit by my experience and to cultivate those qualities necessary to success in which I have been lacking." He concluded to save some, spend less, borrow nothing, and socialize more. In late March, as his situation stabilized, George made a fateful decision: "I will endeavor," he resolved in his diary, "to acquire facility and elegance in the expression of my thoughts by writing essays."[40]

Thus, with this declaration, began George's transition from typesetter to journalist. On March 25, 1865, just a few weeks before the Civil War ended, he returned the demonstrator clothes wringer and went home to write his first essay as an adult. Tellingly, it appeared in the *Journal of the Trades and Workmen*, the West Coast's first labor paper. George's short essay opened with the words "We, the workers of mankind," and proceeded to praise the young labor paper and the efforts of workingmen to better their condition. Although it offered neither a hint of a philosophy of political economy nor a critique of social conditions, the essay revealed its author to be a man not only sympathetic to the efforts of workers, but one who also identified himself as one of them.[41]

For the next few years, George continued in irregular employment in the newspaper field, alternating as journalist and typesetter and moving back and forth between San Francisco and Sacramento. He increasingly identified with the Republican Party and its efforts to reshape the former Confederate states along the lines of the free-labor North, though he was less keen on granting full social and political equality to former slaves. In late November 1866, he joined the staff of the *Daily Times*, McClatchy's new paper and San Francisco's only Radical Republican organ. By June 1867, at twenty-eight years of age, George moved from the pressroom to the position of managing editor.[42] Under George's stewardship (and McClatchy's tutelage), the *Daily Times* expanded its coverage of the land question, coming out strongly against state and federal land grants to railroads. George also editorialized in favor of telegraph and railroad rate regulation and currency reform. In one particularly revealing editorial, he took to task the editor of the rival paper, the *Alta*, for a series of editorials decrying California's high wages as a drag on the state's economic competitiveness. He ridiculed the idea that the state could benefit from lower wages—that is, a lower standard of living for the majority of its citizens. Such notions, argued the young editor, contradicted the "fundamental principles of political economy." Rather, he continued,

Henry George, at age 26 in California (1865). Author's collection

The interests of the State are the interests of its citizens—the greater
the rewards which labor receives, the higher the estimation in which
it is held, the greater the equality of the distribution of earnings and
property, the more virtuous, intelligent and independent are the

masses of the people, the stronger, richer, and nobler is the state.... It would be better for California that she should retain only her present sparse but independent and comfortable population, than she should have all of England's wealth and millions with all of her destitution and pauperism.[43]

This and other editorials revealed George's heightened concern in the postwar economic boom over growing concentrations of wealth and power in the hands of a new capitalist elite. One year later in a July 4, 1868, editorial, George summoned the figure of Andrew Jackson as the consummate anti-monopoly crusader and warned his readers of the need for similar vigilance in their day. "Capital is piled on capital," he cautioned, "to the exclusion of men of lesser means, and the utter prostration of personal independence and enterprise on the part of the less successful masses." Was it just, he asked, for an individual to use for exclusive personal gain the resources provided by God to all "to the injury of his less favored fellow beings?" These concerns constituted the basic questions of political economy that George would seek to answer for the next decade. Was it possible, he wondered, for a society to continue to derive the benefits of individual enterprise while curbing unnatural concentrations of wealth that diminished opportunity?[44]

As George evolved into a reformer, he also sharpened his analytical faculties and ideals as a political economist. Key to this development was the California context in which George lived and operated. In the 1860s, a vibrant public debate emerged over public policy concerning economic development, especially in regards to land. Indeed, controversy over land policy in California at this time was more intense than in any other state. At the heart of this controversy was the problem of large-scale land engrossment, as well as rampant speculation. Much of this problem was a legacy of old Mexican land policies, which the United States inherited when it seized the land in the Mexican-American War, but it also stemmed from inept and corrupt efforts to confirm and secure land titles in the years that followed the conflict.[45] The state's leading economic writers[46] agreed that land engrossment posed a threat to economic development and limited opportunity for republican citizens to advance in society. Their solution, however, was for the government only to clarify and confirm land titles and then simply let the workings of the free market inevitably induce the breakup of large estates. But others, most notably James McClatchy, championed more aggressive measures to combat growing land monopoly. George closely followed this debate and, when he later assumed the position of editor at the *Daily Times*, editorialized in favor of land reform.

Likewise, George was aware of, and without a doubt influenced by, a related debate that emerged in the late 1860s regarding the status of San Francisco's public domain. Municipal officials, citing Mexican property laws (specifically, the granting of pueblo domains to cities and towns) that the United States had pledged to uphold after the war, declared that some eight thousand acres of land near the waterfront was rightfully public land belonging to the city of San Francisco and its inhabitants as a community. When a court decision in 1866 confirmed this claim, the debate shifted to whether the city was required to hold the land in trust in perpetuity for the benefit of the community or if it could sell off the land as it saw fit. George editorialized in favor of proposals that retained large sections of the land in public trust while distributing the rest as free homesteads. Ultimately, the city opted to grant and sell nearly all of the land with no safeguards to prevent engrossment or speculation. The core issues of land ownership, monopoly, community interest, and equality that would come to form the basis of George's argument in *Progress and Poverty* can be clearly seen in this local controversy.[47]

In addition to this California context of intense debate over land policy, it must also be noted that similar questions were being contested at the national level. Only a few years earlier in 1862, Congress had passed three major pieces of legislation related to the disposition of lands in the West: the Homestead Act, the Morrell Land Grant Act, and the Pacific Railway Act. By the late 1860s, all three programs attracted sharp criticism for fostering corruption and facilitating land engrossment and speculation to the detriment of would-be smallholders. George paid a great deal of attention to this debate, writing many columns and editorials critical of federal land policy, indicating his growing interest in the issue and its implications for the future of the republic's ideal of widespread equality of opportunity.

George's growing engagement in the local and national debates over land policy soon led him to go beyond writing editorials. His first major effort in this regard appeared as an essay in the October 1868 issue of *Overland Monthly* entitled "What the Railroad Will Bring Us." His choice of topic was apt; the railroad had emerged as a poignant symbol of the intersection of new technology, big business, and politics in the era. George predicted the impending completion of the transcontinental railroad would bring untold blessings of technology and wealth that would quickly launch San Francisco toward becoming America's first or second city. But he also introduced a key element in his nascent critique of modern industrial development: that as "new" (e.g., undeveloped) societies like California grew and developed, they came to resemble the "old" societies like New York or London. That is, with the overall increase in wealth and progress, "newer" societies suffered the diminution of social equality, high wages, and economic opportunity. Unchecked development, he argued, inevitably put speculators and monopolists on top and hard-pressed armies of wage-earners on the bottom.

> The truth is, that the completion of the railroad and the consequent great increase of business and population, will not be a benefit to all of us, but only to a portion. As a general rule (liable of course to exceptions) those . . . who have lands, mines, established businesses, special abilities of certain kinds, will become richer for it and find increased opportunities; those who have only their own labor will become poorer, and find it harder to get ahead.

In light of the state's future growth, the rapid emergence of monopoly powers, and the crushing effects of the coming depression in the mid-1870s, George's first serious essay in political economy proved remarkably prescient, forecasting the emergence of a talented social critic.[48]

Yet continued turbulence in George's personal and professional life, much of it self-created by poor decisions, forestalled that role for the near term. In August 1868 he quit the *Daily Times* to take a position as managing editor of the newly established *San Francisco Chronicle*. Shortly thereafter, he sent his wife and children east to stay with his parents in Philadelphia and toyed seriously with the notion of moving back there permanently. In December he left the *Chronicle* for another new paper, the *San Francisco*

Herald, where his first assignment was to travel to New York City and negotiate a contract with the Associated Press for access to news over the telegraph. It would prove a memorable assignment.[49]

"THERE AND THEN I MADE A VOW"

The trip to New York City provided George with two experiences that
indelibly shaped his evolving political economy. First, he confronted what
contemporaries called the "double-headed monopoly"—a media monopoly known as the New York Associated Press, which was in turn controlled
by the much larger and immensely powerful Western Union telegraph
company. Because the media giant had already established lucrative contracts with other San Francisco newspapers, the Associated Press rejected
outright George's efforts to secure a contract for the *Herald*. With no other
telegraphic news system in the nation to turn to, the *Herald* was doomed
unless George could secure an alternative source of news. But George rose
to the occasion and accomplished this feat in short order, establishing a
secret system for sending news in coded dispatches over Western Union
lines to the *Herald* in San Francisco. This system was so effective that Western Union, in response to complaints and demands from California's Associated Press-affiliated papers, retaliated by raising the *Herald*'s telegraph
rates to an absurdly high level, forcing the paper to scale back its news services to a fraction of its former level. But George had taken on one of the
greatest corporations in the nation and gained the upper hand for a time,
only to be subjected to the formidable and crushing power of monopoly. It
was an experience he would never forget.[50]

The same could be said of George's exposure to the disturbing contrasts
of wealth and poverty that marked New York City in the late nineteenth
century. As he later related to his friend and confidant, Fr. Thomas Dawson,
the sight of New York's vast slums and masses of desperate people led him
to have a vision, one revealing that God had chosen him to bring social
justice to the poor and dispossessed:

> In a city street, there came to me a thought, a vision, a call—give it
> what name you please. But every nerve quivered. And there and then

I made a vow. Through evil and through good, whatever I have done and whatever I have left undone, to that I have been true. . . . That is a feeling that has never left me; that is constantly with me. And it has led me up and up. It has made me a better and purer man. It has been to me a religion, strong and deep though vague—a religion of which I never like to speak, or make any outward manifestation, but yet that I try to follow.[51]

It would be nearly a decade before George would fully dedicate himself to discovering and eradicating the cause of these immense contrasts of progress and poverty he confronted in the great metropolis. Nonetheless, his time in New York City stoked within him a powerful sense of mission.[52]

By May 1869, with his work finished in the East, George returned to San Francisco—alone. Sensing, in the wake of his defeat at the hands of Western Union, that he was about to enter another period of economic struggle, he made the difficult choice to leave his wife and children behind with his parents in Philadelphia. It proved a wise decision. As he soon parted with the owner of the *Herald*, he was once again plunged into a hand-to-mouth existence. By mid-summer, however, George landed a job as acting editor of the *San Francisco Monitor*, a small Catholic weekly that catered to a largely Irish American audience. Besides giving him desperately needed income, the job exposed George to the social, economic, and political turmoil besetting Ireland, a colonized island where the vast majority of the native population toiled as poor tenant farmers for absent British landlords. Ireland and its woes provided him with a concrete example of advanced land monopolization central to his evolving understanding of political economy. In one editorial, George cited the landlordism of Ireland as a violation of natural law and Christian morality. In another titled, "The Land Question in California," he introduced for the first time his mechanism for achieving a just and permanent land reform: taxation on land calibrated in such a way as to make large, speculative, and unproductive aggregations impossible. He would refine and build upon these ideas substantially in the coming years.[53]

There were, of course, limits to George's evolving radicalism. Like so many Americans of the time, George took a hard line against Chinese immigration. In language often vitriolic and explicitly racist, he denounced the Chinese as unassimilable racial inferiors whose willingness to work for wages far below a level deemed necessary for a white laborer to decently live threatened the well-being of the republic. This argument, one part racial and one part economic, mirrored that of the anti-Chinese movement then growing in California, which ultimately succeeded in prodding Congress to pass the Chinese Exclusion Act in 1882. In the coming years, George would gradually dissociate himself from anti-Chinese rhetoric, coming to believe that it was inaccurate and caused workers to direct their energies and anger against Chinese workers instead of monopolists. When he published *Progress and Poverty* in 1879, he included several declarations on the equality of all races.[54]

George's fortunes picked up in September 1869 when he met Henry Haight, the Democratic governor of California. It was an encounter that led him to assume the position of managing editor at the *Oakland Daily Transcript*, a pro-Haight paper. His tenure there proved important in three ways. First, it cemented a friendship with reform-minded Haight, who in time became one of his key benefactors. The job also brought George into contact with William Swinton, the brother of New York City labor radical John Swinton. Finally, it provided the context for yet another of George's mystical visions similar to the one experienced in New York City, this time connecting the growth of poverty with land monopoly. One afternoon in January 1870, as he rode on horseback in the foothills outside of Oakland, George casually asked a passing teamster the value of the surrounding land. The man replied that he did not know, but that nearby a man was offering lots at one thousand dollars per acre. George recalled:

> Like a flash it came upon me that there was the reason of advancing poverty with advancing wealth. With the growth of population, land grows in value, and the men who work it must pay for the privilege. I turned back amidst quiet thought, to the perception that then came to me and has been with me ever since.[55]

These revelations, both in New York and in California, formed the basis of his conviction that the land question was *the* question facing Gilded Age America—and that he was somehow destined to solve it.

In February 1870, George's growing friendship with Haight garnered him the managing editorship of the *Sacramento Reporter*, a Democratic Party organ. Reflecting his own views and those of Haight, George editorialized on issues of land and tax reform. He also took a hard line against the railroads, especially the mammoth Central Pacific, calling for the government to take control of corporate monopolies in utilities, telegraph communications, and railroads. These issues had come to fore nationally in the wake of a booming postwar economy and the rapid growth of corporations, particularly in these industries.[56]

Feeling as though his situation was now finally stable and that his star was at last beginning to rise, George sent word to his parents in Philadelphia that Annie and the children should rejoin him in California.[57] But his own bad judgment—what he termed in his phrenological exam as his tendency to be "rash and destitute of caution"—once again threw him off course. In the summer of 1870, he sold his controlling interest in the paper to what appeared to be "an honest gentleman." The "gentleman" turned out to be an agent of the Central Pacific Railroad sent to silence its intrepid critic. The new investor promptly fired George, providing him, for the second time in a year, a vivid firsthand encounter with the extraordinary power wielded by monopoly, a devastating power used not only to grind workers and crush competitors, but also to silence critics.[58]

This latest career debacle differed from his previous mishaps in one important respect—on this occasion, he walked away with a respectable amount of money in hand. This not only softened the blow, but also allowed George to move back to San Francisco where, instead of jumping at the first job offered, he spent the fall and winter composing two pamphlets. The first, *The Subsidy Question and the Democratic Party* (1871), was written as campaign literature supporting Governor Haight's reelection. True to his antebellum rearing in a pervasive culture of Jacksonian values, George employed laissez-faire doctrine to argue against government subsidies to railroads.[59]

Far more significant, however, was George's second pamphlet, *Our Land and Land Policy*, which he completed in July 1871. It represented his first formal effort to systematically address the land question and the disturbing vision witnessed in the foothills of Oakland. Two ideas stand out in particular. First, George defined land as not simply an economic unit, but as "nature's storehouse" to which all people deserved equal access. In so doing, he drew upon a longstanding conception in American political thought that linked access to land with freedom, independence, and opportunity.[60]

Second, George invoked the labor theory of value, arguing that all wealth is produced by toil. George joined these two ideas to form a broad theory of land. He utilized statistics showing the rapid engrossment (through misguided state and federal land grant policies) of the nation's public land by corporations and individuals. This trend created an artificial scarcity that further empowered landowners to extract higher and higher rents from land users, thereby depriving the latter of the full value of their toil, thus violating the labor theory of value. Drawing upon economic theory as well as upon evangelical Christianity, George summarized his judgment by upholding the sanctity of private property, but with an important caveat, asserting:

> The right of every human being to himself is the foundation of the right of property. That which a man produces is rightfully his own, to keep, to sell, to give, or to bequeath. . . . But man has also another right, declared by the fact of his existence—the right to the use of so much of the free gifts of nature as may be necessary to supply all the wants of that existence, and as he may use without interfering with the equal rights of anyone else . . . This right is natural; it cannot be alienated. It is the free gift of his Creator to every man that comes into this world—a right as sacred, as indefeasible as his right to life itself.

The growing trend toward the monopolization of land and business undermined the egalitarian and democratic foundations of the nation. "To say that the land of a country shall be owned by a small class," George asserted, "is to say that that class shall rule it; to say that the people of a country shall consist of the very rich and the very poor, is to say that republicanism is impossible."[61]

As for solutions, George proposed a modified Homestead Act where only actual settlers and farmers received modest land grants, a reform that reflected the growing awareness in the 1870s that large amounts of land distributed in the original legislation had been gobbled up by speculators.

He also called for the taxation of large land holdings at the full assessed value as a way to stymie speculation. While *Our Land and Land Policy* produced little public reaction, it indicated George's evolving thought on the critical ideas that would mark his later masterwork, *Progress and Poverty*.[62]

By the summer of 1871, George's friendship with Haight drew him into more direct contact with Democratic Party politics. In June, he served as secretary for the California's Democratic Party convention and was nominated for a seat in the state legislature. He lost in an election that saw the Republicans cleanly sweep to victory over Governor Haight and virtually all Democratic opponents. George blamed his loss on the Central Pacific Railroad, which he believed still waged a vendetta against him.[63]

In the wake of the election, his fortunes soured once more. He had exhausted most of the money from the sale of the *Sacramento Reporter* and hopes for a patronage job disappeared with the ousting of Governor Haight and the Democrats from power. To make matters worse, Annie took ill with an unknown, debilitating medical condition. Although the last year had seen him beginning to develop a reputation as a reformer and social critic, George neared the end of 1871 in a financial condition not much better than the grim winter of 1865–1866.[64]

George fell back on a previous strategy to remedy the situation, sending Annie and the children back east to his parents in Philadelphia for another extended stay. There, Annie could rest and recuperate while his mother cared for the children. Their absence would remove a substantial financial and mental drain on George's resources. With his house in order, he joined with some friends to establish a new, reform-minded newspaper. On December 4, the first copies of the *San Francisco Daily Post* went on sale with a masthead announcing Henry George as managing editor.

In his first editorial, "The Great Work of Reform," George established at the outset the character the *Daily Post* would assume for the next four years. It proposed "a union of the good men of both parties" to pursue a four-point reform plan: a more economical government, lower taxes, reformed civil service, and a reversal of the general trend toward greater concentration of wealth and power in the hands of industrialists and landowners. "The masses are growing poorer," warned George, a trend that endangered the republic.[65]

George and his partners offered the *Daily Post* at the remarkable price of one penny, the first of its kind on the West Coast. It was a calculated risk aimed at attracting reform-minded readers, including the city's workingmen who lacked a daily paper of their own.[66] The paper quickly prospered, reflecting the booming national economy of the early 1870s. By January 1872, as more advertising appeared, the paper enlarged the page size and expanded the Saturday edition to eight pages. The *Daily Post*'s success and reform agenda drew George back into politics. In the summer of that year, he represented California's Fourth District at the Democratic National Convention in Baltimore.[67] By the end of 1872, the *Daily Post* declared itself the largest-selling evening paper west of Chicago. One year later, as its prosperity continued unabated, George editorialized that their accomplishments were due "to the popular appreciation of our desire to deal honestly and justly." Moreover, he concluded, "If we have struck hard, it has always been on the side of the poor, the wronged and the oppressed."[68]

George reveled in his paper's success—not merely for its pecuniary rewards, but also for the fact that it indicated a growing popular sympathy with progressive ideas on free trade, electoral reform, workers' rights, and government ownership of natural monopolies. Indeed, by the time George wrote these words, many organizations and individuals had stepped forward to offer increasingly sharp critiques of declining opportunity, rising oppression, and ineffective democracy across the nation. The National Labor Union and the Grange, for example, had emerged as significant national movements for economic justice, and they were soon to be joined by the Greenback Party (1874).[69]

This financial and career success brought to George's life a stability he had never known as an adult. With the debilitating effects of uncertainty and privation behind him for the next few years, George began for the first time to immerse himself in the study of economics. Unfortunately, precisely what he read remains a mystery as he kept no formal records. But it marked the beginning of a formal intellectual odyssey that eventually inspired him to lead one of the era's most trenchant and influential attacks on laissez-faire capitalism and its attendant dogmas. The goal of this attack was to reform, not overturn, the system. Throughout this period, indeed throughout his life, George remained a firm believer in the essential beneficence of the capitalist marketplace. This view likely had as much to do with his rearing in the antebellum traditions of the Protestant work ethic and free laborism as it did with his own success as an entrepreneur. Yet to the republican dogma of the negative state George made the case for a crucial exception, one necessitated by developments in industrial life unanticipated by the Founding Fathers. "The progress of invention," he wrote, "has created certain great and necessary businesses which are in their very nature monopolies, in which competition does not operate to secure good service at a fair price." Such "natural monopolies" in transportation (railroads) and communication (telegraph) demanded state ownership to prevent a few private citizens from accruing vast and undemocratic powers through their control of vital services.[70]

As an editor and a student of political economy, George also championed a host of other reforms, including free trade, electoral reform (the secret ballot, primaries, and proportional representation), the eight-hour work day, and a reduction in the size of the military.[71] As progressive as these ideas were, they fell squarely within the mainstream of the era's liberal reform proposals. Had they represented the greatest extent of his ideological probing, George would merit barely a mention in histories of Gilded Age labor and populist movements. For George, however, these were a mere launching point for solving the overall vexing problem of modern industrial society: the persistence and growth of poverty alongside phenomenal material wealth. Increasingly in 1873 and 1874, George began to boldly reexamine, just as he had in the case of natural monopolies, fundamental assumptions of capitalist dogma. Two issues dominated his search: the status of private property and the proper method of taxation.

In the first two years of the *Daily Post*, George maintained the faith first expressed in *Our Land and Land Policy* that a reformed and equitable Homestead Act would curb land monopolization that restricted the opportunities of hardworking Americans to achieve independence and economic success. But signs of his moving beyond this mild modification of public policy appeared even then. In May 1872, George addressed the San Francisco Lyceum on the land question and argued that a strict understanding of natural law justified common land ownership because it provided all with access to God's bountiful creation. He qualified this radical idea by arguing that the abolition of private land ownership could only come with the Millennium and the elimination of humanity's selfish impulses.[72]

The *Daily Post* reflected this growing concern of its editor with the land question. The newspaper printed, week after week, sensational accounts of the fantastic land engrossments taking place in California by individuals and corporations.[73] Gradually, as George came to believe that a reformed Homestead Act would do little more than temporarily treat the symptoms of a far deeper problem, he began to focus on the question of land values, rent, and land taxation. On January 2, 1873, the *Daily Post* advocated for replacing California's confusing and unequal morass of taxes with just three—on regulated enterprises (such as liquor and gambling), inherited estates, and land values. This last tax, he argued, would provide the state with a permanent mechanism to prevent the amassing of vast tracts of idle land by eradicating the incentive, namely fabulous profits through speculation. To allay the fears of those who might see the policy as a socialist appropriation of private property, he emphasized its limitations. "We only propose taxation instead of state landlordism," he explained, "because it is more consistent with the ideas and habits of our people, and could more easily be carried out." This idea represented the seed that would eventually blossom into his famous "single tax" by decade's end.[74]

Underlying George's increasingly radical political economy was an intense sense of Christian mission, a spirit reflected in those prophetic visions on the sidewalks of New York City and in the foothills of Oakland. This evangelicalism differed greatly from that of the conservative Christianity of his parents, which George had come to reject, in the words of his own son, as a "religion that taught either of a Special Providence on the one hand or of a merciless fate on the other," in favor of "the belief that social progress is governed by unchanging and beneficial law."[75]

George summarized his vision of a renewed American society in his Fourth of July editorial in 1874:

> The American Republic must be a republic in fact as well as form;
> a Christian republic in the full grand meaning of the words . . . till
> time shall come when warships and standing armies, and paupers and

prisons, and men toiling from sunrise to dark, and women brutalized by want, and children robbed of their childhood shall be things of the past.[76]

In these words and in his earlier reform proposals, we see George developing an increasingly radical, utopian vision of the capitalist future that departed in significant ways from the antebellum republican past.[77]

The outlines of the system of political economy George would develop into *Progress and Poverty* and later pursue as an activist in New York City were clear by the mid-1870s. Raised in a culture of antebellum republicanism and free labor mantras, he held fast to the belief that minimalist government and free-market capitalism offered society the best conditions for material abundance, equal opportunity, and true republican government. But as George observed a republican society in crisis, he began to argue that a modern market economy—in ways unanticipated by the Founding Fathers—could no longer guarantee that the virtuous traditions of American society would flourish indefinitely. More and more, he sought to remove the blinders of complacency from his readers' eyes to reveal and pinpoint the threats posed by monopoly in land and industry to the foundations of republican society. This new situation, he argued, warranted a radical rethinking regarding contemporary orthodoxies on the sanctity of private property and the negative state.[78]

2

"Poverty Enslaves Men We Boast Are Political Sovereigns"

PROGRESS AND POVERTY AND HENRY GEORGE'S REPUBLICANISM

What is the good of having a republic unless the mass of the people are better off than in a monarchy? Does not a real republic mean that all men have an equal chance and not millions born to suffering and poverty?

—*Boston Pilot*, November 2, 1878

There will soon come an armed contest between capital and labor. They will oppose each other, not with words and arguments, but with shot and shell, gun-powder and cannon. The better classes are tired of the insane howling of the lower strata and they mean to stop them.

—General William T. Sherman, 1883

"WE HAVE AMONG US A PERNICIOUS COMMUNISTIC SPIRIT"

As Henry George evolved as a radical reformer in the early 1870s, his personal life took a turn for the better. With Annie's health finally restored and his career track firmly established for the moment, George sent for his family. Together after nearly two years of separation, they reestablished their happy home life in a house in San Francisco's Mission District, not far from the *Daily Post*. Successful at last—not just financially, but in the realm of influencing public opinion as well—George was able to fulfill a goal he established for himself nearly ten years before in that desperate winter of 1865: "to minister to the comfort and enjoyment of those whom I love most."[1]

By late 1874, even greater success appeared imminent. George and his co-owner, enthused by the *Daily Post*'s continued success, decided upon a bold plan to buy their own printing presses and expand their paper's size and circulation. They brought in a wealthy third partner and took out a loan for $18,000; by January 1875, the new system was up and running. They added a weekly edition of the *Daily Post* not too long after, which became the largest selling newspaper in California. By August of that year, they started the *San Francisco Morning Ledger* (the *Daily Post* was an evening paper), including a large Sunday edition with pictures (a first). By the fall, the risk seemed to be paying off.[2]

And then everything collapsed. Even as George's newspaper enterprise expanded, the U.S. economy was falling apart. The Panic of 1873 began on September 18, 1873, when the nation's largest bank, Jay Cooke and Company, went under. The bank failure triggered an earthquake through the nation's entire financial system, one so severe that the New York Stock Exchange closed for the first time in its history. The United States had experienced panics and economic downturns in the past, but none compared to what unfolded in the 1870s, and it brought an intensity of suffering unmatched in previous economic depressions. Over the next five years and five months— the longest period of sustained economic contraction in American history— some 54,000 businesses and 5,000 banks failed and half the nation's railroads fell into receivership. Unemployment skyrocketed to unprecedented levels, perhaps as high as 30 percent, leaving hundreds of thousands of workers vulnerable to eviction and starvation. Farmers fared no better—plummeting commodities prices pushed vast numbers into insolvency and default.[3]

To his distress and dismay, George's *San Francisco Daily Post* was among the many thousands of businesses claimed by the economic crisis. On November 27, 1875, a few days after the Bank of California folded, an "utterly worked down" George closed his newspaper's doors for good, leaving him empty-handed after investing so much time and energy. "Sometimes I wonder at myself," he confided in a letter to John Swinton, "for giving up so easily what I had won so hardly."[4]

Economic historians often consider the wreckage wrought by the Panic of 1873 just the beginning of a larger Great Depression (also known as the Long Depression) that lasted from 1873 to 1898. These years, which included two brutal depressions (1873–1879 and 1893–1898) and a severe recession (1884–1885), constituted the longest period of sustained deflation (1865–1898) in American history.[5] They also marked a sudden and dramatic shift in the national economy from one centered on small proprietary capitalist enterprises (small shops and farms) to one dominated by corporations. Industrialists who withstood the wave of business failures did so by intensifying managerial control over their workplaces, investing heavily in mechanization, and slashing costs—especially wages. Corporations grew larger in size and power and, in contrast to the antebellum era when they were viewed as "creatures of the state," increasingly independent of political and legal control.[6]

In the face of massive unemployment, desperate workers had no choice but to accept these changes. Across the nation, labor unions crumbled and disappeared (national membership dropped from 300,000 in 1873 to under 50,000 in 1877). But working-class Americans did not accept these hard times quietly. Indeed, they responded to the depression and unrest of the 1870s by forming movements such as the Grangers and the Knights of Labor and political organizations like the Greenback Party and Workingmen's Party. These advocates articulated an increasingly sharp critique of laissez-faire capitalism that built upon the republican protest tradition of the antebellum period.[7]

Yet these efforts did little to alleviate the very real suffering of workers and farmers. As a consequence, the number of strikes and labor conflicts increased dramatically during this period, as did the degree of bitterness and violence that accompanied them. Two events in 1877 stand out in particular. On June 21, 1877, a decade-long struggle by miners in Pennsylvania against powerful mining and railroad interests ended with the hanging of ten men alleged to be part of a terrorist conspiracy called the "Molly Maguires." The trials, convictions (most on thin and questionable evidence), and executions of the Mollies (twenty in total) garnered national media attention that depicted the miners as violent, communist foreigners who earned a richly deserved fate at the gallows.[8]

Any calm and reassurance brought by the executions to jittery elites evaporated only a few weeks later, when railroad workers across the country, from Maryland to the Midwestern states, staged the biggest strike in the world in the nineteenth century. The "Great Uprising" was astonishing not simply for its sheer size, but also its violence. Workers in many locales destroyed railroad property, while federal troops and state militias from Maryland to Illinois killed at least a hundred people.[9]

The impact of the Great Uprising of 1877 on Gilded Age society and politics is almost impossible to exaggerate. More than simply terrifying many Americans, it challenged the very foundations of their understanding of republican society. Beneath the periodic struggles over the meanings of terms like "liberty" and "independence," a wide swath of the American public more or less shared a republican vision of a good society based on a citizenry that enjoyed both political freedom and equal access to economic opportunity. Central to this republican self-image was the belief that the United States stood alone in the world, immune to the negative historical forces that beset the fractious nations of the Old World, including the diminution of democracy, equality, virtue, and opportunity and the rise of decadence, inequality, and class conflict. The United States, in other words, stood in stark contrast to Europe, land of monarchs, landed aristocracies, fixed classes, established churches, and social conflict.[10]

The turmoil of the 1870s, culminating in the bloody Great Uprising, dealt a heavy blow to this self-confident republican optimism. As the suffering and unrest spread and festered during the depression years, Americans were confronted with overwhelming evidence that a vast and growing number of their fellow citizens lived as poorly paid wage earners. Worse, they seemed destined to *remain* in this status for life, unable to achieve true economic independence. The recognition of this large, angry, and permanent working class called into question the free labor faith that the dynamism of the market would forever generate opportunity for all, thus fending off the rise-decline-fall fate that awaited all other societies. In short, the depression of the 1870s in general, and the Great Uprising in particular, ushered in a republican crisis that prompted many Americans to wonder whether their nation was doomed to suffer the fate of the Old World.[11]

The Great Uprising of 1877. "The Great Strike—The Sixth Maryland Regiment Fighting Its Way Through Baltimore." *Harper's Weekly*, August 11, 1877. Courtesy of the Library of Congress

The different answers various Americans offered to this question reflected the emergence of increasingly sharp class boundaries.[12] While working-class Americans and reformers like Henry George saw mounting evidence that the republican promises of equality, freedom, and upward mobility were dissipating before their very eyes to benefit unscrupulous monopolists and their political allies, middle- and upper-class Americans came to vastly different interpretations of the republican crisis. Their assessment often took two forms. One consisted of a glowing narrative celebrating "progress." Huge national celebrations attended the completions of the Atlantic Cable (1866) and the transcontinental railroad (1869), the opening of the Brooklyn Bridge (1883), and the unveiling of the fully assembled Statue of Liberty (1886). Millions flocked to the Centennial Exposition in Philadelphia (1876). "The prosperity which now prevails," blithely said President James A. Garfield in 1881, "is without parallel in our history."[13]

But amidst these optimistic proclamations emerged a second interpretation that denounced protesters and strikers as *the mob*. For years they had been haunted by the fear that rising social unrest among the nation's "dangerous classes" could at any moment explode in bloody revolution, as it had only a few years before in the Paris Commune of 1871. Now their worst fears seemed realized. "The Commune had risen in its dangerous might and threatened a deluge of blood," declared one typical chronicler of the uprising. John Hay, future secretary of state for William McKinley and Theodore Roosevelt, was no less hysterical in a private letter to his father-in-law. "Any hour the mob chooses," he wrote, "it can destroy any city in the country—that is the simple truth."[14]

This demonization of the lower orders of society reflected a broader effort by elites in this period to redefine key aspects of the republican tradition. Republican liberty and free labor were redefined to essentially mean laissez-faire individualism. Every member of a republican society, their argument went, was at liberty to make his or her own way in the competitive marketplace, free of any constraints beyond a minimal set of laws. Similarly, republicanism's potentially radical ideal of equality for all was whittled down to simply mean equality of opportunity in the market. "Free labor" now meant simply freedom of contract. This recasting of republican ideals served elite interests by linking economic success with republican fidelity—they, of course, were the truest republican citizens because they had gained success through a faithful adherence to rugged individualism. This emphasis on individualism had the added benefit of justifying the rejection of all claims that the state play a fundamental role in ensuring equality among the people and promoting the common good. As a result, the doctrine of laissez-faire assumed an almost exalted status in the 1870s and 1880s, allowing prosperous and powerful Americans to dismiss the claims of protesting farmers and dissatisfied workers as the misguided rantings of society's losers.[15]

Also gaining popularity in this period was laissez-fairism's most extreme offshoot: social Darwinism. British philosopher Herbert Spencer, social Darwinism's most prominent popularizer, posited that competition among human beings led inexorably to the "survival of the fittest" and the elimination of the "unfit." No amount of utopian theory, enlightened social policy, or Christian charity could alter this basic fact of human life. Spencer's counterpart in America, Yale sociologist William Graham Sumner, pushed the point further, arguing that "millionaires . . . may fairly be regarded as the naturally selected agents of society" while a "drunkard in the gutter is just where he ought to be." Many Gilded Age industrialists, seeking to justify both their tremendous wealth and the minimal wages they paid, understandably embraced social Darwinism. It was precisely this trend that Henry George had in mind when a few years later he condemned social Darwinism as a "comfortable theory" for its ability to ease the guilty consciences of the successful.[16]

This elevation of laissez-faire individualism to the apex of the hierarchy of republican ideals and the embrace of social Darwinism among society's rich and powerful reflected a decisive departure from earlier forms of American republicanism that stressed a unified polity and concern for the common good. Middle- and upper-class Americans in the Gilded Age redefined the republican polity in such a way that placed poor and restive farmers and workers *outside* the sphere of legitimate republican citizenship. According to this new line of thinking, which might be termed "laissez-faire republicanism," the greatest menace to the American republic was not the widening gap between the rich and the poor, but rather the possibility that the poor would mobilize *collectively* against their betters, either by ballot or bullet, and take what did not belong to them. As a result, members of the middle- and upper-classes in the 1870s launched campaigns to disenfranchise working-class voters. (At the same time, and for similar reasons, they made no effort to stop the disenfranchisement of African American voters in the South.) They also sharply curtailed charity, deeming it harmful to the morals and manners of the needy.[17]

Despite the rising chorus of opinion celebrating minimalist government and laissez-faire individualism, middle- and upper-class Americans nevertheless held a markedly inconsistent vision of the role of the state. Laissez-faire doctrine was clear on this matter: the ideal state was a minimal one that allowed free individuals the greatest possible latitude in their pursuits of happiness. But laissez-faire was more a conveniently flexible principle than a clear and firmly adhered practice. Even as Americans in more privileged classes rejected the calls for reform by mobilized workers and farmers as treacherous appeals to state power that violated the sacred values of laissez-faire, they themselves began to use the state to fortify and enhance their established positions in society.[18]

The clearest example of elites' reliance on the state in this period was their shared belief, if not insistence, that working-class protest be answered with state-sponsored violence. This not only violated laissez-faire, it also represented yet another dramatic reordering of traditional republican values. For while republicanism had always valued social order, sanctioning on rare occasions the use of state power to quell civil disturbances (e.g., the Whiskey Rebellion), it had long given primacy to the fear that standing armies spelled the eventual demise of liberty. But in the Gilded Age, elites increasingly demanded that federal and state military power be brought to bear against workers they themselves deemed threats to order, private property, and market freedom. For example, the *Independent*, a religious weekly, called for "bullets and bayonets, canister and grape" to "exterminate" unruly mobs. In the wake of the Great Uprising of 1877, wealthy urbanites around the country embarked on a program of armory construction in large cities to house and equip state militias. Of course, these installations also would offer refuge to upper-class refugees should the dangerous classes explode again. This "militarization of class relations," to use Sven Beckert's apt phrase, occurred at precisely the moment that respectable opinion in the North was invoking the traditional republican aversion to a standing army to justify the removal of federal troops protecting African Americans in the South.[19]

Wealthy and powerful Americans defended this extraordinary appeal to and use of state violence by reiterating, despite mounting evidence to the contrary, a core republican article of faith: America was a classless society. The problem in the 1870s—and the true source of the Great Uprising—was the misguided but growing conviction among many farmers and workers that American society was splitting into classes with opposed interests, they argued. As Allan Pinkerton, head of the Pinkerton Detective Agency, argued in the wake of the Great Uprising, "we have among us a pernicious communistic spirit which is demoralizing workmen, continually creating a deeper and more intense antagonism between labor and capital. . . . It must be crushed out completely, or we shall be compelled to submit to greater excesses and more overwhelming disasters in the near future." Deeming class antagonism unnatural and evil provided the necessary validation for state suppression of dissent. State power would be called upon to maintain America's harmonious, classless, laissez-faire republic.[20]

"THE GREAT ENIGMA OF OUR TIMES":
PROGRESS AND POVERTY

It was in this context of economic contraction, social turmoil, and ideological reconfiguration that Henry George decided to write what would become his famous work, *Progress and Poverty*. Like many Americans, George was deeply troubled by the widespread suffering and unrest of the mid-1870s. While the epic violence of the Great Uprising of 1877 did not reach California, news of it did stir the passions of local workers, record numbers of whom were out of work. Matters took an ugly turn on July 23, 1877 when, following a rally of workers on the Sand Lots near San Francisco's city hall expressing sympathy for the striking railroad workers, an anti-Chinese faction attacked and sacked Chinatown. Known as the Sand Lots Riots, the disturbances lasted four straight days and were the worst in San Francisco's history.[21]

By the time of the riots, George had rebounded from the loss of the *Daily Post*. Through his connections with the local Democratic Party he secured a patronage job as inspector of gas meters, a position that earned him enough money to support his family while placing only nominal demands on his time. Financially stable, intellectually mature, and mystically driven, George shrugged off the tragedy of the *Daily Post* and embraced the near future as a chance to continue his study of political economy and write a book. Years later, with the benefit of hindsight and his incurable optimism, he later concluded that losing the *Daily Post* amounted to "good fortune in the guise of evil."[22]

According to his diary, George commenced writing the book that became *Progress and Poverty* on September 18, 1877, less than two months after the Great Uprising and the Sand Lots Riots. These terrifying upheavals lent great urgency to his work, but his quest had truly begun nearly a decade earlier when he experienced that vision on the streets of New York City in 1869. "When I first realized the squalid misery of a great city," as he would explain, "it appalled and tormented me, and would not let me rest, for thinking of what caused it and how it could be cured."[23] By mid-March 1879, after eighteen months of intense effort inspired by the motto "hard writing makes easy reading," he completed his manuscript.[24]

George initially gave his book the rather drab title of *Political Economy of the Social Problem*. Fortunately for him, he settled upon a title that succinctly and alliteratively captured the vexing duality of the age during the final revisions: *Progress and Poverty*, with the subtitle, *An Inquiry into the Cause of Industrial Depressions and of Increase of Want with Increase of Wealth*. He divided the immense tome (563 pages in the original edition) into twelve sections—ten "books," placed between an introduction and a conclusion. Seeking to elevate political economy above a theory-laden discipline dedicated to upholding the status quo to the detriment of society as a whole, George wrote both a sophisticated economic treatise that engaged the theories of David Ricardo and Thomas Malthus and a moral entreaty that invoked Jesus Christ and the Founding Fathers. Two main questions, therefore, dominate the work: Why does poverty always accompany material progress? How is humanity morally compelled to respond? While he treated the economic and moral analyses separately throughout most of the work, he came to draw the two together in the end, firmly asserting that they were inseparable—albeit with the moral argument taking priority.[25]

In the introduction, George set forth "The Problem" he intended to address and solve: that despite a century of unparalleled material progress, a majority of Americans enjoyed less and less of its benefits. This republican crisis stood in stark contrast to the expectations of the post-Revolutionary War generation. George asked the reader to consider what a figure like Benjamin Franklin would have thought of American society if told of the coming of railroads and factories, of electricity and telegraphs:

> He would have beheld these new forces elevating society from its very foundations, lifting the very poorest above the possibility of want, exempting the very lowest from anxiety for the material needs of life; he would have seen . . . these muscles of iron and sinews of steel making the poorest laborer's life a holiday, in which every high quality and noble impulse could have scope to grow.

In other words, Franklin and other contemporaries would have envisioned the dawning of "a golden age."[26]

This hypothetical vision of Franklin, noted George, represented the hopes and dreams of nineteenth-century Americans as they witnessed a steady stream of revolutionary technology and ideas. It reflected the republican faith in continuous progress. And yet, instead of a golden age, America was trapped in a state where the beguiling glitter of progress was offset by the bleakness of industrial depression, business failure, involuntary unemployment, and mass poverty—a superficiality that Mark Twain and Charles Dudley Warner sought to convey with the title of their 1873 novel *The Gilded Age: A Tale of Today*. These harsh and unwelcome present realities called into question the viability of the republic. The evidence of a republican crisis was both abundant and undeniable.[27]

What America and other developed societies had in common was material progress. To illustrate this point, George asked the reader to compare conditions in "newer" (less developed) and "older" (developed) societies. In the former, there was little poverty, as well as high wages and rates of interest paid on investment. But as newer societies experienced increased material progress, the signs of social dissolution followed close behind:

> The "tramp" comes with the locomotive, and almshouses and prisons are as surely the marks of "material progress" as are costly dwellings, rich warehouses, and magnificent churches. Upon streets lighted with gas and patrolled by uniformed policemen, beggars wait for the passer-by, and in the shadow of the college, and library, and museum are gathering the more hideous Huns and fiercer Vandals of whom Macaulay prophesied.[28]

Far from establishing a golden age of widespread comfort and expanded opportunity as many had hoped and predicted, material progress actually produced a society where "amid the greatest accumulations of wealth, men die of starvation, and puny infants suckle dry breasts; while everywhere the greed of gain, the worship of wealth, shows the force of the fear of want." The virtuous republic of independent producers, so central to the hopes of Franklin, Jefferson, and Jackson, now appeared out of reach. "The promised land," confessed George, "flies before us like the mirage."[29]

Extremes of wealth also violated both Christian morality and republican equality. "It is as though an immense wedge were being forced, not underneath society, but through society," he argued. "Those who are above the point of separation are elevated, but those who are below are crushed down." So long as material progress served only to increase the fortunes of the wealthy few and the misery of the many poor, it was only a spurious progress. It was here that the idea that separated George from nearly all his contemporary political economists was most clearly articulated. Far from being the natural and unavoidable result of the lifestyles of weak and sinful people, he asserted that poverty was actually *generated* by particular public policies and laws. In characterizing poverty as *unnatural*, George decidedly broke from the received wisdom of the age. This break, in turn, justified his quest for a remedy. "This association of poverty with progress," concluded George ominously, "is the great enigma of our times. . . . It is the riddle which the Sphinx of Fate puts to our civilization, and which not to answer is to be destroyed."[30]

Yet, for all its magnitude and foreboding, the all-important question of why poverty increased amid progress remained unanswered by political economists. In noting this, George revealed one of the central purposes of his book—to attack the discipline of political economy itself and expose the failure of political economists to live up to their true mission of providing guidance to "the great masses." Due to an "anarchy of opinion" within the discipline, "charlatans and demagogues" were allowed to peddle unsound ideas "fraught with danger," such as paper money, revolutionary socialism, the abolition of interest, and the false but thoroughly convenient theory of laissez-faire. "I propose to seek the law which associates poverty with progress," George announced, "and increase of want with advancing wealth." He would, essentially, attempt to single-handedly redirect the science of political economy back to its core purpose, thereby offering society the possibility of regeneration. He warned that the saving message contained in the coming pages would be unsettling to most Americans, but the high stakes involved compelled bold action. The fate of the American republic, indeed all of Western society, stood in the balance. So, he finished, "let us not flinch, let us not turn our back."[31]

George intended his book to supersede all others in its field.[32] To do just that, he challenged the very foundation of the age's prevailing economic dogmas of laissez-faire capitalism in Book I. Classical economists had explained that an "iron law of wages" dictated that wages always fell to the lowest level at which a laborer could subsist. The productivity of an individual worker bore little relation to the reward he or she would receive for their toil. So even though industrial technology allowed a shoe factory operative in 1875 to produce many times more shoes than a single cordwainer in 1825, he received far less financial reward for his labor. This outcome was not really an injustice, declared classical economists, but was rather the result of the laws of the free market that men and women were powerless to change.

This iron law of wages itself rested upon two widely accepted tenets of classical economics. The first, the wage-fund theory, stated that employers paid wages to workers from previously accumulated capital (e.g., a wage fund). Wages thus cannot be raised at a rate that corresponded to an increase in economic productivity. George attacked this theory precisely because it placed capital ahead of labor in the hierarchy of basic economic factors. Instead, he proposed to reverse this order, positioning labor *ahead* of capital. To illustrate this radical departure from economic orthodoxy, George used the example of a shipyard. As the constructed ship takes form, men receive wages for the work they perform—wages are not paid out from existing capital (in this case, a previous ship built and sold), but rather from the wealth the workers are in the process of creating. "Wages do not come from capital, but are the direct produce of labor. Each productive laborer, as he works, creates his wages," he asserted. Based on this understanding, workers ought to receive wages as an advance upon this emerging capital and receive *higher* wages that reflected their greater productivity.[33]

The second principle underlying the iron law of wages theory, Malthus' population theory, argued that poverty accompanies economic progress due to an increasing population that draws upon a fixed, finite amount of resources. While some political economists had already challenged the theory, a good many still accepted it as unimpeachable fact. Not so George. In Book II, he soundly rejected Malthusianism as overly deterministic, a characteristic that ran counter to his Christian and republican faiths in the free will of individuals to change their lives and society. Steeped in the tradition of evangelical perfectionism as he was, George also deemed Malthusian theory blasphemous for its contention that God created a world with insufficient resources for his people. The Great Famine in Ireland—frequently cited by Malthusians as proof of the limited resources theory—was caused, according to George, by rigid British adherence to free trade dogmas. It was not "the inevitable results of universal laws, with which, if it were not impious, it were as hopeless to quarrel as with the law of gravitation." Finally, George rejected Malthusian theory because it provided monopolists, conservatives, and the increasing number of devotees of social Darwinism with a seemingly scientific means for justifying their privileged status. Rather than confront vested interests, "it is eminently soothing and reassuring to the classes who, wielding the power of wealth, largely dominate thought."[34]

With the tenets of contemporary economic theory now sufficiently undermined, George offered in Book III his own explanation for the prevalence of poverty amidst increased aggregate wealth. The real problem lay not with a limited fund of wages, nor with population growth, but rather with *distribution*. In the last century, he noted, America had produced an unprecedented amount of material wealth. Yet the distribution of said wealth had been vastly distorted, leaving the lives of most people unimproved or worse.

To explain his theory of skewed distribution, George briefly defined his terms. Production consisted of three elements: land, labor, and capital. All wealth produced must be distributed among them—to landowners, to laborers, and to capitalists. This distribution occurred through three basic mechanisms: rent (to the landowner), wages (to the laborer), and interest (to the capitalist).[35]

ELEMENTS OF PRODUCTION	MEANS OF DISTRIBUTING WEALTH PRODUCED
Land (all natural resources)	Rent to the landowner
Labor	Wages to the laborer
Capital	Interest to the capitalist

By creating separate categories for land and rent, George made another major break from traditional economic theory that generally considered land a form of capital. George argued that capital represented manmade wealth of infinite quantity, whereas land and natural resources existed in finite quantity as a gift of the Creator. Consequently, land existed as a passive entity requiring the application of labor to produce wealth. Land, in short, was not capital for one simple reason: man could not create it. If land existed as a separate and distinct entity within the productive process, then logically the portion of the wealth it received—rent—should also be separate from wages and interest.[36]

The creation of a separate status for land and rent was crucial to the underlying purpose of *Progress and Poverty*, which was to establish where the vast amount of material wealth created by modern industrial society went—and why. George's model narrowed the list of possibilities to three—land, labor, or capital. Labor clearly gained just a fraction of the wealth. Yet what about capital? Marxists charged that capital took everything. But George, true to his essential faith in capitalism, defended capital and interest, the mechanism by which capital received its share of wealth. He contended that a truly free and prosperous economy properly rewarded honest capitalists (as opposed to parasites and speculators) for their foresight, planning, risk-taking, and judicious use of natural resources to create more wealth. But most capitalists in Gilded Age America, while faring better than laborers, failed to receive their fair share of the aggregate wealth produced.[37]

If capital and labor failed to secure the fruits of production (in the form of interest and wages, respectively), where in the distributive process did the wealth go? According to George's model, the only remaining possibility was that the wealth generated by material progress went to the parasitic monopolizers of land in the form of rent, which over time increased at a rate faster than that of wages or interest. As the production of wealth increased, landowners thus took an ever-growing percentage (rent), leaving less and less for labor (wages) and capital (interest). As George summarized in what might be called his labor-capital theory of value:

> Three things unite to production—labor, capital, and land. Three parties divide the produce—the laborer, the capitalist, and the land owner. If, with an increase of production the laborer gets no more and the capitalist no more, it is a necessary inference that the land owner reaps the whole gain. . . . Rent swallows up the whole gain and pauperism accompanies progress.[38]

Identifying land monopoly and the resulting extortionate rent as the culprits placed George squarely within a republican populist tradition that consistently condemned "parasitic" wealth.[39] It also allowed George to reject class conflict and other claims of an inherent antagonism between labor and capital. The real "antagonism of interests," George made clear, "is not between labor and capital, as is popularly believed, but is in reality between labor and capital on the one side and land ownership on the other."[40]

If material progress led to rising rents, which in turn left less and less of created wealth to labor and capital, George still had to explain what *caused* rents to rise and why they rose at rates that exceeded that of wages and interest. In Book IV, "The Effect of Material Progress upon the Distribution of Wealth," George cited population growth, improved industrial production, and rampant speculation as the central causes of the steep rise in land values and rents.[41]

To best illustrate the effect of these factors on production and land values, George looked to the city. A growing urban population greatly increased the utility of each parcel of land, especially when combined with improved technology. As a consequence, far more wealth could be produced on a tenth of an acre of Manhattan in 1879 than on a dozen acres of similarly situated land in 1815. As a result, land values and rents rose rapidly and, according to George's theory of skewed distribution, siphoned off most of the newly created wealth not to the labor that produced it, nor to the capital which facilitated it, but to land, or more precisely to the owners of land, who did nothing to earn it. "The increased production of wealth goes ultimately to the owners of land in increased rent. There is in all this improvement nothing which tends to increase the general return to labor or to capital." This problem only worsened over time as landowners, consumed by greed, hiked rents and speculated in land in anticipation of still greater rises in value and subsequent profits. As speculators took more and more land out of productive use, new societies aged prematurely, suffering "long before their time, the social diseases of older countries." Modern industrial cities like New York, noted George (doubtlessly recalling his visit in 1869), thus emerged as centers of extraordinary wealth but also extreme poverty, stifled opportunity, and bristling tensions between capital and labor.[42]

George's careful progression through the fields of classical economics and contemporary political economy now led him, as the title of Book V indicates, to declare "The Problem Solved." After more than 250 pages of strict analysis, George succinctly identified the problem of modern industrial society in just two simple words: land monopoly. Land to George meant more than simply real estate; he broadly defined it as "all natural materials, forces and opportunities." Material progress ought to promise the betterment of all levels of society in the form of greater comforts, less drudgery, and higher learning. "But labor," argued George, "cannot reap the benefits which advancing civilization thus brings, because they are intercepted" by the monopolizers of land.[43]

This point clearly marked the boundaries of George's radicalism. The injustice against which he worked was not industrial capitalism itself, but rather what he viewed as its illegitimate cooptation. Like many of his fellow reformers in this period, he considered the power monopolists wielded illegitimate because it derived from their ability to control essential tools used in competition such as access to resources, credit, and political power rather than through fair competition in the free market.[44] Land monopoly thoroughly corrupted the free market and the distribution of wealth because "the monopolizers of land can, in rent, levy tribute upon the earnings of labor." This conclusion represented the "simple truth" toward which George's inquiry had been steadily advancing: because labor required land and resources in order to produce wealth, those who already controlled them "command all the fruits of labor save enough to enable labor to exist."[45]

> It is not in the relations of capital and labor; it is not in the pressure of population against subsistence, that an explanation of the unequal development of our civilization is to be found. The great cause of inequality in the distribution of wealth is inequality in the ownership of land. The ownership of land is the great fundamental fact which ultimately determines the social, the political, and consequently the intellectual and moral condition of a people. And it must be so. For land is the habitation of man, the storehouse upon which he must draw for all his needs, the material to which his labor must be applied for supply of all his desires.[46]

With land monopoly firmly established as the central problem afflicting modern industrial societies, George proposed a corrective. He began Book VI, "The Remedy," by dismissing a series of popular solutions then being widely promoted by reformers. Those who championed a smaller, more efficient government understood an important Jeffersonian-Jacksonian principle, but they failed to see how society had drastically changed since the 1830s. Social Darwinists who blamed poverty on the personal weaknesses of the poor conveniently but immorally absolved themselves of any responsibility. Trade unionists stood only to gain temporary relief in limited sectors of the workforce. Advocates of the cooperative movement and other variants thereof (such as producer cooperatives, consumer leagues, and profit-sharing strategies) misunderstood the core issues. The problem, George insisted, "is not because of competition, but because competition is one-sided."[47]

In regard to socialism, George offered an assessment that came to underlie his enormous public appeal in the coming years. He was understandably attracted to the idea of a future society that was fundamentally egalitarian and democratic, and he was keenly aware of the growing popularity of socialist and quasi-socialist ideas, especially among working-class Americans. Yet George was also cognizant of the deep-seated antipathy many Americans held for socialism, an ideology which had long been demonized in American political culture as inextricably linked to violence, revolution, and atheism, or as one minister put it in a book also published in 1879, with "wages without work, arson, assassination, anarchy."[48] George nonetheless found a way to express sympathy for socialism's broad goals while simultaneously distancing himself from its negative associations. Though socialism's promised end was "grand and noble," it could never be suddenly imposed. "Such a state of society," he observed, "cannot be manufactured—it must grow." This growth would begin by breaking the grip of land monopoly, thereby freeing millions of individuals to achieve prosperity and upward mobility as well as steering society back in the direction of republican progress. His answer, in other words, would make possible—gradually—the type of society socialists dreamed of, but without the chaos, bloodshed, and injustice popularly associated with socialist revolution. He offered, in short, a solution Daniel Rodgers has characterized as typical of late nineteenth-century progressive reformers on both sides of the Atlantic: "a middle course between the rocks of cutthroat economic individualism and the shoals of an all-coercive statism."[49]

To achieve this end, George declared his true remedy: "We must make land common property."[50] A proper understanding of history, George contended, revealed private property as unnatural, for all primitive societies held their land in common.

Historically, as ethically, private property in land is robbery. It nowhere springs from contract; it can nowhere be traced to perceptions of justice or expediency; it has everywhere had its birth in war and conquest, and in the selfish use which the cunning have made of superstition and law."[51]

History demonstrated that societies based on private property tended toward slavery of one kind or another. For example, noted George, emancipation in the South accomplished little for the former slaves who now labored under the tyranny of their former masters, who still owned all the land. He explained that to prevent this trend from spreading to all of America, the solution was both simple and radical: "To extirpate poverty, to make wages what justice commands they should be, the full earnings of the laborer, we must therefore substitute for the individual ownership of land a common ownership. Nothing else will go to the cause of the evil—in nothing else is there the slightest hope."[52] Common ownership would thus free the essential ingredient in production—land—for use by society's true producers, labor and capital, leaving nothing to the landlord, speculator, or monopolizer.

But how did George propose to establish this "common ownership"? Certainly he did not envision a socialist confiscation of all private property by the state, an idea that flew in the face of longstanding liberal dogmas that deemed limited government and private property as essential to the preservation of individual liberties in a republic. While Americans did not always agree on the meanings of liberty, equality, and democracy, most were conditioned to condemn any infringement of private property rights as antithetical to republican ideals.[53]

George's solution to this dilemma, presented in Book VIII, "Application of the Remedy," was a plan that stopped short of socialist confiscation. He instead offered a plan where people technically could continue to "own" their land, but would be prevented from deriving any profit from mere ownership (e.g., rent). The state would abolish all taxes except one, a land-value tax that appropriated all rent—in other words, any income derived from non-productive use of land ("the unearned increment"). People would remain free to use their land as they desired, but would be prevented from profiting unjustly.

Let them buy and sell, and bequeath and divide it. We may safely leave them the shell, if we take the kernel. *It is not necessary to confis-*

cate land, it is only necessary to confiscate rent. . . . We already take some rent in taxation. We have only to make some changes in our mode of taxation to take it all.[54]

This was George's most radical break with traditional liberal ideals, a renunciation of a centuries-old definition of private property that lay at the core of republicanism and American political culture.[55]

George never fully explained in practical terms in *Progress and Poverty*, nor in any of his subsequent writings and speeches, how what became known in later years as "the single tax" would be implemented.[56] Nonetheless, the basic outline of his idea was clear. All property would be annually reevaluated by the government, which would assess a property's tax based on an estimate of its rental value on the market. For example, a man "owning" farmland with an annual rental value established at $500 could work the land and keep any profits derived from his harvest. But at the year's end, he faced a choice: pay the government $500 to retain another year's use of the property, or relinquish control of the land to the government. The government in turn would offer it "to the highest bidders in lots to suit." It was certainly not a call for the outright elimination of private landed property by wholesale government confiscation. But the single tax did propose to end private property rights as nineteenth-century Americans knew them. Whereas traditional notions of private property stressed the inviolability of an owner's right to retain, control, and use his land as he saw fit, one of the central purposes of the single tax was to make the holding, controlling, and use of land unstable and fluid, thus preventing monopolization and accumulation.[57]

George explained this dynamic in Book IX, "Effects of the Remedy." With this system in place, the price of land, he wrote, would fall and "land speculation would receive its death blow," as landowners could not afford to pay hefty fees for the privilege of merely holding parcels of undeveloped land from which they could never derive a profit; "land monopolization would no longer pay." George predicted here that most speculators would willingly relinquish their titles to the government, thereby freeing up millions of acres of land for use by honest laborers.[58]

But the single tax promised to do more than merely make vast tracts of land available and affordable to the average American. Abolishing all taxes except the one on land values would liberate the overall productive economy—"like removing an immense weight from a powerful spring"— by rewarding industrious laborers (with higher wages) and honest capitalists (through higher interest) instead of idlers and speculators. With the economic playing field finally leveled and all serious impediments to production removed, poverty would disappear; the single tax would unleash an ever-expanding, prosperous economy of full employment, free of disastrous periodic depressions. In short, George's "simple yet sovereign remedy" would:

> raise wages, increase the earnings of capital, extirpate pauperism, abolish poverty, give remunerative employment to whoever wishes it, afford free scope to human powers, lessen crime, elevate morals, and taste, and intelligence, purify government and carry civilization to yet nobler heights.[59]

As for the social benefits to such a system, George's single tax also promised, in an appeal to the liberal ideals of antebellum republicanism, to reduce the size and complexity of government. In making this claim, however, George did not promise a dramatic shrinkage of all government— only its repressive functions. For example, the single tax would dramatically simplify the collection of taxes, reducing the need for police, jails, or civil courts because there would be less crime and fewer lawsuits over property. As a trade-off, however, the government under the single tax would assume a wide range of "cooperative" functions intended to restore and maintain republican rights and equality.[60]

This was George's second radical break, after his call for an end to absolute rights in private property, with earlier republican dogmas. His plan required the state to take on unprecedented new powers to accomplish both the administration of the single tax and the use of the revenue it generated for the common good. Republican ideology before the 1870s had long held that the greatest threat to republican liberty was a powerful government, as it would inevitably fall under the control of greedy special interests bent on elevating themselves into positions of aristocratic power and privilege. Threats to republican liberty and equality, went the argument, emanated fundamentally from political corruption rather than from any flaw in the capitalist economy. Laissez-faire and a minimal state, therefore, were the best guarantors of republicanism.[61] But not anymore, argued George here. Modern economic realities required *the state* to take on key responsibilities to protect and promote republican liberty and equality.

All revenue collected under the single tax would "be equally distributed in public benefits." Though much of created wealth was attributable to the wisdom of capitalists and the skills of workers, a significant portion was *socially created* by the community itself through the increased demand for goods and production of knowledge. It would be only right that the community would be allocated some wealth in return. These "public benefits," George wrote, would take the form of "public baths, museums, libraries, gardens, lecture rooms, music and dance halls, theaters, universities, technical schools, shooting galleries, play grounds, gymnasiums," as well as include the public ownership of natural monopolies like the telegraph lines, railroads, and utilities. Therein lay what George considered the genius of his radical solution—a modern industrial society could "realize the dream of socialism," while maintaining the essence, dynamism, and freedom of a market economy. The single tax would preserve entrepreneurship and individualism by purging them of their destructive tendencies. At the same time, it validated the prevailing belief denying the existence of class conflict and ruled out the need for the repressive, centralized government that most Americans associated with socialism. George then declared that the "government would change its character and would become the administration of a great co-operative society. It would become merely the agency by which the common property was administered for the common benefit."[62] This was the clearest evocation of his ideas that helped shape and popularize the era's emerging progressivism.

The basis of this new cooperative society would not be a changed government, but rather a changed community. The single tax promised not simply profound economic and social change, but significant moral transformation as well. Not only would crime disappear, but so too would the "greedy and grasping and unjust" impulses that a society dominated by monopoly interests fostered. By making poverty as unlikely a condition for the average person as great wealth had been under the former system, the single tax "would transmute the forces which now tend to disinte-grate society into forces which would tend to unify and purify it." In other words, a spirit of cooperation—"a force which overcomes and drives out selfishness; a force which is the electricity of the moral universe"—would be unleashed, thereby eliminating the "wrong that produces inequality" "We are made for co-operation," George concluded. His invocation of cooperation here is significant because it aligned neatly with the grow-ing popularity of the idea of cooperation and cooperative schemes among workers (most notably, the Knights of Labor) and farmers in the 1870s and 1880s and with the broader values of progressivism and social democracy gaining currency in the late nineteenth century.[63]

In the final book, "The Law of Human Progress," George endeavored to reveal "the great law" that accounted for the rise and eventual decay of all societies. Popular opinion, he observed, believed social progress was natural, inevitable, and seemingly unending. History, however, provided ample evidence of a "universal rule" of human progress: all societies rise, flourish, stagnate, decline, and fall. No society, not even America, stood immune to this inevitability. George warned, "The earth is the tomb of the dead empires, no less than of dead men." In making this point, he placed his analysis squarely within a tradition of republican thought that had long emphasized the danger of declension.[64]

In order to explain why civilizations fell, he first detailed what made them rise. He introduced the concept of "association," which he called "the first essential of progress." When people live apart, they must devote the majority of their waking hours struggling to survive. In contrast, "men tend to progress just as they come closer together, and by co-operation with each other increase the mental power that may be devoted to improvement." Paradoxically, this very process of progress through association tended to foster "inequality of condition and power" in the long run. As an advanc-ing society becomes more specialized in function and organization, a small number of individuals amass extraordinary power and wealth by monopo-lizing land or some other essential, such as credit or fuel. Association, while the initial catalyst for social progress, leads society inexorably toward con-ditions in which the "tendency to progression is lessened, checked, and finally reversed."[65]

When progress halts, "petrification" sets in. A society once marked by fluidity and equality then witnesses the rise of established castes, with more and more people born into lives as powerless, wage-earning laborers with no possibility of social or economic advancement. These unfortunates need to spend all their creativity and energy simply to survive. On the other hand, among the elite few, "mental power is expended in keeping up and intensifying the system of inequality, in ostentation, luxury, and warfare."[66]

In this book, George warned that the United States already was in the beginning stages of petrification, but most Americans failed to see it. General increases in material wealth and continued technological advances were mistaken as proof that nothing was seriously wrong. Yet, despite outward appearances, the vital but less visible measure of progress—equality—receded. "The same cause which turned Roman progress into retrogression is operating now. . . . What has destroyed every previous civilization has been the tendency to the unequal distribution of wealth and power." Look about the nation, he urged. One would see falling wages and interest in the face of ever-rising rent, causing the rich to get richer, the poor to get poorer, "and the middle class to be swept away." Nowhere was this more evident than in big cities like New York, Boston, Chicago, and San Francisco where one found extraordinary extremes of wealth and poverty overseen by a government composed of "a ruling class as in the most aristocratic countries of the world." There one found industrial relations that tended "to assume a form in which one is master and many serve" and a legal system obedient to the moneyed class instead of dictates of justice. Moreover, there was everywhere a weakening of the once universal "confident belief in republicanism as the source of national blessings."[67]

This change occurred not by sudden revolution, but by inches. "To turn republican government into a despotism the basest and most brutal," George pointed out, "it is not necessary formally to change its constitution or abandon popular elections." Indeed, republican government, when coupled with growing misery and inequality, accelerated the descent into barbarism. "To give the suffrage to tramps, to paupers . . . to men who must beg, or steal, or starve, is to invoke destruction." These were the sort who will flock to "the most blatant demagogue" or sell their once-sacred vote to the highest bidder.[68]

Only one result could come of this trend: apocalyptic destruction. "In the festering mass will be generated volcanic forces." Demagogues will arise to lead populist movements based not on democracy, equality, and Christianity, but rather upon violence, inequality, and despotism. While many of his contemporaries would deny it, the elements for such a fearful transformation of American society were all in place. "Whence shall come the new barbarians?" asked George, in terms that place him at the forefront of the era's popular apocalyptic style of reform literature. "Go through the squalid quarters of great cities, and you may see, even now, their gathering hordes."[69]

Despite George's grim description of explosive urban populations, he stood apart from other Gilded Age doomsayers like Josiah Strong. A few years later, Strong would write of the city, "Here is heaped the social dynamite; here roughs, gamblers, thieves, robbers, lawless and desperate men of all sorts, congregate; men who are ready on any pretext to raise riots for the purpose of destruction and plunder." For him, it was the racial, ethnic, and religious makeup of the urban masses that rendered them "social dynamite." But for George, in a line of reasoning that anticipated the environmental interpretation of poverty that would influence the later settlement house movement and the work of Jacob Riis, it was economic injustice and desperation that turned decent Americans into "the new barbarians."[70]

When George wrote of the "gathering hordes," it was not as a doomsayer like Strong, but rather as a would-be prophet offering salvation. He argued in *Progress and Poverty* that while decay and destruction had been the grim fate of all past great societies, it was by no means inevitable that America had to suffer the same. To avoid decline and destruction, American society had to recognize the primacy of equality in the hierarchy of republican values: "Modern civilization owes its superiority to the growth of equality with the growth of association. . . . Progress goes on just as society tends toward closer association and greater equality."[71] In stressing the economic dimension of equality, George challenged a central tenet of the free labor republican political culture of his time—that America would avoid any kind of class conflict simply because all citizens, if not equal in material terms, found equality in the political sphere via the ballot. "Equality of political rights," he ominously warned, "will not compensate for the denial of the equal right to the bounty of nature. . . . Poverty enslaves men who we boast are political sovereigns." In a modern industrial society, democratic freedoms alone were not sufficient to maintain democratic freedoms.

> It is not enough that men should vote; it is not enough that they should be theoretically equal before the law. They must have liberty to avail themselves of the opportunities and means of life; they must stand on equal terms with reference to the bounty of nature.[72]

In making this claim, George became an early proponent of an emerging progressive conviction that republican citizenship included certain material and economic rights in addition to political ones.

For a truly republican society to endure in the age of industrial capitalism, George contended, it needed the courage to break with the past and reshape itself. It needed to change its laws, amend its constitutions, and rethink its traditions, particularly the sanctity of private property and the role of the state. "Social adjustments promote justice."[73] Americans had to overcome their innate conservatism in order to preserve the republic of progress and equality. To do nothing meant certain doom. He warned that "a civilization like ours must either advance or go back; it cannot stand still."[74] The increasing trend toward land monopoly denied more and more people equal access to this bounty of nature, gradually turning the mass of equal citizens of a democracy into the slaves of the wealthy few:

> In allowing one man to own the land on which and from which other men must live, we have made them his bondsmen in a degree which increases as material progress goes on. This is the subtle alchemy that in ways they do not realize is extracting from the masses in every civilized country the fruits of their weary toil; that is instituting a harder and more hopeless slavery in place of that which has been destroyed; that is bringing political despotism out of freedom, and must soon transmute democratic institutions into anarchy.

The single tax, on the other hand, would arrest this trend and provide the context in which equality could flourish and progress continue indefinitely.[75]

George opened *Progress and Poverty* by imagining what Benjamin Franklin would have predicted about American society had he been made aware of the extraordinary material progress to come in the nineteenth century. He asserted that Franklin would have deduced that a society based on democracy and liberty possessing such abundance must surely produce a golden age. Then, for the next five hundred pages, George explained just why this hypothetical forecast failed to come pass, with the republic mired instead in poverty, inequality, and strife. Now, at the very end of the work, George again evoked the image of a golden age, as an obtainable objective rather than as a missed opportunity. If America and the civilized world heeded his call to social, economic, and political regeneration, "the culmination of Christianity—the City of God on earth"—would be achieved.[76]

"NOTHING IN THE ECONOMIC WORLD IS BEYOND THE CONTROL OF MEN"

Henry George's foray into the study of political economy took place in a tumultuous context that caused many Americans to question the long-assumed unique and exceptional character of republican society. Unsurprisingly, he was hardly the only one to search for answers to what commentators increasingly termed the "labor question," or the "social question." Indeed, the late 1870s and 1880s witnessed a profusion of works that marked a decisive turning point in American political thought, public policy, and law. It was in this period that classical liberalism and its ideals of laissez-faire, minimal government, rugged individualism, and absolute private property rights faced a serious challenge by an emerging set of different ideals, values, and aspirations. This new ideological paradigm came to be known variously as social democracy, new liberalism, and progressivism.[77]

Drawing upon the writings and theories of European reformers, as well as on American sources as diverse as the Grangers, Socialist Labor Party, and Knights of Labor, progressivism represented a major break with classical liberalism in two key ways. First, it stressed the primacy of the common good, an ideal that once had grounded eighteenth-century republican ideology but had been marginalized by the growing emphasis in the mid-nineteenth century on individualism. Under the conditions of industrial capitalism, advocates argued that republican liberty for all could no longer be secured merely by establishing a minimal body of laws to prevent individuals from impinging upon the rights of others—especially property rights. Republican liberty in the modern age now required that every individual enjoy a basic set of social conditions that ensured equal opportunities for success and upward mobility.[78]

Second, progressivism called upon the state to provide access to these social conditions. In contrast to classical liberalism's deep-seated fear of the state as an inherent threat to liberty, progressivism turned to the state as a positive and essential *guarantor* of liberty. Unless the state intervened in the market to rein in the power of corporations and ensure broad access to a living wage, education, public health, decent housing, and workplace safety, an untamed industrial economy would transform the American republic into a more European-style society of aristocrats and proletarians riven by class conflict, inequality, and, ultimately, anarchic revolution.[79]

As proponents of progressivism saw it, the challenge posed by the Gilded Age was to develop an effective ideological justification for state action to resolve the alarming problems that accompanied a rapidly unfolding industrial capitalist order. "What was needed was a new philosophy of the state," observes Sidney Fine in his classic study of decline of laissez-faire and the rise of the modern welfare state. "A new liberalism embodying something of the spirit of Jeffersonianism but ready to use government as an agency to promote the general welfare." Central to their understanding of the general welfare was the amelioration of class conflict.[80]

Early signs of this new philosophy of progressivism can be seen in the proclamations of organizations like the Knights of Labor and in the writings of radicals such as Albert Parsons. Significantly, this same impulse also appeared among a cohort of young, idealistic, and—for a time—radical political economists. Young men such as John Bates Clark, Henry Carter Adams, Edward Bemis, and Richard T. Ely all studied political economy in Germany, where the leading scholars of economics had come to reject the central tenets of English classical political economy. They most notably contested the idea that there were universal economic laws (e.g., the iron law of wages) that human beings were powerless to oppose—laws, in other words, that formed the foundation of laissez-faire doctrine. Instead, these

German-educated economists embraced historicism, arguing that because every economic order is created in the unique historical circumstances of its time and place, fixed economic laws that dictated appropriate government policies do not exist. Thus freed from laissez-faire orthodoxy, these thinkers (albeit with considerable ideological differences) advocated statist policies (including, for some, socialism) to promote and regulate national economic development.[81]

This immersion into German economic theory left a profound mark on these young American scholars. The most vivid example comes from Henry Clark Adams, who at the age of twenty-seven sailed for Germany in the summer of 1878. Two months into his studies in Berlin in December 1878—at the moment when Henry George was nearing completion of *Progress and Poverty*—he wrote an enthusiastic essay on socialism. "I hope it does not sound too socialistic," he wrote in his diary. "I am a socialist—to tell the truth." Disillusioned with the conservative political economy dominant in the United States, he found inspiration in the idea that a new political economy, one in step with the realities of the industrial age, could be employed to secure a just, republican society. Adams writes,

> I only know that English economy has served . . . and is serving as an opiate to the consciences of men who are trampling their fellow man in the dust. . . . If it was right for Christ to take the cloak away which covered the sins of men, it is right for me to do the same for that which makes men think their own acts of injustice are not their acts but the outworking of laws beyond human control. Nothing in the economic world is beyond the control of men and men must waken up to the controlling of these laws.

This revelation of Adams and other like-minded political economists marked a pivotal moment in the history of economic thought. It signaled the commencement of a decades-long transatlantic revolution aimed at empowering the state to rein in the excesses of laissez-faire capitalism.[82]

More radical statements, essays, and speeches critical of laissez-faire orthodoxy and admiring (if not fully embracing) of socialism followed in the coming years from Adams, Clark, and their fellow upstarts. It should come as no surprise that many of them read and discussed *Progress and Poverty*; indeed, Clark and Seligman were both significantly influenced by it.[83] But the young radicals soon faced the united opposition of their entrenched superiors in the academy, who wielded the power to grant or deny tenure. (Adams, for example, was ousted from his post at Cornell University in 1887.) By the late 1880s, particularly in the charged atmosphere following the Haymarket bombing in 1886, many of these young men tempered their radicalism, shunning any expressions of sympathy for socialism. And yet they succeeded in directing American political economy toward a progressivism that acknowledged the need for limited state intervention in the economy in the name of the common good, republican liberty, and class harmony.[84]

If Adams, Clark, and their fellow upstarts helped legitimize and popularize progressivism in the academy and in elite circles, Henry George played an important role in doing so among society at large. The two central pronouncements in George's book—that public policy in the age of industry must protect and promote republican equality ("We are made for cooperation") and that the state, as opposed to the market alone, must play the key role in securing this end—aligned precisely with the two underlying ideas of progressivism.[85] So when *Progress and Poverty* became an unprecedented bestseller in the 1880s (discussed in detail in chapter 5), it became the era's first major work read by a wide audience that waged a republican assault on laissez-faire. George was not only one of the first significant proponents of progressivism; he also played an important role in popularizing its core ideas.

"IT WILL ULTIMATELY BE CONSIDERED A GREAT BOOK"

On March 22, 1879, George mailed his manuscript to D. Appleton & Co. in New York City, a leading publisher of works of political economy. As he awaited a reply, fearful that his state job would soon expire, George did what came naturally to him—he established the *State*, a newspaper that began publication that April. No sooner had he begun this budding enterprise when he received the first of many early publishing disappointments. While D. Appleton admitted the treatise was "written with great clearness and force," it found its argument too "aggressive" for contemporary tastes

Henry George, age 40, about the time he finished writing *Progress and Poverty* (1879).
Courtesy of the New York Public Library

and declined to publish it. George's brother Thomas soon reported from New York that Harper's and Scribner's had also rejected the work.[86]

Undaunted, George did what few authors in any era could do: he drew upon his skills as a printer and set the plates for the book himself. By the summer's end, with financial help from friends, George turned out an "Author's Edition" of five hundred copies of *Progress and Poverty* and mailed a number of them to several New York publishers. Hoping to gain the attention of some of the world's most notable social thinkers and reformers, George also mailed complimentary copies to Herbert Spencer and William Gladstone in England, and to two notable social reformers in Scotland and New Zealand. He also sent a copy to his father, accompanied by a letter written in the tone of both a son seeking paternal approval and of a reformer who saw himself in the mold of a biblical prophet:

> It represents a great deal of work and a good deal of sacrifice, but now it is done. It will not be recognized at first—may be not for some time—but it will ultimately be considered a great book, will be published in both hemispheres, and be translated into different languages. This I know, though neither of us may ever see it here.[87]

In light of *Progress and Poverty*'s eventual stunning success—by 1886, the work appeared in thirteen languages and was already the bestselling book on political economy in the nineteenth century—these predictions appear warranted. But when one considers that they were the words of a man with only a marginal formal education and a lifetime to that point of repeated failures, they are a revealing testament to his extraordinary sense of missionary purpose.

As George expected, encouraging news soon arrived. Appleton, upon receiving a revised copy of *Progress and Poverty* and with word that the plates had been set, agreed to publish the work, admitting that its radical tone would "create some sort of a sensation." George would receive a 15 percent royalty cut from every copy sold at the price of two dollars. Within a few months of George sending the plates eastward, and two and a quarter years since he commenced writing, Appleton published its edition in January 1880.[88]

Unfortunately for George, the popularity he so desperately sought for the ideas expressed in *Progress and Poverty* was not generated immediately upon publication. Indeed, it took several years to fully develop. The initial reviews were mixed, with a few applauding the work but far more criticizing or dismissing it. Then, in March 1880, *Progress and Poverty* received its first serious review; although critical in many places, it gave George encouragement. "I have longed," he wrote, "that by this day at least there might be some sign that the seed I had tried to plant there had not fallen by the wayside. This review is that sign." More signs soon appeared: Appleton wrote to say that he had sold the original one thousand copies and intended to print five hundred more.[89]

Despite this good bit of news, George found himself in mid-1880, more than a year after finishing the manuscript, anxious and impatient. While his book had sold reasonably well and attracted the attention of the nation's most prominent newspapers (albeit with mixed results), no firm opinion had yet emerged regarding its thesis; no great reputation had been established. George still lacked the great stage he so earnestly desired from which to trumpet his radical plan of social reform.

He decided upon a bold plan of action. If the world would not come to his door, he would set out in pursuit of it. Accordingly, he fixed his sights on New York, the city that more than any other shaped American public opinion and the portal through which American ideas flowed outward to Europe. Borrowing the necessary funds from friends, he set out in the first week of August 1880.

PART II

The Emergence of "New Political Forces," 1880–1885

3

"New York Is an Immense City"

THE EMPIRE CITY IN THE EARLY 1880s

> There are worlds and worlds—even within the bounds of the same horizon. The man who comes into New York with plenty of money, who puts up at the Windsor or Brunswick, and is received by hospitable hosts in Fifth Avenue mansions, sees one New York. The man who comes with a dollar and a half, and goes to a twenty-five cent lodging-house, sees another. There are also fifteen-cent lodging-houses, and people too poor to go even to them.
>
> —Henry George

CROWDED CITY, IMMIGRANT CITY:
THE DEMOGRAPHIC PICTURE

It had been eleven years since Henry George's last his visit to New York City, when the extremes of poverty and plenty so disturbed him. Now, as he detrained in Manhattan in August 1880, what did he see? What had changed since then? What had remained the same?

To begin with, New York was bigger, both in terms of land mass (through annexations) and population (from 942,000 in 1870 to over 1.2 million in 1880). Across the East River, the nation's third most populous city, Brooklyn, claimed nearly 600,000 residents (table 3.1). Physically, New York remained a city of red brick and brownstone; although its famed skyscrapers had yet to appear, the buildings had grown taller with the advent of cast iron and steel. "New York is an immense city," George wrote to his son Richard shortly after arriving. "Such long streets, such high houses, such crowds as you never saw. It makes San Francisco seem

TABLE 3.1 Growth of Population in New York and Brooklyn, 1860–1890

	1860	1870	1880	1890
New York	813,669	942,292	1,206,299	1,515,301
Brooklyn	266,661	396,099	566,663	806,343

Source: Ira Rosenwaike, *Population History of New York City* (Syracuse: Syracuse University Press, 1972), 63. Adapted from table 19.

quite small."[1] Indeed, New York in 1880 made any city, save London, pale by comparison when it came to size.

George surely would have noticed several new features, ones that would in time come to define modern New York. Central Park, the nation's first large urban park, had been completed in 1873, and St. Patrick's Cathedral, symbolizing the rising presence of Irish Catholics in America, was consecrated on May 25, 1879. The new Metropolitan Museum of Art opened in March 1880. And soaring above everything else, the tallest structures in North America, were the twin towers of the Brooklyn Bridge, a monumental feat of engineering that soon would be finished in 1883. Plans for the erection of another legendary structure, the Statue of Liberty (completed six years later), were well under way.

Apart from the city's new physical features, George encountered a metropolis being reshaped economically, socially, and geographically by advances in technology. New modes of rapid transit were dramatically altering the way people lived and worked, encouraging population expansion out into nearby suburbs. Every day, tens of thousands crossed the surrounding waterways via ferry to Manhattan from New Jersey and Brooklyn. Others were dropped within the city limits from outlying neighborhoods by steam locomotives, the latest being the Elevated Railroad, which carried nearly 61 million passengers in its first full year of service (1880). Once there, commuters joined Manhattan residents aboard streetcars; in 1880 alone, these horse-drawn buses on rails transported 149 million riders. These innovations in transportation also dramatically increased residential segregation based on race, ethnicity, and class; likewise, the city became segmented by function, with some areas devoted exclusively to business and manufacturing and others to residences.[2]

On the heels of these new forms of physical communication came rapid improvements in the communication of information. The recent widespread introduction of the telegraph and telephone speeded up communication within the burgeoning city like never before. New York also possessed more newspapers than any other American city at the time—more than twenty-five daily papers and dozens of weekly papers in English circulated the city, along with a wealth of foreign-language periodicals. This abundance of media sources, however, did not translate into a corresponding variety of ideological and political perspectives. Beyond affiliating with political parties and figures, few papers took bold or independent positions on current issues out of fear of alienating their customers. No paper in 1880 could be considered working-class in orientation, including those that did depend heavily on working-class patronage.[3]

In addition to new technological achievements, mass immigration had continued to transform New York since George last saw it. Waves of so-called "old" immigrant groups (principally from Ireland and Germany), which had begun in the 1830s, had wholly altered the face of the city by 1880. A full one-third of New Yorkers in 1880 were born abroad in Ireland or Germany; among the native-born population, an impressive 80 percent claimed at least one parent of foreign birth (74 percent had two foreign-born parents). All told, New York presented an astonishing picture of a city dominated by immigrants and their children.[4]

As in George's San Francisco, the transformation of New York into a burgeoning city of immigrants did not occur quietly. Working-class native-born New Yorkers blamed immigrants for driving down wages and taking jobs. Middle- and upper-class residents negatively commented on their alien habits, languages, and cultures; they were also made into scapegoats for disease, crime, and intemperance. Ethnic and religious tensions occasionally led to explosive riots. Clashes between Irish Catholics and Irish Protestants in 1870 and 1871 left more than seventy people dead on the city's streets. More commonly, immigrants faced an incessant barrage of ethnic slurs in public speeches, plays, newspapers, and popular magazines. For example, Thomas Nast regularly depicted Irish immigrants as ape-like cretins led by a band of conniving Catholic priests in *Harper's Weekly*.[5]

Such a limited portrait, however, can give the false impression of the city's German and Irish populations as helpless, homogeneous immigrant communities. In reality, there existed within both ethnic groups a significant degree of social, economic, class, cultural, and religious diversity. For instance, while a substantial proportion of Irish and Irish American workers still languished in low-paid, unskilled, backbreaking occupations, ever greater numbers were beginning to enter the ranks of semiskilled and skilled trades. Some "lace-curtain" Irish, as their working-class counterparts disparagingly called them, rose even higher as wealthy dry goods merchants, contractors, and restaurateurs. Still others were breaking into the medical and legal professions.[6] A similar examination of German New Yorkers reveals an ethnic group united by language, but also riven by class, religion, and social distinctions.[7]

As rising numbers of German and Irish Americans climbed the social and occupational ladders in the 1870s, they likewise edged into positions of political power. Far from being a powerless minority, the Irish in 1880 celebrated the election of the first Irish Catholic mayor in the city's history, shipping magnate William R. Grace. In that same year, men of Irish and German descent made up at least 70 percent of the Board of Aldermen. Indeed, it is clear that the virulent nativism of the 1870s did not indicate the poor position of Irish and German New Yorkers, but rather how much their growing self-empowerment frightened native-born Protestants.[8]

In contrast, New York's African American community could point to little in the way of economic and political power. Relative to the native-born white and immigrant populations, African Americans comprised a tiny fraction of the city's population in 1880—just 19,663 persons, or about 1.6 percent. Crowded into the worst tenement housing in the city's lower wards, they struggled in a poverty dictated by racist hiring practices, which confined most black men and women to low-paying menial occupations. The explosion of European immigration shrank their job opportunities; these newcomers, particularly the Irish, pushed African Americans out of many occupations they had come to dominate, such as carting, barbering, and domestic service. African Americans also suffered violence and abuse at the hands of white New Yorkers, ranging from the notorious Draft Riots in 1863 that saw eighteen blacks lynched, to routine clubbings by policemen that went unpunished by an indifferent legal system.[9]

Henry George's New York in 1880 was overwhelmingly an "immigrant city," dominated by Irish and Germans, but it was on the cusp of still greater growth and diversity with migration from Southern and Eastern Europe on the rise. On one hand, this made New York City a unique and cosmopolitan metropolis. On the other, it meant the city was also a place of terrific confusion, with language, neighborhood, class, religion, and race often sharply dividing its citizens.

"EVERYTHING IN MANHATTAN IS IN EXTREMES":
HEALTH, HOUSING, AND LIVING CONDITIONS

In 1880, Gotham was the very embodiment of the "great enigma" George warned about in *Progress and Poverty*—a place experiencing the growth of poverty amidst extraordinary wealth.[10] Evidence of the latter in the Empire City abounded. By 1892, according to the *New York Tribune*, the city would become home to 1,265 millionaires (some 30 percent of the U.S. total). But it was most apparent in the grand homes and institutions built by the city's super rich, especially those who had acquired their fortunes only recently. These *nouveaux riches* —brash arrivistes like the Vanderbilts, Villards, Morgans, and Goulds—sought to mark concretely their arrival in the city's highest circles of wealth and prestige by building themselves magnificent marble mansions on Fifth Avenue. By the 1890s, the upper reaches of that famous thoroughfare were so completely lined by mansions that the American writer Edgar Saltus could write without exaggeration, "There is many a palace in Europe that would hide its diminished roof beside the sheer luxury of Fifth Avenue homes."[11]

New York's elite showed off their wealth in ways well beyond gaudy architecture. They hosted an endless succession of opulent balls, dinners, and soirees. Although not the first of its kind, the event that set the definitive standard for elite displays of conspicuous consumption was the Vanderbilt Ball of 1883. To celebrate the completion of the city's most opulent mansion to date, a marble palace standing at Fifth Avenue and East 52nd Street, Mrs. William K. Vanderbilt threw a grand gala costume ball—as a "housewarming" party. Covered extensively by the press, the festivities brought out a who's who list of New York society. Tellingly—and at odds with longstanding notions of republican simplicity and disdain for luxury—most came dressed as European royalty. The event proved such a hit that elite New Yorkers spent the next decade and a half trying to outdo each other in these astonishing exhibitions of wealth. These events in turn captivated the general public while making it clear to them who possessed true social, political, and economic power.[12]

Yet, for all the glitter of its elites, by the 1880s New York City was equally famous for its displays of conspicuous penury. Only the year before George arrived in the city, the aging poet Walt Whitman looked with growing distress at his beloved city. He added his prescient voice to the rising chorus of Americans who could not help but see in rising poverty a republican crisis in the making. "If the United States, like the countries of the Old World, are also to grow vast crops of poor, desperate, dissatisfied, nomadic, miserably-waged populations, such as we see looming upon us of late years—steadily, even if slowly, eating into them like a cancer of lungs or stomach, then our republican experiment, notwithstanding all its surface-successes, is at heart an unhealthy failure," he wrote in a tone and language strikingly similar to George's.[13]

One did not need to look very hard to find these "vast crops" of poor people. Always a city of contrasts, New York nevertheless probably deserved this appellation most during the Gilded Age. For all its splendor and wealth, for all its capacity to produce and expand, for all its art and high culture, New York was a city where hundreds of thousands of people lived in some of the very worst conditions in the nation. The same year George moved to the city, Richard T. Ely, one of the young radical economists discussed in chapter 2, returned to the United States after finishing his studies in Germany. Upon his arrival in New York, he was stunned by the poverty and suffering existing amidst such ostentatious wealth. "I took upon myself a vow to write in behalf of the laboring classes," he remarked.[14]

The poor of Gotham, many of them immigrants, often lacked occupational skills applicable to their new urban setting, relegating them to erratic and poorly paid employment. Estimates vary, but the average annual wage of the common laborer in New York ranged between $375 and $500 in the

The extreme gap between the rich and the poor. "The Hearth-stone of the Poor." *Harper's Weekly*, February 12, 1876. Courtesy of the Library of Congress

early 1880s, a level far below the estimated necessary subsistence income of approximately \$700.[15] To cover this deficit, male workers relied on their families to produce additional income for the household to survive. More and more women joined the paid workforce. The number of women working in manufacturing rose 21 percent in the 1880s, with significant increases in industries such as silk goods (24 percent), tobacco products (21 percent), boxes (44 percent), and millinery and lace goods (41 percent). In every case they were paid a fraction of the wages enjoyed by their male counterparts. Tens of thousands of women also took work in middle-class homes as domestic servants; others who elected to remain at home took in laundry, sewing, finishing work, and boarders as a means of supplementing the household income. Children were set to work, often at a very young age. Some found jobs as factory hands, others as delivery boys, and still others as rag pickers and scavengers. "It is only by the strictest economy," offered a contemporary observer, "that they [the poor] manage to get along at all."[16]

The poverty of the city's workers was exacerbated by squalid tenement housing. When the city legally established the standard building lot at twenty-five feet (fronting the street) by one hundred feet in 1811, it did so with the understanding that *single-family* homes would be built on them. By 1880, the typical four to six-story tenement building occupied these same lots, often housing more than twenty families. Each floor contained four apartments, usually consisting of three rooms. Only one—either facing the street or the backyard—tended to have any windows to receive any light or fresh air. While reformers successfully pushed the city to adopt a law mandating air shafts between buildings (thereby allowing for small windows in interior rooms) in 1879, the law affected only buildings constructed after it took effect; the city's more than 21,000 existing tenements were left untouched. The vast majority of tenements had no running water, gas lighting, or central heating system.[17] They also suffered from inadequate to nonexistent sewage removal, leading to frequent overflows (particularly during heavy rainfall) that produced oppressive and unhealthful "sewer gasses" and high rates of disease.[18]

Despite the dreadful condition of these filthy buildings, the city's surging population kept the demand for housing high. Optimists had repeatedly predicted since the 1860s that the widespread construction of tenements would solve New York's chronic housing shortage. Yet in 1880, as if to confirm George's contentions about the distortions of land monopoly, demand still outpaced supply and rents continued to rise despite the erection of over seven thousand tenements in the previous decade. One 1883 survey of bricklayers, the city's best-paid wage workers, determined that they paid 28 percent of their annual income to their landlords. Those who lived in far worse housing paid an even higher percentage.[19]

Beyond the terrible conditions and expense, tenement dwellers also endured an environment of epidemics, suffering, and death. Just four weeks before George arrived in Manhattan, the *New York Times* ran a series of stories on the soaring death rate in the city during a recent heat wave, reporting that 1,297 people died in a single week, two-thirds of them children under the age of five. "Undertakers' wagons are busy on the East Side," noted the newspaper, and "the coffin-maker's hammer has no rest."[20] The city's Metropolitan Board of Health had few powers and little will to use them; meanwhile, the politics of patronage undermined efforts to rid streets of filth as contracts were awarded on the basis of political connections rather than commitment to public health. "Streets and avenues in the thinly populated half of the city," one contemporary commented, "are often swept twice a week, while in the crowded and narrow streets sweeping is done but once a week, if that much."[21] In a city that relied upon on sixty thousand horses producing 2.5 million pounds of manure and sixty thousand gallons of urine every day, insufficient street cleaning posed a horrific public health problem.[22]

The problem of tenement life was magnified by the extraordinary population density of the city's slum districts. To George, this overcrowding offered a perfect real-life example of the pernicious effects of land monopoly. "There is plenty of vacant land on Manhattan Island," he would write a few years later. "But on Manhattan Island, human beings are packed closer than anywhere else in the world." Of the 1.2 million persons registered in the Census of 1880, an overwhelming proportion were crammed in the neighborhoods below 14th Street. In working-class immigrant areas such as the Tenth Ward of the Lower East Side, the population density reached 276,672 inhabitants to the square mile, a level then unheard of in human history.[23]

The filthy streets of the Lower East Side. "New York City: How the Metropolis Invites Disease and Epidemics." *Frank Leslie's Illustrated Weekly*, April 23, 1881. Courtesy of the New York Public Library

Statistics compiled by the city's Board of Health and the Census Bureau vividly illustrate the deadly impact of unhealthy tenement life. Table 3.2 shows that for all the effort by reformers and reform-minded government agencies, the city's overall death rate declined only slightly between the years 1875 and 1890. More precisely, it shows an astonishing death rate among infants and children, one of the surest indications of poor health standards.

Moreover, Table 3.3 showcases the stark disparity in health conditions between middle- and upper-class residents and those cramped in the tenement districts. The tenement problem was neatly summarized in a report by the Society for the Improvement of the Condition of the Poor, which noted, "Crazy old buildings, crowded rear tenements in filthy yards, dark, damp basements, leaking garrets, shops, outhouses, and stables converted into dwellings, though scarcely fit to shelter brutes, are the habitations of thousands of our fellow-beings in this wealthy, Christian city."[24] In 1880, two-thirds of the city's residents called such places home (table 3.4).[25]

TABLE 3.2 Death Rates Per 1,000 of Population

	Aggregate	Infants (under the age of 1)	Children (under the age of 5)
1875	28.80	n/a	n/a
1880	26.48	279.80	104.35
1885	26.39	273.60	100.41
1890	26.47	277.48	99.01

Note: The figures exclude stillbirths.

Source: Adapted from tables 3 and 8 in U.S. Census Office, *Vital Statistics of New York City and Brooklyn for the Six Year Period Ending May 30, 1890*, ed. John S. Billings (Washington, D.C.: U.S. Government Printing Office, 1894), 3, 9.

TABLE 3.3 Death Rates Per 1,000 by Selected Grouping and Age, 1890

Wards	Aggregate	Infants (under the age of 1)	Children (under the age of 5)
Entire city	26.47	277.48	99.01
Middle-class	18.67	351.57	129.44
Working-class	41.92	447.70	225.68

Note: City figures for 1890 exclude stillbirths, while those for the ward groupings of that year include them. Working-class wards surveyed: 1, 2, 4, 5B, 8B, 14, and 15B. Middle- and upper-class wards surveyed: 18D; 16D; 21D and F; 19A, D, K, and N; 21 C, F, I, K, and M; and 12 A, E, H, K, and I. Letters correspond to sanitary districts within each ward.

Source: Adapted from table 67 in U.S. Census Office, *Vital Statistics of New York and Brooklyn* (Washington, D.C.: U.S. Government Printing Office, 1890), 66.

TABLE 3.4 Tenement Population in New York City, 1865–1900

	Number of tenements	Tenement population	Total population in tenements	Percent living
1865	15,511	486,000	726,386	67
1879	21,163	720,000	1,150,000 (est.)	65.6
1893	39,138	n/a	1,700,000 (est.)	n/a
1900	42,700	1,585,000	2,507,414	63

Sources: Statistics for 1865, 1893, and 1900 are from Roy Lubove, *The Progressives and the Slums: Tenement House Reform in New York City, 1890–1917* (Pittsburgh: University of Pittsburgh Press, 1962), 257–66. Statistics for 1879 are from the testimony of Colonel Emmons Clark, RCSRLC, 2:2, 646–72. The population statistics for 1879 are based on the July 1878 population estimate from New York City Board of Health, *Annual Report for 1879*, 38th report, cited in the testimony of C. Wingate, *RCSRLC*, 2:1043–45.

The only thing worse than living in a tenement was getting evicted from one. And evictions occurred at a frightful rate in Gilded Age New York, exceeding 16,000 per year in the early 1880s and more than 23,000 by 1892. "Tenant's rights" simply did not exist at this time. Landlords could easily procure an eviction order from a judge for rent overdue by as few as three days or for an expired lease, and would cast a family and their belongings out onto the merciless streets regardless of the season. In addition to seasonal unemployment, wage reductions, illness, and the devastating sudden death of the main breadwinner, evictions added immeasurably to the anxious uncertainty that marked the life of the city's workers.[26]

All of these problems, frustrations, and apprehensions of the city's tenement dwellers found expression in a *New York Times* editorial in May 1880, printed a few months before George set out for New York. It notes that, after more than a decade of population spreading uptown and new apartment construction, decent and affordable housing still eluded a majority of the poor and middle class:

> There are not here, as there are in most cities, decent, respectable neighborhoods which lay claim neither to elegance or fashion. Everything in Manhattan is in extremes....
>
> No other town of any size in civilization which we can recall is so ill-provided in this respect [of good housing]. It would hardly be an exaggeration to say three-quarters of the built-up portion of the Metropolis is either unfit for respectable residents or unattainable for persons of ordinary means.[27]

Henry George could have scarcely put it better himself. The well-deserved reputation of New York as the city of extremes was best and most obviously exemplified in its housing. Too many people with too few resources lived in ill-designed and overcrowded housing. Coupled with poor diets, filthy streets, and inadequate sewage, it made for a potent recipe of misery and death. Perhaps more than any other aspect of Henry George's message of social reform, the idea that nonproducing landlords siphoned off unearned profits at the expense of honest laborers possessed a compelling salience among the city's hard-pressed working class.

"ALL THE BRAINS, AND ALL THE CASH OF THE NATION": THE GREAT COMMERCIAL METROPOLIS

If Henry George's New York provided vivid examples of Gilded Age poverty, it also showcased the age's remarkable industrial progress. The United States between 1860 and 1900 lurched fully into the Industrial Revolution, leaving behind only the fond memory of an economy dominated by farmers and artisanal craftsmen. New immigrants, new technologies, new markets, new modes of organizing production, and new relations between employers and workers facilitated this transformation; by 1900, America possessed the most advanced industrial economy in the world, the very embodiment of the progress of which George wrote. Whereas in 1870 agricultural output dominated the American economy, industrial output exceeded it by $13 billion to $4.7 billion by 1900—a staggering feat in only thirty years. Exemplifying this trend was the steel industry: in 1860, the United States produced less steel than both France and England (approximately 13,000 short tons), but by 1900 the nation was first in the world (10,382,000 short tons).[28]

New York, already America's great commercial metropolis in 1860, experienced proportional changes in its economy, leading the novelist Henry Adams to comment that the city had "exploded its wrapper." Several crucial factors accounted for this. Rapid population growth created both a large supply of cheap labor and a greater demand for goods and services. Technological advances (especially in areas like mechanization), increased power sources, and labor-saving devices made each individual worker and shop considerably more efficient and productive. The establishment of nationwide markets—a development made possible with the advent of the telegraph, mass media, and the locomotive—spurred demand for the products of New York's various industries. Finally, New York became the primary business address of the era's most innovative and influential industrial capitalists. Together, these and other factors combined to sustain the city's reputation as *the* national center for commercial innovation, opportunity, and success, a fact revealed more explicitly by analyzing several key facets of the city's economic growth in this period.[29]

New York in 1880 maintained its dominance of the U.S. import and export trade despite increased competition from Baltimore, Philadelphia,

Newark, and New Orleans. Although its share of trade handled dropped from 70 percent of the U.S. total in 1850 to 56.7 percent in 1880, the value of trade handled (68 percent of total value in 1890) continued to keep New York far ahead of all potential rivals (table 3.5). In addition, New York City's traditional industries—like printing and publishing, clothing, furniture, and tobacco—grew at unprecedented rates between 1860 and 1890 (table 3.6).[30]

The explosive growth of New York City's internal economy likewise played a significant role. With the advent of the streetcar in the 1850s and

TABLE 3.5 Growth of New York City Manufactures, 1860–1890

	Number of establishments	Number of employees	Average capital per establishment	Gross value produced
1860	4,375	90,204	13,991	159,107,369
1870	7,624	129,577	17,042	332,951,520
1880	11,273	223,073	15,932	468,443,248
1890	25,403	340,482	16,774	777,222,721

Source: U.S. Department of the Interior, Census Office, *Census of Manufactures* (1860), 384; *Census of Manufactures* (1870), 550; *Census of Manufactures* (1890), xiv.

TABLE 3.6 Growth of Selected Industries in New York City, 1870–1890

	1870		1890	
INDUSTRY	NUMBER OF FIRMS	VALUE PRODUCED	NUMBER OF FIRMS	VALUE PRODUCED
Clothing	952	38,811,826	4,484	126,012,142[*a]
Furniture	342	(unclear)	598	15,475,981[b]
Print and publishing	191	15,711,246	1,368	60,491,066[c]
Tobacco	656	10,103,751	1,295	35,560,025[d]

[a] Excludes firms providing clothing materials (i.e., buttons).

[b] Includes mattresses and spring beds.

[c] Excludes firms providing printing materials. Bookbinding and blank bookmaking included.

[d] All kinds.

Sources: U.S. Department of the Interior, Census Office, *Census of Manufactures* (1870), 702–3; *Census of Manufactures* (1890), 390–409.

the elevated railroads in the 1870s, Manhattan's sparsely inhabited northern areas underwent rapid development, putting tens of thousands of
tradesmen to work constructing apartments and laying thousands of miles
of streets, sewers, and gas lines. For example, in 1870 a little more than 1,200
masons labored to produce $671,000 in finished work; twenty years later,
2,200 masons produced over $4.2 million. And while real estate had long
been the source of immense fortunes before 1860 (John Jacob Astor being
the prime example), it became an extraordinarily valuable commodity and
a central component in the city's economic expansion (and a vivid illustra-
tion of George's assertions about land values and "association").[31]

The contribution of the city's physical growth to its economy was
matched by a corresponding increase in the demand for local goods and
services. Every one of the thousands of newcomers taking residence in
or passing through the city every year required not just housing, but also
food, clothing, dry goods, transportation, and entertainment. This created
countless entrepreneurial opportunities and tens of thousands of new jobs.
Bread bakeries, for example, which produced primarily for local consumption, more than doubled in number from 455 in 1870 to 1,004 in 1890, with
a parallel rise in bakery employees from 2,344 to 5,804.[32]

To cope with the problems and complexities of the growing metropolis,
the range and scope of the city government expanded. The city's budget
nearly quadrupled between 1860 and 1890, rising from $9,786,000 to an
astounding $34,986,000. The city also hired thousands of workers, some
in established civic fields like public school education, street cleaning,
and police and fire protection, and others (such as engineers, inspectors,
and accountants) in new divisions and departments designed to tame and
rationalize the turbulent urban environment. In either case, New York's
municipal government played an instrumental role in the city's growing
internal economy, by promoting real estate development, extending urban
services, and adding to the public payroll.[33]

New York's expanding economy in the Gilded Age also witnessed the
transformation of several traditional commercial enterprises and the establishment of entirely new ones. While the Empire City had always been a center for banking and investment in the antebellum era, it soared to unprecedented prominence in these fields after 1860.[34] The passage of the National

Bank Act in 1863 and successive legislation promoted the concentration of financial power in New York's large banking houses. Investment banking, led by Drexel, Morgan, & Co., broadened its services to handle investments in burgeoning industries like railroads, mining, and petroleum. The New York Stock Exchange solidified its position as the primary national marketplace for the purchase and sale of stocks and other securities. The insurance industry, led by the nation's four largest companies, was located in Manhattan as well. By 1880, New York was the home to the iconic address (Wall Street), institution (the Stock Exchange), and personality (J. P. Morgan) of finance capitalism. "New York," observed Frank *Leslie's Weekly*, "attracts all the brains, and all the cash of the nation."[35]

Hand in hand with the rising role played by finance between 1860 and 1900 was the decision of many of the nation's major corporations to establish their headquarters in the city. Because of its commercial reputation, access to information and talent, and proximity to credit and marketing resources, New York emerged in this period as the home address of corporate America. By 1900, sixty-nine of the nation's largest 185 corporations based themselves in New York, while many others maintained offices and branch operations there.[36]

Apart from the great wealth brought by these corporations, their ascent signaled a major occupational revolution. A veritable army of workers entered the fields of middle management, sales, marketing, and other white-collar and clerical positions. Corporate growth also increased demand for lawyers, accountants, and other professional experts. Of this rise of "service industries," with their vast expansion of professional, managerial, and clerical occupations and opportunities, George would observe a few years later, "It is everywhere obvious that the independent mechanic is becoming an operative, the little storekeeper a salesman in a big store, the small merchant a clerk or bookkeeper, and that men, under the old system independent, are being massed in the employ of great firms and corporations."[37]

Taken together, these trends and statistics indicate that Henry George had moved to a city that was the virtual embodiment of the Industrial Revolution. As a social critic obsessed with the duality of progress and poverty in an advancing capitalist order, George would find both in abundance in his new home.

"THE WORST GOVERNED CITY IN THE WORLD":
POLITICS AND SOCIETY

Any assessment of New York City during the Gilded Age must consider its politics, in particular the faction of the Democratic Party known as Tammany Hall. Initially founded as a fraternal and charitable society in the 1780s, Tammany steadily evolved in the nineteenth century into a powerful political organization that relied on the poor immigrant vote (especially the Irish), a certain amount of political trickery (e.g., ballot box stuffing), and corruption. By the late 1860s, under the leadership of "Boss" William Tweed, the Tammany machine dominated the city.[38] But in August 1871, a *New York Times* expose revealed Tweed's role in the most costly (possibly to the amount of $20,000,000) and most comprehensive corruption scheme in American municipal history.[39]

The Tweed scandal and its aftermath defined the city's politics in the decade before George arrived. To property owners, businessmen, and old money elites, the most frightening aspect of Tweed was not his corruption; in many ways, his pro-development policies were a boon for business. Rather, they feared his successful mobilization of the "dangerous classes" against their social betters. As one such commentator wrote in 1874, Tammany was comprised of "adventurers, idlers, and criminals, uneducated and without either moral or patriotic conviction[,] ... men who are champions and exponents of the very class against which society is organized to protect itself."[40] To thwart this unwelcome trend, the city's commercial, cultural, and social elite banded together to effectively undercut working-class political empowerment.[41]

A Committee of Seventy comprised of Republicans and reform-minded Democrats drawn from elite organizations like the Union League Club and the Chamber of Commerce succeeded in electing or placing men from their own ranks in several key municipal positions—mayor, comptroller, and the heads of public works and the Central Park Commission, among others. This new leadership broke with Tweed's style of activist government that offered something to everyone, from the poor to prosperous developers. They ushered in a vigorous policy of fiscal retrenchment primarily through reduced taxes, lowered debt, and slashed poverty relief.[42]

With the city's fiscal situation placed under elite control and set in a new direction, the Committee of Seventy moved to make their reassertion of power permanent by trying to disenfranchise massive numbers—between 29 percent and 69 percent by some estimates—of New York voters by imposing a minimum property requirement for voting. The initiative ultimately died in the 1878 New York State legislature, in part due to mobilized working-class opposition. But this effort to restrict the suffrage to the "better sort" of citizens revealed the depth of fear felt by middle- and upper-class New Yorkers regarding the growing power and influence of immigrant and working-class voters.[43]

Tammany survived the Tweed scandal and the Committee of Seventy's efforts to kill it, but it did so only by drawing in respectable merchant reformers like William Havemeyer and Abram Hewitt. The organization needed such men not just for their respectability, but also for their access to ample financial resources. Thus, while Tammany continued to solicit the working-class immigrant vote, it did so while assiduously avoiding any class-conscious appeal. Tweed's replacement as head of Tammany, city comptroller "Honest" John Kelly, acceded to the prevailing liberal dogmas of low taxes and reduced public spending on poor relief and public works, policies that hurt the working class the most—especially during the depression years of the 1870s.[44]

But how then did Tammany rebuild and retain its political base among the city's working class? Instead of promising to defend them as workers from exploitive capitalists (and thereby alienating the organization's merchant benefactors), Tammany leaders promised to protect them as immigrants and Catholics from aggressive nativists. As a result, the traditionally nominal influence of labor and working-class politics within Tammany diminished further in the 1870s.[45]

Other aspects of Tammany served to stymie meaningful working-class influence within the organization. Because the very nature of late nineteenth-century machine politics was local and decentralized, those who identified with Tammany did so largely for local and practical reasons rather than out of any affinity for the abstract ideological positions outlined in its party platform. What drew them to Tammany was both its capacity to provide access to patronage in the form of cash, jobs, and contracts, as well as the occasional timely intervention by a Tammany official on behalf of a beleaguered pushcart peddler, saloonkeeper, or destitute widow. Of vital importance was the fact that Tammany largesse was of the no-questions-asked variety, in sharp contrast to the tightfisted and morally judgmental Protestant charity organizations. This policy, coupled with huge monetary resources, enabled Tammany officials to literally purchase the loyalty of their constituents, giving them an advantage over both reformers trying to woo voters with appeals to honesty and good government and labor activists seeking support with appeals to working-class interests.[46]

The Tammany machine used other tactics besides money and favors to minimize class-oriented politics. New York City did not adopt the secret (or Australian) ballot until 1897, allowing Tammany to employ legions of poll watchers and "shoulder hitters" to ensure that workers voted "correctly." If a voter did not fall into line, his transgression was met with violence on the spot or with later retaliation by party officials, who fired the offender (or his family members) from public jobs or withheld charity. As a result, few workers possessed the will and independence to stand up to such overt intimidation and vote for a labor or socialist party candidate.[47]

Through closed-door caucuses and conventions controlled by party officials, Tammany (and the city's other political organizations) made it all but impossible for labor activists to get nominated.[48] As a result of these factors, New York's workers, in contrast to their counterparts in cities like Chicago where labor enjoyed substantial political influence, found themselves without a significant voice in municipal politics. Lacking any substantive working-class pressure, either from within the party or from without (by an independent labor party), Tammany candidates could give empty rhetorical support to the concerns of workingmen while pursuing a mainstream agenda that never threatened commercial interests. Statistics bear this out: between 1872 and 1886, every mayor was a wealthy businessman connected to the city's highest sources of commercial and social powers, and most of them enjoyed the nomination of Tammany Hall.[49]

For all their cumulative votes, the city's workers enjoyed very little political power as a class of wage earners and lacked representatives willing to fight for their interests. Occasional third-party efforts by socialists or trade unionists failed miserably. Workers were expected to vote for Tammany and other Democratic factions, not to demand a class-based political program or positions of leadership.

"THE METROPOLIS OF LABOR"

Henry George arrived at an uncharacteristically quiescent period in the ongoing struggle between workers and employers in New York. In the months leading up to his arrival in August 1880, the city had experienced only a handful of strikes, only two of which (by piano makers and streetcar drivers) lasted any appreciable period of time. To a large degree, this temporary peace reflected the devastating impact the depression of the 1870s had on the city's labor movement. The decade had begun auspiciously for organized labor, so much so that in July 1870 the *New York Herald*, surveying the condition of the city's labor movement, concluded that "New York City is the metropolis of labor as of everything else, and takes the lead of all other American cities in this respect."[50] Two years later, following the lead of workers in the building trades, 95,000 workers (one-third of the city's workforce and two-thirds of its manufacturing workers) staged an eight-week strike for the eight-hour day. Although the strike failed (only about ten thousand workers gained the shorter day), the Long Strike of 1872 boosted labor solidarity and union membership.[51]

But all hopes of greater activism were dashed the following year with the Panic of 1873 and the ensuing economic collapse. In New York, a city intimately tied to financial markets, industrial production, and the import and export of the nation's goods, the depression hit particularly hard and fast. Massive job losses soon led to widespread hunger and thousands of evictions. Between January and March 1874, over ninety thousand homeless people crammed into the city's police station lodging houses in one of the cruelest winters ever experienced in New York. Amidst such suffering, the local labor movement was devastated, much like its national counterpart. A majority of New York City's local unions completely vanished, and trade union membership plummeted from 45,000 in 1873 to less than 5,000 in 1878.[52]

The climb back for labor from this state of disarray was steep and difficult. In addition to the staggering loss of membership and unions, the organizing of New York City's workers was hampered by a series of formidable obstacles. For one, the downward spiral of wages (to about half the average paid in 1873) caused by the depression pitted workers against each other in intense competition for what few jobs were available. With unions decimated and labor cheap, plentiful, and desperate, employers enjoyed unprecedented power, often replacing men and women with workers willing to accept much lower wages, dismissing others for union activity, and demanding more production out of those retained. This problem intensified as employers, faced with falling prices due to severe deflation, turned to mechanization to cut costs and stay competitive.[53] While this march of mechanization occurred unevenly throughout the local economy (bricklayers, for instance, were barely affected by such trends, while cigarmakers were devastated), it weakened the labor movement by allowing employers to replace skilled workers—who tended to be unionized and well paid—with less troublesome, cheaper, unskilled labor. As one master tailor observed, the introduction of new cutting machines allowed seven men to produce what one thousand cutters once did in the 1860s, lowering production costs by 70 percent and driving skilled tailors "next to pauperism."[54]

An increased tendency toward business consolidation and expansion also hindered labor organization. Prior to the Civil War, few businesses in New York City employed more than fifty workers, but large-scale manufacturing firms became more common by the 1870s. A successful lockout by Singer (sewing machines) and Steinway (pianos) in the Long Strike of 1872 convincingly demonstrated that the owners of larger companies enjoyed new, far-reaching powers of coercion in labor relations—principally deep pockets and a sympathetic legal system. Owners of small firms likewise gained leverage in dealing with organized labor by banding together to form their own "boss" associations in decentralized trades like baking, brewing, garment making, plumbing, stonecutting, and construction. These organizations, themselves essentially employers' unions, allowed petty entrepreneurs to draw upon the strength of a much larger sphere of fellow capitalists to set uniform wages, hours, and conditions and to oppose the efforts of trade unions to change them.[55]

The resurgence of immigration in the late 1870s and its new sources (e.g., Southern and Eastern Europe) provided another hindrance to labor's

efforts to organize. These new immigrants competed with native workers for jobs and wages, further adding to the employers' advantages and
to laborers' woes. "It's that _____ _____ Castle Garden that's killing us,"
cried the vice president of the Jersey City Freighthandlers Union, referring
to the immigrant depot at the foot of Manhattan Island. Moreover, these
new immigrants spoke different languages and often brought with them
cultural attitudes toward work, family, religion, and community that were
often not receptive to the appeals to class-consciousness and trade solidarity then gaining currency within the American labor movement.[56]

The evolution of New York's economy placed additional barriers before
labor's cause. Significantly, while some industries moved toward larger
factory production, others—like cigarmaking, clothing, and other light
manufacturing industries—began to decentralize production by contracting work out to individuals and families to be done in their tenement apartments. This practice allowed an entrepreneur to slash production costs
because little or no factory space was needed and a large segment of this
sweated workforce was comprised of women and children, who occupied
the very lowest rungs on the wage ladder. The business owner also benefited
from an atomized labor force that was next to impossible to organize into
a union. Employers in the cigarmaking trade, for example, augmented this
power advantage further by renting apartments to their workers, thereby
allowing them to thwart any worker organization and strikes simply by
threatening eviction.[57]

Changes in the industrial marketplace also worked to undercut solidarity. More than ever before, New York's vast array of commercial enterprises created products for sale elsewhere. On the micro level, this meant
that a Greenwich Village bakery could begin to sell its bread to grocery
stores throughout the city. On the macro level, it translated into the sale of
everything from beer, cigars, and clothing to printed materials, jewelry, and
gloves all across the country. In both cases, expanded markets translated
into more than simply greater profits for the entrepreneur; it also erased
the last vestiges of pre-industrial ties between producers and their immediate community. While workers in smaller cities and towns could still rely
on substantial community-wide and cross-class sympathy in their struggles
with oppressive factory owners, the same could not be said for workers in

large cities like New York. Strikes (and later boycotts, as we will see in chapters 5 and 6) engendered only the hostility of middle- and upper-class New Yorkers, who both ignored workers' pleas to avoid boycotted products and condemned them as threats to social order.[58]

These hostile responses to labor activism in New York reflected the larger ideological shift in the Gilded Age (previously discussed in chapter 2) among middle- and upper-class Americans to turn from traditional republican values of mutuality, obligation, and the common good to a laissez-faire republicanism celebrating individualism, freedom of contract, and private property rights. New York in this era played a key role in promoting this ideological shift and an attendant formation of bourgeois class identity and class solidarity on a national scale. In the decade before George arrived in Manhattan, elite New Yorkers set aside the differences that had once divided them—in particular differences in pedigree and the age, scale, and source of their fortunes—and began increasingly to think and act as a class.[59]

In commercial life, New York elites formed business associations and strengthened the influence of the Chamber of Commerce. In politics, as we have seen, they became more assertive in pursuing their class interests, uniting behind a program of lower taxes, fiscal retrenchment, and disenfranchisement. In social life, they developed an elaborate calendar of dinners, balls, and cotillions that afforded them the opportunity to mimic European royalty and to flaunt their wealth. They likewise established an intricate web of clubs, churches, museums, and charities. In the latter initiative, they increasingly took a hard line toward the needy, emphasizing the dangers of fostering dependence among the poor through overly generous charity. "Better that a few [of the poor] should test the minimum rate at which existence can be preserved," wrote the city's commissioner of charities and corrections in 1876, "than that the many should find the poor-house so comfortable a home that they would brave the shame of pauperism to gain admission to it." In struggles with their employees, they shed any remaining pretensions to antebellum paternalism and embraced the language of laissez-fairism to denounce strikes and celebrate freedom of contract and the unchangeable "laws" of the market. And, reflecting a growing hostility towards and fear of the "dangerous classes," they demanded larger police and militia forces and pushed for the construction of new armories. Indeed, just a few months after George came to the city, elite New Yorkers gathered for a gala in honor of the new Seventh New York Regiment armory on Manhattan's Upper East Side. This massive edifice had been built at the behest of, and with substantial funding from, a collection of New York's wealthiest, who grew increasingly worried by rising class tension and violence in the 1870s. In a similar expression of cohering class solidarity, many of these same men gathered at Delmonico's (the city's finest restaurant) two years later to honor the British philosopher Herbert Spencer, the single most important promoter of social Darwinism on both sides of the Atlantic.[60]

For the city's workers, the most common manifestation of the growing alienation between themselves and middle- and upper-class New Yorkers took place in the fraught public debate over the right of workers to organize and strike. Since labor possessed few resources with which to combat the vociferous bourgeois hostility, it was a decidedly one-sided discourse. None of the city's twenty daily newspapers expressed much more than tepid rhetorical support for "the honest working man." Indeed, most periodicals dismissed labor's demands not simply as impractical, but also as communistic schemes antithetical to the nation's revered principles of order, freedom, and independence. "Whenever a man undertakes to advocate the cause of the working people," teamster Thomas McGuire complained, "the papers come out and denounce what he says as the 'ravings of a demagogue.'"[61]

Worse than the literary pounding labor received in the daily press, however, were the very real drubbings they received at the hands of the police. In other industrializing cities like Chicago, class sympathy and labor's political influence led municipal police to exhibit restraint when confronting strikers and picket lines in the 1870s. Not so in New York. The supreme example of this recurring violence happened on January 13, 1874, in the wake of the economic collapse triggered by the Panic of 1873. Thousands of unemployed workers gathered in Tompkins Square to demand relief and public works from city officials. For their efforts, they were assaulted by hundreds of club-swinging police without warning or provocation. "Police clubs rose and fell," related one account. "Women and children ran screaming in all directions. Many of them were trampled underfoot in the stampede for the gates. In the street bystanders were ridden down and mercilessly clubbed by

The police riot at Tompkins Square Park, January 13, 1874. "The Red Flag in New York—Riotous Communist Workingmen Driven from Tompkins Square by the Mounted Police, Tuesday, January 13." *Frank Leslie's Illustrated Weekly*, January 31, 1874. Courtesy of the American Social History Project, the Graduate Center of the City University of New York

mounted officers." Samuel Gompers remembered it in more blunt terms: "It was an orgy of brutality." Hundreds suffered battered heads and broken limbs; many protesters were arrested.[62]

The general reaction of the business community, politicians, and the mainstream press was one of unified praise for the police. The editors of the *New York World*, for example, commended law enforcement for pummeling the "rabble of blackguards, mostly foreigners" who sought to "rule the city by riot and terror." These sentiments and the violence that inspired them indicated to the city's workers the willingness of their middle- and upper-class counterparts to take extreme measures, even ones that flaunted long-standing political rights and social traditions, to secure their class interests. From 1874 until the 1890s, tensions and violence between police and labor in New York escalated steadily. Little wonder then that virtually every New York working-class leader to emerge in the 1880s—P. J. McGuire, John Swinton, Samuel Gompers, Justus Schwab, Robert Blissert, to name but a few—harkened back to January 13, 1874 as the moment they began to question the republican notion of America as essentially a classless society and instead see themselves as members of a distinct and besieged class.[63]

This rising hostility toward organized labor, combined with the enormous political power enjoyed by the city's commercial class, explains the curious fact that three years later, during the Great Strike of 1877, New York witnessed hardly any significant labor protest and no violence. With memories of Tompkins Square (not to mention the Paris Commune) still fresh, city officials flooded the streets with heavily armed policemen and state militiamen. This show of force successfully overawed any effort to stage a sympathy strike or violent protest.[64]

If these many external pressures, obstacles, and outright attacks were not enough to hobble efforts by working-class New Yorkers to build an effective labor movement, there was the problem within labor itself. Even as wealthy New Yorkers enjoyed greater unity as a class, workers in this period were plagued by numerous internal divisions. Some disputes were over practical matters, such as which union had jurisdiction over which workers. But the most serious and enduring conflicts were ideological, with socialists, anarchists, trade unionists, industrial unionists, and others all promoting different modes of resistance and divergent visions of the future.[65]

Slowly emerging at this time, however, was a relatively new organization dedicated to the radical idea of uniting all workers, regardless of skill, race, ethnicity, or gender. Founded in 1869 in Philadelphia by a small group of tailors, the Noble and Holy Order of the Knights of Labor was originally committed to secrecy (fearing employer reprisals) and a traditional understanding of labor organization, restricting its membership almost exclusively to white men in the skilled professions. But that outlook gradually changed as the Order welcomed into its membership mill workers from Pittsburgh and miners from the Pennsylvania coalfields.[66]

This dedication to secrecy and the depression of the 1870s sharply limited the growth of the Knights' membership. Nonetheless, the Order had expanded to include fourteen district assemblies and several thousand workers by 1877, enough to justify convening a grand assembly of delegates in Reading, Pennsylvania, on January 1, 1878. Out of this gathering came the organization's first constitution; its preamble neatly summarized the

Order's philosophy and goals, among them securing for workers "a proper share of the wealth that they create," equal pay for men and women, the establishment of bureaus of labor statistics, the eight-hour workday, and the abolition of contract, prison, and child labor. The preamble also made clear the Order's radical philosophy of inclusion that came to be known as industrial unionism, declaring its commitment "to bring within the folds of organization every department of productive industry." In time this guiding principle was captured in the slogan, "An injury to one is the concern of all."[67]

The Knights would eventually grow into a powerful national movement with a strong presence in New York City. But when George arrived in New York in August 1880, no Knights assemblies existed in the city. As Terence Powderly wrote to a local activist just a few months earlier, "there is at present no organization in New York City."[68]

New York City's workers in 1880 faced an uncertain future. On the one hand, the growth of industrial capitalism, increased use of machinery, devaluation of skills, persistent violence by police, debilitating schisms among workers, and declining wages all seemed destined to steadily worsen. In addition, labor remained politically impotent. On the other hand, there were reasons for workers to be hopeful. The economy, after nearly six years of contraction, deflation, and staggering unemployment, rebounded after 1879. Though many labor organizations perished with the depression, those that survived began to rebuild themselves while new ones started from scratch.

Henry George's New York was as intriguing as it was inscrutable. It was a city of immense contradictions. Nowhere else could one find more lavish mansions and more ghastly tenements, more wealthy elites thriving and more workers unable to sustain their families, and a more populist a political system and more people denied meaningful political power. It was also a city of dramatic, unceasing change, as evidenced by its phenomenal population growth and the diversification of its economy. Finally, it was a city of uncertainty, with its direction, leadership, economic focus, ethnicity, and even its very boundaries as yet undetermined.

As he settled into his new surroundings, George reflected this ambivalent outlook on the future. He had moved to New York with one goal in

mind: to gain an audience for his book. This eventually proved an unquali-
fied success, but only after a period of personal struggle and agonizing soul-
searching reminiscent of the periods of misfortune that marked his earlier
endeavors. As always, a lack of money posed the most serious problem; by
October, he was writing to a San Francisco friend that he was depressed.
But at the end of that month, a short-term solution soon presented itself,
one laden with an irony that would not become apparent for another six
years. Congressman Abram Hewitt, the man he would run against for
mayor of the city in 1886, hired George to ghostwrite a report on the status of labor for a House of Representatives committee. Although George
derided it as "hack" work, the $50 per week salary lifted his spirits and led
him to renounce any idea of returning to California. "I had made up my
mind that the thing to do is to go at it here," he wrote to one friend, while
confiding to another that "the only difficulty is to get your feet down in a
new place; but I guess I have got over the worst of it."[69]

By late December, George's situation continued to improve. He was
making a little money, and lecture engagements and writing opportunities
for newspapers and magazines began to trickle in. Yet nothing of perma-
nence or pecuniary promise seemed imminent and he feared for his family
three thousand miles away in California. He had been able to send them
very little money and knew that Annie was probably borrowing money
from friends just to pay the bills for rent and food. For all his ambition
and faith in a society that promised success to those who worked hard and
persevered, he had so little to show for his efforts. He was managing to stay
afloat, but as he wrote to a friend in San Francisco, he was "at 42 poorer
than at 21." He was not complaining, he continued, "but there is some bitterness in it. It is at such times as this that a man feels the weight of a family.
It is like swimming with heavy clothes on." Still, with the new year only days
away and book sales holding steady, George refused to linger on the negative for more than a moment. "I am satisfied," he concluded, "that to come
east is the thing for me."[70]

4

"Radically and Essentially the Same"

IRISH AMERICAN NATIONALISM AND AMERICAN LABOR, 1879–1883

Men of GREEN ERIN! Awaken!
Lift up your souls and your eyes!
Never is Nature forsaken,
While it hath MANHOOD to rise!
Rise from your knees to your stature!
Knees must not bow but to GOD!
Claim ye your BIRTHRIGHT in NATURE—
Claim ye your own native sod!
LAND!—that is yours, when you will it—
Yours without striking a blow!
Ay! from each roof-tree and steeple!
If ye but WILL IT again:
Land for the Landless People!
Land for the CHILDREN OF MEN!
—A. J. H. Duganne, "Land for the People," 1879

"*AT LAST* IT BEGINS TO LOOK AS THOUGH IT HAS REALLY TAKEN"

With the dawning of 1881, George's optimism proved well founded. In early January, D. Appleton's sent word that it had sold every copy of *Progress and Poverty* and were preparing another printing. "*At last* it begins to look as though it has really taken," he wrote to a friend with a mixture of relief and cheerfulness. "My book is getting to be regarded here as the *phenomenal* one." Indeed, it had achieved a unique status: no work on political economy had ever sold one thousand copies in America or Great Britain in its first year. Now that the general public had spoken, he predicted that "pretty soon the economists will be forced to notice it."[1]

Unfortunately, he could relax and feel confident about his future for only a brief moment. His family arrived from San Francisco in early February; they brought him comfort but also greater anxiety about the need to make money. As much as he craved the increased public notice of his ideas, popularity would not pay the bills. As George pointed out to his friend Edward Taylor, "I am getting famous if I ain't making money." The ghost-writing job for Congressman Hewitt soon ended and George was again forced to borrow money from friends, a fact which caused him "terrible mental strain." He even entertained thoughts of suicide.[2]

But good news arrived that bridged the gap between fame and income— at least somewhat. Francis G. Shaw, father of Colonel Robert Gould Shaw and patriarch of the famous Massachusetts family, had read *Progress and Poverty* and was convinced that its message deserved a wider audience. Accordingly, he arranged for the purchase of one thousand copies of *Progress and Poverty* to be distributed to public libraries across the country. Then, another stroke of luck: the New York reform and pro-labor newspaper *Truth*, edited by reformer Louis F. Post and boasting a circulation of more than 75,000, paid to serialize *Progress and Poverty*.[3]

Another front in George's life began to show signs of promise; he was fast growing a reputation among Irish Americans as an advocate of the cause of the beleaguered Irish peasantry.[4] George's foray into Irish American circles happened at a propitious time. The efforts in both America and Ireland to liberate the Emerald Isle from British colonial rule had, after a period of dormancy for much of the 1870s, surged in 1879 and 1880 with the establishment of the Land League movement. It began to take shape in 1879 as a fragile alliance between the two leading factions of Irish nationalism, the moderates known as Home Rulers and the revolutionaries known as Fenians.[5] The former, led by a young Protestant MP named Charles Stewart Parnell, sought to win Home Rule for Ireland through exclusively peaceful and constitutional means—that is, win semi-independence from Britain via the establishment of a separate Irish parliament. The revolutionaries, led by an exiled Irish rebel living in New York named John Devoy, pursued complete Irish independence through the violent overthrow of British rule.[6]

Both camps traditionally kept their distance from each other, Home Rulers out of fear of being branded as revolutionaries and Fenians out of contempt for the very idea of settling for marginal sovereignty within the United Kingdom. In 1878–1879, however, the two factions engaged in secret negotiations that led to a remarkable, if short-lived, alliance known as the New Departure. Key to this unique moment in Irish nationalist history was the sudden onset of a devastating agricultural crisis that saw farm prices collapse, leading to mass evictions of tenants unable to pay their rents and rising fears of yet another famine.[7] Both factions saw in this disaster an opportunity to mobilize the masses of poor Irish tenant farmers— traditionally cool to nationalist efforts—against British rule to achieve Home Rule and soon thereafter (at least in the minds and hopes of Fenians) complete independence. A Fenian ally of Devoy named Michael Davitt began to organize tenant farmer distress into a movement that took the name Irish National Land League. Parnell soon cast his support behind the League and agreed to serve as its president.[8]

The Land League agitation instigated by Davitt and supported by Parnell and Devoy firmly linked the land question to the national question. As the League put it in its declaration of principles:

> The land of Ireland belongs to the people of Ireland, to be held and cultivated for the sustenance of those who God decreed to be the inhabitants thereof. Land being created to supply mankind with the necessities of existence, those who cultivate it to that end have a higher claim to its absolute possession than those who make it an article of barter to be used or disposed of for purposes of profit or pleasure.[9]

This idea underlay the League's primary demand of "peasant proprietary," or making tenants into owners of the land they tilled. In a country where 70 percent of the land was owned by only two thousand families while three million tenants did not own any at all, this was a powerful and popular message—especially in the context of an extreme agricultural crisis.[10]

The Land League soon commenced a program of encouraging tenant agitation to secure peasant proprietary rights through the transfer of property from landlords (who would be compensated by the British government) to tenants. To force the issue, many tenants began to withhold their rents. Some even resorted to rural vigilante violence (a tradition known as Whiteboyism), destroying crops, maiming cattle, and in a few cases murdering landlords or their agents who tried to collect rents or carry out eviction notices. They also employed the tactic of social ostracism. Anyone who aided a landlord by collecting rents or carrying out evictions found themselves cut off from all social contact. This was especially true for any land grabbers who took over an evicted farmer's holding. As Parnell put it,

> When a man takes a farm from which another has been evicted, you must show him on the roadside when you meet him, you must show him in the streets of the town, you must show him at the shop-counter, you must show him at the fair and at the market-place and even in the house of worship, by leaving him severely alone . . . by isolating him from the rest of his kind, as if he were a leper of old, you must show him your detestation of the crime he has committed.

The most famous victim of this policy was the land agent for Lord Erne's Mayo estate, Captain Charles Boycott, whose name became a synonym for the practice. This agrarian-based nationalist struggle became known as the Land War, and its revolutionary potential sent chills through Ireland's Protestant Ascendancy.[11]

"A SINGLE-HEARTED DEVOTEE TO PRINCIPLE": PATRICK FORD AND THE IRISH WORLD

Word of agrarian distress and possible famine in 1879, coupled with the founding of the Land League, sent nationalist sentiment among the Irish in America soaring. The key figure in Irish American nationalist circles, besides Devoy, was Patrick Ford, the founder and editor of the *Irish World*, the largest-selling and most influential Irish American paper in the Gilded Age. Born in Ireland in 1837, Ford emigrated to Boston in 1846 at the outset of the Great Famine. In his youth, he worked at the *Liberator*, America's leading abolitionist organ, where he absorbed the radicalism of its editor,

William Lloyd Garrison. After serving in the Union army in the Civil War, he eventually settled in New York City, where he founded his paper in 1870.[12]

The establishment of Ford's newspaper signaled a significant shift in Irish American social thought.[13] Prior to the 1870s, the Irish in the United States were on the wrong side of many of the main social reform movements of mid-nineteenth century America. When native-born Americans embraced temperance, the Irish drank. As the antislavery movement gained popularity, it was often the Irish who led mobs against abolitionist speakers. As Americans embraced Horace Mann's effort to spread free public education for all, the Irish set about building an alternative parochial school system. "Not an Irish newspaper," wrote abolitionist Theodore Parker in dismay, "is on the side of humanity, freedom, education, and progress."[14]

Native-born Protestants attributed this Irish American recalcitrance to their narrow-minded Catholicism. But Irish resistance to reform movements stemmed from more complex sources. Widespread nativist movements of the 1840s and 1850s had impressed upon the minds of Irish Americans a clear association between reform and bigotry. Many antebellum reformers included dreaded popery on their list of targeted social ills, right next to alcoholism, slavery, and ignorance. Far from admiring noted reformers like Rev. Henry Ward Beecher, Thomas Nast, and Charles Loring Brace, many Irish Catholics despised them as men who regularly attacked them as threats to American society.[15]

Irish American hostility to progressive reform movements diminished following the Civil War. Significant participation in the conflict, increased political power, and the beginnings of a slow but steady upward economic mobility served to gradually draw the Irish further into mainstream American life. By the mid-1870s—in part due to the decade's severe depression that hit Irish Americans (disproportionately represented in unskilled trades) particularly hard—many began to exhibit more interest in progressive causes, especially the labor movement.[16]

Patrick Ford was one of the leading voices in this exploration of radical ideas and causes; his newspaper reached a circulation of 35,000 by the early 1880s. His editorials supported calls for women's suffrage, an income tax, currency reform, elimination of monopolies, land reform, and the rights of workers. Like Henry George, Ford was deeply concerned about the increased poverty, inequality, and unrest he saw and argued that the salvation of the republic depended on radical social change. Unchecked individualism, hard money, and industrial technology unleashed forces within the republic "entirely at variance with and subversive of the objects of its founders as advertised to the world in the Declaration of Independence." The situation worsened every day as "societary corruption overshadows and poisons" the republic's guiding principles "and every day the parasites increase their power."[17] To emphasize this movement beyond purely Irish or Catholic concerns toward broader issues of radical social, economic, and political reform, Ford expanded the name of his paper in 1878 to the *Irish World and American Industrial Liberator*.[18]

Not surprisingly, the Irish nationalism that Ford espoused reflected his overall radicalism, Whereas traditional Irish nationalism attributed all of Ireland's social woes—poverty, famine, and mass emigration—to British colonial oppression, Ford's progressive nationalism lay the greatest blame on Ireland's unjust land system. The Irish people suffered not because of English landlordism, he argued, but *from landlordism itself*. To Ford, the Land League's agitation offered an opportunity not to replace English landlords with Irish ones, but rather to radically reshape Irish society into a just social order, starting with nationalization of the land.[19] "It is," he wrote, "absolutely necessary that the Land, the great storehouse of wealth from which the pay of the army of Labor is drawn, should be in the hands of the people." With the people, through the agency of the state, in control of the land and its natural resources, "every toiler shall get the full reward of his labor," and would have access to opportunities for self-improvement, independence, and modest material comfort.[20]

But Ford's progressive nationalism went still further. He refused to confine his radical critique of modern social conditions to Ireland. Like George, he rejected the notion that the United States was immune to class conflict and social distress. He drew clear parallels between the situation in Ireland—monopolized land, social unrest, hollow democratic institutions, and degraded farmers and laborers—and what was emerging in Gilded Age America. He declared, "The struggle in Ireland is radically and essentially the same as the struggle in America—a contest against legalized forms of oppression."[21]

Patrick Ford, editor of the *Irish World and American Industrial Liberator*. Courtesy of the New York Public Library

In linking the struggle in Ireland to that taking place in America, Ford provided a massive body of Irish Americans and Irish immigrants—at that time, the largest ethnic component of American wage earners—with a new language and ideology of pointed social criticism. Traditionally, the Irish in America expressed their resentment over their low status in Old World terminology, seeing in America a replication of the classic Catholic Irish peasant versus Protestant English landlord struggle. As a result, the main thrust of traditional Irish American social criticism had been ethno-cultural-religious in character. Ford endeavored to modernize that outlook, reinterpreting for Irish Americans their conception of the real enemy from an ethno-cultural-religious one to a socio-economic one. He applied radical new meanings to terms used for decades by the most conservative Irish American nationalists to describe conditions in Ireland: "landlord," "eviction," "aristocrat," "exploitation," "tyranny," "rack-rent," "slavery," "persecution," and more. He also compelled his readers to examine their own situations in America in order to see the universality of the struggle against accumulated, undemocratic power. When presented in this light, these terms took on new significance in the day-to-day lives of the Irish in America. The parallels were all too clear: many faced long hours of toil for meager wages, paid out by absentee capitalists (in effect, industrial landlords) living in luxury befitting British aristocrats. They paid most of those scanty wages to an actual landlord in exchange for a crowded and unhealthy tenement apartment, from which they might be evicted at a moment's notice. And should they unite to ask for an increase in wages, they likely would receive a drubbing from the policeman's club instead. A vivid demonstration of the salience of the concept of landlordism in American working-class thought emerges in the 1883 testimony of Irish nationalist and labor activist P. J. McGuire before a U.S. Senate committee investigating the condition of the nation's workingmen:

> Look at this city, with its long rows of tenement barracks, with its working-people shrinking back into alleys and back lanes and huddled together into damp cellars and basements. In the 17th Ward of this city, the average space of land occupied by each inhabitant is 9 ½ feet square—but little more than a living grave—filth, foul air abounding, the sunshine of Heaven denied them, crowded and packed together; such conditions have been more destructive to

human life than even war itself and all its horrors. In these tenements of the city, 28,000 children are born every year, 10,000 die annually, and thousands are sent to prison annually, and yet the majority of these people have paid by way of rent enough to purchase for themselves, not only one house but several, and still after this outlay [of rent] they are at the cruel mercy of landlords, who, on failure to pay the month's rent, will cast them out into the streets homeless and houseless.[22]

Through his widely distributed newspaper, Ford would foster the establishment of hundreds of Land League branches that shared his progressive interpretation of the struggle.

"THE CHANCE I HAVE LONG WAITED FOR"

Although Ford's radicalism, including radical land reform, developed before his association with Henry George, he was clearly inspired by the latter's philosophy. Ford first came into contact with George's ideas by reading and then favorably reviewing *Progress and Poverty* in his paper.[23] Following their meeting soon after George's arrival in New York, the two grew to be good friends who frequently consulted and corresponded with each other. George found Ford an inspiration: "He is not a politician but a single hearted devotee to principle," and "without exception, the most modest man I ever knew." Ford admired George, promoting him and his book in the pages of his paper. He also helped arrange in mid-April 1881 for the publication of *The Irish Land Question*, a pamphlet based on an article of the same name George had written in 1879 while still in California applying his land monopoly analysis to the situation in Ireland.[24]

George's relationship with Ford allowed him to more easily transition from a mere commentator on Irish affairs to an active participant in the Irish nationalist movement. In so doing, George gathered an immense following among working-class Irish Americans. This was no easy feat for an evangelical English-American Protestant from San Francisco and an outspoken advocate of free trade; on the surface, he seemed to have more in common with Rev. Henry Ward Beecher than with P. J. McGuire. Such personal characteristics, regardless of how much their attitudes toward reform may have shifted, usually garnered a public figure derision and scorn from Irish Americans, not a mass following. How then did George manage to attract such wide support among working-class Irish Americans in his early years in New York?[25]

First, long before ever moving to New York City, George developed an interest in the problems that plagued Ireland. His friendship with James McClatchy of the *Sacramento Bee* and term as editor of the Catholic weekly, the *San Francisco Monitor*, exposed him to Ireland's troubled social, economic, and political situation as well as the struggles of Irish immigrants in San Francisco. By 1879, he was keenly aware of his potential to reach a sympathetic Irish American audience, as evidenced by the success of his "The Irish Land Question" article for the *Bee* (the one later republished as a pamphlet in 1881) and his decision to send twenty-five copies of *Progress and Poverty* to a friend in New York to distribute "to the radicals or the leaders of the Irish movement" residing there.[26]

He also appealed to the Irish because, although an evangelical Protestant reformer, he shunned the virulent anti-Catholicism that so often characterized such leaders. But more importantly, George already established a crucial, personal tie between himself and the religious faith that for many Irish lay at the heart of their cultural identity. His wife, Annie Corsina Fox, was an Irish Catholic. Her sister Theresa was a member of the Sisters of Charity, a Catholic religious order, and she regularly corresponded with her brother-in-law. Beyond question, however, George's most significant development was his friendship with Fr. Edward McGlynn, a radical priest turned zealous convert to the ideals in *Progress and Poverty*.[27]

McGlynn had since the very beginning of his ministry demonstrated an affinity for an emerging liberal Catholicism that was very much at odds with the more defensive, inward-looking separatism in vogue among much of the church hierarchy. As pastor of St. Stephen's Church on East 29th Street, he dedicated himself to aiding the some 25,000 parishioners in his impoverished community, earning him their gratitude and the moniker "soggarth aroon," Irish for "beloved priest."[28] But as work among the poor came to dominate McGlynn's labors, the seemingly intractable, ever worsening problem of poverty began to weigh heavily upon his mind:

I had begun to feel life made a burden by the never-ending procession of men, women and children coming to my door begging not so much for alms as for employment; not asking for food, but for my influence and letters of recommendation, and personally appealing to me to obtain for them *an opportunity of working for their daily bread.* I felt that, no matter how much I might give them, even though I reserved nothing for myself, even though I involved myself hopelessly in debt, I could accomplish nothing. I began to ask myself, "Is there no remedy? Is this God's order that the poor shall be constantly becoming poorer in all our large cities, the world over?"[29]

These were the same questions Henry George had asked himself when he set to work writing *Progress and Poverty.* In 1881, McGlynn received a copy of the book as a gift from a friend aware of the priest's progressive views. The work appealed to McGlynn as "a poem of philosophy, a prophesy and a prayer." Suddenly, he had found the solution to the riddle of why poverty grew worse as the nation experienced remarkable material progress. The priest soon became George's most devoted champion, helping legitimize him in the eyes of more skeptical Irish Americans.[30]

The most significant source of the bond between the New York Irish community and George, of course, came from his immersion in the activities of the Land League. Soon after they met, Patrick Ford introduced George to Michael Davitt, the progressive nationalist and Land League founder then touring the United States. Davitt expressed some interest in George's ideas about land reform and agreed to promote George's book in Ireland, taking one copy for his own study.[31]

Two weeks later, George joined the Land League's newly formed American branch. For George, his association with the League, like his earlier publication of *The Irish Land Question*, made perfect sense. Land monopoly, he argued, threatened *all* nations, not just the United States. Davitt and the radicals in the Irish Land League appeared poised to eliminate it in one corner of the world, at least. Success in Ireland could only strengthen George's attempts to redress economic and social problems in America.

The interest was mutual: Irish nationalists active in the Land League quickly took notice of George. In March 1881, for example, he received an invitation from James Murphy to speak before his Land League chapter because several members "read your lectures" and knew of his "hearty interest in the Land League."[32] He quickly assumed an important role in the League based in New York, frequently attending rallies and giving speeches.[33] In his absence, activists often read George's works at their meetings. The spring of 1881 found George traveling through New England, Canada, and Upstate New York, delivering speeches and raising funds for the League's cause.[34]

These ties grew deeper still when Ford, realizing George's growing popularity among Irish Americans as well as his own personal interest in the application of George's ideas to the Irish context, made an intriguing offer. He would send George to Ireland to cover the Land League agitation for the *Irish World*. Elated, George seized the opportunity. "Thus the chance I have long waited for opens," he wrote a friend. "It will be a big thing for me, I think the biggest I have had yet." George and his family sailed from New York on October 15, 1881, aboard the *Spain*.[35]

For the next year, the *Irish World* carried George's vivid descriptions of landlord abuses, evictions, and general economic inequality in Ireland. The following passage from one of his first dispatches in December 1881 illustrates well the tone and force of those that followed:

> Imagine a government . . . wielded in the interests of a privileged class infuriated with the fear of losing the power of drawing immense incomes from the toil of others. Imagine all constitutional rights suspended, and the whole country at the mercy of an absolute dictatorship, backed by fifty-thousand bayonets in the hands of foreign troops—a dictatorship for which nothing is too arbitrary and nothing too mean. Imagine elected members of the highest legislative body, the trusted leaders of a political party that embraces nine-tenths of the people, lying in jail, and treated with indignities to which convicted felons in civilized countries are not subjected. Imagine the most respected and public-spirited men in their respective localities dragged off daily to prison, without charge or inquiry, upon *lettres de cache* issued by a governmental underling at the suggestion of some landlord or police inspector. . . . Let any American, if he can, imagine

a country such as this, and he will get some idea of the condition of Ireland to-day. It is a reign of terror.[36]

Such fiery rhetoric earned him a wide following among Irish Americans. So too did the publicity he garnered when he visited Parnell and other Land League officials after they landed in prison, and when he himself was arrested twice in Ireland by British authorities for being a "suspicious stranger."[37]

"THERE STILL REMAINS GOOD WORK FOR IRISHMEN TO DO": THE IRISH NATIONAL LAND AND INDUSTRIAL LEAGUE OF THE UNITED STATES

Well before George departed for Ireland, the Irish in America had launched a campaign to aid their Irish brethren during the Land War. The effort began in earnest on January 2, 1880, the day Charles Stuart Parnell arrived in New York City to start a ten-week tour of the United States that saw him speak in sixty-two cities and towns and address a joint session of Congress. The tour proved remarkably successful in rallying Irish American support and raising money—more than $278,000 by July. "The famine-causing land system remains uncrushed," Parnell orated to Irish American activists upon his departure back to Ireland, "and therefore, there still remains good work for Irishmen [in America] to do. . . . I feel sure you will continue . . . to spread the Land League organization all over this country."[38]

Parnell spoke of *continuing* to spread the League in America because Irish Americans had commenced founding local Land League branches across the country ever since his arrival in January.[39] Two months after Parnell's departure, delegates from around the United States convened on May 18 and 19, 1880 at Trenor Hall in New York City to formally establish an American Land League organization. The body approved a series of resolutions condemning British oppression, identifying the Irish land system as the principle source of Ireland's continued agricultural crisis, and proclaiming it the obligation of all Irishmen to aid the cause.[40]

While there was nothing especially radical in these particular resolutions, there were others that made it clear that progressive nationalist and labor interests would play a prominent role in the American side of the movement. One resolution called upon the Land League in Ireland to address, in addition to the cause of the tenant farmer, "the kindred interests of manufacturing, mining, fisheries and commerce [that] are also being protracted by deliberately and wickedly selfish restrictive legislation." Even more telling was the convention's decision to name their organization the Irish National Land *and Industrial* League (INLIL) of the United States and to form a committee "to draw up a statement and programme in connection with the industrial features of the organization, to be submitted at the next convention." Michael Davitt addressed the convention and praised the attention given to the fate of Irish laborers: "Although we omitted the Industrial question from the movement [in Ireland], it was not because we were unaware of its importance."[41]

Irish Americans across the nation, some inspired by traditional nationalist ideals (Home Rule or independence) and others by the promises of progressive nationalism (land reform), rapidly organized hundreds of Land League branches. Of the latter, many were affiliated with Ford's *Irish World* newspaper. By early 1881, more than nine hundred League branches operated nation-wide, committed to raising funds for the cause.[42]

One of the most active and highly organized sectors of the INLIL of America was New York City. Well before the national INLIL took form, activists in New York established local ward branches and a citywide umbrella organization, the Irish National Land League of New York, to coordinate League activities, organize new branches, and collect funds.[43] The movement spread rapidly throughout the city, eventually totaling fifty branches. Every Sunday, Irish American nationalists packed New York City's churches and meeting halls to hear speeches, welcome new members, collect donations, and plan future fundraising events. New York City branches alone contributed at least $30,000 of the total $535,000 raised in the United States.[44] The League also sponsored concerts, balls, picnics, contests, and, when the occasion merited it, mass celebrations (Davitt's arrival) or protests (over Parnell's arrest). These events both raised money and bound participants together in a would-be nationalist movement culture.[45]

The American Land League movement, both nationally and locally in New York, was comprised of three main nationalist factions.[46] The first included fervent Fenians like John Devoy. They agreed to tolerate the land-and-labor reform rhetoric only to the extent that it served a single, ultimate purpose—complete Irish nationhood. Devoy represented Fenian interests at the national level and in New York; he served as president of the First Ward Branch and endeavored to shape public opinion through his newspaper, the *Irish Nation*.

A much larger faction consisted of the growing numbers of respectable middle-class Irish Americans, proudly identified at one point as "clergymen of all denominations, mayors of cities, lawyers, journalists, merchants and traders." Their participation pointed to the unique nature of the Land League, as previous nationalist efforts had all run up against substantial opposition from the Catholic clergy and middle class in America (and Ireland). Both groups recognized that any extremist language of insurrection and assassination made them look bad in the eyes of Americans who viewed the Irish with disdain. These rising Irish Americans craved bourgeois respectability, which they in turn linked to the elevation of Ireland—through peaceful means only—to the status of a free and independent nation.[47] This faction was well-represented in Land League activism in New York. Rallies there often featured William R. Grace, shipping magnate and the city's first Irish Catholic mayor, flanked by notable Irish American doctors, lawyers, judges, merchants, and politicians.[48] Priests often spoke at rallies and opened their churches to weekly League meetings.[49]

The third faction of the nationalist movement consisted of the large body of predominantly working-class Irish Americans who gravitated toward the progressive nationalism of Ford, George, and Davitt. This bloc was especially strong in New York City due to the direct participation of organized labor in League activism. Its efforts were led by a group of men active in both labor and Irish nationalist circles.[50] P. J. McGuire, president of the United Order of Carpenters and Joiners and later cofounder of the American Federation of Labor, is the best known of them. The most consistent and vigorous leadership, however, came from Robert Blissert, an immigrant tailor long active in labor organizing.[51] Both were staunch supporters of Henry George and the principles outlined in *Progress and Poverty*. Under Blissert's direction, labor played an energetic role in League work. New York longshoremen, for example, participated in the conference that founded the INLIL and later presented Parnell with an astonishing sum of $1,000 to aid his cause.[52] Following the lead of the national organization, the League organization in New York added the word "Industrial" to its title,[53] and honored Michael Davitt, the Irish Land League's most progressive figure, with a huge reception at Jones' Woods in one of its first official acts.[54]

At this event, and at many more over the next two years of League agitation, progressive nationalists endeavored to make Irish Americans see the struggle in Ireland as part of a larger worldwide movement for economic justice. Davitt, in an address delivered just before he departed America in November 1880, emphasized this universality of the struggle: "Men of Irish blood and sympathies in America . . . come to the practical assistance of those in Ireland who are now battling not only for the rights of your kindred, but for those of industrial humanity throughout the world."[55] Blissert told the two hundred Land League audiences he lectured before that "there are some persons who say that this land question is an Irish question. Why, it concerns every country, and none more so than America, whose wealth and lands are rapidly falling into the hands of a few men. The movement will go on broadening, deepening and spreading until it brings about the regeneration of man."[56] McGuire offered more specific examples when he argued the same point:

> It is no longer an Irish question because it has come into the arena of world affairs. We [Americans] have known of people driven from their homes at the point of the bayonet. The railroad companies have repeatedly turned out workmen from their homes, and last year in New York City there were 60,000 evictions.[57]

Henry George, stressing the same ideas, noted how unwilling some were to accept them: "The time-serving politicians, who sought to use this Irish movement, tried to keep back the truth. They were trying to keep it a purely Irish movement—they were willing enough to denounce Irish Landlordism, but they tried to prevent all reference to American Landlordism."[58]

The popularity of this connection between the struggles for justice in Ireland and the United States is suggested by the great number of progressively inclined League branches founded by the *Irish World* that were

DAVITT ADDRESSING 10,000 PERSONS AT JONES' WOOD.

"Our object is to teach the people of Ireland, generally, that the Land of Ireland was made by God Almighty free for the people He created to live upon it."

"Davitt Addressing 10,000 Persons at Jones' Wood." *Irish World*, June 5, 1880. Author's collection

centered in highly industrialized factory cities like Fall River, Massachusetts, the western and Pennsylvania mining districts, and in cities like Chicago and Philadelphia that lacked a strong Irish-American middle class or political machine. The outlook expressed in their letters to the League, as well as the fact that they chose to send their money through the *Irish World* (an organ of progressive nationalism) rather than to the main League treasury, reveals a large segment of the Irish American population that viewed the nationalist effort as more than just helping tenant farmers back in "the ould sod."[59] As James Baggs, a New York City produce dealer, put it when he looked back on the heyday of the League:

> The greatest part of the vast sum of money sent through the *Irish World* was subscribed by the poor workingmen and workingwomen of America, who, in so doing, were impressed with the idea that they were doing a work that would benefit the people of Ireland, and the workers throughout the world as well.[60]

On a broader, national level, working-class participation in the League helped popularize the "land question" within the American labor movement. American workers had linked their struggle for economic justice with eradicating land monopoly and speculation at least as far back as the 1840s, when George Henry Evans founded the National Reform Association and urged his many followers to "Vote Yourself a Farm." But interest surged in the early 1880s with the popularity of the League and George. This trend was especially notable within the Knights of Labor, an organization with a very large Irish American membership. Terence Powderly, who took over as the movement's leader in 1879, was the son of Irish immigrants and an ardent Irish nationalist. Soon after joining the Land League in 1880, he began speaking out forcefully at the Knights' annual conventions, urging the membership to place greater emphasis on "the land question"—what he deemed in 1882 "the main, all-absorbing question of the hour." All other labor reforms, he argued, from the eight-hour workday to the abolition of child labor, were of secondary importance to this paramount cause. In 1883, he formally recommended that Knights members read *Progress and Poverty*; the following year the Knights general assembly changed the wording of a plank in its constitution from "The reserving of the public lands—the heritage of the people—for the actual settler;—not another acre for railroads or speculators" to "That the public lands, the heritage of the people, be reserved for actual settlers; not another acre for railroads or speculators, and that all lands now held for speculative purposes be taxed to their full value." These additional words reflect the influence of Land League agitation, in particular the progressive arguments pushed by Ford and George. So too does the decision of the Knights in spring 1886 to add five additional land reform planks.[61]

Participation in the Land League thus compelled working-class Irish American New Yorkers to consider issues beyond gaining Ireland's national independence and ones closer to home. In so doing, it drew significant numbers of them into new forms of labor radicalism, including socialism, which was then influencing the labor movement both locally and nationally. Of course, it inevitably exposed them to one of the key sources of this radicalism: Henry George and *Progress and Poverty*.[62]

Leaders of the more conservative factions of the Land League tolerated this radicalism in part because the movement as a whole depended on Ford's fundraising skills.[63] The hundreds of League branches he established pulled in the great majority of American donations to the League, some $343,000 of a total of $535,000.[64] Additionally, they recognized that just as the movement in Ireland needed an aroused peasantry to succeed, its counterpart in the United States needed an aroused working class. Finally, they believed Ford and his progressive legions could be contained and their influence held in check by the larger organization. As a result, conservatives made overtures to working-class Irish Americans and tolerated (for a time) the radicalism of George and Ford. They even occasionally dabbled in some radical rhetoric of their own in editorials and speeches. Conservative newspapers like the *Irish-American*, for example, published editorials with language strikingly similar to that found in Ford's *Irish World*. For example, a January 10, 1880, editorial in the *Irish-American* asserted, "The natural owner [of land] is the man who develops the resources of the soil by his industry," and demanded a "radical reform of the land system if the people are to be preserved."[65] This, from a paper that often dismissed the city's laborers as "the dupes and tools of idlers and drones."[66] On another occasion, Dr. William B. Wallace, president of the INLIL of New York and conservative member of Devoy's Clan na Gael, praised the League's radical potential when he said, "I must confess I had respect for vested rights [in property] and authority of law, but I am not ashamed to say that I am emerging from such ideas. When a law becomes an injustice and a cruelty he is a slave who will put up with it."

Wallace and others could flirt with this form of discourse without fear of being branded too radical because, for a little more than a year, the inherent ideological and class tensions within the alliance of Irish American factions remained submerged. By the fall of 1881, however, these divisions within the League began to surface, prompting constitutionalists and militant nationalists to avoid once stock phrases like "the land for the people" and "the abolition of Landlordism"; these were now sentiments they had come to intimately associate with the "communistic" schemes of Ford, George, and Davitt.[67]

In addition to these three ideological factions, another significant aspect of the Land League movement on both sides of the Atlantic was the prominent role played by women. From the outset, women attended virtually every meeting and rally and took leading roles in fundraising. In New York, only months after the formal launch of the INLIL, Irish American women met to form the Ladies' Land League. Charles Stewart Parnell's mother Delia and his sisters Anna and Fanny spearheaded the effort, with Fanny acting as president. Ardent nationalists in their own right, they drew thousands of women into the movement, including Patrick Ford's daughter Ellen. Hundreds of these ladies' branches soon formed across the United States, building support and raising money for the cause in Ireland.[68] In January 1881, Anna Parnell returned to Ireland and established a Ladies' Land League there. As in the United States, the movement attracted thousands of women who raised money and spread awareness of the cause, but it also pursued more a radical agenda—more radical than men like Charles Parnell—and many women activists were jailed. Their activism in Ireland, never fully embraced by the male leadership of the League and explicitly condemned by much of the Catholic hierarchy, eventually caused a rift between the two organizations. (Anna Parnell never again spoke to her brother.)[69]

This remarkable mobilization of Irish women on both sides of the Atlantic, as with the participation of Catholic clergy and middle-class Irish, marked a break with previous nationalist efforts that shunned female participation. For many of these women, raised in a traditional Irish Catholic culture that discouraged independence, Irish nationalism served to legitimize their decisions to establish and run their own organizations and to deliver speeches before large crowds in public settings. Many of these same women, having acquired experience in activism as Ladies' Land Leaguers, would continue this activism long after the League's collapse on behalf of other social causes, including Henry George's campaign for mayor in 1886 and the women's suffrage movement.[70]

"THE SEED FOR A NEW AND BETTER SYSTEM": THE EMERGENCE OF LABOR

The fragile Land League coalition finally began to crumble in the fall of 1881. It began on October 17 when Parnell, recently arrested by British authorities along with most of the League leadership, issued from prison the *No Rent Manifesto*, which called upon tenant farmers in Ireland to withhold their rents to protest British policies, in particular a series of recently passed coercion acts. Unfortunately for Parnell, the *No Rent Manifesto* led to the end of the Land League. In Ireland, it prompted the British government to ban the organization. In America, it triggered its self-destruction along ideological lines.

When word of Parnell's manifesto reached the United States, it prompted a highly charged debate among the various Land League factions that brought to light all of the ideological differences so deftly suppressed since the League first began. To progressive nationalists, the *Manifesto* represented a bold new direction for the League, one promising to strike at the heart of Ireland's social crisis. By refusing to pay rent, said progressive nationalists, the tenant farmers of Ireland had declared war on the very idea of private property and land monopoly. Patrick Ford could hardly contain himself:

It is to Ireland what the destruction of the Bastille was to France. With the fall of that prison house of despotism there began a revolution that swept away the last vestige of a corrupt system which for ages had robbed the French people of the fruits of their labor. We believe that the No-Rent manifesto [*sic*] is also the initiation of a mighty revolution that is destined not to end till the disinherited, not only of Ireland, but of all lands, are restored to the inheritance of which they have been robbed.[71]

Almost immediately the ambitions of Ford and his supporters to radicalize the movement were checked by the conservative elements in the League. Prominent members of the Catholic hierarchy in America (and Ireland) condemned the *Manifesto* for its radical implications. Some also took this occasion to condemn the Ladies' Land League as unbecoming to female gentility. Land League officials responded by calling a national convention in Chicago (November 30–December 2, 1881) where, much to Ford's chagrin, conservatives supported the *Manifesto* not as a call for social revolution but merely as an expedient tactic necessary to gain repeal of the Irish Coercion Acts and the release of Parnell and his fellow leaders from Kilmainham Prison. And, lest anyone fail to notice their efforts to completely disassociate themselves from any suggestion of radicalism, they dropped the word "industrial" from the national organization's title.[72]

In New York City, the fallout from the *No Rent Manifesto* was bitter, but it led to the formation of a new movement. Within weeks of the *Manifesto*'s announcement, Irish American labor leader and Land League activist Robert Blissert set in motion a process that eventually resulted in the birth of a new, robust labor movement, one independent of the Irish nationalist organization from which it sprang. On October 30, 1881, just thirteen days after the *Manifesto* ignited the hopes of progressive nationalists, Blissert issued a formal call to the "Trade and Labor Unions of the United States," asserting that "the cause of labor is everywhere the same"—whether it be Irish farmers striking against unjust rents or American laborers striking against starvation wages: "It becomes the duty of every true man to rally around the standard of labor which is now unfurled in Ireland." Toward that end, Blissert announced, a committee of union representatives had already commenced the work of organizing "a grand demonstration" in support of the *Manifesto*. This pronouncement indicated that the city's labor movement sought to strike out in a new direction, no longer confined within an ideologically conservative and ethnically exclusive movement and aimed toward a broad-based effort for the betterment of *all* workers.[73]

Significantly, several non-Irish organizations intended to attend the rally, such as the German House Painters' Society. Germans constituted the other large working-class ethnic group in New York at the time of the Land League and, although not involved at the time in any nationalist movement comparable to the Land League, they were experiencing a similar ideological ferment. Few communities in the United States were more stirred by the many strains of anarchism and socialism developing at that time both sides of the Atlantic than the Germans, especially after Germany's enactment of the Anti-Socialist Laws in 1878 sent thousands of socialist intellectuals and activists to New York. Marx's First International headquartered itself in New York in the early 1870s, as did its later outgrowth, the Socialist Labor Party (SLP). New York's German community also served as the home for the emerging debate within the Gilded Age labor movement over the "practical" unionism of Samuel Gompers and Adolph Strasser and the Marxian socialist organizing which stressed class conflict and hostility to capitalism and wage labor. Thus, as the Irish-led "No Rent" rally took shape, its inclusion of German unions (and its explicit appeal to "German workingmen" in its Declaration of Principles) signaled a transition from ethnic-based to labor-based activism.[74]

On January 30, 1882, thousands of workingmen gathered at Cooper Union. Under a sign that read "The No Rent Battle of Ireland is the battle of workingmen the world over," Blissert, McGuire, and other labor leaders addressed the assembly. They reiterated the theme that land monopolization and the consequent impoverishment of workers were international, not just Irish, problems. They also read a proclamation "to the workingmen of the world," calling upon them to address the land issue in their own country. The key event of the evening came when the body resolved to create a permanent labor organization uniting the city's hundreds of individual, and often antagonistic, labor and trades unions.[75]

Less than two weeks later, on February 11, 1882, delegates representing fourteen unions met to establish the Central Labor Union of New York (CLU), a body that soon grew to become the most important local labor organization in the nation. As with the Knights of Labor and other similar movements, skilled workers (many of them also Knights) spearheaded the creation and leadership of the new organization.[76] Two of the officers, Charles Miller and August Ernst, were German, further emphasizing the creation of a movement that transcended the narrow ethnic particularism of the Land League to embrace a broader ethos of labor and working-class interests. Although the CLU membership was dominated by men of the skilled crafts, its leadership shared a radicalism that placed them at the forefront of the industrial labor movement. Indeed, many of the CLU's founders were committed socialists, among them Phillip Van Patten (National Secretary of the Socialist Labor Party), P. J. McGuire (head of the English-speaking wing of Socialist Labor Party), Charles L. Miller, and Matthew Maguire.[77]

The CLU Declaration of Principles, developed in subsequent weeks, represented one of the clearest expressions of an emerging working-class republicanism in the Gilded Age[78] (discussed more fully in chapter 5) and was a testament to the remarkable degree to which the ideas of Henry George influenced their thought, as evidenced in the first plank: "The land of every country is the common inheritance of the people." From there, the document asserted the labor theory of value and warned of an enormous gulf developing between labor and capital, with the latter accruing to itself unprecedented economic and political power at the expense of the former. "There can be no harmony between capital and labor under the present industrial system," stated the CLU founders, "for the simple reason that capital, in its modern character, consists of unpaid labor in the shape of profits wrongfully extorted from the producer, who possesses neither the land nor the means of production."

The CLU founders proposed "a new and better system" of labor organization, one designed to liberate the producing classes from subtle and politically sanctioned oppressions such as low wages, high rents, expensive transportation, and monopolies in food and fuel. They proposed to accomplish this by reestablishing the traditional link between workers' concerns and political empowerment.

The emancipation of the working classes must be achieved by the working classes themselves. . . . The combined wage-working class represents the great majority of the people. In their hands rests the future of our free institutions, and it is their destiny to replace the present political corruption by a government of the people, by the people, and for the people.

Labor could no longer afford to shun politics as the ignominious domain of the idle and corrupt. The time had come to sever all ties to the established Democratic and Republican parties which "oppressed them all the year round" and to devote all their energies toward building stronger individual unions and an overarching central labor body to emancipate labor in both the political and industrial realms. The precise nature of the political struggle remained unclear, but labor would in the near future reassert its voice in the polity. The platform concluded with a series of concrete demands such as the eight-hour workday, the abolition of child labor, and the establishment of bureaus of labor statistics drawn almost word for word from Knights of Labor's constitution.[79]

The creation of the Central Labor Union signaled the official end of labor's presence within the Land League. Workingmen and labor activists continued to take great interest in the land agitation—the January 30 rally made this clear.[80] However, from this point on, labor's participation would take place under the guidance of the CLU, with the organization eventually arranging its own public events. The reason for this transition was plain: the American Land League's shift to the right in the wake of the *No Rent Manifesto* and its subsequent efforts to discredit Ford, George, and Davitt. What had begun as a labor initiative *within* the INLIL of New York by Blissert to demonstrate the support of American workingmen for what they interpreted as a radical declaration by the League ended in what amounted to an amicable schism. From this point forward, labor would continue to support the League, but on its own terms and in accordance with its understanding of the League.

"WHAT WAS THE LEAGUE IS A THING OF THE PAST"

In the months that followed the "No Rent" rally, the schism within the American Land League grew more pronounced as conservatives moved to end the influence of the progressives. In this effort they were aided by two events in the spring of 1882. On May 2, 1882, Parnell and other League leaders walked out of Kilmainham Prison and announced that a deal had been struck. In exchange for ceasing the radical land agitation—much of it, it must be noted, having been kept up by the women of the Irish Ladies' Land League while the male leadership languished in jail[81]—Britain would halt its coercion policies and make amendments to a recently passed land reform act favorable to tenant farmers.

The Kilmainham Pact outraged both Ford and Devoy (albeit for very different reasons), but before they had time to react, the League suffered another severe blow four days later when Fenian extremists known as the "Invincibles" murdered two British senior officials, the newly appointed chief secretary and the permanent undersecretary of Ireland, in Dublin's Phoenix Park. The murders, as at least one historian has pointed out, served as the Irish equivalent of the Haymarket bombing in how they touched off a conservative, antiradical backlash.[82] The incident provided the enemies of Irish nationalism of all varieties with the ideal pretext for dismissing the land agitation as a Fenian front for violent revolution. Parnell's quest for Home Rule, Devoy's goal of Irish independence, and Ford's dream of social revolution all appeared lost.[83]

Ford and the progressive nationalists had one last fleeting moment of hope. Two weeks after the murders, Davitt emerged from prison with a new sense of purpose in the struggle. If Parnell left Kilmainham Prison having shifted to the right, Davitt walked out of Portland Prison a confirmed radical. In what became the clearest example of the influence wielded by Henry George over the Land League agitation, Davitt announced that he had read *Progress and Poverty* in prison and had been won over by its principles of land nationalization. (George, to be clear, advocated the abolition of absolute private property rights in land through land-value taxation, not state ownership of land.) At a May 21 rally in Manchester in honor of Henry George (then still in Ireland), Davitt announced that the Land League's demand for peasant proprietorship did not go far enough; he would continue the land agitation until Ireland's land question was truly solved. On June 6, 1882, Davitt reiterated his support for land nationalization as he boarded a steamer for New York.[84]

Davitt's "conversion" caused a sensation that nearly eclipsed the events of Phoenix Park. An incredulous Devoy editorialized, "Michael Davitt, if we can believe the *Herald* correspondent in London, has openly abandoned the original programme of the Land League and gone in for Henry George's socialistic scheme for revolutionizing land tenure everywhere."[85] He soon trained his wrath on Ford, branding him a mere opportunist who jumped on the Land League bandwagon only to promote his "communistic" ideas.[86]

Patrick Ford and his partisans, by contrast, were ecstatic. At last, he declared, the gauntlet of true radical land reform—"the program of the 'Land for the People' in the literal sense of those words"—had been thrown down. At last, the principles of Henry George seemed ready to assume concrete form. If Ireland followed Davitt's lead, Ford concluded, "landlordism will be destroyed, and from its ruins will rise an Ireland whose political independence will rest on that surest of all foundations— social independence."[87]

To make the most of Davitt's arrival in the United States, Ford organized a huge reception for him on June 19. In a speech that evening, a chastened Davitt went to great lengths to cool the fury of militant and conservative nationalists, addressing each of the charges leveled against him. He affirmed his loyalty to Parnell and the nationalist goal of Irish independence. His earlier call for land nationalization, he now claimed, represented merely a proposal on his part, not a rejection of peasant proprietary.[88]

But Davitt also said much that heartened the forces of progressive nationalism. To the charge that he had come under the spell of Henry George, Davitt only offered a slight clarification:

> I have not fallen into Mr. George's hands nor into those of his opponents either. Mr. George and myself differ upon essential principles, as any fair-minded critic can see who has studied his great work and read my humble speech. Mr. George, though not an Irishman, has gone to Ireland to help the Irish people. I am, therefore, not going to repudiate a personal friend and a warm and generous-hearted American because the political wisdom of some of my critics declares I have fallen into his hands.

Davitt similarly handled the charge that he was "run by the *Irish World*"and defended Patrick Ford as second only to Parnell in importance to the League.[89]

This was the highest public endorsement yet of Ford, George, and progressive nationalism. Yet, what thrilled Ford even more than Davitt's personal endorsement was a speech offered by Fr. McGlynn, the pastor of St. Stephen's Church who had become a zealous convert to *Progress and Poverty*. McGlynn's speech was notable for two reasons. First, it explicitly endorsed the progressive nationalism of Davitt, George, and Ford in language remarkable for its strident radicalism (and hinting at ideas that would soon form the basis of the social gospel movement). "If I had to choose between Landlordism and Communism," announced McGlynn, brushing aside the charge of critics that the Land League cause amounted to communism, "I would prefer the latter. . . . There is often a noble inspiration at the bottom of what is called Communism. It is intended for the welfare of the masses."[90] Second, McGlynn spoke as a representative of the most powerful antiradical force within the Irish American community, the Catholic Church. Speaking as a priest, highly visible in frock coat and collar, his message lent unofficial Church approval to the progressive nationalist agenda and its radical labor underpinnings. As Ford claimed, "The canting and ignorant cry of Communism has effectively been rebuked. Dr. McGlynn has shown that the settlement of the Land Question on the lines laid down by the Founder of the Land League is not opposed to God's law, and is therefore not in conflict with the teachings of the Catholic Church."[91]

Ford's satisfaction with McGlynn was echoed across the Atlantic in Ireland. Reading of the speech in the *Irish World*, George wrote enthusiastically to Ford: "If Davitt's trip had no other result, it were well worth this. To start such a man [as McGlynn] is worth a trip around the world three times over. He is 'an army with banners.' "[92] Unfortunately for the priest, however, the speech also gained the attention of New York's Cardinal McCloskey and, more ominously, Vatican authorities in Rome. Church officials on both sides of the Atlantic had grown increasingly concerned about the influence of radicalism on American Catholics, specifically the works of Henry George and the rise of the Knights of Labor. Under Vatican pressure, McCloskey ordered McGlynn to refrain from speaking at future

Irish nationalist events, a prelude to the hierarchy's harsher response to McGlynn's involvement in George's mayoral campaign four years later.[93]

A few weeks later, despite Davitt's continued retreat from radicalism, Ford and the progressives staged a massive CLU-sponsored send-off for him at Union Square that drew more than ten thousand people.[94] Participants wore badges that captured the spirit of the event: "Hurrah for Land Nationalization, Davitt, and the Central Labor Union."[95] So too did the text of a formal address read by Matthew Maguire, which expressed the intrinsic link between working-class activism, Henry George, and progressive Irish nationalism:

> Today you and your people are fighting Labor's battle, and it is because you are fighting this battle that we deem it our duty to give you our heartiest support. American workingmen are beginning to see that political liberty, unaccompanied by industrial freedom, is a delusion. . . . They have discovered that industrial servitude can be directly traced to the monopolization of the land by a few men. Ireland has been the first amongst the sisterhood of nations to inaugurate a war against this monopolization. Her cry of "Land for the People" has found an echo on these shores, and has supplied American workingmen with a watchword for the future. Already the Central Labor Union of New York, representing the great majority of the trade and labor organizations of New York and vicinity, has adopted as the principle plank in its platform, the Nationalization of the Land. . . . We are thoroughly persuaded that the emancipation of Labor will never be brought about until the land, the great storehouse from which all wealth is drawn, ceases to be monopolized by a few and is restored to the whole people, to whom it rightfully belongs.[96]

Fr. McGlynn, by now a popular figure in the movement, stressed this same theme in his own remarks. His own radicalism undiminished, McGlynn encouraged Davitt to stand by "the magnificent gospel of the Land for the People"—a gospel fit for all nations, especially America, which was fast becoming engulfed in the "terrible struggle between 'Progress and Poverty.'" And lest that last reference be lost on anyone, he concluded:

And so I quite agree with Michael Davitt to the full, and with Henry George to the full [loud cheering, and three cheers for Henry George], and lest any timid, scrupulous soul might fear that I was falling into the arms of Henry George . . . my private opinion is, that if I had to fall into the arms of anybody, I don't know a man into whose arms I should be more willing to fall than into the arms of Henry George. [Loud cheers.][97]

Davitt, his throat covered in bandages and looking haggard from his whirlwind lecture tour, then delivered a short but pointed speech aimed at striking a resonant chord with his working-class audience. "There is to-day in Ireland," he noted, "a distinct Labor movement, besides the Land League movement—not in opposition to the cause of the tenant-farmers, but in vindication of the rights of the agricultural laborers and artisans of cities and towns."[98]

In the wake of Davitt's departure, it became increasingly clear that the Land League movement had begun to sputter to collapse. Between the start of the winter of 1881, when the *No Rent Manifesto* conflict started, and the spring of 1882, when the Davitt controversy broke, the number of League branches in America declined from a high of 900 down to 500. Contributions to the League suffered a corresponding drop.[99] As a result, on October 7, 1882, Ford issued a stunning declaration in the pages of the *Irish World* that his paper would no longer accept Land League donations. "The reason for this action," explained Ford, "is that *there is no longer a Land League in existence. What was the League is a thing of the past.*"[100]

Militant and conservative nationalists denied the League's death and denounced Ford,[101] but his assessment turned out to be correct. In Ireland, the Kilmainham Pact, as Devoy and the independence-first militants feared it would, tempered the radicalism of the traditionally conservative tenant farmers and validated a moderate, constitutionalist course for subsequent nationalist activity.[102] Reflecting this turn from militancy to moderation, the Irish National Land League of Ireland soon changed the organization's name to simply the "Irish National League."[103]

But on the other side of the Atlantic, frustrated progressive nationalists in New York City did not disappear. Instead, they turned to a new outlet for their energies—an invigorated labor movement embodied in the Central Labor Union. Evidence of this shift in activism appeared even before the breakup of the League. Starting in mid-May 1882, the CLU began to call its own mass meetings for issues related to workers' rights at home rather than the Irish cause. The CLU-sponsored send-off to Davitt in July 1882 was an Irish nationalist event to be sure, but it focused explicitly on Davitt's conversion to the principles of Henry George and his pledge to assist "labor and humanity throughout the world." As the last major Land League event held in New York, it marked a clear transition from broad Irish nationalism to local labor activism. Whereas in the past Land League rallies featured some banners and rhetoric supportive of "labor," now labor rallies dominated the activist scene in New York, peppered with only occasional gestures toward the struggle in Ireland.[104]

That the influence of Irish nationalism on workers' consciousness endured was made clear when freighthandlers announced a "boycott" in the summer of 1882 of businesses with ties to the railroad they were striking against. In so doing, they took the Irish practice of boycotting popularized during the Land League agitation and adapted it to their new urban and industrial context. Social ostracism in rural Ireland became economic sanction in industrial America, with workers refusing to patronize offending employers or businesses they dealt with. It was a tactic (as we will see in chapters 5 and 6) that in subsequent years would become one of labor's most effective weapons.[105]

Progressive nationalists and radical labor activists were disappointed with the collapse of the Land League, but not defeated. Jeremiah Murphy, the president of the Longshoremen's Central Union, summed up their sentiments best when assessing the League's demise. Conservative nationalists, he noted, "were crying all along, 'Those radicals will destroy the movement; they are bringing Socialism and other *isms* into it.' But, mark you, when the Radical element left, where is the Land League?"[106]

As far as Murphy and other Irish American labor activists were concerned, the League ceased to exist. As for the "radical element" that they identified with, its work had only just begun.

5

"Labor Built This Republic, Labor Shall Rule It"

Our father, who is supposed to be in Heaven, dispenser of charity, justice and eternal love, thy name be hallowed. Thy kingdom come alike unto every one, rich or poor. Cause thy will to be respected in Heaven and our rights on earth. We demand to-day our daily bread for which we labor. Forgive us our trespasses if possible, as we shall try to forgive those who starve and oppress us. Withhold from us the temptation to become masters of our fellow men, and deliver us from the evil of ignorance, superstition and the bondage of eternal slavery. Then ours should be the land and the fruits as well as the labor forever and ever, Amen.

—A. Porter, "The Workingmen's Prayer" (published in *Truth*, 1882)

"A SWORD IN DEFENSE OF LABOR"

In the fall of 1882, with the Irish Land League no more, Henry George set sail for New York City. His year in Ireland had been a spectacular success in terms of promoting his book and enhancing reputation in both Great Britain and America. If he did not realize it then, he would soon discover that his most enthusiastic following in the United States was among poor, urban workers. As soon as word spread that he was returning to the city, the CLU resolved to tender him a grand public reception upon his arrival.[1]

Patrick Ford, Robert Blissert, P. J. McGuire, Matthew Maguire and many other leading progressive Irish nationalists and labor leaders were in attendance at the fête, which took place at Cooper Union on October 20, 1882.[2] Throughout every speech delivered that evening, there ran a single, unifying theme: unless workers, inspired by the philosophy of

Henry George and the example of Irish Land League, came to understand the prime source of their oppression (land monopoly) and its remedy (radical land reform), industrial society worldwide would continue to hurtle toward disaster. "No man has unsheathed a sword in defense of Labor so grand and so beautiful as that which Henry George unsheathed in that book of his," said Blissert. That work, declared McGuire, had established a "new political economy" that elevated man's labor above the status "of a mere commodity" and would lead to the "establishment of . . . an industrial government . . . [where] finance and all the tools of labor will belong to the people and not to a few." In other words, proclaimed another speaker, "this great, simple, rightful doctrine of the nationalization of land will prove the emancipation of Labor in America."[3]

The next evening George attended a very different kind of reception, this time at New York's posh Delmonico's restaurant. Organized by Louis F. Post, editor of *Truth* and one of George's devotees, it drew together several men from the ranks of New York City's emerging mugwump reformers, including Rev. Henry Ward Beecher, Charles Francis Adams, and Congressman Perry Belmont.[4] The contrast between the two events could not have been more striking. George recognized few of the guests assembled to "honor" him, and many of them had never heard of him. The elegant setting and the cultured speeches made clear that far from being an expression of widespread popular sentiment like the CLU event the night before, this evening represented Post's attempt to cultivate interest in George among the city's eminent, reform-minded swallowtail set.

The holding of two separate receptions reflected a conscious decision of the CLU leadership. They had declined Post's suggestion for a single reception and instead planned their own distinctly labor-centered event where they could lay claim to George and his message, just as they had done with Davitt the previous summer. Blissert and his fellow Land League and labor activists considered George *their* spokesman and inspiration, not an ally of "bread and water" Beecher. Recent experience with the Land League and Davitt had taught them to be wary of letting politicians, professionals, and establishment reformers into a movement.

On a broader level, this effort to create a distinctly working-class event and to claim the increasingly well-known Henry George as a working-class hero pointed to an emerging belief among many laborers that the nation had entered a dangerous and potentially fatal period in its history. They rejected, however, the conclusion of middle- and upper-class Americans that the nation's ills stemmed from the misguided embrace of radical, un-American ideologies like socialism by the "dangerous classes." Instead, workers offered a different diagnosis and prescription, one shaped by a rising working-class republicanism, that identified a republican crisis caused by a headlong and unrestrained industrialization that enriched and empowered a small elite while impoverishing the masses. This working-class republicanism drew on earlier labor protest traditions that invoked republican ideals, but it went further by stressing inclusiveness across traditional worker divides of skill, ethnicity, race, and gender, in addition to the democratization of industry. Working-class republicanism in the Gilded Age also asserted that republican citizenship must guarantee not only political rights but economic rights as well, and it called upon the state to guarantee them. This language of protest offered a vision of an alternative, cooperative society.[5]

Popularizing this working-class republicanism became a primary goal of the CLU from its earliest days. A significant moment in this effort came in August 1883 when a U.S. Senate committee arrived in New York City to hold public hearings in their tour of the nation investigating the state of relations between labor and capital.[6] Investigations such as this (there were two others launched in 1878 and 1894), notes Mary O. Furner, "subjected the new industrial capitalism to a political and ideological fitness test" regarding its compatibility with republican values and institutions.[7] Keenly aware of this opportunity, the CLU seized the moment and, reflecting its concern that only *authentic* workers provide testimony rather than so-called "workingmen" sent by bosses or local politicians, requested and received permission to present a slate of its own witnesses.[8]

The CLU-organized testimony, as well as the independent corroborations of other individual CLU members, provided a unique opportunity to set before members of the Senate and the wider public (the testimony received substantial press attention) the key elements of working-class republicanism. At its core lay the conviction that a principle central to all earlier forms of republicanism—that economic opportunity and upward mobility were open to all honest, hardworking men of solid character and good habits—had been nullified by laissez-faire industrialization and capitalist-friendly government policy. Finding themselves no longer able to rise, asserted CLU witnesses, American workers were trapped as members of an underclass of poorly paid wage earners, without the freedom and independence of true republican citizens.[9] In his testimony, for example, brassworker Joseph Finnerty pointed out that men in his trade earned about $15 per week, whereas they would have averaged between $18 and $21 per week just fourteen years ago.[10] Teamster Thomas McGuire and others likewise noted that many workers found it impossible to find regular, full-time employment.[11] Another source of concern centered on the increased mechanization of production, which subdivided tasks and undermined skills, leading to, in machinist John Morrison's words, a "very demoralizing effect" on workers and the belief that they had now become "part of the machinery."[12] Workers also found themselves increasingly isolated from their employers, the latter having been replaced by managers who showed little concern for their well-being.[13] Life in overcrowded and unhealthy tenement districts had become the norm for wage earners; as a result, temperance and frugality became meaningless aspirations.[14] Workers also feared being fired and blacklisted for union activity, which undermined their ability to defend their rights, a problem neatly summarized by tailor Robert Blissert: "The members of any trade without a union are slaves."[15]

This working-class republicanism articulated by the CLU witnesses also focused on a particularly distressing aspect of labor's plight—its seemingly *permanent* condition, a fact that called into question America's free labor tradition that had previously always characterized wage work as a temporary stage in an upward journey to eventual self-employment and independence.[16] They spoke of thwarted opportunity and "the crystallization of society more and more into distinct classes, classes just as distinct as any that exist to-day in Europe, and a man born in one of them can never hope to reach the other," as P. J. McGuire put it. This "crystallization," they argued, stemmed from the growing power of monopolies and corporations to crush competitors, potential entrepreneurs, and labor organizations. Finnerty claimed that a man needed just $300 to $400 to set up his own business as a brass worker as late as 1870. But by the early 1880s, the emergence of large companies pushed the average start-up cost to $5,000—a sum far beyond the means of the average brass worker. Thomas McGuire cited similar statistics, recounting his own frustration in trying to compete with large corporations as an independent expressman. Not a single worker questioned the inherent virtue of a capitalist economy. Rather, they charged that it had been corrupted by unscrupulous monopolists.[17]

As it decried the declining status of workers—the true citizens of the republic—Gilded Age working-class republicanism also denounced the rise of a newly empowered elite that enjoyed extraordinary wealth, status, and power. "The poor unfortunate laborer is just like the kernel of wheat between the upper and lower millstone," observed Thomas McGuire. "In any case he is certain to be ground. He *produces* all the wealth while the men who produce nothing *have* all the wealth."[18] Morrison succinctly quipped: "Jay Gould never earned a great deal, but he owns a terrible lot."[19] This working-class republican critique employed the same anti-aristocratic terminology popular in antebellum republicanism, only in the Gilded Age it seemed less a package of useful metaphors to describe unrepublican behavior and more a set of terms to identify the very real efforts of elites to establish themselves as a permanent American aristocracy. Gilded Age elites rejected the ideal of republican simplicity that had long restrained their predecessors (hence Vanderbilt's mansion and grand opening ball in 1883, and the copycat galas that followed). Not surprisingly, a central theme of working-class republican rhetoric and political cartoon imagery excoriated the wealthy for this behavior. "The dangerous classes are not to be found in the tenement houses and filthy districts, but in mansions and villas," asserted the CLU's Conrad Carl in a biting rhetorical reversal of a phrase popular among elites in the Gilded Age.[20]

Additionally, working-class republicanism of this period attacked laissez-faire as an extreme ideology employed by the wealthy to justify unrepublican actions that violated the rights, liberties, and dignity of workers. The ubiquity of this sentiment is seen in how frequently labor speakers, writers, and editors denounced the claim that labor was "a mere commodity," rejecting it as antithetical to traditional republicanism's emphasis on the common good. The CLU's Ed King, for example, attributed all labor disputes to a single cause: "It is because capital insists on regarding a business concern, plant, stock, *and hands* as so much raw material, to be bought and sold, that conflicts do, and always must, prevail between workmen and employers." This laissez-faire notion, he declared, "is rejected altogether by the working classes."[21]

The working-class republicanism articulated by CLU witnesses also criticized the state of American politics as corrupt and undemocratic, with cadres of wealthy special interests working in concert to fleece the poor and deny them their rightful voice in the polity. "The entire political system from top to bottom is a system of bribery and corruption," pronounced Thomas McGuire.[22] Labor intended, therefore, to reclaim its political influence and rid the nation of "class legislation" to establish a government, in the words of Morrison, " 'of the people, for the people, and by the people'— different entirely from the present form of government."[23]

That several of the CLU witnesses referenced "class legislation" points to a distinct working-class republican interpretation of class. Most workers, like their fellow middle- and upper-class citizens, believed that a true republican society was free of classes and, consequently, class conflict. As a result, they expressed great concern over the profusion of class rhetoric in the 1870s and 1880s, but they differed sharply in their interpretation of the causes. Whereas the elites and bourgeoisie blamed the surge of class rhetoric on jealous losers deluded by "foreign" ideologies like socialism, proponents of working-class republicanism attributed its rise to the unrepublican behavior of rich people, monopolists, and other elites. This interpretation explains why populist agitation in this period by workers and farmers often avoided employing class terminology when describing themselves, preferring instead to lump all producers—a category defined very broadly—into "the people" or "the masses." Edward King clarified this idea: "Working people do not represent a class interest at all. They claim to be *the people*."[24] Workers placed monopolists, lawyers, bankers, and other nonproducers outside this circle of republican virtue, deeming them the true sources of class conflict. The latter had banded together as a class to act in their own self-interest, regardless of the cost to the common good. As P. J. McGuire told the senators, "One hundred men with millions of dollars at their command . . . [who] are not engaged in any productive industry . . . have the power to change the value of every pound of merchandise, and every dwelling house and every hour's labor." Class conflict would disappear only when these elite interests ceased to conspire as a class against "the people."[25]

In many ways, this working-class republicanism of the Gilded Age resembled earlier antebellum manifestations of artisan republicanism. Yet there were significant differences, especially in its greater emphasis on communal ideals over individualism and its vision of a more powerful state. Some of its proponents, including CLU witnesses, for example, called for the abolition of the wage system and the adoption of cooperative production.[26] Working-class republicanism also embraced solutions that called for a greater role of the state in protecting republican independence, opportunity, and equality. "If it has not the power," said P. J. McGuire of Congress regarding the need for laws protecting unions, "it should assume the power; and if necessary, amend the Constitution."[27]

Moreover, CLU witnesses voiced another, starker, aspect of working-class republicanism: a foreboding sense of impending doom. Sounding very much like Henry George in *Progress and Poverty* and reflecting the popularity of apocalyptic rhetoric that suggested the very fate of the republic hung in the balance, CLU witnesses laced their testimony with bleak references to imminent social revolution. As Robert Blissert warned:

> Unless some wise legislation is enacted here to protect the many from the aggressions of the few this will become the worse conditioned country that ever existed. . . . This country will see a revolution, the bloodiest revolution which the annals of history have ever recorded, because the growing intelligence and the growing discontent of the masses of people . . . will culminate either in a revolution or in the sudden overthrow of the monopolies.[28]

"WHATEVER ENLARGES LABOR'S SENSE OF ITS POWER HASTENS THE DAY OF ITS EMANCIPATION"

The CLU went beyond speeches and public testimony to promote working-class republicanism. Some of its most significant initiatives in this regard were symbolic, intended to build an oppositional working-class movement.

None captured so fully the effort to awaken workers to the crisis of the republic than the invention of Labor Day.

In the spring of 1882, at the regular weekly meeting of the CLU, Matthew McGuire proposed a resolution advocating that a day in early September "be set aside as a festive day [for] a parade through the streets of the city." They eventually chose Tuesday, September 5, in part because it coincided with convening of a national convention of the Knights of Labor in New York. When the day finally arrived, no one knew how many workers would turn out, given workers' fears of getting fired and blacklisted for labor union activity.[29] Only four hundred men and a brass band had assembled by the time the parade touched off at 10:00 a.m. But as the parade headed north up Broadway, it swelled in size; union after union fell in line from side streets, bringing the total somewhere between five and ten thousand marchers. Many workers held aloft signs with messages that pronounced the broad themes of working-class republicanism: "Labor Built this Republic, Labor Shall Rule It," "Labor Creates All Wealth," "All Men Are Created Equal," "To the Workers Should Belong all Wealth," "Our Power is at the Polls," "Liberty, Equality, Fraternity," "Strike With the Ballot," "Land: The Common Property of the Whole People," "Eight Hours for Work—Eight Hours for Rest—Eight Hours for What We Will," and more. These assertions, indeed the event in its entirety, amounted to a public challenge to the popular progress mantras that suffused so much of mainstream Gilded Age discourse.[30]

Midway through the parade, the throng passed a reviewing stand at Union Square, where Terence Powderly, Patrick Ford, John Swinton, and other labor dignitaries acknowledged each group as it passed. Henry George would not return from Ireland for another month, so he was not present for this particular celebration. After moving up Fifth Avenue, past the opulent homes of Vanderbilt, Morgan, Gould, and other recently minted tycoons, the grand procession terminated at 42nd Street and Sixth Ave. From there, participants and their families (some twenty-five thousand people) headed to Wendel's Elm Park for a day of music, games, and speeches. There were copious amounts of food and beer, of course.[31]

After such an impressive start, annual Labor Day celebrations in New York grew in size and popularity each year. They also grew more diverse as

The first Labor Day parade. "Grand Procession of Workingmen, September 5." *Frank Leslie's Weekly*, September 16, 1882. Author's collection

contingents of women, Jews, and African Americans joined the parades.[32] And each year workers passed a reviewing stand at Union Square, on which sat some of labor's most prominent leaders, such as Henry George, Patrick Ford, John Swinton, and Robert Blissert.[33] By 1886, the CLU's tradition had become a national event, indicating the depth and breadth of working-class discontent across Gilded Age America. That year, nearly twenty thousand marched in Manhattan and another ten thousand in Brooklyn, while twenty-five thousand turned out in Chicago, fifteen thousand in Boston, five thousand in Buffalo, and four thousand in Washington, D.C. Politicians soon took notice. In 1887, five states, including New York, passed laws making Labor Day a state holiday. In 1894, President Grover Cleveland signed into law a measure establishing Labor Day as a holiday for all federal workers.[34]

In the CLU's day-to-day program of heightening workers' awareness of the need to redeem the republic from grasping monopolists and other non-producers, the annual Labor Day celebrations came to represent the high-point of the year. It promoted labor solidarity by featuring a public show of strength, speechmaking, and craft exhibitions, capped by an afternoon of recreation sponsored not by political machine operatives, as was the custom of the day, but by unions. Moreover, by holding the event on a weekday, the CLU was harkening back to the antebellum artisanal tradition of taking time off according to one's interests.[35] As a ritual in the blossoming oppositional working-class republican culture, the celebration also drew together workers in ways similar to, but distinct from, traditional expressions of ethnic loyalty like the Land League and St. Patrick's Day parades or civic holidays such as Fourth of July picnics. On such occasions, participants came together as *workers* who, as the *New York Herald* observed in 1882, "sat together, joked together and caroused together. . . . American and English, Irish and Germans, they all hobnobbed and seemed on a friendly footing as though the common cause had established a closer sense of brotherhood."[36] Commenting on this effect of Labor Day, Swinton observed, "Whatever enlarges labor's sense of its power hastens the day of its emancipation."[37]

The invention of Labor Day, along with the celebration honoring Henry George upon his return from Ireland and the carefully orchestrated testimonies before the traveling Senate committee, was not the only important initiative undertaken by the CLU in its first eighteen months of existence. Another was the formation of an independent labor party. This effort faced two formidable obstacles. First, while some workers (many of them guided by Ferdinand LaSalle) advocated for the formation of independent labor parties, others (reflecting the views of Karl Marx) argued that such parties could succeed only *after* the formation of strong trade unions to back them up. This was the so-called "balance of power" strategy: labor would maximize its influence at the polls by delivering its votes to candidates who pursued a pro-labor agenda, regardless of party affiliation. These conflicting philosophies over political action divided labor organizations, including the Knights of Labor, all across the nation.[38]

Supporters of an independent labor party also had to contend with the power of the Democratic Party, particularly New York's Tammany Hall. As previously detailed in chapter 3, Tammany garnered the lions' share of the working-class vote by distributing patronage jobs, no-questions-asked charity, and occasional rhetorical blandishments celebrating the "sons of toil." These efforts, in the words of Samuel Gompers, had turned workers

into "voting cattle" for the major parties. These demoralized men, according to Blissert, were willing to sell their vote "for a dollar or a glass of beer."[39]
Mainstream political parties also benefitted from public antipathy toward
independent labor politics as promoting un-American feelings of class conflict. They also enjoyed the advantages of a fragmented and multi-tiered
political system that hindered political insurgencies.[40]

Despite these obstacles, a slight majority within the CLU (including key
leaders like Blissert, King, and P. J. McGuire) favored independent political
action. Taking to heart an early CLU proclamation that "the power of using
the people's property, the machinery of State and municipality, should be
wrested from the grasp of our enemies and returned to their rightful owners, the working men and working women,"[41] they established a committee
in June 1882 to consider forming a labor party.[42] Their case for independent
political action gained momentum in July 1882 during a freighthandlers'
strike when the New York Attorney General granted the Hudson Railroad
a ten-day reprieve from state intervention.[43] At a mass rally in support of
the strikers at Union Square on July 19, 1882, CLU Secretary Matthew
Maguire read a series resolutions, including the final one that stated:

> *Resolved*: That as the railroads control the Legislature, Congress, the
> Judiciary, the Democratic and Republican Parties, and all branches
> of the public service, we declare the most urgent duty of the hour to
> organize in our respective trade and labor associations, and to form a
> political party opposed to monopoly in all its forms, and to establish
> a purer form of government, based upon the rights of labor and the
> emancipation from all grades of corporate and political tyranny.[44]

Three weeks later, as it became clear that the freighthandlers had lost their
strike, the CLU's member unions approved the formation of a United Labor
Party. The ULP took as its platform the CLU's Declaration of Principles,
with a modified list of demands at the end. The vote—twenty-seven unions
in favor, one against, with twenty abstentions and absences—reflected the
opposition of many regarding independent politics.[45]

By mid-October, the ULP had nominated candidates for alderman,
mayor, state assembly, and Congress.[46] It also launched a campaign in a style

that anticipated Henry George's 1886 mayoral campaign. Mass open-air rallies, torchlight parades, and curbside speeches from truck beds took place nearly every night from September until Election Day evening. At these campaign events, in order to emphasize the break with the mainstream parties and the clubhouse politics associated with them, the CLU banned all giveaways, especially alcohol. Fearing subversion by the established parties, the ULP also banned the presence of any candidates not officially endorsed by the CLU.[47] And in a ceremony laden with ritualistic significance, it required every ULP candidate to make an "ironclad pledge" that bound them to certain rules and standards in order to gain labor's endorsement.

> I hereby declare my conviction that the shameful treachery characterizing the past history of labor in politics, and the complete collapse of public confidence in the purity of public life and the integrity of political aspirations, demand that all candidates chosen by this organization should publicly pledge themselves to honest aims and loyal service: and, therefore, I, [candidate's name], do here and now solemnly pledge my honor as a man and my reputation as a citizen that I seek no means or private gain, but only the public good, by faithfully serving the working classes.

The pledge then identified and prohibited every conceivable form of political dishonesty. In particular, it warned against "betraying the people in their hour of need by poisoning their minds against hope and trust in deliverance from slavery through honest political action."[48]

Few expected the ULP to sweep a host of labor candidates into office, but many hoped the campaign would serve an educative, conscience-raising function, opening workers' eyes to their rights and making them wary and more critical of the mainstream parties.[49] But labor's inexperience and meager resources led to disappointing results. The ULP's state assembly candidates averaged only 10 percent of the vote and aldermanic candidates just 5 percent. "We have not arrived at the time when workingmen can take political action," one prominent unionist noted, "because they are in favor of the old parties and not true to each other."[50] But despite this political failure and the damage it inflicted on the CLU (many unions left the coalition in protest),[51] advocates of independent political action revived the ULP once again in 1883 for the next election cycle. Their efforts were met with another crushing defeat with attendant reports of bribe-taking, double-dealing, and disorganization.[52]

Two consecutive electoral disasters for the CLU left the advocates of independent political action on the defensive, but no less committed. They believed, as William Forbath writes, that "the redemption of the working class was inextricably caught up with the redemption of the republican tradition."[53] But before labor could successfully return to independent politics, workers needed to develop a new sense of the possible. Such a vision did develop over the next few years as the CLU temporarily set political action aside and embarked on an unprecedented program of working-class activism.[54]

"THE ONLY MEANS TO SECURE THE LIBERTY OF THE WORKINGMEN IS THROUGH THE TRADES UNIONS"

With independent politics proving both unsuccessful and divisive, the CLU increasingly focused its efforts on creating a wide-ranging program designed to give workers greater institutional strength and promote an oppositional working-class republican culture of empowerment. Central to this initiative was worker education. Time and again, labor leaders expressed dismay at the woeful ignorance of workers regarding their rights and the need to see beyond their own narrow interests or those of their trade. As CLU activist Edward King said, since "correct ideas precede successful action," there must be "a systematic forming of logical opinions before you can accomplish any practical result."[55]

To this end, the CLU held weekly Sunday meetings where workers heard many of the foremost radicals and intellectuals in the movement speak about workers' rights, socialism, and land reform. It also sponsored free weekly lectures on labor topics by notables like George, Blissert, and King,[56] and opened a Free Labor Reading Room that offered works by George and Marx, as well as countless labor papers from cities around the country.[57]

But its everyday public activism normally took the form mass meetings, parades, and festivals. At CLU rallies, workers denounced everything from antilabor legislation to needless worker fatalities; alternatively, they rallied to support striking workers or causes like the eight-hour workday. Special occasions like the return of Henry George or the death of Karl Marx were also marked by large rallies. On Sundays, the CLU occasionally organized afternoon steamboat excursions that gave workers and their families a day of common recreation, which were followed by regular CLU meetings on the return voyage. It also sponsored free concerts (with music interspersed by short speeches on labor themes) provided by the Carl Sahm Club, a musician's union affiliated with the CLU.[58]

One medium of labor education that ranked high on the list of CLU priorities was the establishment of a labor paper to compete with the mainstream "organs of capital." The problem, as George explained in the summer of 1883, stemmed from the fact that "the newspaper has become an immense machine, requiring large capital, and for the most part it is written by literary operatives, who must write to suit the capitalist who controls it."[59] In the absence of an official labor paper workers relied on Louis F. Post's mugwumpy daily paper, the *Truth*, and on ethnic weeklies like the *Volkszeitung* and the *Irish World*, which consistently took the side of labor and published summaries of the CLU's meetings and activities.[60]

Then, in October 1883, John Swinton—Scottish immigrant, longtime labor activist, and friend of Henry George—quit his job as an editor at the *New York Sun* to establish *John Swinton's Paper*. "My objects in starting it," he later said, "were to raise the social question, and to induce the working people to bring their interests into politics."[61] Devoted exclusively to labor issues, Swinton's paper not only provided the CLU with space for a weekly bulletin board (fittingly under the headline, "News Not in Other Papers") for their meetings, news of strikes, lists of boycotted businesses, and announcements of worker rallies, it also introduced a large body of workers to the grim realities of the nation's republican crisis and the basis of a solution grounded in a working-class republicanism. Swinton's paper also played a key role in popularizing the ideas of Henry George among workers by publishing his speeches and selected passages from *Progress and Poverty*. It issued a consistent call for labor to take independent political action as, in his words, "new political forces." The mantra "Do Something" appeared repeatedly in headlines and editorials, constantly imploring readers to forsake factional and ideological bickering in favor of united action. Not surprisingly, the CLU celebrated *Swinton's* as a "constant menace to grasping capitalists," particularly "as it is the only vehicle in the English language whereby the wrongs of the wage-earners can be made public and ventilated, without fear or favor."[62]

The CLU further committed its resources to the practical goal of organizing labor. It strengthened existing unions, worked to merge rival unions of the same trade, and organized unions where none existed. By mid-1884, thirteen previously unorganized trades possessed effective organizations. It established a committee on grievances to resolve conflicts within or between labor organizations in matters of jurisdiction, policies, and membership. This committee even managed to broker peace (albeit temporarily) in the infamous struggle between the International and Progressive Cigarmakers' Unions.[63]

Dominated as it was by unions of skilled male workers, the CLU made no effort to organize women workers in its first few years of its existence. Most male workers in this period viewed women wage earners as competitors, as threats to their well-being. By some estimates, some one hundred thousand women labored in New York City for wages that averaged $4.50 per week. Much of this work was concentrated in the needle trades and domestic service. But as the CLU matured as an organization in 1884 and 1885, it began to take steps, like the Knights of Labor nationally, to support striking women workers and organize women workers into unions. The first delegation of women workers marched in the 1885 Labor Day parade; by May 1886, the CLU announced the formation of the New York Ladies' Central Labor Association to operate as a kind of women's auxiliary to the CLU. Ultimately, only a few women's unions were organized, but they were weak and short-lived, reflecting the precarious position of women workers in this period and the decidedly masculine character of working-class republicanism.[64]

Because most conflicts confronting workers arose between labor and capital, the CLU established a committee on arbitration to investigate grievances and speak directly with the accused employer. Frequently, the committee won reversals of wage reductions, increased hours, worker firings, and use of nonunion help. When they failed in their object, or when the employer refused to meet with them entirely, the CLU then threatened stronger measures such as a strike or a boycott. An examination of a single month, August 1885, illustrates the scope of its activity. Early in the month, the committee lodged a complaint against several hotel owners for hiring nonunion painters at wages far below union scale. Some days later, it filed an official complaint against Duden Brothers (lace makers) with the U.S. District Attorney's Office for illegally importing contract labor at below union-scale wages. Next, it threatened action against a theater owner for contracting a boss painter employing cheap, nonunion labor. Then it settled a strike of tin and slate roofers by pressuring the employer to hire only union men. On August 17, the committee called upon the owner of Sulzer's Harlem River Park to pay out funds owed to two unions. Two weeks later, its threat of a strike and boycott convinced a boss baker to rehire a union foreman.[65]

When peaceful arbitration failed, the CLU sanctioned a strike. Often a powerful weapon, a strike could just as easily backfire, demolishing a union lacking adequate money or organization. No incident better illustrated this problem than the Brotherhood of Telegraphers' 1883 strike against Western Union and its ruthless owner, Jay Gould. With a war chest of just $1,000, the telegraphers lost the strike after just four weeks. Western Union rehired only those telegraphers willing to sign an "iron clad oath" renouncing membership in the Brotherhood. This severely weakened the union. The main problem, noted John McClelland, was that striking workers have had "nothing to combat capital with except their empty stomachs, while the capitalists have had unlimited financial resources and have been able to starve the workingmen into submission."[66]

Recognizing this essential reality, the CLU evaluated each situation before deciding whether or not to endorse a strike. This policy of caution produced an impressive record, with the CLU member unions winning or reaching a compromise in three-fourths of their strikes at a time when strikes by individual unions failed at least half the time (table 5.1).[67]

Because money frequently determined the outcome of a strike, the CLU also served as a source and conduit for funds. Indeed, as one of its first official acts the CLU in 1882 raised $7,000 for the striking freighthandlers of New York and New Jersey.[68] By mid-1884, the CLU noted that in the past two years it had spent an astonishing sum of more than $60,000 to aid

TABLE 5.1   Strikes by CLU-Member Unions in New York City, 1882–1884

	Total number of strikes	Strikes won	Strikes lost	Strikes ending in compromises	Ongoing strikes
1882	12	7	4	1	0
1883	8	4	2	2	0
1884*	5	2	1	0	2
Totals	25	13	7	3	2

*as of June 1, 1884

Source: "Semi-Annual Report of CLU Secretary Charles Miller," *JSP*, July 13, 1884, 4.

labor causes. "There is more in perfect organization and discipline than in anything else," observed John Swinton, "—except, perhaps, a large treasury."[69]

While strikes provided the most vivid example of the strife existing between labor and capital in the Gilded Age, the implementation of the boycott inaugurated a new method of struggle and protest. As noted in chapter four, Irish American workers in the early 1880s had begun to adapt what was originally an agrarian tactic in Ireland to fit their urban and industrial context in the United States, replacing social ostracism with economic sanction. A boycott imposed on an abusive employer urged workers, their friends, and the wider community to refuse to purchase his product.[70]

More than any other tactic employed by labor, the boycott represented an effort to strengthen the republican idea of the common good and shared interests, captured best in the motto of the Knights of Labor: "An Injury to One is the Concern of All." It was a palpable response to the challenges posed by rising middle- and upper-class class hostility toward labor agitation, as well as to the increasingly diffuse nature of social and economic relations. With the growth of large corporations and regional and national markets, it became increasingly difficult for a worker to see the connections between his or her life as a producer and as consumer. The boycott represented an effort to reverse this trend, injecting into everyday consumer choices an element of class consciousness and community solidarity—from the daily beer consumed after work to seasonal purchases like shoes.[71]

Boycotts announced. *John Swinton's Paper*, January 24, 1886. Author's collection

Because boycotts required far fewer resources than strikes, many labor organizations imposed them at the slightest provocation, often without adequate organization and coordination. To avoid this problem, the CLU required that member unions submit for approval all requests for boycotts. Once a boycott was approved, the CLU's committee on boycotting worked to publicize it; it placed advertisements in prolabor papers, distributed handbills near offending businesses, and encouraged legitimate businesses to post signs reading "This is a union shop," complete with the CLU seal. According to shoe-laster John Flynn, the CLU sent out "individual committees" to "go right into the neighborhood where we live; we tell our mothers and sisters; we even do it ourselves; I have sent my sister to one, my brother to one and my father to others." Flynn's mention of "mothers and sisters" highlights the crucial, if less visible, role played by women in Gilded Age labor activism; women may have constituted only a fraction of organized workers in this period, but they provided crucial behind-the-scenes support. In the case of boycotts, women's control of domestic spending choices meant that their participation was essential for success.[72]

The number of boycotts overseen by the CLU grew rapidly in the 1880s, reflecting the organization's growing strength. *Bradstreet's* reported 237 known boycotts in the United States for the years 1884 and 1885. The New York State Bureau of Labor Statistics' *Annual Report* for 1885 devoted significant attention to the increasingly popular tactic, but gives no comprehensive statistics. In succeeding years, the Bureau reported 165 boycotts in New York State for 1886 and 242 for 1887.[73]

"THEY ARE THE SERVANTS OF THE PEOPLE, NOT OF ANY 'CLASS' "

As the CLU promoted an oppositional culture of working-class republicanism through education, union building, and strikes and boycotts, it consistently encountered not merely hostile and abusive employers, but also key institutions of the state that backed them. In response, the CLU launched initiatives to reassert labor's place in within the republican polity, focusing on three critical realms of state oppression: the police, the courts, and the New York State Legislature.

Clashes between police and labor activists were common in the years following the Civil War, but they became particularly pronounced in the 1880s as labor, under the direction of the Knights nationally and the CLU locally, challenged the growing power of capital in rallies, demonstrations, parades, strikes, pickets, and boycotts. As a rule, New York City police consistently intervened in labor disputes on behalf of employers, nearly always with violence. The case of Louis Zeiger in February 1884 typified such responses. Zeiger, a cigarmaker and union activist, was picketing outside a cigar factory when the police, at the behest of the factory owner, ordered the protesters to disperse. Zeiger refused, citing the peaceful and legal nature of their demonstration. A patrolman then struck him over the head with his club and dragged him off to jail.[74]

The police also frequently disrupted labor meetings. The most infamous example of this practice (apart from the Tompkins Square assaults in 1874) occurred in February 1885 at a contentious meeting of socialists at Concordia Hall. Without a warning or an order to disperse, hundreds of police attacked the assemblage, striking men and women alike; many were crushed under foot in the resulting panic and stampede. "Broken heads and bloody-bandaged faces were all that remained of the meeting," wrote one indignant witness, "as the police rested on their laurels [for having] 'protected' for the first time on record, a Socialist meeting." The police also employed more subtle forms of harassment, such as denying or delaying the issuance of parade and outdoor rally permits or detailing a massive police turnout to intimidate those attending such events.[75]

These frequent conflicts with the police alarmed Gilded Age workers. They pointedly rejected the assertions of the wealthy and powerful that rising police violence was necessary to suppress the radicalized "dangerous classes" bent on social revolution (see chapter 2). Instead, they interpreted these clashes as further evidence that the republican tradition of equal rights and republican government was under assault. Incident after incident demonstrated that capitalists could summon the ostensibly neutral agents of law and order at a whim to protect their class interests. A local version of the "standing army," so feared by the Founding Fathers little more than a century ago, now acted on its own, beyond true democratic control, to oppress workers—"the people"—on behalf of a small but powerful aristocracy in the making. It created, noted the CLU, a "dangerous and widespread feeling of disgust and resentment among the public."[76] To address this problem and to make the police "understand that they are the servants of the whole people, and not of any 'class,'" the CLU repeatedly sent committees to the city's police commissioners to demand disciplinary action against offending officers. None met with any success.[77]

The CLU campaign to challenge state power also focused on the anti-labor legal system. Virtually everything about the courts troubled and enraged labor, from the machine-controlled system for filling judicial posts, to the haughty attitude of judges and their summary form of justice that nearly always favored employers, to the laws limiting jury duty to property owners. Workers hauled before judges were treated with scorn and contempt. For example, two men arrested in 1884 for distributing boycott handbills languished in jail for weeks because the judge set bail at $500—nearly a year's wages for many workingmen—and then allowed the case to drag on for even longer.[78]

Worse than contempt, workers also faced a pro-business State Supreme Court that frequently declared the few prolabor laws that passed the legislature unconstitutional. In one illuminating case, after years of struggle, cigarmakers in 1883 succeeded in gaining passage of a law banning the production of cigars in tenements, only to have the court nullify it in October 1884. "Who can wonder," wrote Swinton after the decision, "that so many workingmen are coming to the conclusion that the Legislature and the Courts are so subservient to capital as destroy every hope of their securing through them any redress of even the most loathsome wrong?"[79]

As with police harassment, the CLU spearheaded an effort to regain respect and equality before the courts of law. It pursued this end mainly by providing free legal counsel to those arrested for picketing. Its motives were twofold: not only were they trying to secure acquittal, but they were also looking to create "test cases" against both police harassment and the pretexts upon which it was based—the "conspiracy" clauses in the state penal code. New York's penal code, like those in many other states, contained broad clauses that defined criminal conspiracy as any combination of individuals that resulted in injury to a person or their property. Technically speaking, the law covered any and all combinations, including those formed by employers or merchants, but pro-business courts sanctioned its use almost exclusively against labor organizations striking against an employer and later, by the mid-1880s, for boycotting.[80] To workers in the Gilded Age, the use of conspiracy laws against labor exposed the extent to which capital controlled state power. The laws represented precisely what workers termed "class legislation,"[81] and thus the CLU worked for its repeal by organizing mass rallies, backing prolabor political candidates, and providing legal counsel to workingmen arrested under such charges.[82]

The CLU also challenged the hostility of the state toward labor by focusing on the legislature in Albany. This effort took the form of both seeking repeal of class legislation (e.g., the conspiracy laws) and gaining the passage of laws designed to relieve the plight of laboring men and women. (The Knights of Labor commenced a similar effort aimed at Congress.)[83] This emphasis on the positive role of the state to secure social justice indicated an important departure among Gilded Age workers from the antebellum dogma of minimalist government. The CLU Committee on Labor Bills drafted labor legislation and lobbied sympathetic politicians to sponsor it. When votes on such bills (or ones threatening to labor) were pending, the committee issued resolutions and organized rallies. For example, in the spring of 1884, the committee drafted an eight-hour workday bill, forwarded it to a prolabor senator, and organized mass meetings of support; when it was defeated,[84] the CLU issued an angry statement denouncing the politicians as "the slimy tools of brutal slave-drivers and the patrons of criminal greed," vowing "to prepare a political coffin for [them]."[85]

THE KNIGHTS OF LABOR IN NEW YORK

The rise of the CLU in New York was facilitated by a simultaneous and complementary emergence of the Knights of Labor. As noted in chapter 3, the Knights had remained a small, clandestine labor organization of roughly twenty thousand workers concentrated in Pennsylvania as late as 1880. But with the elevation of Terence Powderly to the position of Grand Master Workman, a recovering national economy following the depression of the 1870s, and the growing appeal of working-class republican ideology, membership soon began steadily to grow and spread. The Knights' ideology gradually evolved to reject the narrow particularism of trade unionism and instead embraced an inclusive vision of worker solidarity, calling for the organization of all workers into unions, regardless of skill. In an even greater departure from traditional trade union philosophy, the Knights also welcomed women and African Americans into their ranks. The Order's reputation and membership grew rapidly over the next few years, reaching 60,811 members in 1884 and more than 700,000 in 1886.[86]

Another key development in the growth of the Knights of Labor, in addition to its inclusive philosophy, was its largely successful effort to avoid official condemnation from the Catholic Church, an institution central to the lives and identity of many workers. Beginning in the 1870s, Church officials in the United States and Canada criticized the Knights for its secret oath and rituals, and reminded Catholics of the Church's long-standing ban on membership in secret societies. Soon after he took over leadership of the Knights, Powderly, a devout Catholic himself, took steps to appease the concerns of Catholic authorities. In 1882, he made the momentous decision to eliminate the oath and policy of secrecy, as well as to deemphasize the rituals, paving the way for massive membership growth.[87]

In spite of these steps, criticism of the Knights by some Catholic clerics continued to grow in the early 1880s, no doubt in response to the organization's growth. Outright condemnations came from several bishops. These and other conservative Church leaders pleaded with Rome for an official papal condemnation of Catholic membership in all trade unions except those under clerical supervision. (Significantly, they also called for the condemnation of Henry George's *Progress and Poverty*, which they had come to see as a primary textbook of modern radicalism in the United States.) These conservatives were opposed by a group of more progressive-minded church officials like Bishop James Gibbons of Baltimore, who cautioned that condemning the Knights would shatter the Church's credibility among workers and drive countless numbers of them from it. Nonetheless, some members of the Church hierarchy continued to condemn Catholic membership in the Knights and interest in Henry George.[88]

In spite of this climate of hostility, the Knights experienced rapid expansion in the New York area, which mirrored the organization's rise nationally.

While Powderly had reported in the spring of 1880 that no Knights assemblies existed in the city, Knights organizers soon established the first of what ultimately numbered more than four hundred local assemblies.[89] By 1886, New York and the surrounding vicinities possessed five district assemblies comprised of 415 locals with nearly seventy thousand members, almost one-tenth of the Knights national membership of 700,000 (table 5.2).[90]

By far, the most active branch was District Assembly 49. Dominated by a group of LaSallean socialists (nicknamed the "Home Club"), DA 49 emerged as one of the most radical sections within the Knights of Labor. Seeking to push the Knights in a more progressive direction, they rejected the "practical" agenda of trade unionists and instead emphasized the Knights' more radical positions, such as organizing unskilled workers and immigrants, including the Chinese. They declared the differences between labor and capital irreconcilable, calling for the abolition of the competitive wage system. Many supported the general principles of land reform as articulated by Henry George, but found his single tax reform insufficiently radical. Indeed, the year before they founded their assembly, several of DA 49's future leaders wrote George a letter lauding him as a "distinguished economist" who rightly demonstrated that rent is robbery, but chiding him for the limitations of his radicalism. "We know very well that you are an individualist whilst we have placed ourselves upon the side of Collectivism," they charged.[91]

In its first four years of existence, DA 49 organized hundreds of local assemblies; by July 1886, it was the largest Knights district assembly in the

TABLE 5.2 The Knights of Labor in New York City, 1886

	Members	Local assemblies	Trade
No. 45	132	13	Telegraphers
No. 49	60,809	366	Mixed
No. 64	1,938	11	Printers
No. 85	1,704	9	Plumbers
No. 91	3,329	16	Shoemakers
Totals	67,912	415	

Source: Knights of Labor, *Record of the Proceedings of the General Assembly of the Knights of Labor of America* (Richmond, VA, 1886), 326–28.

New York area and the second largest in the nation. But despite DA 49's successes in organizing a wide array of workers, especially those ignored by the trade unions, its confrontational tactics and radical ideology eventually caused dissention. Their hostility toward trade unionists (whom they considered elitist) elicited complaints to the national Order that DA 49 leaders sought to destroy their unions. DA 49 was also at the center of the most widely publicized and significant intralabor dispute of the era involving two rival cigarmakers unions.

The dispute started in 1881 when a dissident group of cigarmakers broke away from Local 144 of the Cigar Makers International Union (CMIU).[92] Calling themselves the Progressive Cigar Makers Union (Local Assembly 2814 of the Knights), they rejected the trade-centered "new unionism" of the CMIU and its leaders Samuel Gompers and Adolph Strasser. Instead, they welcomed formerly unorganized cigarmakers, especially the lower skilled. For the next five years, the Progressives and the Internationals engaged in bitter struggle over issues of membership, jurisdiction, and strikes. The Internationals benefited from support from the CLU, with which they were affiliated.[93]

Overall, the institutional and ideological growth of the New York labor movement was helped by the presence of dedicated and active Knights of Labor. Not surprisingly, when the CLU formed in 1882, many of its influential leaders—including George K. Lloyd, P. J. McGuire, Matthew Maguire, George Blair, Philip Scannell—were active Knights. So too was Henry George, who joined in 1883. Over time, as the CLU grew, Knights would come to comprise more than half its member unions and individual members and would play a crucial role in promoting and coordinating the CLU's agenda.[94]

"WIDELY ACCEPTED ARTICLES
IN THE WORKINGMEN'S CREED"

One of the busiest and most visible Knights in New York was Henry George. As a self-made intellectual who had ceased to work as a printer long ago, he was hardly a typical Knights' member. But there was much about the Order that George agreed with and admired, including its leader

Terence Powderly. The two met for the first time in August 1883, but Powderly had embraced many of the ideas in *Progress and Poverty* years before; he had even proposed a restructuring of the city's tax code along the lines of the single tax when serving as mayor of Scranton, Pennsylvania.[95] Powderly had also been a Land Leaguer allied with the radical George-Davitt-Ford faction that advocated the abolition of absolute private property rights regarding land. He would later support several declarations by the national Knights body in favor of land reform, including a 1884 one that read in explicitly Georgist terminology "that all lands now held for speculative purposes be taxed to their full value."[96] Powderly and George would remain friends and regular correspondents for the rest of the decade.

But beyond ideology and friendship, George was no doubt compelled to join the Knights because he believed it would help promote, given his rising popularity among workers, *Progress and Poverty* and the single tax. In March 1883, just five months after returning from Ireland to a hero's welcome from the Central Labor Union, George learned that an inexpensive "workingmen's edition" of *Progress and Poverty* had sold an astonishing twenty thousand copies with no sign of slowing down. Evidence of working-class enthusiasm for *Progress and Poverty* abounded. In Chicago, the members of District Assembly 24 voted to devote the first twenty minutes of every meeting to a reading of *Progress and Poverty*. In New York City, cigar markers chose one from their number to read *Progress and Poverty* as they worked. CLU activist Edward King said that any public speaker seeking to win over a crowd of workers "could not do better than to start with a quotation from Henry George's 'Progress and Poverty.'"[97]

George's rising popularity among American workers, so vividly illustrated by the CLU reception and soaring sales of *Progress and Poverty*, raises a compelling question: how can we account for the appeal of an enormous book on political economy among landless urban workers, the majority of whom possessed only a rudimentary education? Part of the answer lies in George's intent. Although he longed for the endorsement of eminent intellectuals like political economist Edward Atkinson and Britain's Herbert Spencer, he always expected his work to be read by the common worker. Unlike the so-called mugwumps of the Gilded Age, who favored social reform but feared the masses they advocated for, George had faith in "the great masses of men" who, as "the repositories of ultimate political power" could drive social change.[98]

A more significant explanation for George's success in attracting a vast working-class following stemmed from the timing of *Progress and Poverty*'s publication. As a work of political economy designed to solve the plight of labor and restore the republic, his tome rolled off the printing presses at D. Appleton's at precisely the moment when American wage earners were confronting the harsh realities of industrial capitalism's ascent, realities that convinced them the republic was in crisis. "The general faith in republican institutions is . . . narrowing and weakening," wrote George in *Progress and Poverty*. "Thoughtful men are beginning to see its dangers without seeing how to escape them; are beginning to accept the view of Macaulay and distrust that of Jefferson."[99] *Progress and Poverty* represented one of era's first comprehensive attempts to recast earlier forms of republicanism to offer a new and more radical solution to the frightening challenges of industrial life. "The ground was ripe," wrote economist Richard T. Ely in 1885, "for the seed sown by Henry George."[100]

George also gained working-class readers because he presented his message in a highly readable form. Here too he distinguished himself from the ethical economists that in coming years would publish books and articles aimed exclusively at educated elites like themselves.[101] Even as many sections of *Progress and Poverty* stood above the comprehension of people not versed in political economy, in the most critical parts of the book where he set forth his ethical arguments George employed a compelling rhetorical style, full of vivid images ("in the festering mass will be generated volcanic forces") and moral outrage ("amid the greatest accumulations of wealth, men die of starvation").[102] Workers did not need a formal education to grasp the essential meaning of passages like: "when everyone gets what he fairly earns, no one can get more than he fairly earns. How many men are there who fairly earn a million dollars?"[103]

In a similar manner, George also appealed to his working-class readers by lacing his prose with the familiar idioms and turns of phrase of evangelical Christianity and perfectionism—a common practice among populist reformers in this era. These ideas were central to the antebellum social reform movements that drew large working-class support, especially the temperance and abolition movements. George drew on this tradition both by invoking Christian morality to indict growing social inequality and promising a millennial "City of God" on earth should his reform plan be adopted. Here again he distinguished himself from the ethical economists, many of whom were professed agnostics and all of whom shunned any invocation of Christian ideals or imagery in their writings.[104]

Workers also appreciated George's efforts to wrest the discipline of political economy from conservative scholars defending laissez-faire and employing flawed theories (e.g., the iron law of wages) "against every effort of the working class to increase their wages or decrease their hours of labor." They appreciated his condemnation of political economists for performing the same function, as he put it, as "the cursed-be-Ham clergymen [who] used to preach the divine sanction of slavery in the name of Christianity."[105] Properly oriented, wrote George, "Political Economy is radiant with hope."[106] Countless workers in the Gilded Age agreed. By 1884, a prominent political economist observed that "tens of thousands of laborers read *Progress and Poverty* who have never before looked between the covers of an economics book, and its conclusions are widely accepted articles in the workingmen's creed."[107]

Working-class readers likewise appreciated George's humble origins, his struggle to make a living as a wage earner in California, as well as his membership in a printer's union and, by 1883, in the Knights of Labor. Such biographical information lent authenticity to his book's arguments. George the reformer came not from the condescending ranks of the "Best Men," like Beecher and Godkin, but from the people's ranks. His sympathetic style came across as genuine. His work on behalf of the Irish Land League reinforced this image.

George's book also attracted a wide working-class following because it drew upon familiar elements of the American republican tradition. He based his critique of the laissez-faire industrial economy not on the writings of Europeans like Smith, Ricardo, Malthus, and Marx and instead used the ideas, language, and idioms of American republicanism, in particular, its producerist tradition: God placed men and women on a bountiful earth and endowed them with the intelligence and skill necessary for progress; work was a sanctified and necessary activity and those who performed it were the truest republican citizens; and to producers (and honest capitalists) belonged the fruits of their toil. Similarly, George drew upon familiar republican and producerist concepts to explain the dangers facing the republic.[108] Just as the radical artisans of the 1830s had argued that the new market economy threatened republican society, George argued that monopoly of any kind, but especially of land, threatened to transform a society of virtuous producers into one marked by inequality, dependence, and unnatural class conflict. His program, he argued, was designed specifically to safeguard the fundamental elements of republican citizenship— liberty, independence, equal opportunity, equality, and democracy. "Equality of political rights," wrote George, "will not compensate for the denial of the equal right to the bounty of nature. . . . Poverty enslaves men who we boast are political sovereigns." Employing terms and concepts straight out of the lexicon of traditional republican terminology, George spoke to the American working class in a language they readily understood.[109]

But of particular importance was George's emphasis on inequality. One of the central tenets of American political culture (and often noted in the writings of European visitors like Tocqueville) in the century following the American Revolution was the celebration of the republic as a land where extremes of wealth did not exist and equality of opportunity abounded.[110] In the late 1870s, however, as evidence of widespread and deepening economic inequality mounted, George emerged as the first significant figure to confirm its glaring presence, to explain the lethal threat it posed to democracy and republican institutions, and to offer a solution. Above all, even if they remained skeptical of the efficacy of the single tax, working-class Americans welcomed George's analysis and dire warning that *something* needed to be done to steer the nation away from the path toward European-style inequality and back onto its proper republican course. It was not until the late 1880s and 1890s that significant numbers of reform-minded Americans took up this cause and began publishing articles and studies in popular journals.[111]

This emphasis on inequality points to another aspect of George's appeal to working-class Americans. From Thomas Jefferson's purchase of the Louisiana Territory to Thomas Skidmore's call for equality of property ownership in the 1830s, from George Henry Evans's campaign for free western homesteads in the 1840s to the Free Soil movement of the 1850s, Americans of all classes and callings shared a belief that republican society depended on widespread access to land as a source of opportunity and independence. George's charge that land monopoly, rather than mere population growth, had created an artificial, dangerous land scarcity and high prices likewise appealed to Gilded Age workers steeped in this tradition. Indeed, it added another dimension to the rising outcry among workers and reformers against the massive land grants given to railroads by state and federal authorities. Like Evans, George made an explicit appeal to urban workers, arguing that his reform, by eliminating the incentive to speculate, would release millions of acres for tillage by Americans currently trapped in overcrowded cities. It would also lower the rents of those who elected to stay and increase their chances to own their homes.[112]

And yet, had he relied solely on appealing to America's republican tradition, George could hardly have expected to garner a mass working-class following in the Gilded Age. Just as scholarship in recent decades on the Knights of Labor has challenged earlier depictions of the movement as hopelessly "backward looking,"[113] careful analysis of George's work reveals a duality—strikingly similar to that found in the ideologies of the Knights of Labor, Populists, and other late nineteenth-century insurgencies—that drew upon past traditions as a means of articulating a progressive, forward-looking vision of future industrial society. In essence, every element of George's appeal to tradition also had a radical edge, one that both anticipated and furthered the emergence of working-class republicanism in the Gilded Age and, later, progressivism.[114]

To begin with, George offered a radical redefinition of republican citizenship and its attendant notions of democracy and equality. This effort put him at the forefront of Gilded Age reformers who insisted that traditional conceptions of liberty, justice, and equality needed updating and redefining to address the challenges of the new industrial age. So even as he wrote and spoke of workers as the pillars of the republic deserving their full, rightful measure of political and social equality, George augmented this traditional notion of republican citizenship by arguing that it carried certain *economic* rights as well, a notion central to working-class republicanism and emerging progressivism. The only difference was that while some workers (notably the Knights of Labor) proposed measures to republicanize industry by enhancing the voice and rights of workers in the productive process and establishing cooperatives, George proposed his single tax to republicanize resources (e.g., land).[115]

To accomplish this goal, George's program called for a radical departure from a core tenet of traditional republicanism by insisting on state intervention in the economy. As noted in chapter 2, George, like many of the workers he appealed to, came of age in a political culture wedded to the liberal abhorrence of strong, centralized, interventionist government as antithetical to a proper republican polity. The crisis of the 1870s and 1880s, however, prompted new thinking on this matter, leading George and American workers to propose a radical break from traditional republicanism's anti-statism. Whereas workers and farmers had once celebrated laissez-faire as essential to their liberty, they now insisted state intervention was necessary.[116] As a result, when George proposed to radically break with traditional republicanism by both abolishing absolute private property rights and empowering the state, his message was in sync with the working-class republicanism then animating workers' response to industrial capitalism.[117]

He also offered a radical reinterpretation of Christianity that also found resonance among his working-class readers. George did much more than merely pepper his narrative with familiar references to scripture; he articulated the nascent ideas that would come to form the social gospel movement. Although Gilded Age workers frequently exhibited contempt for the Christian clergy, that did not necessarily mean they rejected Christianity. For many, Christianity was a creed of social justice that identified society's sinners as idlers ("Pharisees") who grew rich by manipulating the law, not as honest toilers living in poverty. "It is not the Almighty, but we who are responsible for the vice and misery that fester amid our civilization," wrote George. God provided plenty; man merely distributed it unjustly. Such a message resonated with workers' increasing interest in what Christianity had to say on matters related to society, as opposed to questions of dogma, piety, or sectarianism.[118]

Finally, George appealed to a mass working-class audience through his vision of an alternative future society that, while not constituting the overthrow of the contemporary American economy and political system, called for its radical reshaping along mutualist and cooperative lines. These ideals were at the very heart of working-class republicanism that found wide expression by individual workers, labor editors, and organizations like the Knights of Labor. They spoke of a future cooperative social order that, while not explicitly socialist, embodied many of its promises. The Knights, for example, in their Declaration of Principles, called for "the introduction of a co-operative industrial system" that would "supersede the wage system." In his conclusion to *Progress and Poverty*, George conjured up a similar vision of a transformed society: "We are made for co-operation."

George's broad appeal among American workingmen stemmed from the convergence of his message and the popular ideas that formed the foundation of working-class republicanism. Both shared a disdain for the notion that the economy was controlled by immutable laws that men and women were powerless to change. Both also believed that the conditions of modern industrial society necessitated breaking free of the republican orthodoxies of inviolable private property rights and a minimalist state. Those who read *Progress and Poverty*, listened to passages read in workshops and at Land League meetings, or heard George and his followers speak discovered a usable and increasingly familiar political economic vocabulary that resonated in essential ways with their working-class republicanism. George's message allowed them to comprehend the compelling social problems they faced and the need to resolve them. One C. P. Atkinson described the impact of *Progress and Poverty* among workers as follows:

It came to the weary and heavy laden as the talisman of a lost hope. All their lives long they had been taught that poverty was a 'dispensation of Providence' needful to keep them humble and teach them patience, but if cheerfully borne, it would somehow contribute to their happiness in the dim beyond. 'Progress and Poverty' reversed all this, teaching that poverty is an artificial condition of man's invention. . . . Workingmen and women, learning all this, . . . commenced to wrestle with their chains.[119]

This appeal among working-class Americans led to extraordinary book sales and many invitations to lecture—in short, the fame and impact George had so yearned for in his downtrodden California years. From 1883 to 1886, George spoke before countless Knights of Labor assemblies, Irish nationalist societies, and reform groups throughout the Northeast and Midwest. While these events earned him very little money, they did expose an ever-growing number of workers to his ideas.[120] His growing popularity also led to many invitations to write for magazines, opportunities that held out the prospect of increasing his following and bringing in needed income to alleviate what he termed in a letter to a friend as the persistent "bread and butter question."[121] So when *Frank Leslie's Weekly*, one of the nation's most popular and widely circulated publications, asked George in March 1883 to write a series of articles for the princely sum of $100 apiece, he leaped at the chance. While he was grateful for the money and exposure, he could not help but see in this deal a clear confirmation of his rising status as a public intellectual; *Leslie's* intended the articles to compete with a rival series then running in *Harper's Weekly* by the nation's foremost advocate of laissez-faire and social Darwinism, Yale sociologist William Graham Sumner.[122]

The first essay in the series, "Problems of the Time," appeared on April 14, 1883.[123] In this and the succeeding essays, George reiterated many of the ideas and themes he previously outlined in *Progress and Poverty*, but in a manner designed to relate them to specific issues then dominating public debate over industry, monopoly, and labor unrest. Line by line, in essay after essay, George laid out before his readers the evidence of a republic in crisis. The free labor promise to workers of upward mobility was being undermined by monopoly capitalism and the spread of a form of industrial slavery. "The man who is dependent upon a master for a living," he observed, "is not a free man." New industrial technology, while holding the potential to improve society, was "degrading men into the position of mere feeders of machines."[124] A powerful, untouchable American aristocracy was coalescing, threatening to make meaningless the republic's democratic traditions. George warned his audience, "All the tendencies of the present are not merely to the concentration, but to the perpetuation, of great fortunes" as in unrepublican Europe. That wealth carried with it enormous political power, twisting "our government by the people [into] . . . government by the strong and unscrupulous." The latter, he declared, hid behind the mantras of laissez-faire, that "the gospel of selfishness," and social Darwinism, "the comfortable theory that it is in the nature of things that some should be poor and some should be rich." Underlying all these dark assertions was the same apocalyptic language found in *Progress and Poverty* that demanded radical reform and action from the people before it was too late. "Our society is evolving destructive forces," he warned, " . . . [and] present tendencies . . . threaten to kindle passions that have so often before flamed in destructive fury."[125]

Sprinkled throughout these essays were George's trademark turns of phrase that transformed complicated and controversial ideas into seemingly commonsensical maxims:

We may not like it but we cannot avoid it. Either government must manage the railroads, or the railroads must manage the government.[126]

Supposing we did legalize chattel slavery again, who would buy men when men can be hired so cheaply?[127]

When a man gets wealth that he does not produce, he necessarily gets it at the expense of those who produce it.[128]

Contempt of human rights is the essential element in building up the great fortunes.[129]

"The poor ye will always have with you." If ever a scripture has been wrested to the devil's service, this is that scripture. How often have these words been distorted from their obvious meaning to soothe conscience into acquiescence in human misery and degradation.[130]

In addressing these vital issues, George brought to his essays a higher degree of radicalism, both in terms of rhetoric and ideology. He expanded, for example, his list of natural monopolies that required government ownership from the railroad and telegraph system to include the telephone system and electric utilities.[131] George also emphasized more forcefully the central themes of emerging progressivism, in particular that republican citizenship carried with it not merely political rights, but also economic ones: "The freedom to earn, without fear or favor, a comfortable living ought to go with the freedom to vote."[132]

Moreover, he offered a more forceful condemnation of industrial monopoly (in comparison to his focus on land monopoly in *Progress and Poverty*). "The big mill crushes out the little mill. The big store undersells the little store till it gets rid of its competition," while "the greater railroad companies are swallowing up the lesser railroad companies; one great telegraph company already controls the telegraph wires of the continent." George cautioned in these essays that the heads of these immense enterprises were fast transforming themselves into an American aristocracy and the great mass of the American people into their feudal vassals.[133]

Significantly, George repeatedly expressed admiration for the ideals and goals of socialism. But in doing so, he took care to emphasize that his single tax reform did not threaten the capitalist free market, individualism, and profit-seeking. "Capital is a good; the capitalist a helper, if he is not also a monopolist," wrote George. "We can safely let anyone get as rich as he can if he will not despoil others in doing so." Yet George made it clear that he admired socialism and that he could foresee a time in the future when it would be implemented in the United States. He predicted that "the natural progress of social development is unmistakably toward cooperation, or, if the word be preferred, toward socialism." The need for the state to assume a more active role in economic life was "the truth in socialism."[134] Such bold assertions explain why the eminent political economist Richard T. Ely described George as the most influential socialist in the United States two years later in his book *Recent American Socialism*.[135] George's essays in *Leslie's* also reflected a degree of tolerance for socialism in public discourse that prevailed until the Haymarket bombing in May 1886.[136]

One key benefit of the *Leslie's* series, besides the income, was the opportunity for George to publish another book (the collected *Leslie's* essays were published together under the title *Social Problems*) espousing his radical critique and reform program at a time when many other reformers, activists, journalists, politicians, and political economists were publishing their own works purporting to explain the "labor question" and other pressing social issues.[137] While the impact of George's essays is difficult to gauge, it can be said with certainty that, along with a large general public, a number of influential public figures read them. For example, the well-known minister and social critic Josiah Strong read them while writing his bestselling book, *Our Country: Its Possible Future and Its Present Crisis* (1885).[138] Yale sociologist and social Darwinism proponent William G. Sumner also read them, in part because George pointedly ridiculed him on several occasions.[139] Francis A. Walker, the nation's foremost political economist, took umbrage at George's criticism of a Census Department report he had compiled and wrote a testy letter to *Leslie's*.[140] And nearly all Walker's esteemed colleagues in the political economy discipline read them as well, including the rising cohort of younger political economists such as Richard T. Ely and John Bates Clark, then flirting with socialism and who eventually developed the foundations of new liberalism. Significantly, although unknown at the time, George's writings had begun to find their way into the hands of readers who, in part inspired by them, would soon emerge as prominent American reformers and radicals, including Ignatius Donnelly, Daniel DeLeon, T. Thomas Fortune, Tom L. Johnson, Lincoln Steffens, Clarence Darrow, John Dewey, and Jacob Riis (a more complete list is discussed in chapter 8).

But as his star continued to rise, George found himself confronted by two misfortunes in July 1883, one rather minor and the other quite significant. In the former case, he learned from the editors of *Leslie's* that they would not extend the series beyond the original agreement of thirteen essays. They found his critique of modern industrial society too radical.[141] The professional rebuff disappointed George, but he was already nearing completion of a new book, a free trade manifesto entitled *Protection or Free Trade*. However, the one disaster all writers fear struck: he lost the manuscript as he was moving to a house in Brooklyn. This mishap hit him hard, but George's spirits were sustained by the popularity of the *Leslie's* essays and his plans to publish them in book form. Before long, he summoned the will to begin rewriting, right from the very beginning, the manuscript for *Protection or Free Trade*.[142]

Further evidence of George's rising public recognition appeared in late summer 1883. In August, as he worked on the galley proofs of *Social Problems*, George was called to testify before the same Senate committee investigating the relations between labor and capital before which the CLU brought its slate of witnesses. For several hours he related his views on the causes of labor-capital conflict, from the increase of monopolies in industry and land to the growing gap between the rich and poor, and articulated why his single tax reform offered the best hope for restoring justice and harmony.[143] Two weeks later, George attended the second annual Labor Day parade as an honored guest of the CLU. He was no doubt gratified to see so many signs with slogans that reflected the ideas he put forth in *Progress and Poverty* and the *Leslie's* series, including one that read, "The Modern Industrial System Increases Capital and Poverty."[144] He certainly did not miss the huge Georgist cartoon carried by workers labeled, "The Situation." It showed "Capital" flying a kite labeled "Rent" with a tail that read, "meat, coal, flour prices."[145]

There was yet another sign of George's ascendant influence, especially among workers, but it was one that remained secret for the time being. Unbeknownst to George, the very same conservative Catholic Church officials who expressed alarm over the soaring numbers of Catholic workers in the Knights of Labor (and who, as noted in chapter 4, pressured New York's Cardinal McCloskey to rein in Fr. Edward McGlynn) also feared the evident rising popularity of *Progress and Poverty* among them, a book they considered heretical and dangerous. A heated transatlantic debate ensued between conservative clerics who wished to condemn both the Knights and George and more moderate clerics who warned that such a move would trigger a disastrous backlash. The Vatican eventually placed George's works on its Index of Forbidden Works in February 1889.[146]

Unaware of these potentially damaging machinations, George continued to lecture and write. In late 1883, he capped off the most successful year of his career, one in which he both significantly raised his profile and income, by accepting an invitation to lecture in England, Scotland, and Ireland. Here was a chance to build on his successful tour of Ireland and England in the previous year and expand his international following. In December 1883, shortly after publishing *Social Problems*, George set sail for London.[147] He arrived to find himself one of the most talked about men in England, which was then convulsing with debate over social, political, and economic reform proposals. Among socialists, Fabians, land reform advocates, and other radicals, George's ideas found many supporters, leading

"The Old Story." *Punch*, January 26, 1884. Courtesy of the Library of Congress

to speaking engagements and extensive press coverage, clearly marking his entry into an emerging transatlantic network of progressive reformers and ideas. "Here I am in London," he wrote his wife, "and at last begin to realize that I am a very important man."[148]

But not all the attention was adulatory. Indeed, many British intellectuals and conservatives published highly critical reviews of George's speeches and *Social Problems*. Their criticism annoyed and stung George, in part because he was so convinced of the correctness of his analysis, but also because he remained very self-conscious of his humble origins and self-education in political economy. Nonetheless, when he sailed for New York after a four-month tour, he believed he was making headway in bringing his message to the world.[149]

When George arrived in New York Harbor in late April 1884, he once again received a hero's welcome by the CLU with a mass rally at Cooper Union. As he approached the podium to deliver a short speech, reported the frequently antilabor *New York Times*, "men arose in their seats and shouted until they were hoarse. Hats were waved about and thrown in the air, and for fully five minutes the hall was a perfect pandemonium."[150] For the remainder of the year, George kept up his lecturing and writing, including rewriting *Protection or Free Trade*. In September, he again accepted an invitation from the CLU to review the annual Labor Day parade, and he left for Europe again in November for a three-month lecture tour. Returning in February 1885, he resumed lecturing and writing articles.[151]

As 1885 drew to a close, George looked forward to the coming year with eagerness and optimism. By now, there was no question that he had achieved international recognition as reformer whose ideas were to be taken seriously, even by those who rejected them, due to their popularity among workers and a significant subset of influential middle-class reformers. His latest book, *Protection or Free Trade*, due to be published in January, promised even greater public recognition. The year 1886 seemed full of promise.

PART III

The Great Upheaval, 1886–1887

6

"The Country Is Drifting into Danger"

"ARE WE IN DANGER OF REVOLUTION?"

In April 1886, the New York Academy of Design unveiled its spring exhibition of paintings and sculptures. Of the many pieces on display, one large painting drew particular attention from both critics and casual viewers alike. Robert Koehler's *The Strike* depicted a vivid scene of industrial discontent inspired by events the artist witnessed during the Great Uprising of 1877. Set in an unidentified industrial town, the painting captures a moment of confrontation as workers pour out of a factory to gather outside the office of their employer. The work is fraught with tension and an atmosphere suggestive of impending violence. One worker in the foreground stoops to pick up a rock. In the center foreground, a woman tries to calm another angry worker. To the left, Koehler shows what appears to be a labor leader in a red shirt pleading with the factory owner on behalf of the striking workers.

The timing and place of the debut of Koehler's painting was extraordinary, even if purely coincidental. New York City, indeed the nation as a whole, was at that very moment plunging into an unprecedented period of social turmoil. Many Americans by 1886 were coming to the conclusion

"The Strike." *Harper's Weekly*, May 1, 1886. Author's collection.

that *something* had to be done to reverse the trend toward European-style class conflict and violent upheaval. But what to do? This anxiety seemed to be the central theme of Koehler's painting. Labor and capital both deserved praise and scorn. Many capitalists, perhaps including the stern one shown in the painting, did indeed exploit their workers. Yet Koehler depicts him as willing to bend his ear to his workers' grievances. Many workers, perhaps including those gathering outside the factory, labored under oppressive conditions. Yet too many, as suggested by the man reaching for the rock, seemed all too willing to resort to violence. Koehler's scene calls out for an answer, but Americans were no closer to agreeing on how to solve the labor question in April 1886 than they had been in 1877.[1]

It was in this context of tension and uncertainty that the year 1886 unfolded as one of the most tumultuous in American history, rivaled only by the years 1776, 1861, 1877, 1919, 1946, and 1968. The number of strikes that year (1,432) was nearly triple the average of the five hundred strikes that took place in the years 1881–1885. The number of boycotts imposed likewise exploded.[2] Writing of this upsurge in labor protest, Richard T. Ely wrote, "It is doubtful if history records any more rapid social movement than this ominous separation of the American people into two nations. Already they scarcely speak the same language."[3]

In early March of that year, two hundred thousand workers, most of them affiliated with the Knights of Labor, commenced a massive railroad strike against the lines owned by Jay Gould, one of the nation's most notorious capitalists. The Knights had prevailed over Gould in another large strike the year before, an event that helped spark a massive spike in membership in the Order (to more than 700,000 members by mid-1886). But this time around, resolving to crush the Knights, Gould refused to back down. Instead, he hired strikebreakers and compelled governors in the affected states to call out their militias to protect them. Gould soon emerged as the winner in what came to be called the Great Southwest Strike.[4]

Reacting to the labor strife along Gould's railroads and elsewhere, President Grover Cleveland delivered on April 22, 1886, a "special message" that revealed the extraordinary nature of the times. It was the first official presidential statement in the nation's short history related to the plight of labor. "The present condition of the relations between labor and capital," he wrote, "is far from satisfactory." But rather than blandly call upon both sides to amicably reach an accord—the standard rhetorical procedure in the 1880s—Cleveland asserted that most of the problem stemmed from "the grasping and heedless exactions of employers and the alleged discrimination in favor of capital as an object of governmental attention." Still more remarkable, the president called for an unprecedented role for the national government in the free market economy: Congress should establish a federal board of arbitration to facilitate the settlement of future industrial disputes.[5]

Nine days after Cleveland's special message, as if to confirm its main contention, workers across the country participated in the largest protest in the nation's history for the eight-hour workday. On May 1, 1886, some 340,000 workers took part in eight-hour strikes, and large demonstrations were held in cities like New York and Chicago.[6] Three days later, however, an explosion at a Chicago labor rally organized by anarchists in Haymarket Square unleashed a furious wave of antilabor rhetoric and action damaged the labor movement for decades to come. The bombing and subsequent panic left seven policemen dead. Hysterical headlines across the nation screamed that revolution was at hand. "Anarchy's Red Hand: Rioting and Bloodshed in the Streets of Chicago," declared the *New York Times*. "The villainous teachings of the Anarchists bore bloody fruit in Chicago tonight," read the accompanying article's opening lines, "and before daylight at least a dozen stalwart men will have laid down their lives as a tribute to the doctrine of [anarchism]."[7] Chicago police soon arrested eight men, all self-proclaimed anarchists, and charged them with murder. The drama of their subsequent trials and eventual convictions dominated headlines for the rest of the year.[8]

Middle- and upper-class Americans viewed these developments with alarm. Once again, they voiced from the pulpit, boardroom, and editorial page renewed fears of a Paris Commune-style social uprising in America. Such fears only mounted as the number of strikes, boycotts, and labor demonstrations increased into the summer months. For example, the *Forum*, the respectable journal of elite opinion, included nine articles devoted to the topic between March and August 1886, appearing under such titles as "An Employer's View of the Labor Question," "Shall an Eight-Hour System Be Adopted?," "What Rights Have Laborers?," "The Evolution of the Boycott," "Shall We Muzzle the Anarchists?," and "Is Labor a Commodity?" The most provocative was an article by Bishop John Lancaster Spalding asking "Are We in Danger of Revolution?"[9]

Like many Americans in the spring of 1886, Henry George wondered the same thing. But in his case, he hoped the mounting crisis possessed a silver lining; this could be just the moment when the nation, especially its political leaders, would finally be forced to admit the necessity for bold reforms to preserve republican liberty. Inevitably, George believed, they would have to pay some attention to his single tax solution. As he awaited this development, George continued to write, finishing *Protection or Free Trade* in March and lecturing throughout New York, New England, and the Midwest. Sensing that a new, larger opportunity was at hand with the "labor question" once again rising to the fore in public discourse, he turned aside the advice of friends urging him to travel abroad again. "I feel that I can be more useful here for awhile yet," he wrote to one. "We are making steady progress here, and before long I think the time for bringing the question into practical politics will come."[10] Events nationwide and locally in New York City soon would prove him remarkably prescient.

"A PROTEST AND REVOLT AGAINST SYSTEMATIC INJUSTICE AND TYRANNY"

Well before workers on Jay Gould's railroad lines went on strike in March 1886, labor unrest began to rock New York City. Trouble first occurred on the streetcar lines, eventually leading to three citywide strikes that paralyzed the metropolis. Streetcar strikes were a common feature of Gilded Age urban life,[11] but the intensity of those in New York City and the subsequent extensive national press coverage led the commissioner of the New York State Bureau of Labor Statistics to claim they provided the "initial impulse" that sparked the labor unrest known as the Great Upheaval that swept the nation in 1886. "The car strikes of 1886," he wrote, "assume[d] the aspect of a protest and revolt against systematic injustice and tyranny."[12]

New York streetcar corporations were among the most powerful and profitable in the city, and the plight of their drivers was legendary. While labor activists in the mid-1880s led a national campaign for the eight-hour workday, the majority of streetcar drivers and conductors worked between fourteen and sixteen hours per day, often with no breaks, standing the entire time on platforms exposed to all of the elements, whether in the searing heat or biting cold. Companies routinely deducted "fines" from their drivers' meager pay for minor offenses, such as having an insufficient number of passengers on board or for running behind schedule (even if the delay resulted from unavoidable traffic tie-ups). As an editorial in the *Boycotter* put it, "the lot of the car horse—which cannot be called a happy one—has been far more enviable than that of the conductors or drivers."[13]

These conditions led drivers and conductors to form a union, the Empire Protective Association (Knights of Labor, DA 75; hereafter referred to as the EPA). The organization reported its first success in late January 1886 after it successfully negotiated an agreement with all the streetcar lines to pay their drivers and conductors $2.00 per day for twelve hours of work, with a reasonable amount of time off for breaks. When several companies began violating the agreement in February, the EPA led two successful strikes. These actions won restoration of the twelve hours for $2.00 rate originally agreed to.[14]

Despite these successes, the union soon clashed with William Richardson, the streetcar company owner with the worst reputation as an employer. Known as "Deacon" Richardson because of his work in a Brooklyn Baptist church, he owned the large Atlantic Avenue line in Brooklyn, as well as the Dry Dock line in Manhattan, one of the city's busiest crosstown lines, which ran from the ferries on the Hudson and East Rivers down the length of Grand Street.[15] His workers complained of sixteen-hour days without breaks and tyrannical managers who imposed numerous fines and often summarily discharged men without cause.[16]

Richardson not only rejected the EPA's demand of $2.00 for twelve hours, but went a step further: he took out advertisements in the local papers seeking replacement workers. In response, eight hundred drivers, conductors, and stablemen walked out on Tuesday, March 2. Unlike the earlier streetcar strikes, however, Richardson refused to give in, claiming he could not afford the new wage scale and, invoking the individualist dogma of laissez-faire capitalism, that he would not be "dictated" to by his employees.[17]

After a two-day standoff, Richardson ordered his managers to run a single car out of the stables. He did so to defy the strikers and to maintain his line's state charter, which could be revoked if the company failed to run its cars. What ensued came to be known as the Grand Street Riot. As soon as Car No. 155 appeared, strikers and their supporters began piling lumber, cobblestones, barrels, bricks, overturned wagons, and any other obstructions they could find on the tracks. To the jubilation of the strikers, the car retreated back to the stables.[18]

Subsequent events, however, quickly proved their joy premature. At Richardson's request, Superintendent of Police William Murray sent 750 officers (25 percent of the city's police force) to assist in a second attempted run. Five hundred patrolmen took positions along the length of Grand Street, while the remaining 250 formed a phalanx surrounding the streetcar as it emerged from the stables a second time. They encountered a throng of strikers and their supporters, who "groaned, hissed, and jeered from the sidewalks." In solidarity with the strikers, drivers from the other streetcar lines unhitched their teams and allowed the crowd to overturn their cars along the tracks. The police removed these and other obstacles while the crowds of men and women jeered and pelted them with rocks, eggs, and

The Grand Street Riot. "The Street Railroad Strike in New York—The Police Opening the Way for a Horsecar." *Harper's Weekly*, March 13, 1886. Courtesy of the Georgia State University Library Digital Collection

rotten vegetables. In response, the police frequently charged the crowd and beat onlookers with their clubs. Finally, the Dry Dock car reached the Hudson River ferries, reversed direction, and lumbered back to the East River stables. The four-mile round trip journey took two hours to complete.[19]

Two aspects of the incident reveal much about the attitudes and outlook of New York City's workers during the Great Upheaval. First, it brought out not only the eight hundred men on strike, but thousands of labor supporters. Although the press called it a "riot," it was more accurately a classic case of purposeful crowd action, unified in the objects of its anger (the police and the streetcar company) and its goal (stopping the progress of the streetcar). Notably, the crowd included large numbers of women, who played a central role in the action. "Women came out of side streets to dump ashes on the rails," related one newspaper account. Another noted that "female heads protruded from the windows of factories along the line of march, and girls and men hissed and hooted . . . and one fiery woman threw a tea cup at the driver."[20]

An additional novel feature of the Grand Street Riot was the extraordinary role assumed by the police. One reporter's account captured, albeit unintentionally, the sentiment of many onlooking laborers when he described the car as being "surrounded by the strong escort of the police, who zealously fought off would-be intruders as though the Sub-Treasury, with all its millions had been put on wheels."[21] To many working-class New Yorkers, this spectacle suggested that Deacon Richardson had the power to summon the police to serve as guardians of his personal "millions" rather than as protectors of public institutions or the public peace. While the city's laborers had grown accustomed to, though never accepting of, the frequent intervention of police in labor disputes on behalf of capital, the police actions in this streetcar strike were unprecedented. By escorting Deacon Richardson's car "like a military procession," according to *Harper's Weekly*, the force of 250 policemen in effect served as scab labor for the first time in the annals of the city's history. Furthermore, in addition to protecting the Dry Dock's car, the police removed every obstacle from its path and at one point even lifted the car onto an adjacent track to allow it to pass an overturned truck. Such unprecedented intervention on behalf of an individual's business explains the crowd's virulence toward the police. As one journalist wrote, "Everybody in the neighborhood, particularly boys and young men, seemed to harbor a grievance against the railroad company, against the police for helping it in its distress, and against the reporters who kept close to the police."[22] It also reflected the profound ideological shift in Gilded Age political discourse whereby business leaders and other elites proclaimed an absolutist fidelity to laissez-faire and the negative state as they simultaneously increased the state's power and demanded that it intervene on their behalf in labor disputes.[23]

What made the actions of the police in the Dry Dock strike even more extraordinary was the fact that the entire episode occurred on the *publicly-owned* streets. Workers saw the police as the lackeys not just of capital, but of capital built on the nickels of mostly working-class New Yorkers by virtue of a streetcar franchise granted by the city's Board of Aldermen, the ostensible representatives of the people. "Nobody can doubt that we have been proceeding upon an erroneous system," declared the *Boycotter*. "We have been giving away the use of our streets to capitalist speculators." This struggle transcended the usual practical labor issues like wages and hours. It instead raised larger questions of democracy, citizenship, and equal justice—the very concerns at the heart of working-class republicanism.[24]

In response both to the extraordinary events that transpired along Grand Street and rumors that the other streetcar lines in the city were pooling funds to prop up the besieged Dry Dock, the EPA voted to declare a city-wide work stoppage on every streetcar line until Richardson relented and met the terms of his workers.[25] Nothing like this had ever occurred in New York's history and no one knew quite what to expect.

As the sun rose over Manhattan on March 5, 1886, the city's entire fleet of streetcars lay dormant. Over sixteen thousand drivers, conductors, and stablemen refused to report for work. With the exception of the elevated railroads, which lacked the necessary cars to handle the increased demand, the city was utterly paralyzed. The Great Tie-Up, the largest urban mass transit strike in the nation's history to that point, lasted only ten hours. Richardson, facing immense public pressure and a warning from the New York State railroad commissioners (to whom the EPA had appealed) to restart his line or face the loss of his charter, gave in; he relented to the strikers' central demands and agreed to send the rest to the state railroad commissioners for arbitration. In celebration, the streetcar workers piled onto streetcars and rode them through the city streets while thousands cheered them on. On the Dry Dock line's Grand Street cars, jubilant men waved brooms and American flags, the former symbolizing their "clean sweep" in the struggle, the latter signifying of their conception of themselves as true republican citizens and guardians of American liberty.[26] It was, in the words of John Swinton, "the greatest victory yet inscribed on the records of organized labor in this city," made possible "through the solid and majestic stand made by all hands."[27]

For the next few weeks, the city's streetcar employees enjoyed the benefits of their victory. EPA leaders spoke confidently about going further, including a demand for $2.50 for a ten-hour workday.[28] But they called yet another strike on April 15, this time against the Third Avenue line for refusing to dismiss seven nonunion employees openly hostile toward the Knights of Labor. The union also demanded the rehiring of fired union employees and a wage increase.

The strategies of both sides in the struggle were clear from the outset. The EPA hoped, as in the Dry Dock strike, to gain the assistance of the state railroad commissioners in forcing the president of the Third Avenue line, Lewis Lyons, to either negotiate in good faith with the union or forfeit his charter for failure to keep his line running. President Lyons and the company's directors, on the other hand, decided to wage an all-out assault on the EPA. Lyons announced his intention to replace all the striking men with nonunion workers and to never again to deal with the EPA. "We will sacrifice the road and the franchise," declared company board member Dr. Samuel Hall, "and sell out our cars at auction rather than yield." Lyons added that "rather than submit . . . I would let them tie me up through eternity."[29]

The terminology employed by Hall, Lyons, and the pro-business press reflected the increasingly common practice among Gilded Age employers, editors, and politicians to invert the rhetoric of working-class republicanism, painting capital as the victim of "tyrannical" labor bosses seeking to "dictate" terms that violated both employer liberty and the laws of the free market. Indeed, they were following the lead of Jay Gould in his efforts to both defeat and discredit the Knights of Labor in their strike against his railroads. Denouncing the Knights as a "secret organization" led by "agitators who had constituted themselves the rulers of the men," Gould cast the strike as "a question of the dictation of a mob against law and order."[30] Such a rhetorical recasting was intended to stir up middle- and upper-class resentment against union activists for acting on, in the *New York Times*'s phrasing, the "outrageous" presumption that they possessed the right to give orders to their employer.[31] "Public opinion now believes that there never was such an unrighteous strike," opined Superintendent of Police Murray. "The police share that opinion, and should they be turned loose upon the mob, the mob can expect little mercy."[32]

On day three of the strike, in response to the intransigence of Lyons and the directors, the EPA called for another citywide "tie-up" of all the streetcar lines, the second such dramatic sympathy strike in six weeks.[33] Full-scale rioting broke out the next day when, to no one's surprise, the Third Avenue Line attempted a symbolic run of twenty-five cars from its stables at East 65th Street. The presence of scores of policemen on the cars and along the route did little to stop the vast seething crowd of strikers and sympathizers, including many women, from attacking the cars (destroying four completely) and halting the attempted run. The riot ended only when two additional squads of policemen arrived to beat back the crowd and make arrests.[34]

While the tie-up and riot seemed reminiscent of the Dry Dock strike and Grand Street riot six weeks earlier, key points of contrast stood out. Whereas the Dry Dock's Richardson gave in quickly, Lyons and the Third Avenue line stood firm. Mimicking Gould's hardnosed ultimatum recently issued to Terence Powderly in the Southwest Railroad strike, Lyons defiantly declared that he would henceforth deal only with the men he employed and not their so-called representatives from the Knights of Labor. Furthermore, whereas Richardson rehired all of his striking employees, Lyons fired his men; they could reapply for their jobs on an individual basis, but "they will not be received back in a body under any circumstances." And, in a parting slight to the Knights of Labor that likewise echoed what Gould had said a few weeks earlier, he added that the strike now allowed him to employ higher quality workers as old hands had become less reliable since they joined the Order.[35]

Faced with such formidable employer hostility and fearing growing public anger at the inconvenience, the EPA called off the citywide tie-up. The strike against the Third Avenue line, however, continued. For the next six weeks the EPA adopted a series of strategies to prolong the strike against a vastly superior adversary. It appealed again to New York's state railroad commissioners to force the company to accept arbitration by threatening to revoke its charter.[36]

The EPA also announced a boycott, backed by the CLU and its member unions, to drive the Third Avenue line into bankruptcy.[37] As part of this effort, the EPA launched a project of purely symbolic value—the establishment of a free stage coach line along Third Avenue.[38] By staking their claim to the public thoroughfare—the peoples' property—the strikers made a potent statement. They were upholding one of the basic tenets of working-class republicanism, one found in the writings of Henry George and the rhetoric of the Knights of Labor: the monopolization of vital resources (e.g., mines, telegraphs, or, in this case, transportation) by a few individuals denied opportunities to the people and undermined social, economic, and political equality.

As the strike and boycott staggered toward inevitable defeat, the politically and ideologically charged nature of the conflict sharply increased. One major cause was the behavior of the police on behalf of the Third Avenue line. Stephen B. French, president of the Board of Police, in a public letter to the owners of the streetcar lines on April 20, effectively handed over his police force for the duration of the troubles.

> Dear Sir: That no misapprehension may exist in the minds of any portion of our community that the Police Department is unable to afford your road the necessary police protection in the running of your cars, we hereby notify you that we have been, and are, at all times ready to maintain the laws, preserve the peace, and protect the lives and property of all law-abiding citizens in this city, and are ready to give your company the necessary police protection in carrying on your business. Advise us promptly when and where you desire police protection.
>
> Your obedient servant,
> S. B. French,
> President, Board Police.[39]

In the case of the Third Avenue line's President Lyons, his "obedient servant" went beyond merely protecting Third Avenue cars and employees.[40] Plainclothes policemen showed up on strikers' doorsteps to pressure them to return to work. Others went further, actually performing labor on behalf of the company.[41] As Swinton thundered:

> We ourselves have seen them acting as drivers, couplers, and general assistants on the cars; we have seen them training the green hands who had taken the strikers' places, and curbing the horses which the blacklegs could not manage. They were not satisfied with arresting every driver upon the Union lines against whom they could find the least cause of complaint, but they acted otherwise as though they were mere tools of the Shylock corporation which had cheated the city treasury out of millions of dollars, and which would be suppressed but for the lobby it keeps at Albany.[42]

The reference to cheating stemmed from revelations after the strike that the Third Avenue line not only derived hundreds of thousands of dollars in profits from the use of the public streets, but also had cheated the public out of as much as one million dollars in taxes by underreporting revenue which it split with the city.[43] With this revelation also came other rumors, backed with some evidence, charging that the company had been propped up financially by the other streetcar companies. Such corporate collusion, usually in the form of business or employers' associations, was becoming increasingly common in the Gilded Age. It was yet another example of the selective adherence to the dogmas of laissez-faire individualism.[44]

Most significant, however, was the intervention of the state (beyond the already considerable role played by the police) on behalf of the Third Avenue line. Shortly after the second citywide tie-up and just as the EPA's position began to weaken, the courts intervened. On April 28, a grand jury indicted five members of the EPA Executive Board for conspiracy, characterizing them as "evil[ly] disposed persons" who "maliciously" contrived "by threats and intimidation" to prevent the Third Avenue line from conducting business.[45]

The day after the indictments saw yet another hard blow from the state that further politicized the interpretation workers gave to the struggle. The New York State railroad commissioners issued a report on the strike; they sided with the Third Avenue line and declined to revoke its charter—despite the fact that the company had failed to run its cars due to a strike of its own making, violated a labor agreement, and refused arbitration. The rejection of the EPA appeal made it clear to the strikers that the state commission created to regulate the railroad corporations now *served* them instead.[46]

The Third Avenue strike ended in defeat for the workers in early June after a third citywide tie-up and more indictments against union leaders from the grand jury. All 1,200 strikers either lost their jobs or, if the company rehired them, lost their seniority and became parttimers.[47] But not every aspect of the failed strike was entirely negative for labor. First, while entirely local in its scope, the strike possessed a powerfully symbolic link to the struggle of labor nationwide. President Lyons, as many workers pointed out, seemed cut from the same cloth as Jay Gould. Second, the incidents exposed a hardening of class lines, specifically a coalescing of upper-class interests that did not hesitate to undermine the rights of everyday workers, the foundational citizens of the republic. Third, the response of the state, the police, and the courts vividly demonstrated to workers the extent to which capital and its political allies had twisted republican institutions to undercut their status as citizens. Fourth, the three unprecedented citywide tie-ups inescapably demonstrated the power of direct, collective action. Finally, they validated key arguments set forth by Henry George and the Knights of Labor regarding the need for public ownership of natural monopolies and the need for working-class political mobilization to preserve the republic.

"There is a remedy," wrote John Swinton alluding to labor's political power in the city. "But there is very little hope of the workingmen adopting it."[48] What Swinton did not know when he wrote those lines in April was that the streetcar strikes marked the beginning of a period of extraordinary labor conflict nationwide. Nor did he know that they constituted but one of a series of galvanizing episodes that would lead labor by midsummer to seize the remedy he so consistently proposed.[49]

"EXPOSURES OF POLITICAL AND CORPORATE RASCALITY": THE BROADWAY SURFACE RAILROAD SCANDAL

On their own, the intense streetcar strikes in the spring of 1886 did not possess sufficient power to prompt New York City's workers to take Swinton and George's advice and bring their grievances to bear at the ballot box in November. As leading voices of labor so often lamented, workers typically expressed their outrage eleven of the twelve months in the year. During the twelfth—November—they set aside their grievances and, like "voting cattle," reelected representatives from the major parties who acted on behalf of business. What broke this pattern in 1886 was the breaking of the biggest municipal scandal since the Tweed Ring exposures of 1871–1872. The revelations of the Broadway Surface Railroad franchise scandal enabled those involved in the streetcar strikes and subsequent boycotts to explicitly connect their struggles to municipal politics and to subsequently launch an unprecedented independent labor party challenge.

The Broadway and Seventh Avenue Surface Railroad Corporation was the largest streetcar line in the city. Its owner, Jacob Sharp, had been active in the city's streetcar systems for decades, owning three companies in addition to the Broadway line. The corruption scandal itself began two years earlier, when the Board of Aldermen announced plans to extend Broadway streetcar services south from Union Square. Numerous streetcar lines, keen to extend their lucrative networks, submitted bids for the franchise. Behind the scenes, they also offered massive bribes to the aldermen. Sharp outdid them all with a bribe of $20,000 each to twenty-two out of the twenty-four aldermen; he was promptly awarded the franchise.[50]

Fifteen months later, as rumors of corruption and bribery began to swirl about the city, the state senate opened hearings regarding the awarding of the franchise. They began their work in early February 1886, exactly two days after the city's streetcar workers successfully achieved the $2.00-for-twelve hours standard on most lines in the city (though, significantly, not including Sharp's). The testimony given by Sharp and numerous aldermen suggested bribery, but there was no concrete evidence. Sharp, for example, could not account for three million dollars in cash he raised from loans and bond sales.[51]

The hearings appeared to end on an inconclusive note, but the scandal soon exploded when Henry Jaehne, vice president of the Board of Aldermen, was arrested on March 8 (three days following the Dry Dock strike) for accepting a bribe from Sharp.[52] Soon, twenty aldermen and former aldermen (two others had died since 1884) were indicted. The following day, the *New York Times* printed an extraordinary chart on its front page showing the status of the members of the 1884 Board of Aldermen. The roster listed fifteen as "out on bail," three as having "fled the country," one as an "informer," one as "at-large," and two as "dead."[53]

For the rest of the spring, the scandal involving the "Boodle Aldermen" unfolded simultaneously with the streetcar strikes. The city's newspapers included coverage of both on their front pages nearly every day. The first real drama erupted on May 13 with the commencement of Jaehne's trial. It lasted just three days, resulting in a conviction and sentence of nine years and ten months.[54]

A number of aspects to this particular scandal heightened its significance in the eyes of local labor activists. For one, Jacob Sharp was no ordinary

THE ALDERMEN OF 1884.

The table below shows the Aldermen of 1884 who voted for the Broadway Railroad grant and the present standing of those now alive. Sheriff Hugh J. Grant, who represented the Nineteenth Assembly District in the 1884 board, and Mr. John C. O'Connor, Jr., who represented the Eleventh Assembly District, are not included in the list, because they voted against the grant. At the "snap" meeting of the board held early in the morning, and at which the franchise was granted over the veto of Mayor Edson, Messrs. Kirk, Finck, McLoughlin, Miller, Grant, and O'Connor were absent. Messrs. Kirk, Finck, McLoughlin, and Miller, however, voted to confirm the grant at the meeting held on Dec. 5. Of the 22 who voted away the franchise, 15 have been arrested and are out on bail, 3 have fled, 1 is in custody as an informer, 1 is still at large with a warrant out for his arrest, and 2 are dead:

Dist.	Name and Politics.	Disposition.
1.	Thomas Cleary,* Co. Dem.	Out on bail.
2.	W. P. Kirk, Tam.	Out on bail.
3.	John O'Neil*, Co. Dem.	Out on bail.
4.	Thomas Shells, Jeff. Dem.	Out on bail.
5.	Henry W. Jaehne.* Co. Dem.	Out on bail.
6.	Patrick Farley, Co. Dem.	Out on bail.
7.	Charles B. Waite. Rep.	Informer in custody.
8.	Frederick Finck, Rep.	Out on bail.
9.	William H. Miller, Rep.	Out on bail.
10.	Thomas Rothman, Rep.	Fled.
12.	Robert E. De Lacy,* Co. Dem.	Fled.
13.	James Pearson, Rep.	Out on bail.
14.	A. J. McQuade, Co. Dem.	Out on bail.
15.	M. F. McLoughlin, Tam.	Dead.
16.	Charles Dempsey. Tam.	Fled.
17.	Louis Wendel, Rep.	Out on bail.
18.	Patrick Kenney, Tam.	Dead.
20.	Francis McCabe, Tam.	Out on bail.
21.	Henry L. Sayles, Rep.	Out on bail.
22.	Charles H. Reilly. Co. Dem	Still at large.
23.	Michael Duffy, Tam.	Out on bail.
24.	L. A. Fullgraff, Tam.	Out on bail.

*At present Aldermen.

"The Aldermen of 1884." *New York Times*, April 14, 1886. Author's collection

streetcar operator. He owned the largest line in the city and possessed one of the worst reputations among streetcar workers, perhaps second only to Deacon Richardson.[55] The scandal was also *local*—involving what Swinton termed "the exposures of political and corporate rascality [that] are such as to put Boss Tweed to the blush." It involved legislators in Manhattan, not Albany or Washington and concerned issues that were readily understood by all.[56]

Moreover, the scandal further illuminated another area of concern—the justice of a private corporation profiteering off of the people through the use of public property. Such vivid examples of corporate ruthlessness by what one worker termed "the pirates who have stolen our streets," aided by their compliant political cronies, explain in part why the land reform tenets of *Progress and Poverty* (and in similar Knights of Labor pronouncements) resonated so powerfully among landless urban workers. If the land belonged to the people, then its monopolization by private corporations or speculators violated the laws of nature and undermined the egalitarian foundations of the republic. In their minds, the local streetcar corporations differed from land-grabbing railroads in the West only in size and place. Indeed, Sharp (like Lyons and Richardson) was frequently compared with Jay Gould, who not only owned a vast national railroad network, but also major shares in some of New York's elevated railway lines. George articulated this explicit connection in a speech at a huge labor rally in April amidst the streetcar strikes and the lead up to the May 1 eight-hour workday demonstrations. "Where workingmen have not the right of access to land they must pay tribute for its use, and only make a bare living. . . . You are taxed for everything, even for riding on the elevated railroad or in the streetcars." Urban transportation, he insisted, should be publically owned and free.[57]

But the legal outcome of the Broadway Surface Railroad scandal revealed a justice system skewed to favor the interests of the wealthy and powerful. During and after the trial of Alderman Jaehne, persistent rumors circulated alleging that the "Boodle Aldermen" and Sharp had arranged for a team of "jury-fixers" to guarantee hung juries or acquittals in subsequent cases.[58] Moreover, after Jaehne's conviction and severe sentencing, the legal process ground to a virtual halt. Between mid-May and early October, no other trials occurred. "The tempted Alderman is duly punished," observed "Looker-On" following the Jaehne conviction. "The tempter is still 'unknown' and undiscoverable by the District Attorney. Millionaire Sharp still walks our streets." So too, did the remaining indicted aldermen, a situation that allowed six to flee to Canada.

No such torpid process impeded the trials of scores of arrested boycotters and strikers. In many of these cases, the time elapsed between indictments and convictions was a matter of weeks instead of months, and on more than one occasion the arrested men were held without bail. "Looker-On" accused the district attorney of pursuing a hidden agenda. To take the heat off his aldermen cronies, he "cunningly got the editors of dailies crazy about boycotting and so got rid of the boodle trials very neatly."[59] The district attorney eventually restarted the aldermen trials in early October, some of which led to convictions in the next few years.

Close examination of the scandal also offered evidence of *systemic* corruption, not just the traditional Tammany shenanigans. Of the twenty-two aldermen arrested, seven were members of the County Democracy, seven of Tammany Hall, and another seven of the Republican Party (one was an independent).[60] Such tripartisan complicity in the scandal undercut any argument that it was the work of a single party or faction. It led to the inescapable conclusion among many workers that the entire municipal government had surrendered its obligations to govern in the interests of the people and instead offered its services to the highest bidder. The scandal thereby undermined the most influential argument against independent political action: that labor could achieve more by using its votes to hold the "balance of power" in elections, eventually pledging them to the regular party which promised to address their needs best.

Thus as the Third Avenue streetcar men fought a losing battle against the combined forces of the courts, the state legislature, and the police, the Broadway Surface Railroad bribery scandal served as an explicitly ideological backdrop indicating the extent to which undemocratic forces had united to undermine republican government. The Tweed scandals of the previous decade shocked the city, but they held little resonance for labor activism. Indeed, many laborers responded with sympathy for "Billy" Tweed and his Robin Hood-style that lined his pockets, but yet also assisted the poor.[61] For them, the infamous Tweed Courthouse on Chambers Street hardly represented a monument of municipal oppression. But in the wake of the streetcar strikes and the corruption scandals, that designation fell to City Hall, a building standing just a few hundred feet south of the Tweed Courthouse. That building housed the Board of Aldermen chambers where the corrupt franchise vote took place, as well as the rooms where the state railroad commissioners met but failed to exercise their authority on behalf of the strikers against the Third Avenue line. Workers now possessed evidence not simply of the state shirking its duty to the people in favor of serving corporate interests, but also of their local elected officials profiting from it. As they saw it, Jacob Sharp had effectively purchased the local legislature of the nation's largest city to enrich himself—all the while grinding his workers to the bone. Not surprisingly, in just a few months Henry George would make public ownership of the streetcar lines a major plank in his mayoral platform.[62]

"A FORMIDABLE WEAPON OF DEFENSE"

The streetcar strikes and the accompanying "Boodle Aldermen" scandal formed only a part of that spring's ideologically fraught events. Of equal importance were the series of high-profile boycotts launched by a host of unions against offending employers. In recent months, unionists, led by the CLU, had employed the boycott with great effect against printers, brewers, newspapers, manufacturers, and theaters.[63] No complete statistics exist on the number of boycotts waged in New York City, though the State Bureau of Labor Statistics reported what it could for the year 1885 (table 6.1).

Through early 1886, labor benefited from the fact that the boycott was a novel and subtle method of challenging employers. As a result, the police and courts tolerated boycotting for the most part. Harassment was confined to the arrest of pickets posted to inform the public of a boycott in progress. But with the boycott's increasing use and effectiveness by mid-spring 1886, authorities soon moved to ban it.[64] Three boycotts during this period drew special attention from the press, public, and legal authorities who eventually initiated a legal crackdown: those waged against Theiss's music hall, Gray's bakery, and Landgraff's bakery. Each gained widespread public attention and ended with sweeping arrests of those involved.

TABLE 6.1 Boycotts in New York City, 1885

	Successful	Partly successful	Lost	Ongoing	Total
Statewide	35	6	2	16	59
Citywide	20	4	0	7	31

Sources: New York State Bureau of Labor Statistics, *Annual Report for 1885*, 3:335–37; *Annual Report for 1886*, 4:737–43; *JSP*, December 27, 1885, 1, 3; *Bradstreet's*, December 19, 1885, 394.

George Theiss owned a popular music hall, the Alhambra Court, located at 134–136 East 14th Street. His trouble with organized labor began in March when the CLU accepted a request for assistance from the Carl Sahm Club, a musicians' union, as well as from the Waiters' and Bartenders' Unions, to obtain Theiss's compliance with union wages and work rules.[65] The owner rebuffed a CLU committee on March 6, prompting the announcement of a boycott. To enforce the boycott and inform the public, the CLU posted between seventy-five and 150 pickets on the streets surrounding Theiss's hall to distribute thousands of copies of fliers that read:

BOYCOTT! BOYCOTT! BOYCOTT!
TO ALL UNIONISTS, KNIGHTS OF LABOR, AND THE PUBLIC IN GENERAL.
Boycott Mr. G. Theiss's Alhambra Court, 134–136 East Fourteenth street, and his concert place, West Fourteenth street, near Sixth avenue.
He is a foe to organized labor. Also for refusing to arbitrate with the committee of the Central Labor union, and grossly insulting the same by using obscene language, unbecoming a man. We expect from every tradesman and storekeeper, and their families, who can earn their living from the working people, not to patronize the concert gardens owned by Mr. Theiss, and it will be the duty of every friend of organized labor not to buy goods at any store, the occupants of which, or their families, continue to spend their money for the benefit of Mr. Theiss, by visiting his places.[66]

Theiss suffered a significant loss of business,[67] prompting him to meet the CLU committee. On March 23, a committee of CLU officials, accompanied by Max Dannhauser, Paul Wilzig, Michael Stroh, Hans Holdorf, and Adolph Rosenberg (the representatives of the musicians, waiters, and bartenders unions), met for seven hours with Theiss and successfully negotiated an end to the dispute. Theiss agreed to employ only union men and pay union wages. He also agreed to pay a "fine" of $1,000 to cover the expenses of the three-week boycott. While the latter condition would soon return to haunt the unionists (Theiss would later bring charges of extortion against the boycotters), for the moment they had achieved, in union parlance, a "clean sweep."[68]

Soon, however, another boycott began that attracted even more attention. On April 5, a delegate of the Bakers' Union No. 1 called on a Mr. Gray, owner of a bakery at 508 Hudson Street to inform him that he was in violation of union work rules and wages. When Gray refused to change his employment practices, the Bakers' Union announced a boycott. From that point forward, in a move clearly designed to elicit public sympathy, Mr. Gray, who also ran a plumbing shop, placed his wife in charge of the bakery. It proved a brilliant ploy.[69]

Like the Theiss boycott, the effort against Gray started out with much vigor and enthusiasm. Dozens of pickets patrolled the sidewalks near the bakery, distributing circulars informing neighbors and potential customers of the grievances against the Grays. They also, as in the Theiss action, expanded the scope of the boycott, warning local grocers to cease selling the Grays' bread and suppliers to stop delivering flour or they too would face a boycott against their establishments.[70]

The Gray boycott, however, soon collapsed completely. On April 14, the police began arresting pickets and continued to do so with such vigor that picketing all but ceased within two days.[71] By then it was clear that the boycotters were failing to deter customers from patronizing the bakery. Situated in the Ninth Ward in Greenwich Village, Mrs. Gray's bakery catered to an economically diverse clientele. As soon as the boycott commenced, Mrs. Gray lost virtually all her working-class customers, while the flow of her middle-class and wealthy customers continued unabated. Soon, however, the Gray boycott assumed the character of *cause célèbre* among the middle class and wealthy throughout the city, indeed, even the nation.[72]

The mainstream press played the key role in transforming the Gray boycott from a neighborhood dispute to a symbolic municipal clash of class interests. From the moment the boycott commenced in early April, the press extensively covered the "plucky little woman" and her struggle against the "outrageous" demands made by "drunken and half drunken men" of the Bakers' Union. Elite New Yorkers and others from around the nation sent hundreds of dollars to Mrs. Gray's bakery with instructions to buy bread and distribute it to the "deserving poor," or to specific charities. "The boycott," the *New York Times* gleefully noted, "was proving an excellent promoter of charity."[73] John S. Barnes, one of the best known stockbrokers in the city, sent $10 and a note which read, "Your course toward the cowardly creatures who are persecuting you wins the respect of every lover of liberty and order." Charles Crocker, the millionaire president of the Southern Pacific Railroad, sent $50 and a letter praising Mrs. Gray for her stand against "the worst kind of tyranny" that even European monarchs "would be ashamed to exercise." Wealthy women (among them Mrs. Russell Sage) also did their part, arriving in private carriages to conspicuously purchase baked goods. "It is becoming quite the fashionable craze," observed the *New York Times*, "for wealthy shoppers to . . . procure bread and cake for the swell dinners in the evening." Far from bringing Gray to terms, the boycott had transformed her bakery into the "most widely known bake shop in the United States." As a consequence, the boycott eventually failed.[74]

This extraordinary commitment of middle- and upper class New Yorkers to the defeat of the Gray boycott was a vivid example of the continued coalescence of bourgeois solidarity in the Gilded Age. Increasingly confident that the republic was in excellent health and that laissez-faire capitalism rewarded the fit and punished the unfit, the privileged united to delegitimize and stymie expressions of working-class unity and collective action. Unions, alliances, strikes, and boycotts, they argued, were the unnecessary and sinister products of restive workers and farmers led astray by radicals and demagogues who either did not understand the immutable laws of capitalist political economy or who consciously sought its destruction.[75]

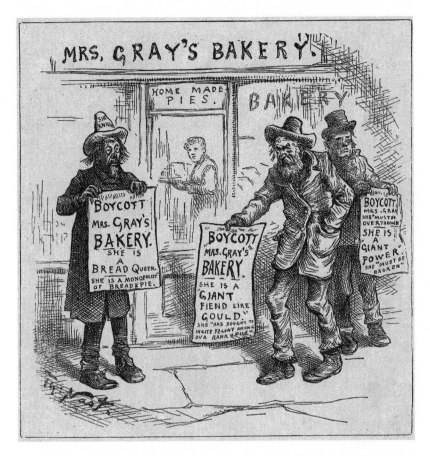

Demonizing the boycotters. "The Chivalry of Modern Knights." *Harper's Weekly*, April 24, 1886. Courtesy of HarpWeek

The third notable boycott in the spring of 1886, that against the Land-graff Bakery, commenced just as the effort against the Grays began to fail. Mrs. Landgraff owned a bakery at 157 Second Avenue on the Lower East Side that employed both German and Bohemian bakers. In April, Mrs. Landgraff's Bohemian bakers went out on strike over wages and rules, but because her German bakers stayed on the job, she continued to produce and sell bread. To thwart this effort, the striking Bohemians imposed a boycott.[76]

In contrast to the recent failed boycott against Mrs. Gray, the boycott against Landgraff accomplished its goal with textbook precision. The crucial difference was location: unlike Gray's bakery, Landgraff's was situated in a working-class neighborhood. With pickets posted in front of the bakery distributing circulars printed in both German and Bohemian, Landgraff's business virtually disappeared. Over-the-counter sales dropped from an average of $15 to $20 per day to just a few dollars, while the local groceries to whom she sold bread refused to carry her products until the strike and boycott ended.[77] "The boycott," observed the *New York Times*, "has been a perfect success as far as the grocers and the poor people of the vicinity are concerned."[78]

For a time, Mrs. Landgraff, much like Mrs. Gray, enjoyed patronage and donations from wealthy patrons inspired, she acknowledged "in a voice choked with tearful joy," from sympathetic newspaper coverage.[79] The boycotters, however, remained vigilant, maintaining pickets and staging parades calling attention to the conflict on the streets of the working-class Lower East Side. Eventually, upper-class New Yorkers lost interest and outside patronage and donations disappeared. On July 9, after an eleven-week boycott, Mrs. Landgraff announced that she was closing her bakery.[80]

The Landgraff boycott provides an instructive contrast to the outcome of the bakers' struggle with Mrs. Gray. The fundamental principle behind the boycott was the idea of widening the scope of a labor dispute to include the greater community. Through mass meetings, circulars, and pickets, the boycotters succeeded in reestablishing the link between producers and consumers that had been largely eroded in industrial urban centers. The entire neighborhood was not simply made aware the dispute, but also its potential complicity in it through the purchase of the offending employer's products. As a result, even though Mrs. Landgraff enjoyed initial press support and outside donations, her defeat was ensured when her local patronage abandoned her.

"MAKING WAR UPON LABOR"

Many labor leaders, in spite of the setbacks in the streetcar strikes and the Gray boycott, viewed labor's unprecedented activism in the spring of 1886 as a welcome harbinger of the movement's growth and success. Others were not so sanguine. In late April, just ten days before the Haymarket bombing, the ever-prescient John Swinton warned labor activists in New York and across the nation of an impending crackdown.

> There are dangerous times ahead for labor Unionists. Every man or woman, whether a Knight of Labor or a Trade Unionist, must be prepared to meet it. . . . There is a feeling abroad that is antagonistic to the organization [of labor]. The police are itching to get a "whack at the heads" of the workingmen. . . . The militia are desirous of coming out with their rifles to shoot down the unarmed mob. The press is almost unanimously arrayed against the workers, because they dare interfere with what is called "freedom of contract." The great public outside of organizations have been taught that every man, especially those possessed of capital, can do just as he sees fit.[81]

Only days after this editorial appeared, city and state officials did indeed launch a crackdown on labor so sweeping that it became known as a "grand legal roundup." These indictments and arrests began a full two weeks *before* Haymarket and its subsequent hysteria. The chief impact of Haymarket in New York, as we shall see, was not in triggering the roundup, but in influencing the outcomes and sentences in the trials that followed. The main impetus behind the roundup was the growing perception among business elites and politicians that the boycott represented more than a clever and effective labor tactic—it was an assault on established authority, private property, and the free market.[82]

The roundup began on April 20, the day after the second streetcar tie-up paralyzed the city, with the indictment of thirteen men for boycotting Mrs. Gray's bakery. The next day, George Theiss, now resolved to fight the results of the boycott to which he recently succumbed, went to court to lodge extortion charges against the five leaders of the boycott. That same day, Mrs. Landgraff filed a complaint against the men boycotting her bakery. A grand jury also indicted forty-seven tailors for their boycott against the firm of Cavanagh & Sanford. These legal proceedings came to a head on April 29, when the grand jury indicted seventeen members of Bohemian Bakers' Union (involved in the Landgraff bakery boycott) for "conspiracy" and "coercion," and indicted seven members of the CLU committee that negotiated with Theiss for "extortion." The next day, the crackdown extended to the streetcar strike; five members of the EPA were arrested on charges of conspiracy. "Never till the past week," thundered Swinton, "have we had so many proofs of the complete subordination of the courts, police, and municipal authorities of this city to the corporations now making war upon labor."[83]

Such comprehensive repression on the part of the state against organized labor, following months of strikes, boycotts, and clashes with police, lent added significance to an event planned many months before: the May 1 eight-hour workday demonstrations.[84] That day some forty-five thousand New York City workers participated in a one-day strike to draw attention to the issue. In the evening, a CLU-sponsored mass rally drew over twenty thousand workers and their sympathizers to Union Square. While more than 1,500 policemen (half the city's entire force) stood by, the crowd listened to a series of speakers (in English and German) who discussed the necessity of the eight-hour workday; most of their attention, however, was devoted to the current crisis brought on by the legal crackdown. Charlie Spinner of the Clothing Cutters' Union captured the mood of the evening when he advised his audience to "vote for the workingmen's candidate, boycott the Third Avenue road, and damn the conspiracy law."[85] Three days later, Haymarket exploded.

Despite labor's protest, the arrests continued until over one hundred boycotters and labor activists were behind bars. The central case, however, involved just five men: the Theiss boycotters, who faced the charge of extortion under the penal code because they demanded the theater owner pay them a $1,000 "fine" to cover costs associated with the boycott. It quickly became clear that the district attorney's office hoped the convictions on this charge would set a legal precedent, branding all future boycotts as extortion and thereby severely curtailing the practice, if not outlawing it altogether. The starkest evidence of this intent emanated from the indictments handed down by the grand jury:

This so-called boycott is an accursed exotic, and we urge every effort of our legislators, the Bench, the Bar, the Press of the land and every American citizen to aid in exterminating this hydra-headed monster, dragging its loathsome length across the continent, sucking the very life-blood from our trade and commerce, equally baneful to the employers and the employed.[86]

Such a beginning to the proceedings left few workers optimistic about the outcome of the trials.

They began on June 22, with Judge George C. Barrett presiding.[87] Paul Wilzig, the representative of the Waiter's Union and the man who accepted Theiss's $1,000 check, was the first to stand trial. The prosecution's strategy was straightforward: it argued that Theiss succumbed to the demands of Wilzig and the others because they threatened to maintain a boycott against his business, a threat the state deemed intimidation. The trial lasted just two days; conviction seemed a foregone conclusion, especially in light of Judge Barrett's instructions to the jury. Barrett began by denying that the union men possessed any right to demand that Theiss dismiss his nonunion workers, and they certainly did not have the right to demand an additional $1,000. He then declared picketing and boycotting acts that brought "the power of combination to bear in an unlawful way to injure the employer's business." Thenceforth, he said, the courts would no longer confine their prosecutions of workingmen to acts of violence, but would consider even the suggestion of ill intent. Said Barrett, "*The men who walk up and down in front of a man's shop may be guilty of intimidation, though they may never raise a finger or utter a word*. Their attitude may be that of menace."[88] Not surprisingly, after a mere fifteen minutes of deliberation, the jury returned a guilty verdict.[89]

When the next trial, that of Hans Holdorf, followed a nearly identical script and ended in conviction,[90] Michael Stroh and Adolph Rosenberg decided to cut their losses and pled guilty. This left only Max Dannhauser, who defiantly withstood great pressure to take a plea and went ahead with a trial. He likewise was found guilty. All that remained of the drama was the sentencing.[91]

The next day, July 2, workingmen and sympathizers packed Barrett's courtroom to hear the fate of the boycotters. Before announcing the sentences, Barrett took time to issue a scalding rebuke to the five convicted boycotters and their sympathizers, making much of the fact that the men were all immigrants.

> The moral guilt attaching to the crime of which you have been convicted is heightened by the fact that you are not American citizens. Such Socialistic crimes such as these are breaches of national hospitality. . . . Common gratitude would have prevented your outraging public opinion and bringing into force the actions and methods of a Socialistic character which you brought with you from abroad.

If the practice of conspiratorial combination is not punished, he concluded, "we would be on the high road to savagery."[92] His invocation of nativist wrath to condemn the boycotters reflected another increasingly common theme in Gilded Age bourgeois discourse. By branding the demands and actions of labor as foreign, middle- and upper-class Americans could easily dismiss working-class agitation as both dangerous and illegitimate.[93] To underscore this notion, Barrett imposed considerably harsh sentences:[94]

Paul Wilzig	2 years, 10 months
Hans Holdorf	2 years, 10 months
Max Dannhauser	3 years, 8 months
Michael Stroh	18 months
Adolph Rosenberg	18 months

Although the law allowed for sentences of up to five years, few expected such severity given that these were the first prosecutions against boycotting.[95]

Labor leaders denounced the biased convictions and harsh sentences. The actions of the court bore out Swinton's earlier prediction that "dangerous times" lay ahead for labor. Justice, it appeared now more than ever, would be meted out according to class distinctions. "The conviction is rapidly forcing itself upon every man who works with his hands," observed the *Boycotter*, "that our boasted equality before the law is a fallacy, and that the judicial bench is to a great to extent run in class interests."[96] It had been "a trial in which one class of society was to sit in judgment upon another," argued Swinton, referring to New York State's requirement that only property owners were eligible to sit on a jury. "Every man called to act as a juror in these cases was a pronounced enemy of organized labor."[97]

Judge Barrett, who did little to hide his hostility toward the boycotters, drew particularly harsh condemnation. In addition to his prejudicial charges to the jury, his treatment of Max Dannhauser heightened the perception that workingmen were no longer entitled to the basic rights promised by republican government. Because Dannhauser refused to plead guilty and forego a trial, Barrett gave him an additional ten months prison time; he in effect penalized Dannhauser for demanding his right to a trial by jury.

Yet, however much the jury selection system and the conduct of Judge Barrett outraged labor, none of these things were particularly new. What made these trials significant was that they seemed to fit into a larger constellation of recent events that pointed to the stripping of wage earners of their rights as republican citizens. The real "conspiracy," argued labor leaders, was not within the ranks of labor, but rather within the halls of justice. Its purpose was to deprive labor of the boycott, a proven, potent weapon in the struggle to achieve justice. Swinton warned that this conspiracy would not stop with the suppression of boycotting; the coming struggle ran much deeper than that. He wrote, "Class lines are being closely drawn. There is a determination among bosses to stamp out labor organizations and suppress speech and press to the furthest possible limit. This determination is shared by officers of the law." "By the time the Summer is over," he warned, "a pretty extensive body of criminal law will have been built up between workingmen and their masters." Expressing the same sentiment, a letter writer to *Swinton's* posed a telling question: "I would ask if the present state of things can continue, and our Republic endure."[98]

To thwart this attack from the bench, CLU leaders called a mass protest meeting at Cooper Union for the evening of July 7. Over 2,500 people packed the hall that evening to hear speeches by Swinton, Blissert, and John McMackin. George, then touring the coal-mining districts of Pennsylvania and researching a series of articles on the status of labor for the *North American Review*,[99] sent a letter expressing his "indignation" over "the cruel sentences imposed by Judge Barrett," which "can only be approved by excited class feeling." McMackin's reading of the letter received enthusiastic applause.[100] The assembly then passed a series of resolutions that included:

Resolved, That we condemn this verdict and sentence as a brutal outburst of class hatred by representatives of the capitalistic class, against
the growing power of organized labor, and that we do not consider
the victims of this "class justice," our fellow workingmen Wilzig,
Holdorf, Dannhauser, Stroh, and Rosenberg, as criminals, but martyrs in the labor cause:

Resolved, That we spurn the attempt to wrest from us one of the
mightiest weapons in our battle against spoliation, the boycott, by
unjust and barbaric punishment of the champions of our cause; that
we will hold onto it, undismayed by arbitrary judicial decision.[101]

The most provocative note of the evening was sounded by Swinton,
who used his speech to chastise not only Judge Barrett but also the city's
workingmen, whose votes placed Barrett and his ilk in office in the first
place. "I am tired of denouncing the authorities of this country," said the
editor. Every time he did, he told his listeners, beginning with the Tompkins Square Riot of 1874, the injured workingmen continued to vote for
their oppressors. "They cheered me in April," referring to his own labor
party candidacy for mayor in 1874, "and fired a poison bullet into my
heart in November." Swinton then remarked, "I presume it will be the
same 100 days from now." The crowd responded to Swinton's provoking
tone of pessimism with cries of "Oh, No!" Over the years such exchanges
had become commonplace at labor rallies. Nevertheless, the result in
November always remained the same. And yet, by early July 1886, there
were those in attendance who believed the context of labor activism had
fundamentally changed.[102]

If any worker needed further evidence of the legal campaign being
waged against labor, the courts provided it just days after the Theiss boycotters' sentencing and the ensuing protest rally. On July 11, another jury of
businessmen found six of the seventeen Bohemians guilty of conspiracy in
the Landgraff boycott. Just before sentencing the men to jail terms of ten to
thirty days, Judge Barrett expressed his hope "that our clemency will sink
into the hearts of those like you who have similarly erred, and that in the
future we shall have no more of this kind of boycotting."[103]

Barrett's hope that the crackdown on labor would subdue its recent aggressive behavior was misplaced. Not only did workers continue "this kind of boycotting," they immediately set about augmenting it. "Boycott at the polls," urged Swinton, "You can't be sent to the penitentiary for it—not yet."[104]

It had been an extraordinary spring for the New York City labor movement in 1886. For four years, the CLU-led movement had experienced unprecedented growth while traditional tactics like the strike and novel ones like the boycott succeeded as never before. Ideologically, the movement had matured as well. Although the CLU never achieved anything approaching ideological harmony, its leaders successfully built an organization that allowed for ideological differences while simultaneously making the body more and more the engine of a radical working-class oppositional culture. This was particularly evident in the realm of political activism. Although they had pulled back from their earlier attempts to create a permanent United Labor Party, the pro-politics faction of the CLU, which included virtually all of its leaders, never ceased in its efforts to call attention to the inevitable necessity of seizing political power from their oppressors. Still, a significant percentage of CLU members remained convinced that labor lacked the maturity and strength to mount a credible campaign of independent political action.

Then came the streetcar strikes that pitted some of the city's most abused workers against powerful figures and corporations that enjoyed the protection of key elements of the state—the police, courts, state legislature, and New York State Railroad Commission. These events gave concreteness to the ideological assertions of working-class republicanism—namely that "the people," the foundation of republican government, increasingly were being driven from their central position in the polity and deprived of their basic rights. These assertions gained even greater credence with the revelation that the city's largest streetcar corporation—and one notorious for its hostility towards labor at that—had bribed nearly every member of the Board of Aldermen to gain a lucrative franchise. The specter of monopoly undermining republican government so fearfully portrayed in *Progress and Poverty* and the radical labor press now took tangible, local form.

And finally, there came the "grand legal roundup" of over one hundred labor activists and their subsequent judicial railroading. All this, of course, occurred against a national backdrop of soaring labor-capital conflict and the wave of antiradical hysteria that followed the Haymarket bombing.

Taken as a whole, these events transformed the often abstract ideas and ideological tenets of working-class republicanism into cold, harsh reality. "To turn republican government into a despotism the basest and most brutal," warned Henry George at the close of *Progress and Poverty*, "it is not necessary formally to change its constitution or abandon popular elections." Devious monopolists, rapacious capitalists, and aspiring aristocrats were just as likely to secure it by inches. Only one thing, said George, Swinton, and a host of others of like mind, stood in their way—"the people." If only the people could be awakened to the reality of the steady usurpation of their rights, their freedoms, and their livelihoods, then they might unite to halt this assault on republican liberty. In the spring and summer of 1886, the course of events in the civic, political, economic, legal, and social life of the city's working class took on a character so compelling as to awaken even the most jaded among them to a sense of republican crisis and the need for extraordinary action.[105]

A movement toward independent political action by the city's workingmen quickly began to unfold. On July 11, four days after the protest rally and on the same day as the Landgraff verdicts, the CLU held its regular meeting and established a committee for the purpose of devising a strategy for labor to turn its grievances into political action. In its subsequent report to the CLU membership, this committee proposed that labor abandon the traditional political parties as hopelessly corrupt and commence direct, united political action as "one grand political organization." This organization's goal would be to "redeem our city government from the hands of plunderers whose acts of spoliation have brought disgrace upon this city, and through whom the administration of justice has become a farce." As a first step, the committee called upon all the city's labor organizations to send one delegate for every one hundred members to a conference to determine whether or not the workingmen of New York favored independent political action.[106]

Only a few days before, Swinton had reminded workers of their past failures to unify at the polls. It seemed in the summer of 1886 that, come November, labor just might find a different target for its "poison bullet."

7

"To Save Ourselves from Ruin"

Where legislation is to be bought, the rich make the laws; where justice is to be purchased, the rich have the ear of the courts.
—Henry George, *Social Problems* (1883)

Politically America is a democracy; industrially America is an aristocracy. . . . He *makes* political laws; he is *under* industrial laws. At the ballot box he is king; in the factory he is a servant, sometimes a slave.
—Rev. Lyman Abbott, "Dangers Ahead" (1885)

"HE EMBODIES THE ASPIRATIONS OF THE MASSES"

Within days of the CLU's decision to consider reviving the United Labor Party, talk of a Henry George nomination began to circulate. On August 1, *John Swinton's Paper* hit the newsstands with a banner headline calling upon organized labor to nominate Henry George for mayor:

A fitter candidate could not be found. He is as true as steel. He embodies the aspirations of the masses. He is a worker, a printer, a unionist, a Knight of Labor, a man of business experience; and it will not be held against him that he is a native of the country, and the most renowned living American author. IT MAY BE A BOOM.[1]

George emerged so quickly as the odds-on favorite to receive the ULP's nomination because of labor's extensive experience with him over the previous six years. Even though he arrived in the Empire City as a virtual unknown just a few years earlier in August 1880, George had firmly established himself in the minds of the city's workers as a man committed to alleviating their plight. They knew George to be both a skilled worker:

ON'S PAPER.

TO A FOOTING ON THE EARTH ; 2, HIS RIGHT TO LABOR ; 3, HIS RIGHT TO THE FRUITS OF HIS WORK.

CTOBER 10, 1886.   OFFICE, 21 PARK ROW.—$1 A YEAR.—3 CTS. A COPY.

WATCHERS.

The friends of George must see that he is not *cheated* in counting his vote.

Each candidate under the law can designate a *Watcher* for each election district, to see that the vote is correctly canvassed.

This authority must be in writing signed by Henry George, that is, each watcher must have written authority to see the votes counted.
—A VETERAN.

CHICAGO TO NEW YORK.

CHICAGO, Oct. 7.—For God's and the country's sake elect Henry George Mayor of New York.—
BERT STEWART.

NEW HAMPSHIRE TO NEW YORK.

MANCHESTER, N. H., Oct. 5.—We do hope that the working people of New York will elect Henry George Mayor.—9611.

KANSAS TO NEW YORK.

WICHITA, Kan., Oct. 6.—Now that Henry George has been nominated for Mayor of New York, it will be a terrible blow to the cause of humanity if he is defeated, and such knaves or fools as vote against him, from among the common people, will prove themselves foes to liberty and justice, and must be branded as the obsequious hirelings of tyrants.

Do go on in your good work, and may millions urge you forward till John Swinton's Paper finds a reception at every fireside.

Boys of New York ! make Henry George your Mayor, and our country is safe.—J. O. CUMMINGS.

MILLIONS ARE WATCHING.

BRIDGEPORT, Conn., Oct. 7.—I feel heartily glad that New York voters of the Labor ticket still seem united. I would implore them not to allow any sneaks from the old parties to cause discord in their ranks by holding up religious, national or other prejudices. It is a question which concerns each and every wage-earner, and let them not prove traitors to the cause, now that they have an opportunity to set the house in order.

I have read of a custom that existed somewhere in olden times of paying tribute to their king in the shape of a bottle of wine from each male adult. The wine bottles were emptied into a large tank. After a time, sluggishness sprung up, and one said to himself, " Oh, my bottle of wine will not be missed among so many;" another thought the same, and so on, until one year they had all thought so, and no tribute in the shape of wine was received.

Let the New York voters take a lesson, and every man look after his own vote. Let them

HENRY GEORGE.

The George Campaign

TUESDAY'S DEMONSTRATION AT COOPER INSTITUTE.

Mr. George's Speech of Acceptance—Strong Reason, Sound Sense, and Noble Eloquence—The Mighty Issues now Brought into Politics—An Unprecedented Tide of Popular Enthusiasm.

The Henry George meeting at the Cooper Union on Tuesday night was the most remarkable gathering in the last quarter of a century, in this city. It was exceptional for many reasons : The event, the chief actors, the audience, the resurgent enthusiasm, the pile of 35,000 pledges, the interest of the press, and, above all, the New Declaration of Independence. If the workingmen do their duty ; if they stand shoulder to shoulder in the political struggle as they have in many an industrial struggle ; if they unanimously throw off

talked of, I regarded it as something which was not to be thought about. I did not desire to be Mayor of New York. I have had in my time political ambition, but years ago I gave it up. I saw what practical politics meant ; I saw that under conditions as they were a man who would make a political career must cringe and buy and intrigue and flatter. I resolved that I would not so degrade my manhood. Another career opened to me. The path that I had laid before me, that my eyes were fixed upon, was that of the pioneers who go in advance of politics (applause), that of the men who make the roads that will be trod by millions; and it seemed to me that there lay my duty and there my career. Since this matter has been talked about, many of my friends throughout the country all beyond the sea have written letter after letter asking me not, as they were pleased to say, to lower the position I occupy by running for municipal office. I believe that workingmen ought to go into politics. I believe, and have long believed, that through politics is the way, and the only way, by which anything real and permanent can be secured for labor. (Applause.) I had made up my mind at first to refuse the nomination, but when it came to me with the unanimous voice of the nominating convention I decided not to refuse. I made very important conditions. I asked for the guarantee of the good faith of the men who put me forward. (Applause.) I asked for some tangible evidence of the real support of my fellow-citizens of New York who wanted me to go to the front. That evidence you have given

he was a printer, as well as a member of both the Typographical Union and the Knights of Labor. Workers also knew George had suffered poverty and hardship, and that even after achieving international renown he lived a humble, unostentatious life. Still more, given labor's bitter experience in the past with corrupt and unresponsive career politicians, his lack of past involvement in politics added to his credentials.[2] "We do not absolutely require a 'great' man," noted James Smith, "yet we do want an *honest* man—a man unbesmirched by political jobbery, and who is not a *reformer*!" His election, he continued, would place "in the Mayor's chair, next November, *a man from your own ranks*."[3] Above all, George emerged as a likely candidate of labor because workers found his message compelling and attractive, whether they read it in *Progress and Poverty*, came in contact with it through the Land League activism, learned of it in workshop debates, or heard George speak in public. It was a message that resonated with key aspects of their own working-class republican ideology, one that spoke directly to their experiences as exploited workers and held out the promise of a redeemed American republic.

Four days after Swinton published his exuberant call for a George nomination, a conference comprised of delegates from 165 local labor organizations gathered at Clarendon Hall and voted to formally reestablish the United Labor Party.[4] Two weeks later, the Labor Conference delegates convened again, this time to elect the ULP leadership and to authorize a group to ask Henry George if he would accept their nomination.

"An active party among the workingmen here are very anxious to run me for Mayor," he wrote in early August to a friend back in San Francisco, "but I do not care to do it." The offer was tempting, yet it also clearly frightened him. Labor candidates had run up a bleak record in past elections; not a single one ever received more than a fraction of the workingmen's vote. Moreover, labor lacked the experience, connections, and money of the major political parties. If George allowed himself to become part of yet another dismal electoral defeat, his reputation as the leader of social and economic reform would suffer. On the other hand, a respectable showing, perhaps even a victory in the nation's largest city, would raise his profile substantially, exposing millions to his single tax reform ideology. Though intrigued by the possibility of spreading his ideas, George nonetheless decided to wait. Protesting that he had a great deal of important business that demanded his attention, he politely declined the offer. He sent away empty-handed a second delegation a few days later.[5]

It was at this point that Tammany attempted to stop the nascent George movement in its infancy. William M. Ivins, the city chamberlain and a Tammany official, invited George to lunch and advised him to stay out of the race. He could not win the election anyway, Ivins said, regardless of the number of ballots cast in his favor (e.g., he would be "counted out"). If, however, George agreed to refuse labor's nomination, Tammany would see to it that he was elected to Congress.

George asked why, if he could not win, did Tammany want him to withdraw?

"You cannot be elected," responded Ivins candidly, "but your running will raise hell!"

"You have relieved me of embarrassment," responded George. "I do not want the responsibility and work of the office of the Mayor of New York, but I do want to raise hell! I am decided and will run." He may have tweaked some of the details of this story here and there, but there was no question that Tammany Hall was keen on keeping George out of the race.[6]

Soon after this incident, a third ULP delegation called on George. This time he promised them a formal written statement indicating his intentions. Dated August 26, 1886, George began by saying his natural inclination was to refuse the nomination, but yet "there are considerations which, under certain conditions, would compel me to say 'Yes.'" George then proceeded to outline those considerations. He wrote that it had long been his belief that workers could expect little substantive change without entering politics to bring the issue of "industrial slavery" to the fore. The logical place to begin this challenge was on the local level, and no place cried out louder for a movement to transform politics into something more than a struggle for spoils than New York City, where "politics has become a trade, and the management of elections a business." Also, there was the appeal of a United Labor Party that emerged not from the "halls" or at the behest of the wealthy, but from the "great body of citizens," including those not narrowly defined as laborers.[7]

"My sense of duty," continued George, "would not permit me to refuse any part assigned me by the common consent of earnest men really bent upon carrying into politics the principles I hold dear." But the key question remained—was labor "really bent" this time around? He cautioned that "such a movement as is now proposed ought not to be lightly entered into." Labor had to demonstrate its unity and purpose, not simply to him, but to the countless voters who traditionally sympathized with such efforts, but seeing little hope of success, cast their ballots for the party deemed the lesser evil. To guard against this possibility, George announced that he would accept the ULP nomination, with a single, extraordinary qualification: labor must produce at least thirty thousand signatures from citizens pledged to support him at the polls on November 2. "This would be a guarantee that there should be no ignominious failure, and a mandate that I could not refuse."[8]

Days later, the public reading of this letter to the assembled delegates of the Labor Conference jolted the ULP into action. Party officials immediately set about ordering pledge rosters, organizing a canvas of the entire city, and establishing neighborhood pledge centers. They also established a committee to draft a party platform. Confident of their success, they also began planning a convention for September 23 to approve a platform and nominate George as the ULP's candidate for mayor of New York City.[9]

The excitement generated by George's conditional acceptance of the ULP's nomination and the subsequent launching of the signature campaign was evident days later at the annual Labor Day parade on September 6. It was very likely that some measure of George's doubts about the ability of the city's workingmen to meet his challenge and mount a convincing campaign were diminished as he stood on the stage and reviewed the largest Labor Day parade to date. Twenty thousand laborers marched and cheered the man they hoped would bear their standard in the coming political contest. Many bore signs with statements like "Henry George, Our Next Mayor" and "All Workingmen are Aroused for Independent Political Action."[10]

For the next few weeks, while ULP leaders made plans for the nominating convention, working-class men and women gathered signatures for George. Fr. Edward McGlynn, George's close associate, aptly described the request for signatures as a "master stroke," as it channeled a surging working-class anger into a nascent political movement. ULP volunteers did more than simply collect signatures; they seized the opportunity to create a database for the upcoming campaign, typing each signer's name, address, and labor organization onto a card. They would use this information during the campaign to facilitate the distribution of George's literature and ULP campaign material as well as to conduct neighborhood canvasses. It also allowed ULP activists to make meaningful, face-to-face contact with supporters and foster among them a sense of solidarity and movement. The signature campaign likewise allowed women to play an important role in the campaign.[11]

The signature drive also possessed important symbolic value. In addition to mobilizing the forces of the ULP, it also stood out as a powerful show of their reassertion of popular democratic power to restore republican governance. In contrast to the mainstream parties' practice of nominating candidates in back rooms hidden away from public scrutiny, the ULP was energetically canvassing the city for their nominee. As James Smith wrote in a letter to a labor paper, it represented a "novel but thoroughly democratic means of ascertaining the will of *the people.* . . . This striking method marks the beginning of a political revolution worthy of the American spirit of liberty and independence." The editor of the *Boycotter* agreed: "It is the fulfillment of the Jeffersonian idea of the people calling on a man to fill an office."[12]

After several weeks of frenetic grassroots political activity, 409 delegates from 175 labor organizations convened in Clarendon Hall on the evening of September 23, 1886, to formally nominate George and approve a party platform.[13] The meeting got under way ninety minutes late due to another scheme by Tammany; it tried to pack the hall with anti-George men committed to nominating a Tammany-controlled "labor" candidate.[14] Eventually called to order, the meeting opened with the reading of a telegram from the St. Louis Central Labor Union: "Organized Workingmen of the West congratulate you on your firm and independent movement. Your success is ours. Henry George and Labor will be the battle cry for all enslaved toilers from the Atlantic to the Pacific."[15]

The first item of official business concerned the reading and approval of the ULP platform. The first plank assailed the "corruptions of government and impoverishment of labor," both of which stemmed from society's neglect of the principles set forth in the Declaration of Independence. "We aim at the abolition of the system which compels men to pay their fellow-creatures for the use of God's gifts to all," read the document, clearly in reference to George's criticism of absolute private property rights. Such an injustice created "tramps and paupers" and stimulated a competition among workers that served "to reduce wages to starvation rates." Asserting the labor theory of value, the plank ended by decrying the system in which "the wealth producer [becomes] the industrial slave of those who grow rich by his toil."[16]

The assembled workingmen registered their approval with loud and enthusiastic applause followed by a vote of approval.[17] All that remained was the nomination. James H. Casserly of United Carpenters took the floor:

> I arise to put in nomination for the position of Chief Magistrate of this city a man above all political cliques, a man who, while occupying the proud position of Mayor of this city, will yet be able to look after the interests of the workingmen. He is now busily engaged in the work of elevating the masses by his writings and his ideas. Should we have him for two years as our municipal governor he would do a great service to labor. I nominate Henry George for Mayor.[18]

"At the mention of Mr. George's name." wrote a *New York Herald* reporter, "the delegates sprang to their feet, threw their hats in the air and cheered themselves hoarse." "Hats, handkerchiefs and canes were flung in the air," commented another journalist from the *New York Times*. "Men stomped on the floor until the building shook, and for a time the noise was deafening." The wild scene lasted several minutes. When quiet returned, other delegates seconded the nomination.[19]

George won by an overwhelming margin, receiving 360 of 409 votes cast. After "Three cheers for George!" rang out, it was announced that delegates would next convene on Tuesday, October 5, to make the nomination official by presenting to George the requested thirty thousand signatures. The meeting was then adjourned.[20]

Significantly, three days before this grand ULP convention that formalized George's nomination and officially launched his mayoral campaign, a smaller gathering of George supporters assembled. In a scene reminiscent of the two receptions tendered George upon his return to New York City in 1882, George and a group of his mugwump supporters organized a separate convention to endorse his campaign. Held on October 2, this "Citizen's Meeting" was attended by notable figures from the city's middle and upper classes. Its purpose, ULP chairman John McMackin somewhat awkwardly suggested, was to show the established parties "that it is not only men of muscle with whom they have to contend, but men of brains also." After several addresses by a series of respectable figures like Rev. Dr. Heber Newton, McGlynn arose to deliver a stirring speech on behalf of George: "We are inaugurating a movement which shall be the second, and with due reverence I say, a better declaration of independence. The head of this movement is a prophet. . . . He is in New York now—alive and kicking; and Henry George can kick pretty hard I can tell you." The meeting then adopted a resolution endorsing George's candidacy and adjourned.[21]

This pageant of respectability, held separately from the working-class event yet to come, reveals George's strategy of appealing to both the angered worker and the outraged mugwump. Though highly popular among wage workers, George also enjoyed significant middle-class support,[22] if not for his candidacy then certainly for his ideas regarding the threat posed to the republic by rising inequality and his insistence that class conflict was unnatural and dangerous. But in order to win their actual votes on Election Day he would have to avoid being branded a dangerous radical—something that soon proved impossible once his opponents' campaigns moved into high gear.[23]

Three days after this "citizen's meeting," the convention of far greater consequence took place at Cooper Union—a convention unlike any in the city's history. It opened with dramatic, ritualistic display. With George sitting before them, delegates passed over their heads, from the rear of the building all the way to the stage, large bundles of pledge forms. Stacked in tall pyramids they contained over 34,000 signatures, gathered in a single month, in support of George's candidacy for mayor.

John McMackin then formally extended to George "the nomination of organized labor and the indorsement of the business and professional men of New York."[24] After an ovation which lasted several minutes, George addressed the assembly:

Working-men of New York—organized laborers of New York, I accept your nomination. For weal or for woe, for failure or for success, henceforth I am your candidate. I am proud of it from the bottom of my heart. I thank you for the compliment you have paid me.[25]

In the brief speech that followed, George endeavored to set the tone and direction of the campaign to come. He first cautioned his listeners not to expect an immediate revolution with his election; there were great limitations placed upon the office of mayor, and sweeping change could not come overnight. But it would begin, George promised, with his use of the authority invested in the mayor—the power to appoint, to inspect, and, of course, to rouse public opinion—to the maximum.

Then George struck the central theme of his candidacy, one that emanated directly out of the radical republican vision he had been promoting since the publication of *Progress and Poverty* seven years prior. If elected, George pledged, he would be mayor to *all* classes and interests in the city, not just the wealthy. He vowed to uphold law and order, and to eliminate the rampant abuses of the law enforcement establishment—direct appeals to the central tenets of working-class republicanism that had been so dramatically violated in the recent crackdown on organized labor.

The battle against class rule promised to be tough, he warned. Tammany and the other political parties and factions had unlimited resources and intense interest in maintaining the current spoils system. Labor had to unite as true republican citizens, as "the people," to thwart a pernicious class movement of greedy monopolists and unscrupulous capitalists. "Chattel slavery is dead," said George, "but there devolves upon us the task of removing industrial slavery. That is the meaning of our movement. This is at once a revolt against political corruption and social injustice." After listing examples of this injustice in land use, housing, etc., he concluded on a high note; he harkened back to the internationalist themes emphasized in *Progress and Poverty* and in his activism on behalf of the Irish Land League:

We are beginning a movement for the abolition of industrial slavery, and what we do on this side of the water will send its impulse across the land and over the sea, and give courage to all men to think and act. Let us, therefore, stand together. Let us do everything that is possible for men to do from now until the second of next month, that success may crown our efforts, and that to us in this city may belong the honor of having led the van in this great movement.[26]

After a raucous ovation of approval, the convention adjourned. George followed the delegates outside and delivered short speeches from the tailboards of several wagons to those unable to gain admission to the event.

There is no doubt that many delegates went home that evening realizing that they had just participated in an unprecedented event in the annals of the city's history. They had accomplished in the space of one summer what only a year earlier seemed impossible—uniting a loose federation of unions known for their factionalism (especially on the issue of politics) into a viable, independent political organization. Thousands had mobilized in the effort to raise money, collect signatures, produce campaign literature, and canvass on behalf of the ULP. And they had chosen as their candidate a man with an engaging personality, a respected intellect, and an untarnished record as a champion of the workingman. To many in labor's cause, there was a palpable feeling of optimism, a sense that this would be no ordinary labor party effort that might garner only a few hundred symbolic protest votes. Might they actually win?[27]

Adding to this sense of extraordinary possibilities was news from around the nation of similar stirrings among workers. Harsh crackdowns on labor activism similar to that in New York were occurring in scores of industrial centers from coast to coast. The resulting anger generated by these incidents, along with the outrage sparked by the unfair trials of the Haymarket anarchists, led to the formation of United Labor Parties and other organizations with similar names in 189 towns and cities nationwide, in 34 of 38 states and 4 territories, from Boston to San Francisco; it was what Leon Fink has termed "the American worker's single greatest push for political power."[28]

None of these campaigns, many of which resulted in labor victories in November, commanded the same level of national attention as George's campaign in New York City. As one supporter observed, "The whole country is watching with most intense anxiety to see if there is sufficient intelli-

gence and honesty in the people of the commercial and financial metropolis of the nation to secure safety and purity of government 'of, for and by the
people.'" From the successful movement launched by the workers of New
York City, declared the *Boycotter*, "will spring hopes in the hearts of our
now faint brethren in other parts of the United States, who are now eagerly
watching us. . . . Let us with our ballots begin the battle of freemen—a
battle that cannot cease until we have this republic a democracy in fact as
well as in name." As George himself said in his acceptance speech before the
ULP delegates, "The campaign this fall is only the first step. The movement
of the working masses has started here."[29]

"THE HENRY GEORGE MOVEMENT HAS
SO STIRRED UP THE OLD MACHINE MEN"

Given such expressions of enthusiasm, it is important to ask whether
George himself believed he might actually win. Or did he consider his bid
for the mayoralty merely a symbolic statement by labor and an opportunity
for him to promote his land-value tax reform program? In a letter to his old
San Francisco friend Dr. Edward Taylor a few days after Labor Day, George
made his perception of events clear:

> All the probabilities are that I will be in the fight, and it is by no
> means impossible that I will be elected. But the one thing sure is that
> if I do go into the fight the campaign will bring the land question into
> practical politics and do more to popularise its discussion than years
> of writing could do. This is the only temptation to me.[30]

In a word, George saw himself in a no-lose situation. He might very well
lose the election, but at the very least he would attract significant attention
to his single tax reform. The latter was clearly paramount, but in George's
mind winning was a very real possibility, one that he would pursue with
great vigor to the very end of the campaign. As he wrote to a friend in early
October, "The great question is at last in politics and the struggle has begun.
It is taxing every nerve, so that I can only write a few words. But I think we
shall win this first skirmish."[31]

Stoutly standing in the way of victory, however, were the mainstream political parties. Clearly alarmed by the ULP insurgency, they moved quickly to ensure a George defeat and the maintenance of the political status quo. Tammany, given its dependence on the working-class vote, had the most to lose. After its initial attempts to derail the George candidacy failed, the organization was left with no alternative than to forge a seemingly unlikely political alliance with the County Democracy. Founded years earlier as the anti-Tammany reform faction of the Democratic Party, the County Democracy at first shunned the very idea of an alliance. "We can't touch pitch without being defiled," argued a highly placed official. However, unite they soon did, "pitch" and all, as Tammany shrewdly nominated the County Democracy's own Abram Hewitt as its mayoral candidate. The alliance stunned many political observers, but it made perfect sense given the era's trend toward greater bourgeois solidarity in the face of labor mobilization.[32]

Hewitt was a sixty-four-year-old, five-term New York congressman. Born to modest circumstances on an upstate farm, he had risen to become a prosperous iron manufacturer. As both an industrialist and member of Congress, Hewitt had styled himself as a friend of the workingman. A paternalist at heart, he refused to shutter his mills during the depression years of the 1870s. Unlike most men of his class in the wake of the Great Uprising in 1877, he did not call for the military to mow down the mob. Instead, he convened lengthy congressional hearings to investigate the relations between labor and capital, the results of which exposed the fact that many industrialists exploited their workers.[33] Hewitt even declared his support for trade unions. These sentiments explain why (as noted in chapter 4) he hired George back in 1880 to ghostwrite portions of a congressional report into the status of labor.

In Hewitt, a respected industrialist with a prolabor reputation, Tammany gambled that it could retain the bulk of its working-class vote and maintain its ties to the city's business establishment.[34] As the *New York Sun* observed, talk of Hewitt as a Tammany candidate "would be laughed at as silly by most politicians in an ordinary year, but this fall the Henry George movement has so stirred up the old machine men that they seriously consider any project, no matter how wild."[35]

The Republican Party had no intentions to compete for the labor vote. As one newspaper commented, "The Republican party is nowhere a workingman's party, and especially not in New York City. Most of its members pride themselves that they are distinct from the working masses."[36] Republicans settled upon a brash and outspoken twenty-eight year old named Theodore Roosevelt. Born into a wealthy family with an ancestry that reached far back into the days of Dutch New Amsterdam, Roosevelt had won his first political office (as a state assemblyman) in 1882, just two years after graduating from Harvard College. He supported both good government initiatives and labor reform legislation, but left politics from 1884 to 1886 after suffering the sudden deaths of his wife and mother on the same day. In 1886, eager to reenter public life, he accepted the Republican Party's nomination on October 15.[37]

Despite Roosevelt's penchant for publicity, all eyes were focused on Hewitt and George. To George's great frustration, Hewitt refused to debate him in public. But he did engage in an exchange of letters that appeared in the papers. The verbal fray began when Hewitt, in accepting his nomination, made it clear that his chief campaign strategy would be to depict George as a dangerous radical bent on social upheaval. His main reason for running, he declared, was to thwart the ULP's effort to pit "one class of citizens against all other classes." George and the ULP threatened American values and institutions by "substitut[ing] the ideas of Anarchists, Nihilists, Communists, Socialists, and mere theorists for the democratic principle of individual liberty." He warned that "the horrors of the French Revolution and the atrocities of the Commune offer conclusive proof of the dreadful consequences of [these] doctrines."[38]

George answered Hewitt's red-baiting with a public letter on October 18; the missive deftly combined a careful refutation with dismissive ridicule. "I am confident that in a cooler frame of mind," he chided, "the phantoms which now affright your imagination would shrink into the ridiculous scarecrows that they really are." Were Hewitt to actually read the ULP platform, he would see no evidence whatsoever of un-American ideas or plans to dismantle American democracy. To the contrary, the congressman would learn that the ULP was dedicated to restoring the democracy and fundamental rights of citizenship that monopolies and political machines like Tammany—Hewitt's primary backer—had subverted. Far from representing a narrow class movement as Hewitt insisted, the ULP was a movement *against* class politics. It represented an effort, George pronounced, of the "masses against the classes."[39]

Hewitt's response appeared in the next day's papers. Continuing his antiradical alarmism, he informed George that his ideas were dangerous, even if George was unaware of it. "Neither did Robespierre, St. Just, or Couthon foresee or admit the horrors in which they were forced to take part." He continued to reiterate that his entire motivation for running was to put "the seal of public condemnation upon doctrines which are destructive of social order."[40]

George struck back the next day with force, bluntly stating that Hewitt's letter had been filled with "deliberate misrepresentations." Apparently, George asserted, Hewitt had opted for a campaign based on demagoguery—not an "appeal to the highest qualities of your fellow-citizens, but upon an appeal to the lowest passions and vilest motives." George dismissed the notion that Hewitt was running to "save society" from a "mere theorist," and charged him with willingly serving as a respectable figurehead of a corrupt Tammany organization determined "to save their power and plunder." If Hewitt did not know this to be true, it was because his own riches had blinded him to the plight of the great mass of citizens. "The great body of your constituents are not millionaires like you." They suffered from economic exploitation and political disenfranchisement at the hands of the system he benefited from and now represented.[41]

Clearly irritated by both George's skill and boldness in rhetorical combat (and likely relieved he declined George's repeated invitations to a face-to-face debate), Hewitt in his next letter objected to the ULP candidate's "personal remarks" and "objectionable language"; he declared the debate by public letter finished. He nonetheless took the opportunity in his final letter to reiterate his alarmist charges against George, ending with one final red-baiting flourish. George's ideas, "though merely ink when set on paper, turn to blood when put into action."[42] George responded with one last letter; he reiterated his previous defense of his ideas and criticized Hewitt for "raising the cry of anarchy and destruction, posturing in the role of 'saviour of society.'"

Hewitt's ending of the letter debate did not end the campaign to brand the George and the ULP as the vanguard of a new Commune. The daily press, much of it controlled by the mainstream political parties and all of it beholden to business interests upon whom it depended for advertising revenue, parroted many of the same themes articulated by Hewitt.[43] In one instance, the *New York Daily Graphic* printed a mock "speech" by George in which the candidate exhorted his followers to "fall into line, abandon the Democratic party that has stood by you, and to help me, your free trade socialist candidate in the crusade for the Commune."[44] Even worse, many papers intentionally misquoted George to make him sound like a radical bent on social upheaval.[45] One paper quoted him as saying:

With all its drawbacks, and horrors, and shortcomings, the great epoch of the French Revolution, now but a century gone, is about to repeat itself here. Liberty, equality, and fraternity embodies the aspirations of every working-man in the world to-day. . . . This is a class movement—the uprising of the working-men, the revolt of the disinherited classes claiming their share of the wealth their toil produces.[46]

Elite magazines like *Puck* went further and ran vivid cartoons depicting George as both foolish and dangerous. Not one of the city's more than twenty daily English-language papers endorsed George for mayor. Only after the ULP established its own daily paper two weeks before the election did the George campaign enjoy any kind of positive media coverage outside of small circulation papers like *Swinton's*, *Truth*, the *Irish World*, and the *Volkszeitung*.[47]

Joining Tammany and the media in the mobilization against George and the ULP were key elite institutions and organizations. The Union League Club, which counted among its members most of the city's wealthy and powerful men of business, law, and politics, cast its influence and capital behind Roosevelt's candidacy. So did the Citizen's Committee of One Hundred, an influential good government organization likewise comprised of affluent, influential men dedicated to defending the interests of property. Merchant organizations such as the Dry Goods Merchants and the Business Men's Cleveland Association also mobilized to stop the labor

The media portrays Henry George as a dangerous revolutionary. "Reform—By George!" *Harper's Weekly*, October 23, 1886. Courtesy of HarpWeek

insurgency. Well-to-do lawyer Samuel Barlow spoke for many when he warned that a George victory would trigger a clash between, "order and disorder and between labor and idleness, between the madness engendered by German philosophy, French Anarchism, and beer on the one side and common sense conservatism on the other."[48]

The George campaign also had to contend with the Catholic Church. As noted in chapter 5, the Church's opposition to the George movement had begun long before the 1886 mayoral campaign and was part of a much larger effort in the 1880s to steer Catholics away from radicalism. One of the Church's leading figures in the effort to staunch Catholic labor activism independent of clerical control and prohibit Catholics from reading *Progress and Poverty* was Archbishop Michael Corrigan of New York. Corrigan's visceral hostility toward radicalism in general, and Georgism in particular, became evident during the campaign in his efforts to silence the radical priest and George supporter Fr. Edward McGlynn, who (as detailed in chapter 4) had drawn a warning from Corrigan's predecessor Cardinal McCloskey in 1882 for his outspoken identification with the radical wing of the Land League.[49]

In late September 1886, upon learning that McGlynn intended to deliver an address at the October 2nd "Citizen's Meeting" in support of the George candidacy, Corrigan forbade him to speak. McGlynn protested; all the papers had carried advertisements of his appearance, so to pull out at the request of the archbishop would bring scandal to the Church. He then asked George to call upon Corrigan to explain his theories and their compatibility with Church teachings on private property. George complied, but the meeting did not go well. Corrigan remained convinced that George was a dangerous radical. McGlynn resolved to speak at the meeting anyway, explaining in a defiant letter to Corrigan:

> I, in view of my rights and duties as a citizen, which were not surrendered when I became a priest, am determined to do what I can to support Mr. George; and I am also stimulated by love for the poor and oppressed laboring classes, which seems particularly consonant with the charitable and philanthropic character of the priesthood.[50]

McGlynn's bold decision to speak brought a swift reaction. Corrigan suspended him from his priestly duties for two weeks, then banned him from public speaking for the remainder of the campaign. Behind the scenes, he redoubled his efforts to begin formal disciplinary proceedings against McGlynn at the Vatican. McGlynn submitted to his superior's authority this time around, but he kept his suspension and silencing a secret to avoid a scandal that might raise doubts among Catholics about supporting George. For the remaining weeks of the campaign, McGlynn continued to advise George and appear in public with him—an important gesture which helped to maintain George's legitimacy among many Irish Catholic workers. Nonetheless, silencing McGlynn removed one of George's crucial campaign assets.[51]

Part of the motivation behind Corrigan's vendetta against McGlynn and George may have had more to do with politics than piety. Years after the George campaign, a number of prominent Tammany leaders revealed that they approached Corrigan in 1886 to urge him to discipline McGlynn. Corrigan had good reason, apart from his own philosophical conservatism, to accede to their request: the Church in New York City had long relied on Tammany Hall for protection and special favors, such as subsidies for parochial schools and giveaway land deals for building new churches. So when the archbishop was approached by a posse of Tammany operatives on the McGlynn matter, he felt compelled to act. He not only agreed to silence McGlynn, but also, according to the account, to issue a pointed condemnation of George's ideas just before the election.[52]

"A MOVEMENT OF THE MASSES AGAINST ROBBERY BY THE CLASSES"

As the United Labor Party worked to overcome these substantial obstacles, it also articulated the reasons behind its creation and campaign. This was not a mere gesture of symbolic protest, but a real movement seeking to reassert workers' place within the polity by seizing political power. By 1886, the experiences with the streetcar monopolies, hostile judges, abusive policemen, and corrupt public officials—all indifferent to their needs and mistreatment—had demonstrated the immense degree to which politics, business, and the law were intertwined, and the extent to which the voice of society's producers had been stifled and trampled. "As Labor stands today," wrote James Smith, "it is practically disfranchised, because it has hitherto handed over to one or the other of the old political parties its strength." Condemning the political establishment, "Printer" observed in a letter to the *Boycotter*: "What a sarcastic misnomer is the phrase 'the people's servants!' Do servants dress better than their masters? Do they strut and swell out with self-conscious importance? Do they make laws against the interests of their masters? As a matter of fact, *they* are the *people's* masters."[53]

The ULP thus represented a fundamental effort by labor to redeem workers' citizenship—a citizenship that carried with it not merely political and social, but also economic rights. "In this country, the most important of modern republics, the degradation of citizenship flourishes, becoming more and more general every year, till to-day we are not far distant from pure and unadulterated oligarchy," one activist warned. The United States would soon see "the separation of the people into two classes—monarch and serf."[54]

By responding to the republican crisis with the formation of a labor party bent on reasserting the power of the producers, the city's working-men declared their intent to resume their proper role as "the people," with elected officials of their choosing representing *their* interests, not those of commerce, privilege, or monopoly. The interests of capital had gained unfettered access to state power in recent decades, influence which they used to expand and solidify their power in society. A victory by the ULP would shake up this emerging hierarchy and begin to reverse this trend. "We are going to the polls," Henry George told the crowds on the eve of the mayoral election, "and we will show the politicians that we are the masters and not the servants."[55]

This implicit effort to revitalize citizenship and re-empower the work-ing class was explicit throughout the ULP's platform, campaign literature, and stump speeches. "Class movement!" cried George in his acceptance speech, referring charges by Hewitt and Roosevelt that he was foment-ing class conflict. "What class is it? The working class!" In an earlier age, everyone had to work for a living; no such distinction of a "working class" could be made. But now, remarked George, men had devised ways of liv-ing off the labor of others. "If this is a class movement, then it is a move-ment of the working class against the beggar-men and the thieves. . . . It is a movement of the masses against robbery by the classes."[56] An edito-rial in the *Boycotter* echoed this line when it deemed both Hewitt and Roosevelt as "class candidates" representing the interests of corrupt busi-nessmen and politicians.

> The truth about this class issue is that the men who have raised it really desire that the wage-earner should allow the wage-payer to do his voting for him. Here we have indeed an alarming and dangerous class movement to deal with. Henry George's candidacy means that an effort is now being made in New York City to arrest this most un-American class movement . . . at the ballot box.[57]

As important as this broad philosophical ideal of restored citizenship was, what practical results did George and the ULP envision should they win? George himself admitted that the powers of the executive in New York City were circumscribed; the city charter reserved authority over taxation, budget, and law-making to the Board of Aldermen and the state legislature. Yet he disagreed with the editor of the *New York Times*, who charged that he "does not seek the office of Mayor with any thought that he can directly promote the application of his peculiar theories." Quite to the contrary, George and his ULP supporters outlined a very specific set of goals for labor's mayor should he be elected.[58] These goals were detailed in the ULP platform that George helped draft in August. While at least one historian has argued that George made the platform weaker and more cautious in comparison to its predecessors in the ULP campaigns of 1882 and 1883, the document is more accurately understood as a strategic mix of both radical demands and moderate platitudes designed to attract the maximum number of voters.[59]

In this effort, the ULP proved remarkably successful. It did not suffer a single defection from its coalition despite changes in the platform. It appealed to relatively conservative trade unionists in the State Workingmen's Association, the trade-union political body headed by Samuel Gompers. The State Workingmen's Association recognized the ULP and cast its support behind George even though they had eschewed the idea of independent labor politics for years.[60] The revised platform also garnered the support of radicals such as the Socialist Labor Party, which backed the ULP. As the editor of *Der Socialist* put it, "Henry George is no socialist. His program is not socialistic. But Henry George stands for socialistic demands and if his program is carried out, it would be an advantage for the workers and a heavy blow for capitalism."[61]

Still, George's decision to depart from the 1882 and 1883 platforms requires an explanation. To begin with, many changes were made for purely practical reasons. The demand in the original platform for national currency reform, for instance, was completely irrelevant to New York City and its mayor. Its call to establish a state bureau of labor statistics and abolish contract convict labor had been recently accomplished. The decision to limit the number of specific demands in the new platform—leaving out the establishment of the eight-hour workday and the abolition of the truck-pay system while retaining calls for equal pay for men and women and public ownership of mass transit, among others—was likely meant blunt any political attacks from Hewitt and Roosevelt whereby labor's cause could be misrepresented as dangerous radicalism. It also gave the platform a more universal appeal, targeting disaffected middle-class voters who did not identify as wage earners but who nonetheless opposed monopoly and corruption.

Of far greater consequence than what George and other ULP leaders removed from the platform was what he *added* to it. For example, the passionate demand that "the people of New York City should have full control of their local affairs" (e.g., home rule) and be freed from undemocratic control by state officials in Albany was an explicit call for the restoration of democracy and self-representation. The powers of the mayor ought to be broadened, argued the platform, to more effectively carry out the will of the people. The city needed "one executive responsible to the people." To achieve this end, the platform called for a referendum to convene a state constitutional convention.[62] If George won the election and the referendum passed, he could lead a city delegation to the state constitutional convention to gain home rule. The city would then be free to make its own decisions under leadership attuned to popular concerns on key matters such as the eight-hour workday, first lien laws, child labor, improved factory and tenement safety, and public ownership of mass transit.

Even before these structural changes in city politics were made, George declared his intention to use the mayor's existing limited powers to the fullest extent possible, particularly the power to appoint the heads of important city departments like Public Works, Streets, and Charity. After a thorough housecleaning of corrupt officials, he told a reporter, he would appoint "men of character, capacity and courage, on whom I could rely to work for the purification of the city administration."[63]

George also had a bigger target to morally wield the city executive's power against: the established political machines. As their platform put it, the ULP campaign "affords the only hope of exposing and breaking up the extortion and peculation by which a standing army of professional politicians corrupt the public whom they plunder." Winning the mayoralty would firmly establish the ULP in municipal (and eventually state and national) politics, resulting in the subsequent election of aldermen, assemblymen, and judges from the ranks of "the people." This would dismantle the system of patronage that the corrupt machines relied on. "Jack Plane," writing to *John Swinton's Paper*, summed up this aspiration in the following call to action:

> Up and cleanse your city offices of the filthy slugs, roaches and bloated spiders of politics that fatten on the stealings from city treasury and banks. Pitch from their snuggeries the adulterous issues of the debauched ballot-box. The hour of order is closing in upon you. . . . The period of wholesale peculation is fast passing away.[64]

The 1886 ULP platform also went beyond the original in committing the next mayor to establishing classless rule by vetoing "class legislation" passed by the Board of Aldermen. Reflecting the republican ideal of the common good, George and the ULP vowed to abolish "all laws which give to any class of citizens advantages, either judicial, financial, industrial, or political, that are not equally shared by all others." Mayor George, for example, could veto the Board of Aldermen's decisions to award streetcar franchises to corrupt and abusive corporations. He could also use his authority to compel the streetcar and elevated railroad companies to reform by launching investigations into whether they paid their proper amount of taxes, treated their employees fairly, charged reasonable fares, and provided quality service. Furthermore, as both the platform and George made clear, these would be but the first steps toward a comprehensive public takeover of the transportation and communication systems, wresting them from corporations that garner "enormous profits" while they "oppress their employe[e]s and provoke strikes that interrupt travel and imperil the public peace"—a clear reference to the streetcar corruption scandals and strikes that rocked the city that past spring and that contributed to labor's political mobilization.[65]

George and ULP leaders also augmented the 1886 platform to take on other aspects of class rule, especially the police. Although the head of the New York City Police Department was one of the few positions not under executive control, the mayor's office possessed sufficient authority, moral and otherwise, to curb the department's excesses. This understanding was particularly compelling given the extraordinary actions taken by the police during the spring's tumultuous protests. As the *Boycotter* put it, with a genuine representative of labor as mayor, "the police of the city would be confined to their legitimate functions of preserving the peace instead of being turned over to the corporations to do the work of the striking car-drivers."[66] The platform went further by pledging to simplify the legal system and to abolish property requirements for jurors—a particularly salient point in the wake of the boycotter verdicts. This would eliminate class rule by expanding the jury pool, enabling workers brought before the bench a chance to be judged by their economic peers and diminishing the power of hostile, activist judges.

The labor campaign also believed the mayor possessed a potential that far exceeded its actual powers as delineated by law. As the chief executive of the nation's largest city, as well as the *de facto* leader of a new political party, George could further the objectives of labor and the ULP by using his position as a bully pulpit for social reform. "The Mayor of New York has not only the large powers of the office," George noted, "but is in a position to appeal effectually to the still larger power of public opinion, that can always be relied on to support reforms of which the people feel the need." Just as his election, in and of itself, would have a powerful symbolic impact on the American working class, so too would his high office. With ready access to national media, Mayor George could provide labor with an unparalleled mouthpiece for making known its plight and advocating radical social reform.[67]

A final critical element added to the 1886 ULP platform was an explicit condemnation of economic exploitation. "We aim at the abolition of the system which compels men to pay their fellow-creatures for the use of God's gifts to all," read the ULP platform in a clear allusion to George's criticism of unchallenged private property rights. Such a system, argued the ULP, "permits monopolizers to deprive labor of natural opportunities for employment," thus boosting unemployment, driving down wages "to starvation rates," and making "the wealth producer the industrial slave of those who grow rich by his toil." It also forced hundreds of thousands of citizens to live in crowded, unsanitary tenements. "We declare the crowding of so many of our people into narrow tenements at enormous rents while half the area of the city is yet unbuilt upon to be a scandalous evil."[68]

The ULP's proposed remedy, unsurprisingly, was George's single tax reform. The platform demanded an end to all taxes excepting those on land, which would be taxed at full value "so that those who are now holding land vacant [to gain by speculation] shall be compelled either to build on it themselves, or give up the land to those who will." For all its flaws and idiosyncrasies, George's single tax plan added an explicitly progressive character to the campaign. Although *Progress and Poverty* advocated a conversion to land-value taxation and the abolition of absolute private property rights in land on a *national* scale, George's mayoral platform essentially called upon the city government, in P. J. McGuire's words, to "municipalize" the land. This was no abstract consideration; New York in 1886 was driven perhaps more than any other city in the United States by real estate development and speculation, and was racked by overcrowded and unhealthy housing. Throughout the campaign, George spoke out against the horrors of tenement life:

> Nowhere else in the civilized world are men and women and children packed together so closely.... Now, is there any reason for such overcrowding? There is plenty of room on this island. There are miles and miles and miles of land all around this nucleus. Why cannot we take that land and build houses upon it for our accommodation? Simply because it is held by dogs in the manger who will not use it themselves, nor allow anyone else to use it, unless they pay an enormous price for it.[69]

In contrast, the old ULP platform raised no explicit challenge to absolute private property rights, nor to the private ownership of utilities, railroads, or telegraphs.[70] Nor did it argue in communitarian terms, as the 1886 version did, that "the enormous value which the presence of a million and a half of people gives to the land of this city belongs properly to the whole community," and that it "should be taken in taxation and applied to the improvement and beautifying of the city, to the promotion of health, comfort, education, and recreation of its people." Revenue generated from land-value taxation would be "for the use of the whole people, and for the beautifying and adornment of the city, for providing public accommodations, playgrounds, schools, and facilities for education and recreation."[71]

Careful consideration of the 1886 ULP platform and George's rhetoric on the campaign trail makes it clear that the city's workers did not form a labor party and nominate Henry George simply out of anger or to "send a message" to the established parties. They developed a specific agenda that called for radical political, economic, and social change.

Now all they had to do was pull off the impossible.

"A TAILBOARD CAMPAIGN"

The United Labor Party campaign, which had commenced back in September 1886 with the organized effort to collect the signatures in support of George, began in earnest in early October. From the official headquarters at the Colonnade Hotel at 141 East 8th Street, the party coordinated an army of volunteers and established Henry George Clubs and political organizations in all twenty-four state assembly districts. Significantly, these institutions were situated in storefront offices—a sharp contrast to Tammany's traditional use of saloons as campaign centers. Some of the larger individual trade organizations—in particular, the cigar makers, printers, and builders—established Henry George Trade Legions to lead parades and place men at the polls.[72]

One of the greatest obstacles facing the Labor campaign was the lack of money. As George wrote to a friend just after the nomination, "Money will flow like water to beat me."[73] To another he confided, "Tammany, or no Tammany, I think I will be the next Mayor of New York. . . . Our only difficulty is shortness of money."[74] To counteract this problem, labor leaders devised a grassroots fundraising campaign, requesting a twenty-five cent donation from each of the CLU's more than one hundred thousand unionized workers, as well as assessing each labor organization for five cents per man, per week. Workers unable to give money often donated time. Others gave both in the form of "$1-and-a-day's-time pledges." Labor organizations, including those far beyond the city limits (workers from St. Louis, for example, sent $500), sent financial support.[75]

The ULP also lacked experience in running a campaign. Nineteenth-century urban politics was structured in such a way as to make it nearly impossible for third parties to mount successful challenges. The law required political parties to print and distribute their own ballots, to post poll watchers to challenge potentially fraudulent voters, and to guard against the wily distribution of intentionally flawed ballots (which would be voided during the count by the opposition).[76] A viable party thus needed an army of volunteers to staff the polls to ensure a fair election result. Tammany alderman Fatty Walsh glibly summed up the challenges facing the George campaign: "What can those fellows do without an election inspector or poll-clerk? And where are they going to get the money to run the polls with?" Walsh was referring to the fact that the established parties had $226,000 in public funds at their disposal to pay for poll watchers. This money was distributed by Tammany-controlled police precinct captains under the careful direction of the political machine's district leaders. By one contemporary estimate, 20 percent of the electorate, or forty thousand voters, received money for their efforts on Election Day.[77]

George nonetheless expressed optimism over the ULP's chances for success. "We are not experienced campaigners," he admitted, "but we know all the methods of the machine men and we shall use them for our own purposes."[78] Unlike Alderman Walsh's Tammany, George's organization would wield no influence over who worked as official poll inspectors; still, "we cannot be denied [poll] watchers." Labor planned to place men with badges indicating the labor organizations to which they belonged at every polling site. "Let the tailor, the carpenter, the bricklayer and all of our trades have a representative at the polls to see that every friend of labor votes for Henry George and for him only," urged Samuel Gompers. George concurred. "You will find that the labor movement is well organized—better organized than it ever was before—and I count upon giving the old political organizations a surprise that will make them feeble."[79]

To bring off this surprise, the ULP established its own daily newspaper, the *Leader*, to counter the hostile mainstream press.[80] It also commenced a nonstop "tailboard campaign" of public speaking throughout the city every day until the election. From the day following his formal acceptance of the nomination to Election Day, George averaged seven public appearances a day; he spoke before unions, fraternal organizations, ethnic associations, reform clubs, and other assemblies. Midday found George stumping outside factories to greet and address workers on their lunch breaks. In the evenings, he made the rounds of neighborhoods, speaking from the back of a wagon (on the "tailboard") at street corners, near railroad stops, and in public squares. On one evening alone, George spoke before audiences at St. Cecilia's Catholic Church on East 106th Street, the Waiters' Union No. 3 at East 40th Street and Third Avenue, a mass meeting of eight thousand workers at East 42nd Street, an impromptu gathering at an Elevated Railroad stop, and at ten o'clock before a "First Voters" meeting at Chickering Hall.[81] Through a speakers' bureau under the direction of Samuel Gompers, the ULP deployed dozens of tailboard speakers to every corner of the city. Those who stepped up to speak on behalf of George included well-known working-class leaders such as P. J. McGuire and Robert Blissert, as well as the novelist William Dean Howells, free thinker Robert Ingersoll, socialist Daniel DeLeon, Episcopal cleric Rev. Heber Newton, reformer Josephine Shaw Lowell, and economist E. R. A. Seligman. On one evening alone the New York *Star* estimated that over thirty thousand workers gathered at sixteen George rallies across the city.[82]

Significantly, as they had in the Land League years before and more recently in the streetcar strikes, women played a crucial role in the campaign. In addition to the aforementioned collection of signatures, women organized rallies, collected funds, and distributed campaign literature. Many of the tailboard speakers were women. "I have fought side by side with the men of the party to which I belong," recalled former Ladies' Land Leaguer, Irish nationalist, and women's rights activist Marguerite Moore a few months after the election. "I have done all that a man could do in an election campaign, with the exception of smoking cigars and casting the ballot." These efforts included delivering two to three speeches every night on George's behalf until Election Day.[83]

The ULP's tailboard campaign benefited tremendously from the good weather that prevailed throughout the month of October. This unprecedented style of grassroots politics and community outreach underscored the fundamentally democratic nature of the labor revolt. By actively canvassing every working-class neighborhood in the city, George projected

The tailboard campaign. "New York City: The Mayoralty Campaign—A Henry George Meeting on the East Side." *Frank Leslie's Weekly*, October 30, 1886. Author's collection

an image of a political movement of, by, and for the people. In contrast, Hewitt barely campaigned at all, speaking only a half-dozen times, always before select groups of supporters.[84]

But more important than his campaign style was the substance of George's appeal to working-class New Yorkers. As he did so successfully in *Progress and Poverty* and his subsequent writings, as well as in his nomination acceptance speech, George eloquently explained to his working-class audience his program for radical social change in the context of New York City in plain terms and unadorned language:

> The great mass of the citizens of New York are tired of living as they have hitherto lived. Half of the area of this city is unbuilt upon. Is there not room enough and land enough here to give every man an independent home? A man who holds ground vacant that somebody else wants to use should pay in taxes just as much as though he were to put a building upon it. That goes to the heart of the labor question. In this city thousands will be starving this winter for want of work. Is there not enough work to be done? Why there is not labor is because human beings are shut off from the natural opportunities to labor. It is here just as in Ireland, namely, that what the Creator intended for all his children, the land, just as he intended

the air or water, is made the private property of a few. Are these little children who every day are coming into the world not entitled to anything?[85]

Supporters of George echoed these ideas in speeches, editorials, and letters. "A vote for Henry George for Mayor," wrote "Printer" to the *Boycotter*, "will be a census of those who believe that rights under our laws shall include a recognition of men's natural rights." Another observer wrote that others not so well versed in political economy or natural law supported George because "they are opposed to the oppression which is now practiced in one form or in another on laboring men and the poor generally."[86]

As always, George cast his radicalism in the familiar terminology of republicanism. He promised to empower workers not by attacking the middle class, but by overthrowing their *common* foe, the monopolist. His election would not revive the Commune, it would reinvigorate the Constitution. One Gordon Clark captured this essential quality of the campaign when he wrote:

Henry George represents the whole present field of economic progress and the elevation of the masses under American constitutional methods. His election will inspire the depressed masses throughout the country with the feeling that industrial emancipation has begun, and in the American way. Mr. George knows how to insist on all the great self-evident truths that Jefferson laid down.[87]

One week before the election, the ULP issued a call to the city's workingmen to participate in a grand pre-election spectacle—a "monster parade"—on October 30. Entitled a "Proclamation to the People of New York City," the document neatly summarized the central demands of the ULP campaign. Invoking the tenets of working-class republicanism and a call for revitalized citizenship and classless rule, the proclamation invited "all bodies of organized labor and all political organizations attached to the new party of equal rights, social reform, true Republicanism, and universal Democracy." It also was suffused with Georgist themes of landlord exploitation, noting that the parade would include:

thousands who are deprived of their birthright of a footing on the earth, who must work one hundred days a year for a landlord, while the common methods of transportation could carry them conveniently to suburban homes if the city should justly resume its right to its thoroughfares and possess itself of the land nearby by now held by speculators; who pay thrice the value of fuel because avaricious men have possessed themselves by means of unrepublican laws of the free gifts of nature.[88]

Unintentionally, the city's financial and political elites had planned their own gala event that same week. It served as a stark foil to the ULP's monster parade. On October 28, 1886, more than a million people, among them President Cleveland, several members of Congress, and foreign dignitaries, gathered along the city's waterfront to witness the unveiling of the Statue of Liberty. The event was a celebration of progress, with many speeches praising the health and vitality of the republic. Prominent New York businessman Chauncey Depew delivered an address that lauded democracy and self-government as the antidote to the strikes and protests then afflicting the nation. "The problems of labor and capital, of property and poverty," he declared, "will work themselves out under the benign influence of enlightened law-making and law-abiding liberty, without the aid of kings and armies, or of anarchists and bombs."[89]

That few activists in the ULP agreed with these ebullient sentiments was made quite clear two days later when the ULP staged its monster parade. The big event took place on the Saturday night before Election Day. In an inversion of the fair and dry weather that dominated much of the campaign, the heavens opened up and heavy rains poured down upon the participants and spectators. Nonetheless, over thirty thousand marchers braved the weather to march in support of their candidate and cause. ULP officials chose a particularly symbolic route for the parade. It began at Cooper Union, where labor had honored George upon his returns from Ireland in 1882 and 1884, and where labor had nominated him in 1886. From there, it strode up to Union Square, the scene of so many labor rallies in the past and where George and other party leaders stood on the reviewing stand during the past few Labor Day parades. The parade finally terminated

"Our Statue of Liberty—She Can Stand It." *Puck*, October 27, 1886. Courtesy of the Library of Congress

in Tompkins Square, the location of the infamous and radicalizing 1874 police riot and the heart of the multiethnic Lower East Side. Thousands of spectators stood in Union Square to view labor's display of pride, solidarity, and purpose, a spectacle which recalled the artisanal rituals once so common in America through the Age of Jackson and most recently revived by the CLU's annual Labor Day celebrations. In parading through the city's thoroughfares, squares, and parks, workers publicly asserted their rights as republican citizens. By any standard it was an extraordinary event, one that boded well for the election only three days away.[90]

Just ten hours later, the Tammany-Corrigan alliance unleashed a second assault on the George campaign that made the silencing of Fr. McGlynn pale by comparison. It also revealed the extent of their fears that, with two days to go before Election Day, George might actually win. In a carefully orchestrated charade, Joseph J. O'Donohue, a major Tammany leader, penned a letter to Monsignor Thomas S. Preston, Vicar-General of the New York Archdiocese, inquiring if it was true that the city's Catholic clergy supported George's candidacy and his radical social and political ideas. Preston, Archbishop Corrigan's right-hand man, obligingly wrote a blunt condemnation of George: "His principles [are] unsound and unsafe, and contrary to the teachings of the church. . . . His principles, logically carried out, would prove the ruin of the working-men he professes to befriend."[91]

Tammany immediately printed copies of Preston's letter and distributed them to tens of thousands of New York Catholics as they exited churches following morning Mass the day after the ULP's monster parade.[92] The letter's implication was completely obvious to all who read it: Catholics who voted for George on Election Day put their souls in peril, as they would be guilty of disobeying Church authority and embracing heretical doctrines.

The brazen ploy stung the George campaign, but there was simply no time to wallow in despair. With the election only two days away, George and his supporters worked tirelessly delivering speeches and making preparations to post signs, distribute ULP ballots, and staff polling sites with watchers to guard against the expected Tammany shenanigans. They also organized one last major rally for Election Day eve; Terence Powderly, Grand Master Workman of the Knights of Labor, was the featured speaker. Powderly, out of concern that many viewed labor politics as controversial (especially in the wake of the Haymarket bombing and trials), had originally decided to stay out of the George campaign. But when he learned that Tammany was planting rumors that he opposed George's run for mayor, he immediately headed for New York City "to refute the slanders." At Cooper Union he delivered a stirring endorsement of George and urged New Yorkers to get out the vote in an election bound to have an impact far beyond the borders of the city:

> You are not voting for the city of New York alone. The eyes of the . . . entire world . . . are turned to this city, in the hope that you people will redeem the name of the fair metropolis of the country from the disgrace that has been cast upon it. . . . You have nominated Henry George, and in doing so you have placed him not only before the city of New York, but before the world.[93]

The next day—November 2, 1886—New York went to the polls. The day of reckoning had finally arrived. The polls opened on at 6:00 a.m. and closed at 4:00 p.m. In the intervening ten hours, an army of ULP men and women worked to get out the vote, distribute ballots, and monitor polling sites. Some glitches did arise; a few polling sites were poorly monitored, and in some places labor party ballots were not available. And yet, by midday the word on the street told of an enormous outpouring of votes for Henry George.[94]

George himself spent the day in an open horse-drawn carriage, driving around the city. Seated next to him was the indefatigable Fr. McGlynn, riding, according to George, "in this silent way to show that a conscientious Catholic could and did support me." The spectacle was "a novelty in the history of the city," according to a *New York Star* editorialist outraged at so pedestrian a style of campaigning. But for George, this last gesture was designed to emphasize the populist and democratic appeal of the campaign and bolster support among wavering Catholic voters. Terence Powderly also appeared at polling sites with George.[95]

When the votes were finally counted, George polled a stunning 31 percent of the vote (68,110), a tally that put him well ahead of Republican Theodore Roosevelt (60,435). It was a landmark result: no labor candidate in the city's history had ever received more than a few thousand token votes. Victory, however, went to Hewitt, who pulled 41 percent (90,552 votes) of the vote.

At midnight, George conceded the election to Hewitt. He spoke before a disappointed but still hopeful crowd of four thousand supporters:

> The future, the future is ours. This is the Bunker Hill. We have been driven back as the Continental troops were from Bunker Hill. If they won no technical victory, they did win a victory that echoed around the world and still rings. They won a victory that made this Republic a reality, and, thank God, men of New York, we in this fight have won a victory that makes the true Republic of the future certain—certain in our time.[96]

ASSESSMENT

In seeking to make sense of Henry George's mayoral campaign, a number of essential questions arise. Most immediately, did Tammany steal the election from George? Nearly every biography of George and many memoirs of his associates, including those by Henry George Jr. and Louis F. Post, firmly assert that labor's great political effort fell victim to the wily ways of Tammany. By far the most colorful description comes from Charles Edward Russell in 1933, forty-seven years later: "When the last vote had been deposited that day, Henry George was elected mayor of New York. In the next three hours he was deprived of his victory by the simple process of manipulating the returns."[97] Because such accusations were published years, if not decades, after 1886, some historians have argued that they are largely apocryphal and that little hard evidence exists suggesting widespread fraud.[98]

Nonetheless, George certainly believed he had been, in the terminology of the day, "counted out," and he said as much several times immediately following the election. In his concession speech, he claimed that had there been a fair vote, "I would be elected mayor tonight." Four days later at a Cooper Union rally in his honor, he referred to "the influences that have given us nominal defeat" and called for "no whining and no repining." Two months later, he wrote to a friend that "on a square vote I would undoubt-edly have been elected."[99]

Tammany certainly had the reputation and proven capacity to steal the election. It was experienced in tilting electoral results in its favor. Further-more, the amount of fraud necessary to defeat George was relatively small—just 11,222 votes out of 219,097 cast (assuming most crossover Republicans voted for Hewitt over George). Put another way, Tammany needed to steal from George just 5.1 percent of the total vote to give Hewitt his 22,442 margin, or 468 ballots per assembly district (out of New York's twenty-four A.D.s) or fourteen votes per polling site (out of 812 total stations).

In the end, the lack of concrete evidence means the question of fraud in the mayoral election of 1886 will remain forever shrouded in mystery. A more compelling question regarding the results of the George campaign, given his staggering tally of 68,000 votes, is who voted for George and why? Any evaluation of the performance of George and the ULP, runs up against one immediate obstacle: in 1884, the city changed the boundaries of its electoral districts to match state assembly districts, thereby ending their longstanding correlation with census districts. As a result, detailed statistical information about the ethnic, social, and political breakdown of the vote is impossible to produce. Nonetheless, analyses of various indirect data when taken together do present a broad, informative portrait of voting behavior.

The election returns indicate that George succeeded in garnering sub-stantial ethnic working-class votes, particularly from Jewish, German, and second-generation Irish voters. For example, he won the heavily German and Jewish 10th and 14th A.D.s, and beat Tammany's Hewitt in the 8th (finishing second to Roosevelt). George also won in the 15th and 17th districts, which covered the heavily working-class Irish district of Hell's Kitchen along the Hudson River.[100]

Analysis of the vote based on class provides a more precise picture. Research by James Donnelly shows that cross-referencing voting data with housing density (as a rough measure of wealth) during the period corrobo-rates the finding of strong working-class support for George (see table 7.1). Three of four districts he won (10th, 14th, and 15th) averaged 27.8 people per dwelling (PPD) versus 18.52 citywide, and he finished second in every district averaging 30.0 or more. Overall, he won or finished second in every

TABLE 7.1   Electoral Results of the 1886 New York City
Mayoral Race

A.D.	George	Hewitt	Roosevelt
1st	2,031	2,728	984
2nd	1,682	4,072	879
3rd	1,619	3,810	1,573
4th	3,131	4,379	1,024
5th	1,705	3,432	1,365
6th	3,197	3,409	1,606
7th	1,274	3,052	3,790
8th	2,671	2,241	3,436
9th	2,416	3,405	3,143
10th	3,695	3,105	2,478
11th	707	2,060	2,977
12th	2,702	3,596	1,525
13th	2,158	2,830	3,677
14th	2,807	2,688	1,008
15th	4,207	3,828	2,311
16th	3,218	3,380	1,255
17th	4,620	3,872	3,435
18th	3,024	4,221	1,488
19th	3,635	4,992	4,142
20th	3,304	3,749	1,964
21st	850	3,470	3,937
22nd	5,970	6,498	3,658
23rd	4,992	7,294	5,799
24th	2,495	4,441	2,981
Total	68,110	90,552	60,435

Source: Louis F. Post and Fred C. Leubuscher, *Henry George's 1886 Campaign: An Account of the George-Hewitt Campaign in the New York Municipal Election of 1886* (1887; repr., Westport, Conn.: Hyperion Press, 1976), 156–68.

district averaging 27.0 PPD. The data also suggest George drew substantial support from middle-class voters, coming in first or second in six of seven A.D.'s with PPD of 17.0–26.0.[101]

Not surprisingly, Hewitt and Roosevelt split the votes of the very wealthy (districts with PPD density of 16.0 or lower).[102] A closer examination of the

30.0 PPD districts (e.g., the very poorest) shows the seemingly incongruous result of Hewitt winning every one of them.[103] His backing by the very poor, however, makes sense when one considers the extent these people were dependent upon the largess of the Tammany machine. As George had warned in *Progress and Poverty*, offers of immediate relief and assistance carried far greater weight to denizens of pestilential slums than the promise of future deliverance by radical social change.[104]

But if the majority of the poorest and most dependent New Yorkers withheld their support from George and the ULP, how do we explain the fact that George nonetheless finished second in many of these 30.0 PPD districts and won in the slightly better off working-class districts (PPD's between 26.0 and 30.0)? Generally, but especially in the case of the latter, the data suggest that working-class New Yorkers' traditional support for Tammany was due to a lack of a credible alternative. Tammany's long-standing policy of offering a psychologically comforting defense to ethnic groups against nativists and reformers made it popular among working-class New Yorkers. Its unrivaled access to jobs and unofficial forms of charity added to this appeal. Until another political movement arose to appeal directly to their needs as workers, they stood loyally by the organization that offered them *something* tangible in return for their support. The rise of the ULP, coupled with the vivid experience of state oppression to which Tammany raised no objection, offered workers the opportunity to bypass their machine patrons and seek empowerment through an agency of their own making. In a word, the George campaign, by providing an alternative source of political power, allowed workers to take Swinton's advice and extend to political activity something theretofore reserved for struggles with unresponsive employers: the boycott.[105]

These findings underscore both the strength and weakness of the George campaign. On the one hand, its appeal to working-class republicanism successfully convinced thousands of workers to break from Tammany and vote for their own man. On the other, a still greater number remained faithful to the machine. If George and the ULP hoped to definitively win in the future, they needed to make greater gains among these still-leery working-class voters.

Another factor not yet considered is the impact of religious authority on voters. How big a role did opposition from the Catholic clergy play in

George's defeat? Many of George's friends believed the Church was primarily to blame for Hewitt's victory. Poultney Bigelow, for example, wrote that George was winning the race until the Sunday before Election Day, when "from every pulpit came a soft whisper more potent on the Tuesday after than Moses on Mount Sinai."[106]

Some scholars have dismissed this clerical meddling as having had no meaningful influence on George's defeat.[107] But data from the election suggest that Catholic condemnation of George may have substantially influenced voter behavior, especially among Irish Catholics. George won a majority of the second-generation Irish vote, but Hewitt bested him in the contest for the first-generation Irish immigrants.[108] It is quite likely that these more recently arrived Irish voters were not only poorer than their second-generation counterparts (and hence more dependent on Tammany), but also more beholden to clerical authority. Ireland had recently experienced a "devotional revolution" that confirmed the centrality of the Catholic Church in Irish life.[109] Once in America, these first-generation Irish would be far less likely to defy the authority of their archbishop and support a third-party candidate. This was especially true for New York; the archdiocese led a similar devotional revolution in the United States and its archbishops enjoyed tremendous power and authority.

Nevertheless, despite Tammany's still strong hold on the city's politics, the election results revealed the great opportunities that lay before the ULP. George's 68,110 votes illustrated the strength of the oppositional movement culture that labor activists had been building since the early 1880s, and demonstrated the significant place of George and his radical republican vision within this culture. But the results also revealed the challenges facing the ULP. If they were to build upon their limited success in 1886, George and the ULP needed to overcome the political hegemony of Tammany and the religious hegemony of the Church. They also would have to garner and hold the votes of those without firmly established voting habits and political loyalties. Like Fiorello LaGuardia's insurgency more than four decades later, George would need to mobilize a mass of new voters—unnaturalized immigrants, recently arrived residents, and the politically inactive.[110] George and many in his camp also believed they would need to attract more middle-class voters.

The city's labor activists, aware of these opportunities and challenges, concerned themselves with the essential question: what next? What did they need to do to make sure the ULP insurgency was not merely a symbolic act of protest without any long-term significance? How could they ensure that it represented merely the first step in a profound political revolution to restore democracy and inaugurate radical economic reform? To do so they would have to build in the coming year a stronger, broader-based movement—one capable of transforming the city's heterogeneous body of workers into a united body committed to independent political action in the name of radical reform and restoration of a just republican order.

8

"Your Party Will Go Into Pieces"

No man has exercised so great an influence upon the labor movement of today as Henry George.

—Knights of Labor, January 15, 1887

"THE OPENING OF A NEW POLITICAL ERA"

Although they lost the big prize, the city's workers interpreted the astonishing tally of 68,110 votes against extreme odds and an active political machine working against them as a moral victory and maybe something more. "It was an unprecedented uprising of the working classes which shook this city," optimistically declared John Swinton. "It was a revolt that signifies the opening of a new political era." The election, he argued, raised the consciousness of the masses to the real source of their oppression, to the true meaning of democracy, to the full scope of their rights as citizens of a republic, and to the imperative of wielding the ballot to secure their salvation.

> They have been driven to this course as the only way of resisting the ceaseless usurpations of the plutocracy. They have been driven to it by the discovery that their only safety lies in this direction, and that if they are ever to make a stand in self-defense, they must use that all-powerful weapon which has been put into their hands by the constitution.[1]

Even the *New York Times*, generally hostile to the labor movement and Henry George in particular, argued that the ULP's sudden appearance on the political scene and extraordinary vote tally was "an event demanding the most serious attention and study." *Leslie's* concurred, contending that the election amounted to a call for fundamental change not simply in New York City, but nationwide. Godkin's *Nation* gloomily warned that "with the boycotting Socialistic and Anarchist vote, and the 'crank' vote, there is in our city affairs a danger which it will not do to joke about."[2]

These claims and concerns were no doubt heightened by the results of the other insurgent labor campaigns across the nation. Many succeeded in

"What Will They Do About It?" *New York Journal*, November 7, 1886, vol. 20 of the Henry George Scrap Books. Author's collection

"Uncle Sam (to Labor Party Representative)." *Frank Leslie's Weekly*, November 13, 1886.
Courtesy of the Georgia State University Library Digital Collections

electing mayors and representatives to state legislatures. Chicago's United
Labor Party, for example, polled twenty-five thousand votes (of 92,000
cast) and elected a state senator and seven state assemblymen. Its candidate
for Congress lost by just sixty-four votes. In Milwaukee, the People's Party
polled thirteen thousand votes, enough to elect the mayor, a state senator,

six state assemblymen, and one congressman. Many labor candidates, running as nominees of the mainstream parties, also won offices and seats that year, including Knights of Labor B. F. Shively and Martin Foran of Cleveland, who were elected as Democrats to Congress.[3]

The excitement generated by these results among supporters of radical reform even reached London, where Frederick Engels had been keeping an eye on the Great Upheaval. He sent his upbeat assessment in a letter to F. A. Sorge just after the 1886 mayoral campaign:

> The Henry George boom . . . was an epoch-making day. . . . The first great step of importance for every country newly entering into the movement is always the constitution of the workers as an independent political party, no matter how, so long as it is a distinct workers' party. And this step has been taken, much more rapidly than we had a right to expect, and that is the main thing. That the first program of this party is still confused and extremely deficient, that it has raised the banner of Henry George, these are unavoidable evils but also merely transitory ones. The masses must have time and opportunity to develop, and they can have the opportunity only when they have a movement of their own—no matter in what form so long as it is their own movement—in which they are driven further by their own mistakes and learn through their mistakes.[4]

Keen to build upon their "first great step," ULP activists wasted no time in establishing a permanent party organization. At a rally held in George's honor a week after the election, the ULP adopted a resolution denouncing the mainstream parties as out of touch and corrupt, proclaiming that:

> Since the Republican party has outlived the days of its usefulness, and the Democratic party has become but a corrupt machine . . . we hereby declare that the time has come for an organization which shall be in the true sense republican and in the true sense democratic—of a real party of the people, of a progressive democracy which shall revive and carry out the principles of Thomas Jefferson.

The address concluded with further resolutions establishing a temporary central committee to begin work on "the formal organization at the proper time of a National Party."[5]

By January 20, 1887, ULP delegates to a county convention had succeeded in ratifying a new party platform based on the 1886 platform, but with additions regarding electoral reform, women's suffrage, and currency reform. With an eye toward garnering the labor vote, the platform also included more explicit expressions of working-class republicanism. It upheld labor as "the creator of all wealth" and castigated the "perverse economic system which, on the one hand, deprives man of his birthright, and on the other robs the producer of a large share of the fruits of his labor." Offsetting this nod toward labor, however, was the more prominent presence within the platform of George's single tax plan, as well as the call to establish statewide "Land and Labor Clubs" to promote it.[6] For the moment, this apparent shift in emphasis raised few eyebrows.

Swinton and other ULP activists envisioned the party as one open to a wide range of ideological, political, and philosophical interests, all united under "fundamental principles" so as to include the maximum number of people of progressive ideas and good will committed to saving the republic from the monopolists. To them, George seemed the ideal future candidate. He had already demonstrated a remarkable ability to unite socialists, Land Leaguers, and trade unionists, as well as middle-class reformers, free traders, and liberal Christian clerics into a powerful progressive coalition under the ULP's banner. They now proposed to take this diverse movement national, with an ultimate goal captured in several stanzas from "The Future," a poem by labor poet Jack Plane that appeared in *John Swinton's Paper* two weeks after the election.[7]

> Keep your Unions intact,
> Fate will yet its gifts disgorge;
> Take to your hearts the coming fact,
> *We'll make a governor of George . . .*

> Lay this unction to your soul,
> Workers by the bench and forge;
> Fate will bend to our control,
> WE'LL MAKE A PRESIDENT OF GEORGE.

The creation of a permanent ULP was further cemented by George's new weekly newspaper, the *Standard*. With Louis F. Post as editor, the first issue rolled off the presses on January 8, 1887. In its "Salutatory," George wrote that the *Standard* would serve as "a focus for news and opinions relating to the great movement, now beginning, for the emancipation of labor by . . . the abolition of industrial slavery." It would also be an "advocate of a great party yet unnamed that is now beginning to form." If early signs were any indication, the paper looked to be a great success; the first issue went into three printings and sold nearly seventy-five thousand copies.[8]

By early spring 1887, the continued rise of Henry George and the ULP seemed assured. The party once limited to Manhattan now had organizations in many upstate counties, bolstered by dozens of Land and Labor Clubs. Swinton captured the optimistic mood, writing that the ULP's swift progress "has shown us that in spite of all differences and divisions it is possible to unite the political power of labor upon a platform confined to fundamental principles."[9] Looking ahead to the fall elections, the ULP leaders issued a call on May 5, 1887, for a state convention to be held in mid-August.[10]

George and the ULP also were heartened by the fact that labor's Republican and Democratic opponents gave every indication that they were chastened by their tangle with the ULP in 1886. Aware that substantial numbers of working-class party regulars had crossed over to the ULP in the mayoral election, Tammany and the other political organizations moved quickly to placate and regain the labor vote. New York District Attorney Randolph B. Martine dropped the charges against one remaining Theiss boycotter and also withdrew the indictments against the officers of the Empire Protective Association. "The working classes have saved themselves from this reign of terror by their vote on the 2nd instant," commented Swinton.[11]

More encouraging news came in January when, in his message to the New York state legislature, Democratic Governor David B. Hill admitted that George's 68,110 votes suggested "a growing discontent among the industrial classes." Hill urged lawmakers to enact "practical measures of relief" for labor. Before the legislature adjourned that session, it would enact a wide range of prolabor initiatives, including the establishment of the ten-hour workday for railroad workers, the Saturday half-holiday for all state workers, and Labor Day a state holiday. It also passed more stringent tenement house regulations and tougher laws regarding women's and child labor. Lawmakers also abolished ironclad contracts. Finally, it renewed the State Board of Arbitration for three more years and increased its powers; it then created eight additional state factory inspector positions, filled by the governor with prominent labor leaders.[12] This blitz of prolabor legislation by no means met the full demands of working-class New Yorkers, but there was no mistaking the fact that it was an unprecedented shift by the state government toward their cause.

Even the struggle between Fr. McGlynn and Archbishop Corrigan seemed to hold positive possibilities for the labor movement and the ULP in New York. The feud that simmered in secret for the last month of the election finally boiled over and became public shortly after the ballots were counted. Two weeks after the election, Corrigan issued a pastoral letter warning of the threat posed by the popularity of "certain unsound principles and theories which assail the rights of property" and violate Church teachings. Although he never mentioned George by name, there was no mistaking the real target of Corrigan's sharp pen. Days later, McGlynn, whose case was already pending before high authorities in Rome, gave a provocative interview in the *New York Tribune*. He criticized the Church's conservative approach to poverty and advocated George's "great panacea," the single tax. An enraged Corrigan extended McGlynn's suspension from priestly duties to January 1, 1887, and in the meantime sent a letter to Rome requesting prompt disciplinary action.[13] The Vatican responded in early December by ordering McGlynn to travel to Rome to explain himself. McGlynn, however, refused to obey and told Corrigan as much in a letter, citing health concerns (he had a heart condition, making long travel risky) and the fact that his ideas and teachings did not violate any Catholic tenets.[14] The priest's defiance only made Corrigan more determined than ever to see the rebel cleric severely disciplined, if not excommunicated, and George's works placed on the Church's Index of Forbidden Works. "Georgean economics are a civil disease bordering on madness," he wrote to Cardinal Simeoni in Rome. They had convinced McGlynn that "the savior of society is not our beloved [Pope] Leo but his friend George, pontiff of a democratic church without dominion or tiara."[15]

George, unaware of the perilous position of his works in the eyes of the Church, nonetheless understood this ecclesiastical conflict as one bearing profound implications for the course of radical reform in America and worldwide. Accordingly, he dedicated the first three issues of the *Standard* to a review of the McGlynn-Corrigan affair and his own vehement defense of the embattled priest. The suppression of McGlynn, charged George, did not stem from questions of theology, but rather from the priest's political activities on behalf of labor. McGlynn, he pointed out, had campaigned for Grover Cleveland in the 1884 presidential contest and incurred not so much as a raised eyebrow or a frown from his superiors, many of whom were tacitly allied with the Democratic Party. His support of George and the ULP, however, drew their instant condemnation and retaliation. George asserted that McGlynn was being punished "for taking the side of the working men against the system of injustice and spoliation. . . . His sin is in taking a side in politics which was opposed to the [political] rings that had the support of the Catholic hierarchy." George urged the members of St. Stephen's Parish to stand up to this "barefaced attempt to use the Catholic Church as a political machine" by withholding their weekly financial contributions—in other words, to launch a boycott of their very own place of worship. "Is it not time," George asked in the second issue of his paper, "that we should demand that American priests be released from the abuse of ecclesiastical authority which makes them political slaves?"[16]

On Saturday, January 15, the same day that the second issue of the *Standard* hit the newsstands with George's denunciations of clerical despotism, Corrigan installed one of his stalwarts, Monsignor Arthur Donnelly, as McGlynn's indefinite replacement at St. Stephen's. The rectory staff promptly quit in protest. The next morning, none of the ushers and only a few altar boys and choir members showed up for Sunday masses. Many of the parishioners who did attend services withheld their contributions to the collection plate.[17]

On Monday, January 17, more than seven thousand men and women gathered outside St. Stephen's to demonstrate their outrage at McGlynn's official removal as their pastor; inside, a committee of thirty five formalized their boycott of the parish and issued a series of resolutions that read:

> *Resolved*, That we, the parishioners of St. Stephen's church, abstain from any further support, pecuniary or otherwise, for the church of St. Stephen's while the Rev. Arthur J. Donnelly remains in the church; and,

> *Resolved*, That we pledge ourselves to refuse to *contribute* to the maintenance of the church while we are deprived of the administration of the Rev. Dr. Edward McGlynn.

Finally, they resolved to send a committee to the archbishop the next day.[18]

That same evening, in nearby Cooper Union, a mass rally in support of McGlynn took place under the auspices of the Central Labor Union and the United Labor Party. Numerous Catholic labor leaders spoke on behalf of the priest, often in language that mirrored that of McGlynn and George. No one denied clerical authority in religious matters, but they vehemently resisted the abusive use of such authority to suppress the individual political opinions and activities of Catholics. John Bealin, a man who had recently been blacklisted himself for his involvement in the George campaign, drew a clear parallel between abusive employers and an abusive Church hierarchy. "When men attempt to better their condition by organizing their trade they are blacklisted. . . . They are driven from the shop and the streetcar; and now we see a priest, the only one among the thousand who dare to speak the truth, struck *down* by his superiors."[19] By casting the issue in such terms, Bealin and others emphasized that the great majority of McGlynn's support came from people who interpreted the clerical conflict in terms of class, not religion. Accordingly, they encouraged the parishioners of St. Stephen's to boycott the parish.[20] Demonstrations continued on a nightly basis, and financial contributions to the debt-ridden church plummeted.

For his part, McGlynn remained silent but undaunted. Then, in March 1887, he broke the silence Corrigan had imposed on him and took the extraordinary step of founding the Anti-Poverty Society to provide himself with an alternative pulpit. Two weeks later, before a crowd of thousands at the Academy of Music, he gave what became his most famous speech, "The Cross of the New Crusade." In a compelling oratorical style, McGlynn called for joining Christian morality with secular reform to bring social justice to the suffering masses. No longer could Christianity be a faith concerned only with the next life. A true reading of the message of Christ, he argued, compelled one to act to improve conditions on earth. These themes in McGlynn's address (and subsequent ones) place him squarely within the tradition of the emerging Social Gospel movement.[21]

The Anti-Poverty Society was formally organized a few weeks later, with McGlynn as president and George serving as vice president. Weekly Sunday evening meetings began on May 1, and soon drew crowds of two to three thousand people; a majority of these attendees were Catholic, but there were sizable numbers of Protestants, Jews, and freethinkers as well. These revival-style meetings centered around a sermon-like lecture often delivered by McGlynn. Occasionally George and Rev. Hugh O. Pentecost, minister of an evangelical church in Newark, would be featured.[22] All of these addresses espoused the tenets of George's single tax and the moral argument that lay behind it, ideas captured in the Anti-Poverty Society's dedication to proclaiming "the truth that God has made ample provision for the need of all men during their residence upon earth, and that involuntary poverty is the result of human laws that allow individuals to claim as private property that which the Creator has provided for the use of all."[23]

The Anti-Poverty Society continued the trend begun by the progressive nationalists within the Land League at the beginning of the decade and carried on by George and the CLU through 1886—that of making social justice reform movements palatable to traditionally conservative Catholic first- and second-generation immigrants. McGlynn, said George, was a priest "who appeals to the love of God and the hope of heaven, not to make men submissive of social injustice which brings want and misery, but to urge them to the duty of sweeping away this injustice."[24]

The creation of the Anti-Poverty Society, with its explicit message of social justice and opposition to hierarchical authority, along with the radical agitation of the poor parishioners at St. Stephen's, were unprecedented events in the history of the archdiocese—indeed, in the entire history of the Catholic Church in America. What made the events especially notable was that fact that women, as they had in the Land League movement, the streetcar strikes, and the George campaign, comprised a large number of the protesters; some accounts even suggested they were a majority.

The New Crusade handbill distributed by the Anti-Poverty Society, 1887. Author's collection

Marguerite Moore, the former Ladies' Land League activist and Henry George supporter, spoke at several protest meetings. She urged resistance to Corrigan, especially in the form of withholding financial support, sharing her own experiences with the repressive Church hierarchy in Ireland. Given the power of prevailing Victorian ideals of proper conduct for women— ideals that were arguably even stronger in the American Catholic subculture—the involvement of so many women in the pro-McGlynn protests was extraordinary. They were out front and center, not exactly being submissive to male authority or confining themselves to the domestic sphere.[25]

The pro-McGlynn movement cheered those who viewed the Church, especially after its blatant meddling in the mayoral election, as a major obstacle to future working-class mobilization. Wage-earning Catholics supporting McGlynn appeared to be making a profound statement: they would not be forced to choose between their faith and work. They would and could remain good Catholics—after all, they were demanding the *reinstatement* of their pastor—while simultaneously affiliating with a secular movement aimed at bettering their earthly condition. If this brazen challenge to the received culture of conservative Catholicism was to succeed, untold numbers of working-class Catholics across the country might be emboldened to engage more fully in the surging labor movement of the mid-1880s. Perhaps then the ULP might not have to contend with the efforts of the dominating conservative clergy to sway working-class Catholics from voting for labor candidates in upcoming elections. McGlynn's antagonists within the archdiocese certainly recognized this implication: Corrigan forbade Catholics from attending the weekly Anti-Poverty Society meetings, even going so far as to deny two people Catholic burials due to their participation.[26]

With the creation of a permanent, statewide ULP and the continued resistance of McGlynn and his working-class Catholic supporters, the leaders of labor's mobilization had much to be optimistic about. George's prediction after the election that "it is not the end of the campaign, it is the beginning" seemed prescient. By the early spring of 1887, the road to working-class empowerment, the restoration of republican government, and the establishment of a more just economic system seemed wide open and free of any obstructions.

COMING APART

For every sign of hope that pointed to the dawning of a "new era" for American workers, however, more and more portents of impending trouble began to appear. Nowhere was this more apparent than within the ranks of organized labor, both locally and nationally. One such area of dispute and division was exemplified by the socialist-dominated District Assembly 49, the largest Knights organization in the New York area. Openly hostile to trade unionism, DA 49 had been at the center of the brutal struggle between two groups of cigar makers, the trade unionist Cigar Makers International Union (CMIU) and the socialist, anti-trade unionist Progressive Cigarmakers Union (as discussed in chapter 5). Negotiating a truce and an eventual merger of the two feuding organizations in July 1886 had been one of the Central Labor Union's most significant achievements.

But DA 49 refused to concede defeat in its struggle against the trade unionists. Outraged by the merger of the Progressives and the CMIU, DA 49 leaders declared war on *both* unions. It also attempted to destroy the CLU by thwarting an internal restructuring effort and by scuttling the 1886 Labor Day parade and celebration. Given its sheer size and numerous members, DA 49's declaration of war triggered fears among trade unionists of a wider anti-trade union movement within the CLU and Knights of Labor.[27]

Those fears soon were realized. DA 49 used its considerable influence to push the national Order to adopt a more hostile policy toward the trade unions. At the Knights of Labor General Assembly (held in October 1886 in Richmond, Virginia), DA 49 leaders used their experience and their sixty-one delegates to mold, direct, and control the agenda. After blocking the passage of fourteen measures favored by the trade unionists, they forced the approval of "Document 160," a sweeping anti-trade union measure that prohibited cigarmakers from belonging to the Knights if they were also members of their national trade union. As one Knight observed, the act was the culmination of the efforts by DA 49 and their allies "to bring on open warfare between the Order and the trades unions."[28]

Open warfare came, but not until after the George campaign finished in November. The actions of DA 49 at the Richmond convention convinced the emerging trade union leadership—P. J. McGuire, Adolph Strasser, and Samuel Gompers—to form their own, separate national federation of labor unions. Just a little over a month after George's defeat, delegates from twenty-five trade unions convened in Columbus, Ohio, to form the American Federation of Labor (AFL). While the ostensible goal of the new body was to further the trade union movement, its goals clearly indicated a determination to distance trade unions from the Knights of Labor, which they had come to see as increasingly hostile to their interests.[29]

In mid-December 1886, shortly after the founding of the AFL, DA 49 ordered its affiliated local assemblies to leave the CLU, a move they hoped would deal a fatal blow to the trade unions in the New York area. Next, as part of their strategy to gain control of the leadership of New York workers, DA 49 assumed control of a waterfront strike that New Jersey coal handlers and New York longshoremen had begun over wage reductions.[30] It initially convinced workers in numerous related occupations to stage sympathy strikes so that nearly thirty thousand men had walked out of their workplaces by late January 1887. But DA 49 stunned observers and union members alike only two weeks later by agreeing to end the strike in exchange for the restoration of the original wage rate, leaving these thousands of sympathy strikers in the lurch. Discredited among the rank and file, DA 49 soon began to hemorrhage its membership; by July 1887, its strength had plummeted to nearly half of what it was one year before.[31]

Though DA 49 failed to displace the CLU as the leading organization of New York workers, its departure from the body did change fundamentally the latter's character. It soon shifted from a federation of diverse organizations, skills, trades, ideologies, classes, and goals to one skewed toward the trade unions and their more moderate labor agenda. The same was true for Gompers's State Workingmen's Association, which also contained an influential Home Club faction. Emotions ran so high at the January 1887 assembly of delegates that a fight erupted between the trade unions and the Knights over credentials; enraged DA 49 Home Club member John Brophy leapt onto the stage and pointed a gun at Gompers. Calm eventually returned to the shaken assembly, but relations between the trades and the Knights were clearly worsening—not a positive sign for the future of the new political forces.[32]

Further signs of trouble within labor's ranks also appeared in mid-December 1886, this time in a proclamation by Terence Powderly, the

Knights Grand Master Workman. In his assessment of George's mayoral campaign, he praised the role played by the New York Knights assemblies in delivering much of the 68,110 vote tally as "a triumph unparalleled in our history." However, he reversed his decision of the past summer to sanction political action by Knights assemblies. Thenceforth, he declared, the Order would revert to its traditional policy of encouraging members to vote as politically independent individuals instead of as active Knights officially joined to any party. Powderly feared that independent labor politics, like strikes and boycotts, alienated labor's potential allies in government circles, the Catholic Church, the middle class, and sympathetic businesses.[33]

Leaders of trade unions likewise indicated that the AFL would soon go the way of the Knights to shun independent labor politics. John R. O'Donnell, ex-president of the Typographical Union No. 6, reflected this attitude when he called for a return to the "balance of power" strategy. He reasoned in an early December 1886 speech that "trades unions and politics do not mix." During the recent election, the Typos had been among George's most active supporters.[34]

Powderly's proclamation on independent labor politics heralded a wider campaign to expunge radicalism from the Order. Aghast at the vehemence of the red scare following Haymarket and the Great Uprising—a backlash that deemed nearly all labor organizations, especially the Knights of Labor, as hotbeds of socialism, anarchism, and bloody revolution—Powderly felt compelled to protect the Order by presenting it as a moderate, non-threatening, nonviolent institution. In December 1886, he ordered all local assemblies to cease raising funds for the legal defense of the Haymarket anarchists; in the winter and spring of 1887, he repeatedly denounced Knights-led strikes as irresponsible and damaging to the Order's wider reputation. In October 1887, he even refused to denounce the sham verdict brought down against the Haymarket anarchists. "Better that seven times seven men hang," he said, "than to hang a millstone of odium around the standard of the Order by affiliating in any way with this element of destruction." He also suspended dozens of local assemblies (fifty-one in Chicago alone) ostensibly for non-payment of dues; in truth, he wanted to prevent them from sending socialist delegates to the upcoming Knights national convention. Defections from the Knights accelerated all through

1887, with virtually every large urban district assembly losing half its membership and more than 2,600 local assemblies being suspended for failing to pay their dues. Powderly, unfazed, persisted in his policy, proclaiming that he preferred to have one hundred thousand moderate, thoughtful, patriotic men than have over one million radicals prone to strike over the slightest offense. "He is a true Knight of Labor who with one hand clutches anarchy by the throat and with the other strangles monopoly," he asserted.[35]

While the labor movement began to fracture both locally and nationally, the fortunes of the would-be new political forces suffered an additional blow. Working-class Catholics at St. Stephen's Parish had kept up their unprecedented defiance against Archbishop Corrigan, spurred on by rumors of an impending order of excommunication for McGlynn from Rome. "Nothing happening today in the United States," wrote Cuban nationalist Jose Marti from his exile in New York, "can compare in transcendence and interest to the struggle developing between the authorities of the Catholic Church and the Catholic people of New York." On June 18, 1887, McGlynn's supporters staged a protest parade in which some seventy-five thousand people marched. Two weeks later, as the boycott pressed on, an official of the Anti-Poverty Society mused, "I think they will have to excommunicate one or two besides Dr. McGlynn, they will have to excommunicate some millions of American Catholics."[36]

In the end, however, it took just one excommunication. On July 3, 1887, a cable arrived from Rome: McGlynn was excommunicated from the Church. For Catholics, there was no severer penalty than excommunication, prompting many who willingly had defied Monsignor Donnelly at St. Stephen's and had participated in Anti-Poverty Society meetings to reconsider their future course of action. Risking the wrath of a pastor or archbishop was one thing, but suffering the ultimate sanction in Church law—thereby forfeiting any chance of eternal salvation—was quite another. In the contest for the allegiance of working-class Catholics between progressive labor activists and conservative church officials, the latter had at last played its trump card. Unfortunately for labor and McGlynn, the hegemonic power of established religion could not be swept aside so easily. After an initial outburst of indignation over McGlynn's excommunication, the unprecedented organized defiance of clerical authority in support of McGlynn rapidly dwindled. The pews quietly filled up again at St. Stephen's Church. So too did the contributions to the collection plate. Any hope among radical activists that working-class Catholics were willing to place their class and political interests ahead of their religious loyalty had been sorely misplaced.[37]

There were exceptions, of course. The father of future radical Elizabeth Gurley Flynn, a strong supporter of McGlynn and George, left the Catholic Church for good after the excommunication. As Flynn later wrote, "Large numbers of Catholics, like my father, did not return to the fold. So it was partly on account of what happened to Fr. McGlynn that we were not brought up Catholic." Unlike Flynn's father, however, most of the city's Catholics did not share his convictions or possess his courage.[38]

Among these retreating Catholics was Patrick Ford. For nearly twenty years, he had published the most radical and most widely read newspaper among Irish immigrants and Irish Americans, the *Irish World and Industrial Liberator*. He had long promoted the works of Henry George, and he distinguished himself as an outspoken advocate of radical social reform in Ireland and America during the Land League movement. He had also touted the activism of McGlynn not simply for his radicalism, but also for the fact that McGlynn was a representative of an otherwise conservative Church. Now, in the aftermath of McGlynn's excommunication, Ford openly broke with George and McGlynn for what he regarded as their unwarranted anticlericalism. Thereafter, he spent the rest of his life retreating from radicalism. His newspaper no longer focused on "social questions" in Ireland and the United States, but moderate Irish nationalism.[39]

"THE LAMP OF THE UNITED LABOR PARTY WILL BE BUT A SMOLDERING WICK"

The final act in the dissolution of labor's would-be new political might came in the ULP campaign of 1887. Growing hostility among Henry George and his largely mugwump, middle-class, single-tax devotees toward key elements of the ULP's working-class constituency was the primary problem. The original ULP formed just the year before had consisted of

a similar mix of middle-class and working-class elements. The two nominating conventions for George attest to this fact. But the CLU's leadership in 1886 had been directly drawn from the ranks of labor—men like
Gompers, McGuire, Blissert, and Block. Over the course of the winter of
1887, as the party took permanent shape and looked to extend its influence
statewide (with national aspirations for the future), working-class leaders
found themselves struggling to maintain their voice within a party created
by them and for their interests. Only one of the ULP Central Committee's four officers—John McMackin—was a bona fide workingman.[40] Its
proposed constitution (written by George) contained some specific labor
demands (i.e., equal pay for women and preventing police interference on
behalf of corporate interests), but it was largely focused on electoral reform
and the implementation of George's single tax. The ULP's official call to the
August 1887 convention, also written by George, was even more revealing
in its shift away from specifically labor-related concerns. It spelled out the
need for the single tax, currency reform along the lines of the Greenbackers,
government ownership of natural monopolies such as the telegraph and
railroad, and electoral reform. In the one passage that actually addressed
the interests of workers, George wrote that in order "to do away with that
monstrous injustice which deprives producers of the fruits of their toil
while idlers grow rich," the ULP promised only "to change the existing system of taxation."[41]

As one socialist leader later commented, "The call for a state convention . . . proved to be a very skillful rhetorical evasion of the main issue
between capital and labor upon which organized labor stands. . . .
Mr. George for the first time took a serious interest in the party which he
had captured for his plans and policy."[42] The ULP's decision to establish
Land and Labor Clubs also suggested to some an effort to create parallel,
if not rival, institutions to individual labor unions, the original foundation
of the ULP.[43] Many found similar motives in George's establishment of
the *Standard,* which not only relentlessly preached his single tax doctrine,
but also diverted readers and advertisers away from struggling papers that
more consistently focused on working-class issues, such as *John Swinton's
Paper* and the *Leader.* To those committed to maintaining the ULP's focus
on labor and working-class issues, it was becoming increasingly clear that

George had begun "the work of side-tracking the movement from the whole issue of Labor to the one question of a single tax."[44]

More explicit evidence of George's sudden shift away from radicalism came in an essay he wrote for the July 1887 issue of the *North American Review*. In it, he called for the formation of a national party united behind the "vital question" introduced in the 1886 election. In contrast to his oft-stated assessment (as late as January 1887) that the election had been about "the abolition of industrial slavery," George now offered a new interpretation:

> In going into the municipal contest in New York last fall on the principle of abolishing taxation on improvements and putting taxes on land values irrespective of improvements, the united labor party . . . brought the labor question—or what is the same thing, the land question—into practical politics. And it is there to stay.[45]

Clearly, many within the ULP did not share this revisionist interpretation of the 1886 campaign. Indeed, as far back as late November 1886, John Swinton began to warn against drawing too close a link between the "new political forces" and the single tax.

> We did not support Mr. George's election because of his theory of taxation, as we explicitly stated during the campaign. The Central Labor Union did not nominate him because of that theory. The 68,000 votes of which we boast were not cast because of that theory. The theory constituted but a very small plank of the platform upon which he stood as a candidate. . . . Up to the day of the election we supported him because he was the representative of the general labor movement upon a platform which embraced nearly all its leading principles.[46]

The editors of the *Cigar Makers' Official Journal* offered even harsher criticism:

> Henry George's theory that the taxation of land values will relieve the work-people employed in factories, mines and mills of their present

misery and poverty is a snare and a delusion. No sensible trade unionist will take any stock in George's patent medicine. . . . No financial
scheme or novel plan of taxation will shorten hours of labor.[47]

Equally distressing to labor, George concluded his article by announcing
his intention to de-emphasize the new party's stress on labor. He asserted
that the ULP "will not be a labor party in any narrow sense, and in the
name which it will finally assume the word labor, if not dropped, will at
least be freed from narrow connotations." Many within the ULP rejected
this insinuation that their very serious goals constituted a "narrow" agenda
and they firmly opposed tampering with the party name. "In the word
'Labor,'" the editors of the *Leader* argued, "are crystallized the noblest aspirations, the grandest and broadest ideas of our century."[48]

Following this essay, the *Leader*, by now firmly in socialist control under
the editorial direction of the Russian-born socialist Serge Schevitsch, began
to openly take issue with George's overt attempts to transform the ULP
into a single tax party. For example, a June 28, 1887, editorial acknowledged George's contributions to the cause of the worker, but criticized
his single tax plan as impractical and praised instead the ideas of socialist
Lawrence Gronlund.[49]

Weeks of escalating discord culminated in early August when, less than
two weeks before the ULP state convention, McMackin and George moved
to purge the socialists from the party's ranks. On August 4, McMackin
announced that he would strictly enforce a rule in the ULP constitution
that forbade ULP members from holding membership in another political
party. That rule had long been understood to apply only to membership in
the *mainstream* parties, but McMackin and George, under the pretense of
avoiding factionalism, took a hardline position with an eye toward excluding the socialists, a great many of whom were also members of the Socialist
Labor Party.[50] George Block, head of the Bakers' Union and an enthusiastic George supporter in 1886, saw these planned expulsions as a movement
"to reduce the United Labor party to a middle class tax reform party. . . .
George begins to find fault with the word 'labor,' and is apparently using
the labor organization to further his pet scheme." Echoing the sentiments
of many outraged socialists, Block drew a parallel between their pending

expulsion from the ULP and another celebrated case of suppressed dissent—that of McGlynn. George, he asserted, was "anxious to have them excommunicated" for their contrary views.[51]

Where had this uncharacteristically intolerant attitude on the part of Henry George come from? Why was he now bent on reducing the influence of organized labor in general, and socialism in particular, within the ULP? While some of his contemporary critics claimed George had cynically hitched his single-tax wagon to the labor movement in order to ride it as far as he could before jumping off, there is little evidence to support such an explanation. Just because George saw in the mayoral campaign an opportunity to advance his single tax idea does not mean he acted solely from opportunistic motives. His long involvement with organized labor and oft-stated hope of starting his movement by reaching the working masses undermines such an argument.[52]

The answer to George's abrupt change of direction more accurately lies in his rethinking of his position *vis-à-vis* socialism in light of the events of 1886. The rhetorical and legal assault on the labor movement in the aftermath of the Haymarket bombing in Chicago and the bitterly contested boycotts and streetcar strikes in New York seems to have given George pause. So too did the reactionary efforts by the Catholic Church to suppress Fr. McGlynn. George also could not help but notice the zeal with which Hewitt and Roosevelt portrayed him as a socialist revolutionary bent on violently overthrowing republicanism and capitalism. Added to this was the fact that, one year earlier, economist Richard T. Ely devoted significant attention to him and his ideas in his book, *Recent American Socialism*; Ely specifically identified the "distinct services" George had rendered as helping to spread "the cause of socialism" among American workers.[53] Throughout his life and writing up to 1887, George had displayed a consistent toleration of socialists and an open admiration of their goals. Indeed, he wrote in *Progress and Poverty* in 1879 that the single tax would allow society to "realize the dream of socialism." A few years later in 1883, he wrote in *Social Problems* that "the natural progress of social development is unmistakably toward cooperation, or, if the word is preferred, toward socialism." His radical republicanism remained fundamentally opposed to the socialist contention that class conflict was intrinsic to a capitalist society, but he never condemned socialist ideology.

Yet this changed in 1887, apparently because he sensed a dramatic shift in public sentiment against socialism.[54]

George was not alone in reassessing his relationship with the various strands of Gilded Age radicalism in 1887. That same year, as noted earlier, Patrick Ford beat a hasty retreat after more than two decades of radical activism and journalism. Terence Powderly, head of the most radical labor movement in the nineteenth century and member of a secret revolutionary Irish nationalist organization (Clan na Gael), was making a similar retreat from radicalism, renouncing independent political action, denouncing strikes, and condemning the Haymarket anarchists. Much like Powderly, who told the Knights General Assembly in 1887 that anarchism "has tarnished the name of socialism and caused men to believe that socialism and anarchism were one," George appears to have come to a similar conclusion; socialism was tarnishing Georgism. Powderly in 1887 increasingly spoke of labor's need to earn the esteem of employers, respectable public opinion (e.g., the middle class), and the Catholic Church. While George remained defiant in regards to the Church, he and Powderly employed a similar calculus in the years following the Great Upheaval. Seeing business, the church, and the state collectively mobilized against radical working-class activism, they were determined to chart a new, safer course. Although George had benefited greatly from socialist support during his run for mayor of New York, he had come to see it as more of a liability than an asset.[55]

Also drawing away from any association with radicalism after 1886 was the young generation of "ethical economists," men like John Bates Clark, Richard T. Ely, and Henry Carter Adams. In the late 1870s and early 1880s, they had written effusively about socialism and the need for a greater role for the state in the economy. But after 1886, their superiors in the academy mobilized to rein in these upstart radical intellectuals. Threatened with firing or the denial of tenure, their enthusiasm for radicalism was noticeably checked.[56]

Given this repressive climate, George increasingly felt that the future of his movement lay in the middle class. In his own mind, he was not excluding the socialists so much as he was shifting the inclusive canopy of the ULP to the political center. While it left socialists outside the big tent, it welcomed the middle class as well as many workers of moderate ideological persuasion into the fold.[57] "The action taken by the [ULP] . . . was a step toward real unity," wrote George of McMackin's enforcement of the ban on dual party membership. "This decided action removes a cause of dissention and opens the party's doors to thousands of men in the labor movement who have held aloof simply because of their dislike for [socialist] ideas."[58]

But in order to disassociate himself from socialists, George had to do what he had never done before: publically condemn socialism itself. He did this relentlessly in the pages of the *Standard*, dismissing the "utter impracticability and essential childishness" of socialism and the delusional nature of its followers. "Either they must go out, or the majority must go out," continued George, "for it is certain that the majority of the men who constitute the United Labor Party do not propose to nationalize capital and are not in favor of the abolition of all private property in the 'instruments of production.'" Further, he disingenuously claimed that the socialists had demanded the ULP endorse "their peculiar theories as a condition of continuing to act with the party." But the socialists had made no such demands. In fact, they stated they would settle for the retention of the 1886 ULP platform upon which George had run.[59]

The ULP's dissolution became official at the party convention in Syracuse in August. Although embittered by George's sudden turn against them, socialists arrived at the convention hopeful that reconciliation and compromise were still possible. In recent weeks, both socialist papers, the *Leader* and *Volkszeitung*, had expressed displeasure with the situation, but refrained from lashing out at George and the ULP leadership.[60] They were immediately disappointed. Georgists packed the convention hall and upheld McMackin's declaration against dual membership as a means to expel members of the Socialistic Labor Party.[61] In the time allotted to the socialists to speak, Serge Schevitsch warned:

> I tell you that by doing what you are about to do you are ruining your party. . . . In the course of time the great movement of wage-workers will again evolve and take the upper hand, but for the present your party will go into pieces. . . . There were Socialist writers who criticized Henry George's theories, but the very life of a great idea is discussion and criticism.

Hugo Vogt asked perhaps the most poignant question of all: "Was the labor movement to be wrapped up in one person—Henry George—and no one else?"[62]

George rose to respond. He again repudiated not just the socialists, but the very idea of socialism. Sounding very much like Powderly, he argued that "the greatest danger that could befall this party would not be the separation of its elements—but would be a continuance within its ranks of incongruous elements" that would breed disunity. With compromise so forcefully ruled out, the socialists and their sympathizers walked out in protest, leaving behind an overwhelmingly a pro-George assembly.[63]

In short order, the body approved a party platform that included an explicit refutation of socialism:

We do not aim at securing any forced equality in the distribution of wealth. We do not propose that the state shall attempt to control production, conduct distribution, or in any wise interfere with the freedom of the individual to use his labor or capital in any way that may seem proper to him and will not interfere with the equal rights of others. Nor do we propose that the state shall take possession of land and either work it or rent it out.

What the ULP did propose was adoption of the single tax, the virtues of which the platform extolled in detail. The final paragraphs of the document included a call for legal, electoral, and currency reform. The platform gave only one sentence of support, almost begrudgingly, to traditional labor legislation in the areas of child labor, shorter work hours, convict labor, the penal code's conspiracy clause, and factory, mine, and tenement inspection. Capping this utter makeover of the ULP, the delegates nominated a slate of candidates, none of whom besides George (nominated for secretary of state, the highest office being contested that year) could claim to come from the ranks of labor.[64] Unmistakably, it had been George and not the socialists who sought to steer the party toward a narrow ideological agenda. In so doing, he irrevocably shattered the vibrant movement he had ridden to prominence less than a year before.[65]

George's reconstituted ULP soon encountered a series of setbacks that undermined its chances of victory. First, the socialists who were purged from the ULP formed the Progressive Labor Party and nominated rival candidates. The hastily assembled PLP would never threaten the ULP for supremacy at the polls, but their campaign highlighted the deep divisions within the ranks of labor—in stark contrast to the united front put up in 1886—and likely helped convince many working-class voters to turn back to the mainstream parties.[66] Then the ULP lost the Central Labor Union. The institution that gave birth to the ULP and played such an important role in the 1886 election had become so deeply divided over George's social-ist purge and dogmatic emphasis on the single tax that it voted to remain apolitical until after the election.[67]

Not long after, George and the ULP lost the support of another key ally from the previous year's campaign. Having already lost Patrick Ford, he now lost John Swinton, albeit for very different reasons. As a labor activist who passionately advocated the unity of all progressives into one powerful, prolabor movement, Swinton was sickened by the course taken by the man he once touted for mayor and of whom only one year earlier he commended "as true as steel. He embodies the aspirations of the masses." Swinton fol-lowed his schism with George by closing his newspaper, citing insufficient revenues and the depletion of his personal savings.[68] Whereas George relied the year before on editorial support from *John Swinton's Paper*, the *Irish World*, *Volkszeitung*, and *Leader*, he now found himself engaged in a cam-paign for state office with only the backing of his own *Standard*.[69]

The final blow to the ULP's prospects was delivered by George him-self. Back in January 1887, in just the second issue of the *Standard*, George weighed in on one of the leading labor issues of the day—the fate of the Haymarket anarchists. He staunchly condemned what he termed the "illegal convictions" of these men merely because they taught "unpopular doctrines."[70] Now in early October, one month before the election, George reversed his position entirely. Sounding very much like Powderly again, he published an editorial supporting the convictions. While he did call upon the governor of Illinois to commute the death sentences to life imprison-ment, his reasoning was that doing so would avoid creating martyrs to inspire new acts of anarchist violence.[71]

George's working-class supporters were utterly stupefied. In New York and across the nation, the labor press excoriated George as a turncoat and unprincipled politico. The *Chicago Labor Enquirer* published a widely circulated editorial recalling how on a Midwest lecture tour, only three months before, George told a July 4th rally in Cincinnati that the jailed anarchists could rely upon him "to do all in my power to set them free." Now, reported the paper, "the scholar and philanthropist is transformed into a seeker for office." Radical Emma Goldman echoed these sentiments when she later wrote, "Henry George, the social iconoclast, the lover of freedom and justice, had been slain by Henry George, the politician."[72]

The ULP campaign of 1887 therefore lacked the crucial characteristics that had so vividly distinguished the 1886 effort: the grassroots organizing, the unity of a diverse prolabor coalition, the voluntarism, the mass rallies at Cooper Union, the tailboard speeches in working-class neighborhoods, and the parades. Efforts by a few stalwart unions to galvanize organized labor and revive the spirit of 1886 failed. The ULP born in the Great Upheaval of 1886 was dead—no longer "united," hardly representative of "labor," and barely a "party" at all.

When Election Day finally came, the results were devastating. George polled just 72,281 votes statewide (7.1 percent of the total) versus 480,000 (47.5 percent) for the Democratic winner and 459,000 (45.4 percent) for the Republican runner-up. Most stunning was the news from New York City. George received a meager total of 37,316 votes, a total that paled in comparison to the 68,110 he received in 1886.[73] The hopes of many in 1887 that they would soon see the formation of a national labor party, with George nominated for president in 1888, were shattered.

As for the labor movement itself, its aspirations were similarly dashed. Far from constituting what Engels had termed a "first great step" in the political empowerment of the working class, the emergence of the ULP in 1886 had been a singular event. Its subsequent campaign in 1887 was a mere denouement marking the abrupt end of independent political action by labor in New York and in much of the nation for many years to come. Not until the early twentieth century would organized labor mount another meaningful political challenge.[74]

Although George sought to put a good face on the election results, telling his readers in the *Standard* that time would prove their struggles "a blessing in disguise," the contrast to the election of 1886 was far too stark to ignore. The election ended any ambitions that Henry George would be the one great figure who, by virtue of his spirited writing and tireless activism on behalf of American workers, would mold them into a new, powerful political force.

The Gilded Age witnessed an extraordinary period of working-class activism that saw workers formulate stronger critiques of laissez-faire capitalism and engage in unprecedented collective mobilization. But it peaked in 1886 and 1887 before diminishing in the face of a powerful combination of internal dissention, co-optive politics, conservative religion, government-sanctioned repression by employers, and economic depression. Internal dissention rocked and fractured organized labor at the leadership level and amid the rank and file. Henry George locally and Terence Powderly nationally renounced their earlier policies of tolerant inclusiveness and destroyed their organizations by purging radicals from their ranks. In addition, the struggle between trade and industrial unionism that raged at the national level in 1887 between the Knights of Labor and the nascent AFL reverberated in New York City; with the exit of unions representing unskilled labor, the pathbreaking Central Labor Union's coalition was shattered. After 1887, the CLU scaled back its activism and inclusiveness to focus on practical issues affecting its skilled trade union members. Nationally, the AFL adopted a similar strategy. Significant efforts to organize the ever-growing numbers of unskilled, largely immigrant wage earners, both in New York City and across the nation, would not resume in earnest for another twenty years.[75]

The hegemonic power of machine politics and established religion also limited the power of the labor movement after 1887. Fr. McGlynn's persecution sparked a momentary burst of protest among working-class Catholics, but his excommunication imposed an unofficial Church condemnation of all forms of radicalism. In New York City, where clerical authority was as strong as it was conservative, radicalism was diminished and discouraged among many working-class Catholics in the coming years.[76] Furthermore, the bitterness that clerical meddling engendered among non-Catholic workers, especially socialists, fostered acrimony within the labor movement for generations to come. Pope Leo XIII's issuing in 1891 of *Rerum Novarum*, an encyclical supportive of moderate social reform, including participation by Catholics in labor unions, did little to bridge those divisions. Nor did his lifting of Fr. McGlynn's excommunication in 1892.[77]

Co-optive politics both locally and nationally also played an important role in diminishing labor radicalism. In New York City, Tammany Hall moved quickly to defuse independent labor politics by co-opting key parts of the labor agenda (factory safety, tenement reform, etc.) while continuing to cater to ethno-cultural concerns by railing against nativism and temperance. The *Irish American* predicted as much in the days that followed the 1886 election:

> The large vote polled by Henry George was a surprise to many; but much of it was made up of those who will, hereafter, be found enrolled under the banners of the Democracy, from which they were, in this instance, led away by false hopes and ill-judged enthusiasm. We have seen the same thing in the "Granger" and "Greenback" craze; but sober second thought always showed these erring voters that their true interests were best cared for by the great Democratic party of the people.[78]

Vital to this reclaiming of the labor vote were the important lessons Tammany leaders learned from the 1886 campaign, which they subsequently adapted to future electoral strategy. For example, noting the popularity and effectiveness of the ULP's policy of establishing Henry George Clubs in storefront offices in every election district, Tammany ended its practice of using saloons as political club houses and instead established Tammany district offices throughout the city—a decision that made the organization appear more professional and open to the public. Working-class interests also gradually gained a more receptive hearing within Tammany in the late 1890s and early twentieth century, especially when progressives like Alfred E. Smith and Robert Wagner Sr. remade the political machine into an agent of moderate social reform. Third-party challenges, most notably by the Socialist Party, would appear periodically in the coming decades, but Tammany would dominate New York City politics until the 1930s. On the state and national levels, the Republican and Democratic parties likewise retained working-class voters by adopting a limited number of prolabor reforms to their agendas, such as workmen's compensation and eight-hour workday legislation, all while remaining overwhelmingly favorable to industrial interests and Wall Street. Eugene Debs and the Socialist Party would garner nearly one million votes in 1912 presidential election, but that amounted to a mere 6 percent of the total.[79]

In addition to internal woes, labor's collective mobilization after 1887 confronted an increasingly unified and resolute business community, both locally and nationally, that enjoyed unprecedented access to state power. Beginning in the 1890s, employers established numerous business associations, the most prominent being the National Association of Manufacturers, to lobby for pro-business legislation and, equally important, to stymie prolabor laws such as the eight-hour workday and the prohibition of child labor. They also imposed an unprecedented number of lockouts—Homestead being the most famous—assisted as ever by the protection of local police and state militia. But these business leaders, recognizing the reputational damage of relying upon deadly force by the police, militia, and federal troops, increasingly turned to the courts to protect their interests, securing injunctions from willing judges to crush strikes and boycotts. In this they were aided by the severe depression of 1893–1897, which put many capitalists out of business but also greatly limited the ability of workers to collectively resist.[80]

These post-1887 trends constitute the primary answers offered by many historians and political scientists to one of the most vigorously debated questions in American history: why did workers in the United States, in contrast with those in all other industrializing nations in Western Europe, not develop a long-lasting and viable socialist or labor party? But together these points only partly answer the question. They also divert our attention from the broader legacy of labor radicalism and Henry George in the Gilded Age.

AMERICAN RADICALISM, PROGRESSIVISM, AND THE LEGACY OF HENRY GEORGE

The rise and fall of Henry George, the Knights of Labor, and the United Labor Party in New York City reveal a great deal about the Gilded Age and the popular response to the revolutionary changes being brought about by industrialization. In the decade leading up to the Great Upheaval of the mid-1880s, American workers developed a distinct working-class republicanism and established new institutions such as the Knights of Labor. They developed an inclusive vision of solidarity that sought to organize workers regardless of skill, gender, ethnicity, and race. They challenged capitalist productive relations by attempting to democratize the workplace and develop cooperative ventures. To achieve their ends, they adopted militant tactics—frequent strikes and boycotts, sometimes on a massive scale—and called for a more activist state to check the power of capital. Finally, Gilded Age workers dreamed of a future society based on cooperation in which "wage slavery" was abolished.

This working-class republicanism, embraced by workers across the country in varying degrees and forms, became the basis of a thriving labor movement. Nowhere were these efforts more evident or more successful than in New York City, where the proliferation of Knights of Labor local assemblies and remnants of former Irish Land League branches led to the formation of the Central Labor Union. This ideologically inclusive local federation of unions—including trade unionists, socialists, and Knights—set the tone and pace of organized labor's revival in the city. The CLU organized unions, coordinated strikes and boycotts, educated workers, lobbied for labor legislation, staged parades, and promoted independent political action. By 1886, no other city in America could boast of a more unified and powerful labor movement. When an alarmed commercial and political elite responded with a legal crackdown on organized labor, it triggered the Great Upheaval, starting with mass strikes in early 1886 and climaxing in the Henry George's run for mayor as the nominee of the United Labor Party.

The fact that George and his ideas gained such currency among workers in the 1880s, to the point that they nominated him for mayor, explains a great deal about the essential character of the Great Upheaval in New York City and the nation as a whole. George was representative of his generation, one shaped and motivated by the era's conflicts and contradictions. Born in the latter years of the Age of Jackson into a lower-middle-class family, George was influenced from an early age by an evangelical Protestant tradition, a belief in individualism, a faith in upward mobility, and the idealistic zeal of the abolitionist movement and the Civil War. As he grew into early adulthood he, like so many of his contemporaries, confronted challenges to these ideals. Economic depressions, new technology, concentrations of capital and power, and many other obstacles arose to make the sure road to upward mobility and success seem less guaranteed. Throughout the 1860s and early 1870s, George struggled to "make it" as both his heart and political culture suggested he ought. Instead, he jumped from job to job and suffered humiliating poverty, agonizing self-doubt, and even thoughts of suicide. By the mid-1870s, George and many of his generation began to ask whether or not the promises of America's political and economic system were still true.

George reacted to the crisis by formulating his own radical republican solution in *Progress and Poverty*, a work that spoke directly to the concerns of working-class Americans in a language they readily understood. As a result, the book (and by extension, its author) gained a large following among workers because it promised to restore to them core republican promises such as democracy, equal opportunity, and citizenship. Like many progressive reformers and labor leaders in this period, George did not want the United States to return to some idyllic agrarian, pre-industrial past; his consistent calls for a return to the principles of Jefferson and Jackson were not calls for a return to a lost antebellum world. Rather, he felt the solution lay in reviving and updating the core elements of traditional American political economy such as free labor, upward mobility, entrepreneurship, and respect for the producer in the new industrial era. His vision of future industrial society accepted corporations, wage work, and new technology, but it also demanded that measures be taken to protect producers. By reining in the monopolist but not the capitalist, by eliminating the speculator but not investment and interest, by abolishing absolute private property rights in land but not freedom of use, George did not seek to overturn American society or its economy. Instead, he endeavored to cure its ills by ending its excesses and reversing its class stratification. His message enjoyed great appeal among Gilded Age labor radicals who similarly worked to fix rather than overthrow of the economic system to benefit the working classes.[81]

Nowhere in his model was there any room for the class consciousness and class conflict socialists described as inherent in a capitalist society. Indeed, the fundamental purpose behind George's program was the complete *cessation* of class conflict, an idea linked to traditional republican notions of a classless society. Labor and capital, wage earner and professional, employee and boss, George told his readers and listeners, they all had mutual interests and, more importantly, a mutual adversary: land monopoly (and, by extension, all monopoly of opportunity). All suffered at the hands of non-producing monopolists and speculators, and thus all shared an interest in seeing them eliminated. The only threat to the American republic that exceeded laissez-faire monopolism, according to George, was self-destructive class conflict. Monopoly insulated itself from interference by fostering class conflict between workers and employers. George dedicated himself, first in California and then in New York City, to the goal of awakening the masses to the existence of this sinister adversary and the means of defeating it. In short, he offered workers a radical corrective that promised to eliminate *both* the deleterious effects of monopoly and the self-defeating struggle between labor and capital in favor of a just social order. It would be brought about by a radical reform (the single tax) that abolished a foundational element of the capitalist market economy (absolute private property rights) and inverted a core principle of traditional republican political economy (the negative state).

Many workers in the Gilded Age were drawn to the appeal of class-conscious radicalism and socialism, yet as the events in New York City in the 1880s attest, a far larger body of laborers and their allies clung to the hope that a warped but essentially sound capitalist system could be fixed. They embraced varying forms of radicalism grounded in a not-quite-dead-yet republican tradition that stressed simultaneously democracy and equality as well as individualism (within limits) and respect for private property. No matter how radical the rhetoric and action, working-class activism in the United States largely took place within the traditional political sphere and focused on the struggle to define republican ideals such as liberty, equality, citizenship, and justice.[82] By no means did they deny that their interests as producers and wage earners were in sharp conflict with the interests of their capitalist employers. Nor did they reject the perception that the working and employing classes were in bitter and intensifying conflict. They did, however, resist the claim that this conflict was an irreversible and welcome prelude to a dramatic toppling of the capitalist order.

The Gilded Age marked an era when working-class Americans, antagonized by the crush of unfettered industrial capitalism, responded by building a movement that suggested a wide range of possibilities, including for some a future socialist society. But as the popularity of *Progress and Poverty* and George's subsequent immersion into the world of working-class activism demonstrates, it was a movement more fundamentally based on a radicalized republicanism. As such, it offered the vision of a more egalitarian industrial order brought about by a variety of radical means, ranging from producer cooperatives, to independent labor parties, to George's single tax system. By promising the renewal, not the overturning, of American society to meet both the wonders and dangers of modern industrial society, George provided an alternative vision to both laissez-faire capitalism on the one hand and revolutionary socialism on the other. He offered American workers the promise of justice and equal rights found in socialism, but with the individualism and opportunity for material success central to antebellum American political thought. The price of economic justice, political empowerment, and social equality, asserted George, was *not* a renunciation of the capitalist market. Rather, it was within that very system that one found the true source of social renewal. Thus, George appeared to many— both as an intellectual and as the leader of an insurgent movement—as a man who offered the hope that society's producers could be returned to their rightful place in the polity *without* revolution or class war. It was that hope that propelled George to prominence and ultimately served to limit the movement's radical potential.

Many historians looking at the American labor movement in the late 1880s have argued that were it not for the aforementioned crippling factors—internal dissention, co-optive politics, conservative religion, government sanctioned repression, and economic depression—American workers would have taken a less exceptionalist path. That is, they would have embraced socialism as the main ideology of the labor movement and established an enduring labor or socialist party like their Western European

counterparts.[83] The evidence from the experience in New York City, however, suggests that there were other factors beyond the aforementioned
ones that brought about the dissolution of the city's working-class political
activism after 1887. Indeed, it was the inherent limitations of working-class
radicalism—limitations exemplified by its elevation of Henry George—
that ultimately contributed to its demise. Instead of demonstrating the
strength of class consciousness and the potential for socialism to take firm
root in the United States, the rise of George and his central role in the Great
Upheaval in New York City underscore the enduring appeal of core ideals
associated with the republican tradition. George embodied the potential of
Gilded Age working-class radicalism to challenge the era's prevailing social
inequality and economic exploitation, going so far as to call for the abolition of absolute private property rights in land and the commitment to
the negative state, two of the dominant culture's cardinal principles. And
yet, with his reverence for the ideals of free labor, individual achievement,
upward mobility, and limited government, as well as his abhorrence of class
conflict and socialist revolution, George also embodied the limitations of
that same radical tradition.

But focusing on the "Why no socialism (or labor party) in America?"
question obscures the broader significance and the effects of Gilded Age
labor and farmer radicalism and of Henry George. In the face of the profound challenges wrought by the advent of industrial capitalism, American
political culture in the late nineteenth and early twentieth centuries shifted
dramatically away from a longstanding republican commitment to laissez-
faire economics, private property absolutism, and minimalist government
and toward a new vision of republican society that recast the state as the
vital *guarantor* of liberty and equality, rather than a threat to them. This
new ethos of progressivism placed a much greater value on protecting and
enhancing the common good and the rights of "the people" as opposed to
the rights of individuals. Private property rights were considered important, but not wholly sacrosanct. It envisioned the state not merely as a necessary evil to be kept as small and weak as possible, but rather as an essential,
neutral arbitrator between competing interests (most especially labor and
capital), as an agent of positive social change, and as a vital guarantor of

liberty and equality—all in the service of avoiding class conflict. Progressivism in the United States was a far cry from European socialism, but it also was a far cry from laissez-fairism and social Darwinism.[84]

Many individuals and organizations played a role in this transformation, but Henry George was certainly an early and influential figure. His masterwork, *Progress and Poverty*, was read by more Americans than any book on economics in the nation's history. In clear prose that combined strands of republicanism, evangelical Christianity, and economic theory, he outlined the fundamental problem posed by industrial capitalism—the increase of poverty and inequality amidst great wealth—and offered a compelling remedy: the single tax. The single tax movement garnered a large following, but far larger was the number of people—significantly, from both the working and middle classes—who came to embrace the essential, radical idea that lay at the heart of *Progress and Poverty*: the state must actively promote equal opportunity via market intervention and social reform to defend republican ideals and institutions in the face of a grasping, monopolizing capitalist system. Laissez-faire made sense in the eras of the Founders and Andrew Jackson, but in the subsequent age of industrial capitalism it threatened to destroy the republic. The Founders, argued George, were wise to fear state power in their day, but if they were alive in the Gilded Age they would have agreed that monopoly power posed an even greater threat. George's fundamental proposition (as opposed to his more specific single tax) that state authority must be brought to bear in the economic sphere to protect republican liberty, equality, and citizenship was by far his greatest and most enduring legacy.

Perhaps the most effective way to illustrate the broad and profound influence of Henry George on the emergence of social democracy or progressivism in the United States is to consider the number of progressive reformers influenced by his ideas. The list reads like a Who's Who of Progressive Era reformers, intellectuals, and writers. They include populist leaders Jerry "Sockless" Simpson[85] and Ignatius Donnelly;[86] leading socialists and anarchists Eugene Debs,[87] Laurence Gronlund,[88] Joseph Labadie,[89] Daniel DeLeon,[90] William Dwight Porter Bliss,[91] and Edward Bellamy; investigative journalists Lincoln Steffens,[92] Upton Sinclair,[93]

Ida Tarbell,[94] T. Thomas Fortune,[95] and Jacob A. Riis;[96] novelists Hamlin Garland[97] and William Dean Howells;[98] politicians and reformers Joseph Tumulty,[99] Tom L. Johnson,[100] Frederic C. Howe,[101] Newton D. Baker,[102] Samuel M. "Golden Rule" Jones,[103] Brand Whitlock,[104] William Simon U'Ren,[105] Lucius F. C. Garvin,[106] Peter Witt,[107] and Benjamin Marsh;[108] anti-poverty crusaders Florence Kelley[109] and Josephine Shaw Lowell;[110] liberal Christian clerics and early social gospel advocates Bishop Rev. Heber Newton,[111] Rev. John Augustine Ryan,[112] Rev. Hugh O. Pentecost,[113] and Rev. Walter Rauschenbusch;[114] intellectuals and scholars Charles Francis Adams,[115] John Dewey,[116] Frederick Jackson Turner,[117] Felix Adler,[118] and John R. Commons;[119] civil liberties pioneer Clarence Darrow,[120] and the inventor of the board game that came to be called Monopoly, Elizabeth Magie.[121] Internationally, George's ideas had a profound effect upon figures as far-flung and diverse as Leo Tolstoy,[122] Sun Yat Sen,[123] and George Bernard Shaw.[124] Only some of these reformers advocated the single tax. Most, in the words of Michael Kazin, "adapted his economic theories, crusading language, and fierce empathy with the working classes to different and broader purposes."[125]

One of the most perceptive assessments of Henry George's influence on several generations of American reformers comes from the historian Eric F. Goldman. Writing to a friend in 1954, two years after publishing *Rendezvous with Destiny: A History of Modern American Reform*, he recalled with wonder:

For some years prior to 1952 I was working on a history of American reform and over and over again my research ran into this fact: an enormous number of men and women, strikingly different people, men and women who were to lead 20th century America in a dozen fields of humane activity, wrote or told someone that their whole thinking had been redirected by reading *Progress and Poverty* in their formative years. In this respect no other book came anywhere near comparable influence, and I would like to add this word of tribute to a volume which magically catalyzed the best yearnings of our fathers and grandfathers.[126]

Even more succinctly, John Dewey declared of George's influence: "Henry George is one of the great names among the world's social philosophers. It would require less than the fingers of the two hands to enumerate those who, from Plato down, rank with him."[127]

Epilogue

The disastrous ULP campaign of 1887 marked the end of one phase of Henry George's public life and the dawning of another. For the next ten years, George focused on winning the hearts of the American middle class to his single tax program. Although the term never appeared in *Progress and Poverty* and was only used once or twice by George in passing until late 1887, it soon came to serve as the slogan of his movement. Apart from its simplicity, the term had the appeal, according to George, of dispelling the misapprehension that his plan involved socialist land confiscation. In the last issue of the *Standard* for 1887, George published an editorial entitled "Socialism vs. the Single Tax," signaling his complete acceptance of the term by that time.[1]

In 1888, George busied himself as the editor of his weekly paper, which by this time had begun to lose money. It only continued printing by virtue of donations from friends and supporters of the single tax cause. In the fall of that year, George and McGlynn parted bitterly: McGlynn remained loyal to the ULP, while George announced his support for Grover Cleveland in the coming election because of his free trade principles.[2] In a manner striking in its similarity to the purge of the socialists the year before, George and his supporters were expelled from the ULP. As much as

McGlynn was a resolute free trader, he absolutely could not bear the idea of supporting Cleveland, a candidate backed by Tammany Hall (and tangentially, Corrigan).[3]

Soon after Cleveland's defeat in November 1888, George set sail for England for the fourth time that decade. After a short stay of five weeks, speaking before enthusiastic audiences of land and tariff reformers (many of whom were avowed single taxers), George returned to the United States to lecture across the country on both the single tax and tariff reform. In March 1889, he once again returned to the British Isles, this time for an extended stay that lasted into the summer. Traveling throughout England, Scotland, and Ireland, George spoke before supportive crowds and met the leading figures in the European labor and land reform movements. The respect and support that greeted him at nearly every stop boosted his optimism and confidence regarding his movement's progress. The capping event of the trip came in June when he attended an international conference of land reformers in Paris. The body elected him honorary president and listened to him deliver the keynote address. When he returned to the United States in July, he found the single tax movement on this side of the Atlantic growing rapidly. By the end of 1889, the *Standard* announced that 131 Single Tax Clubs operated across the country.[4]

The following year continued to bring honors and accolades to Henry George from land reform advocates worldwide. Invitations poured in for him to visit and deliver lectures. The most exciting prospect was a request for him to travel to Australia and New Zealand. With handsome fees guaranteed and expenses paid, George leapt at the opportunity, setting sail in February 1890. There, he gave lectures and participated in debates. That June, he and his wife embarked on a long trip "around the world," touring parts of Asia, Africa, the Middle East, and Europe. They finally returned to New York City on September 1, 1890, just in time for George to attend the first annual national single tax convention at Cooper Union. He was welcomed as a conquering hero by over three thousand delegates who, in the course of the proceedings, established the Single Tax League to unify the individual clubs nationwide. George was gratified by the passionate reception, but made clear in his address that free trade had now become an equally important element of his reform agenda.[5]

After nearly two years of near constant travel, George handed over control of the *Standard* to a group of devoted single taxers and began writing another book, *The Science of Political Economy*. It was to be a summation of his philosophy of economics and morality. But soon other matters arose which captured his attention. The first centered on Pope Leo XIII's encyclical letter, *Rerum Novarum (On the Condition of Labor)*, published in May 1891. Its intent was to simultaneously affirm the importance of labor and the rights of workers while warning against the false promises and heretical teachings of radicalism. Since George believed, not without justification, that at least part of the letter was directed against his teachings, he responded by publishing *The Condition of Labor, An Open Letter to Pope Leo XIII* in October. In this small book, he argued that the fundamental underpinning of his teachings was the message of morality and justice taught by Christ.[6]

By this point in his career, George was extremely bitter toward what he termed the "political and corrupt machine" aspect of the Church. Bitter feelings had also sprung up toward Herbert Spencer, whom he considered an unprincipled turncoat for renouncing his earlier declarations in favor of radical land reform. George thus spent much of 1892 writing *A Perplexed Philosopher*, venting in its pages his ire against the British political economist.[7] Then in late December came astonishing news. "Something wonderful has happened on this side of the water," George wrote to Fr. Dawson. Officials in Rome reversed the order of excommunication against McGlynn. Although he and McGlynn remained estranged since their 1888 falling out, George took immense satisfaction that a cause he had championed for years—that of opposing clerical meddling in the political lives of Catholics—had now succeeded.[8]

Remarkably, George had withdrawn almost completely from the national single tax movement by 1892. Louis Post, Thomas Shearman, and others now supplied the energy and direction. Nonetheless, many still considered George the movement's central figure. At the National Single Tax Convention held in Chicago in early 1893, George addressed the delegates and was reunited with Fr. McGlynn for the first time since their separation. But these happy events were tarnished by an incident that indicated that the movement begun by George had now since passed him by. Delegates

approved, over George's vehement objections, a measure to remove statements in the organization's platform calling for public ownership of natural
monopolies like utilities, transportation, and telegraph communications.
For all his flight from radicalism since 1886, this act drew fire from George;
he viewed it as a sellout of a vital principle. Unsurprisingly, this was the last
Single Tax Conference George ever attended.[9]

For the next few years, George continued to work on *The Science of
Political Economy*. He and his wife opened their New York house as a kind
of salon for progressive-minded people to meet and talk. He also kept up
a vigorous correspondence with the international land reformers he had
met in his travels, a group that included Russian novelist Leo Tolstoy, who
expressed admiration for his ideas. At the same time, however, George's
health began to decline.[10]

As early as January 1897, despite his retreat from public activism, George
began to hear rumors that he again would be the nominee of a third party
for mayor of New York City. The city was in the grip of yet another massive corruption scandal involving Tammany officials and the police department,[11] and support was growing for an independent reform candidate.
George's doctors warned that a campaign would likely kill him, but he felt
duty-bound to accept such a nomination if offered. As he wrote to his wife
regarding the risky decision,

> The people want me; they say they have no one else on whom they can
> unite. It is more than a question of good government. If I enter the
> field it will be a question of natural rights. . . . New York will become
> the theatre of the world, and my success will plunge our cause into
> world politics.[12]

On the stage at Cooper Union on October 5, 1897, eleven years to the day
when he stood there with bundles of some 34,000 signatures piled before
him, George accepted the nomination of The Party of Thomas Jefferson, a
coalition of united reform groups. "I would not refuse if I died for it," he
told them, reflecting his awareness of his poor health.[13]

For the next three weeks, George ignored the advice of doctors and
friends and campaigned as if it were 1886 all over again, often delivering up

to five speeches a day. On the evening of October 28, 1897, five days before Election Day, George set out to deliver yet another five speeches. Weary and haggard, he only managed to deliver four, the last of which amounted to little more than a few rambling sentences. Fearing for his health, his wife and friends took him back to the Union Square Hotel for the night. In the early morning hours, his wife found him out of bed and delirious. When the doctor arrived, he saw immediately that George had suffered a severe stroke. Hours later, Henry George died, surrounded by his wife, sons, and close friends.[14]

Two days later, as the eulogies poured forth from across the nation and around the globe, George's body lay in state in Grand Central Station. Contemporaries attest that over a hundred thousand people walked past the coffin to pay their last respects, with still thousands more unable to gain entry. "Never for statesmen or soldier," remarked one paper, "was there so remarkable a demonstration of popular feeling." Indeed, the spectacle rivaled similar public viewings of Lincoln in 1865 and Grant in 1885. A funeral service was held in the great terminal later that evening, followed by a mass funeral march downtown along streets lined with thousands of mourners, past City Hall, and over the Brooklyn Bridge. On November 1, at a private service presided over by Rev. Heber Newton and Fr. Edward McGlynn, the body of Henry George was laid to rest in Green-Wood Cemetery.[15] On the following day, Election Day, the Party of Thomas Jefferson, now headed by Henry George Jr., still managed to poll 5 percent of the vote behind a victorious Tammany ticket.[16]

On a marble tombstone placed on his grave a short time after the funeral read the following words from George:

The truth that I have tried to make clear will not find easy acceptance. If that could be, it would have been accepted long ago. If that could be, it would never have been obscured. But it will find friends—those who toil for it; suffer for it; if need be, die for it. This is the power of truth.[17]

It was a fitting inscription. Ever since experiencing that mystical vision on the streets of New York City nearly thirty years before, George had dedicated his life, however imperfectly, to the cause of securing to all human beings their natural rights to equality, liberty, and opportunity, and in turn inspired and influenced many generations after him to strive toward that same goal.

Notes

More information and full-text documents can be found in the appendix, at http://www
.edwardtodonnell.com/books_and_writings_books_henrygeorge/primarysources/appendix
.html.

INTRODUCTION

1. *New York Times*, October 29, 1886, 2.
2. *John Swinton's Paper* (hereafter referred to as *JSP*), October 31, 1886, 1.
3. President Benjamin Harrison, *Inaugural Address* (speech, Washington, D.C., March 4, 1889).
4. Mark Twain and Charles Dudley Warner, *The Gilded Age: A Tale of Today* (Hartford: American Publishing, 1874); Walt Whitman, quoted in Alan Trachtenberg, *The Incorporation of America: Culture and Society in the Gilded Age* (New York: Hill & Wang, 1982), 70.
5. *New York Times*, July 23, 1877, 2.
6. Allan Pinkerton quoted in Heather Cox Richardson, *West From Appomattox: The Reconstruction of America After the Civil War* (New Haven, Conn.: Yale University Press, 2008), 164.
7. Henry George, *Progress and Poverty: An Inquiry into the Cause of Industrial Depressions and of Increase of Want with Increase of Wealth* (New York: D. Appleton, 1879), 9–10.
8. Leon Fink, "The Uses of Political Power: Toward a Theory of the Labor Movement in the Era of the Knights of Labor," in *Working-Class America: Essays on Labor, Community, and American Society*, eds. Michael H. Frisch and Daniel J. Walkowitz (Urbana: University of Illinois Press, 1983), 133; Leon Fink, *Workingmen's Democracy: The Knights of Labor and American Politics* (Urbana: University of Illinois Press, 1983), 26.
9. Richard T. Ely, *Recent American Socialism* (Baltimore: Johns Hopkins University Press, 1885), 19.
10. *JSP*, November 7, 1886, 1; Karl Marx and Frederick Engels, *Letters to Americans, 1848–1895: A Selection* (New York: International Publishers, 1953), 162–63.

11.   See, for example, David Remnick, ed., *The New Gilded Age: The "New Yorker" Looks at the Culture of Affluence* (New York: Modern Library, 2001); Michael McHugh, *The Second Gilded Age: The Great Reaction in the United States, 1973–2001* (Lanham, Md.: University Press of America, 2006); Paul Krugman, "The Death of Horatio Alger," *Nation*, January 5, 2004, http://www.thenation.com/article/death-horatio-alger; James Laxer, "Reflections on the Public Good in the New Gilded Age," *Queen's Quarterly* 106 (Spring 1999): 17–25.

12.   Larry M. Bartels, *Unequal Democracy: The Political Economy of the New Gilded Age* (Princeton, N.J.: Princeton University Press, 2010); David Grusky and Tamar Kricheli-Katz, eds., *The New Gilded Age: The Critical Inequality Debates of Our Time* (Stanford, Calif.: Stanford University Press, 2012); Katherine S. Newman and Elisabeth S. Jacobs, *Who Cares? Public Ambivalence and Government Activism from the New Deal to the Second Gilded Age* (Princeton, N.J.: Princeton University Press, 2010); Susan P. Crawford, *Captive Audience: The Telecom Industry and Monopoly Power in the New Gilded Age* (New Haven, Conn.: Yale University Press, 2013); Wendy Martin and Cecelia Tichi, eds., *Best of Times, Worst of Times: Contemporary American Short Stories from the New Gilded Age* (New York: New York University Press, 2011).

13.   Walter Licht, *Industrializing America: The Nineteenth Century* (Baltimore: Johns Hopkins University Press, 1995), 183.

14.   Edward N. Wolff, "Recent Trends in Household Wealth in the United States: Rising Debt and the Middle-Class Squeeze—An Update to 2007" (working paper, Levy Economics Institute of Bard College, Annandale-on-Hudson, New York, March 2010), http://www.levyinstitute.org/pubs /wp_589.pdf. See also G. William Domhoff, "Wealth, Income, and Power," Who Rules America?, table 4, http://www2.ucsc.edu/whorulesamerica/power/wealth.html.

15.   Daniel Boorstin quoted in David McCullough, "The Course of Human Events" (32nd Jefferson Lecture in the Humanities, Washington, D.C., May 15, 2003), http://www.neh.gov/about/awards /jefferson-lecture/david-mccullough-lecture.

1. "TO BE SOMETHING AND SOMEBODY IN THE WORLD"

1.   Charles A. Barker, *Henry George* (New York: Oxford University Press, 1955), 5–6; *The Complete Works of Henry George*, ed. Henry George Jr., vol. 9, *The Life of Henry George* (Garden City, N.Y.: Doubleday, Page, 1911), 1–6.

2.   Barker, *Henry George*, 3–4; George Jr., *Life of Henry George*, 1.

3.   Stuart M. Blumin, "Mobility in a Nineteenth-Century American City: Philadelphia, 1820–1860" (Ph.D. diss., University of Pennsylvania, 1968), 22; Licht, *Industrializing America*, 33–34; Jeffrey Sklansky, *The Soul's Economy: Market and Selfhood in American Thought, 1820–1920* (Chapel Hill: University of North Carolina Press, 2002), 114.

4.   For more on artisans and their work and training traditions, see Bruce Laurie, *Artisans into Workers: Labor in Nineteenth-Century America* (New York: Hill & Wang, 1989), 35–36; and Sean Wilentz, *Chants Democratic: New York City and the Rise of the American Working Class, 1788–1850* (New York: Oxford University Press, 1984), 23–60.

5.   In 1791, John Vallance opened his first engraving shop, Thackara & Vallance, in partnership with his wife's uncle, James Thackara. He later formed a second business in 1817 called Tanner Vallance Kearny & Co. Biographical information on Vallance was gathered from his obituaries in *Poulson's American Daily Advertiser*, June 16, 1823, and in the *Philadelphia City Directory* (1793).

6.   Kim Voss, *The Making of American Exceptionalism: The Knights of Labor and Class Formation in the Nineteenth Century* (Ithaca, N.Y.: Cornell University Press, 1993), 23–24; Laurie, *Artisans into Workers*, 44, 47, 57; Wilentz, *Chants Democratic*, 42–103; David Brody,

In Labor's Cause: Main Themes on the History of the American Worker (New York: Oxford University Press, 1993), 13–16.

7. Henry George, *Social Problems* (1883; repr., New York: Robert Schalkenbach Foundation, 1992), 35–36.

8. Ronald Schultz, "The Small-Producer Tradition and the Moral Origins of Artisan Radicalism in Philadelphia, 1720–1810," *Past and Present* 127 (May 1990): 84–116; Wilentz, *Chants Democtratic*, 93–94. "Sinews" quote from Howard B. Rock, *The New York City Artisan, 1789–1925* (Albany: State University of New York Press, 1989), 11.

9. Michael Les Benedict, "Laissez-Faire and Liberty: A Re-Evaluation of the Meaning and Origins of Laissez-Faire Constitutionalism," *Law and History Review* 3 (Fall 1985): 293–311; Martin Burke, *The Conundrum of Class: Public Discourse on the Social Order in America* (Chicago: University of Chicago Press, 1995), 68–96, 108; John Lauritz Larson, *The Market Revolution in America: Liberty, Ambition, and the Eclipse of the Common Good* (New York: Cambridge University Press, 2010), 104–12, 141; Daniel Rodgers, *Contested Truths: Keywords in American Politics Since Independence* (New York: Basic Books, 1987): 72–75; Christopher Tomlins, *The State and the Unions: Labor Relations, Law, and the Organized Labor Movement in America, 1880–1960* (New York: Cambridge University Press, 1985), 34–36; Voss, *Making of American Exceptionalism*, 34; Wilentz, *Chants Democtratic*, 148–53, 284–85, 302–3. *New York Journal of Commerce* quote from *Journal of Commerce from John R. Commons, et al.: Documentary History of American Industrial Society* (New York: Russell & Russell, 1958), 5:209.

10. Brody, *In Labor's Cause*, 3–42; Larson, *Market Revolution in America*, 104–12; Laurie, *Artisans into Workers*, 35–46; Licht, *Industrializing America*, 49–51; Voss, *Making of American Exceptionalism*, 23–24; Wilentz, *Chants Democratic*, 113.

11. Brody, *In Labor's Cause*, 44–48; Philip S. Foner, *History of the Labor Movement in the United States* (New York: International Publishers, 1955), 1:122–42; James L. Huston, *Securing the Fruits: The American Concept of Wealth Distribution, 1765–1900* (Baton Rouge: Louisiana State University Press, 1998), 260–72; Larson, *Market Revolution in America*, 104–12; Laurie, *Artisans into Workers*, 74–75, 80–91; Licht, *Industrializing America*, 51–57; Voss, *Making of American Exceptionalism*, 27–36; Wilentz, *Chants Democratic*, 57–58, 219–96; B. H. Moss, "Republican Socialism and the Making of the Working Class in Britain, France, and the United States," *Comparative Studies in Society and History* 35, no. 2 (April 1993), 390–413.

12. Vallance's obituary in *Poulson's American Daily Advertiser*, June 16, 1823.

13. George Jr., *Life of Henry George*, 1–4.

14. Bruce Laurie, *Working People of Philadelphia* (Philadelphia: Temple University Press, 1980), 20–21.

15. George Jr., *Life of Henry George*, 5; Laurie, *Working People*, 33–52. For more on the role of Christianity in the formation of middle-class values and culture, see Paul E. Johnson, *A Shopkeeper's Millennium: Society and Revivals in Rochester, New York, 1815–1837* (New York: Hill & Wang, 1978).

16. Barker, *Henry George*, 8–9. Evidence of the Georges' financial status is found in the following letters: Richard George to Henry George (hereafter referred to as HG), July 19, 1858, and Catherine George to HG, February 2, 1858, Henry George Papers (New York Public Library, hereafter referred to as HGP).

17. Barker, *Henry George*, 10–13; Rhoda Hellman, *Henry George Reconsidered* (New York: Carlton Press, 1987), 88–92.

18. For a vivid expression of George's evangelical millennialism, see HG to Jane George, September 15, 1861, excerpted in George Jr., *Life of Henry George*, 116–18.

19. Eric Foner, *The Story of American Freedom*, (New York: Norton, 1998), 65–68; Jonathan A. Glickstein, *American Exceptionalism, American Anxiety: Wages, Competition, and Degraded Labor in the Antebellum United States* (Charlottesville: University of Virginia Press, 2002), 60–142; Huston, *Securing the Fruits*, 66–69, 131, 184–91; Laurie, *Artisans into Workers*, 74–112. Abraham Lincoln quoted in Allen C. Guelzo, *Lincoln: A Very Short Introduction* (New York: Oxford University Press, 2009), 125–26.

20. Barker, *Henry George*, 13–15; George Jr., *Life of Henry George*, 6–9.

21. Barker, *Henry George*, 15–16; George Jr., *Life of Henry George*, 45–49.

22. HG to his parents, April 6 and 7, 1855, HGP; HG to Aunt Mary, April 9 and 10, 1855, HGP.

23. HG to his parents, June 14, 1856, HGP. The most important source of information regarding George's sea voyage is the sea journal he kept, as well as letters written to and by him during the trip. See especially the journal entries dated February 27, April 3, April 5, May 9, May 31, June 7, 1855, and December 11, 1861. Captain Miller also wrote an account of the voyage (found in HGP).

24. Barker, *Henry George*, 26; George Jr., *Life of Henry George*, 42. Henry George's diary (hereafter George Diary), May 17, 1879, HGP.

25. Barker, *Henry George*, 26–27; George Jr., *Life of Henry George*, 49–50. The rowdy activities of the Lawrence Society are described in the following letters: HG to B. F. Ely, September 30, 1857, HGP; Jo Jeffries to HG, January 4, 1858, HGP; Charles Walton to HG, July 29, 1863, HGP.

26. For George's plans to head West, see HG to Mrs. Rebecca D. Curry, April 3 and June 1, 1857; Mrs. Curry to HG, April 19, 1857; HG to Emma Curry, March 16 and June 29, 1857; Emma Curry to HG, April 19 and May 19, 1857; Florence Curry to HG, August 17, 1857, all HGP.

27. Barker, *Henry George*, 31–32; George Jr., *Life of Henry George*, 51–52. T. J. Jackson Lears, *Rebirth of a Nation: The Making of Modern America, 1877–1920* (New York: HarperCollins, 2009), 55–57; "Average pluck and energy" quote from the *Boston Globe*, cited in Richardson, *West From Appomattox*, 207; HG to Representative Thomas B. Florence, October 5, 1857, HGP; HG to Thomas Lattimore, October 10, 1857, HGP; HG to Captain Thornton A. Jenkins, November 23, 1857, HGP; HG to his Parents, January 7, 1858, HGP.

28. Barker, *Henry George*, 32.

29. Henry George, "Phrenological examination of head by self," ca. January 1858, in Diaries and Memoranda, 1855–1896, HGP. For full text of this document, see George Jr., *Life of Henry George*, 53–55.

30. George Jr., *Life of Henry George*, 69–82; HG to Mrs. Rebecca (Curry) Malthrop, June 29, 1858, HGP; Catherine George to HG, August 15 and September 18, 1858, HGP; Richard George to HG, September 18, 1858, HGP; HG to Caroline George, October 10, 1858, HGP.

31. Jo Jeffries to HG, May 19, 1858, and February 3, 1859, HGP.

32. Barker, *Henry George*, 43–44; George Jr., *Life of Henry George*, 83–84, 88–93; Licht, *Industrializing America*, 64–65.

33. George Jr., *Life of Henry George*, 95–96, 105, 112–13; Barker, *Henry George*, 44–54; HG to Catherine George, November 20, 1859; Catherine George to HG, May 20, 1861; Richard George to HG, June 10, 1861.

34. See the letters between George and his sisters dated April 10, August 19, and November, 1861. Barker, *Henry George*, 51–54, 57–59, 64, 108; George Jr., *Life of Henry George*, 109–25, 257–60. George's worries about his family's reaction to Annie's Catholicism are reflected in letters between him and his sister Jane George in September 1861. Annie George recalled the details of the courtship and marriage in a letter to George dated December 3, 1868, HGP.

35. Barker, *Henry George*, 58–62; George Jr., *Life of Henry George*, 126–41.

36. Barker, *Henry George*, 58–64; George Jr., *Life of Henry George*, 142–44.

37. George Diary, December 24, 1864, HGP; George Jr., *Life of Henry George*, 146; Barker, *Henry*

George, 64. For more on the nineteenth-century ideal of "rags to riches" and upward mobility available to all willing to work hard, see John G. Cawelti, *Apostles of the Self-Made Man: Changing Concepts of Success in America* (Chicago: University of Chicago Press, 1968), 101–64; and Paulette D. Kilmer, *The Fear of Sinking: The American Success Formula in the Gilded Age* (Knoxville: University of Tennessee Press, 1996), 1–21.

38. Barker, *Henry George*, 64–69; George Jr., *Life of Henry George*, 148–49.

39. Barker, *Henry George*, 62–64; George Jr., *Life of Henry George*, 149.

40. George Diary, February 17, 1865, HGP.

41. George Diary, March 25, 1865, HGP; *Journal of the Trades and Workmen* 25 (March–April 1865), copy in HGSB, vol. 25; Barker, *Henry George*, 66–67; George Jr., *Life of Henry George*, 154–59.

42. Barker, *Henry George*, 75–79; George Jr., *Life of Henry George*, 167–75.

43. *San Francisco Alta*, August 8, 1867; *San Francisco Daily Times*, August 9, 1967; Barker, *Henry George*, 97.

44. *San Francisco Daily Times*, July 4, 1868; Barker, *Henry George*, 102.

45. For a vivid depiction of this problem, see George Fox Kelly's pamphlet, *Land Frauds of California: Startling Exposures. Government Officials Implicated. Appeals for Justice—The Present Crisis* (1864).

46. See John S. Hittell, *The Resources of California Comprising Agriculture, Mining, Geography, Climate, Commerce, etc., etc., and the Past and Future Development of the State* (San Francisco: A. Roman, 1863); and Titus Fey Cronise, *The Natural Wealth of California* (San Francisco: H. H. Bancroft, 1868).

47. Barker, *Henry George*, 89–95. For more on San Francisco's pueblo lands controversy, see Christian G. Fritz, "Politics and the Courts: The Struggle Over Land in San Francisco 1846–1866," *Santa Clara Law Review* 26 (1986): 127–64; and Peter L. Reich, "Dismantling the Pueblo: Hispanic Municipal Land Rights in California Since 1850," *American Journal of Legal History* 45, no. 4 (October 2001): 353–70.

48. Henry George, "What the Railroad Will Bring Us," *Overland Monthly* 1, no. 4 (October 1868): 302; Barker, *Henry George*, 102–4; George Jr., *Life of Henry George*, 176–79; Trachtenberg, *Incorporation of America*, 57.

49. Barker, *Henry George*, 105–6, 108–10; George Jr., *Life of Henry George*, 180.

50. Barker, *Henry George*, 110, 113–20, 124; George Jr., *Life of Henry George*, 180–87; HG to Nugent and HG to Charles A. Sumner, January 14–April 29, 1969, HGP; Maury Klein, *The Genesis of Industrial America, 1870–1920* (New York: Cambridge University Press, 2007), 132. See also Oliver Gramling, *AP: The Story of the News* (New York: Farrar and Rinehart, 1940), 64–78; and Menahem Blondheim, *News Over the Wires: The Telegraph and the Flow of Public Information in America, 1844–1897* (Cambridge, Mass.: Harvard University Press, 1994), 96–168.

51. Barker, *Henry George*, 121–22; HG to Fr. Thomas Dawson, February 1, 1883, HGP.

52. Louis F. Post and Fred C. Leubuscher, *Henry George's 1886 Campaign: An Account of the George-Hewitt Campaign in the New York Municipal Election of 1886* (1887; repr., Westport, Conn.: Hyperion Press, 1976), 28–29. See also George's recollections of his time in New York in an August 29, 1893, speech before the Chicago Art Institute, HGP.

53. HG to Sumner, Hanson, Sinclair, and Caroline George, May–August, 1869; Barker, *Henry George*, 125–27; *San Francisco Monitor*, August 14, 1869; August 21, 1869; and September 11, 1869.

54. Henry George, "The Chinese on the Pacific Coast," *New York Tribune*, May 1, 1869; Henry George, "The Kearney Agitation in California," *Popular Science Monthly* 17 (August 1880), 433–37; George, *Progress and Poverty*, 498–99, 503–4; Rosanne Currarino, *The Labor Question: Economic Democracy in the Gilded Age* (Urbana: University of Illinois Press, 2011), 36–59, 170n77; Michael

Kazin, *The Populist Persuasion: An American History* (New York: Basic Books, 1995), 36; R. Jeffrey Lustig, *Corporate Liberalism: The Origins of Modern American Political Theory, 1890–1920* (Berkeley: University of California Press, 1983), 72, 76n56. For a collection of George's anti-Chinese writings, see *Henry George: Collected Journalistic Writings*, ed. Kenneth C. Wenzer, vol. 1, *The Early Years, 1860–1879* (Armonk, N.Y.: M. E. Sharpe, 2003), 161–81.

55.   Barker, *Henry George*, 136; George Jr., *Life of Henry George*, 208–10.

56.   Barker, *Henry George*, 138–45.

57.   Annie George to HG, April 2, 1870, HGP; Barker, *Henry George*, 138; George Jr., *Life of Henry George*, 211–13.

58.   Barker, *Henry George*, 139–45; George Jr., *Life of Henry George*, 211–16. For George's later accounts of the Central Pacific duplicity, see his columns in the *San Francisco Post*, January 14, 1873, and the *San Francisco State*, April 5, 1879.

59.   Henry George, *The Subsidy Question and the Democratic Party* (San Francisco, 1871); Huston, *Securing the Fruits*, 255–58.

60.   Henry George, *Our Land and Land Policy* (1871), reprinted in *The Complete Works of Henry George*, ed. Henry George Jr., vol. 8, *Our Land and Land Policy* (Garden City, N.Y.: Doubleday, Page, 1911), 1–131; Foner, *Story of American Freedom*, 9, 20–21, 32, 62–63, 113, 143; Huston, *Securing the Fruits*, 292–94; Laurie, *Artisans into Workers*, 67–68, 99–100. As past biographers have noted, scholars have almost no evidence as to what books George was reading in this period or which of them may have influenced the evolution of his ideas. See Barker, *Henry George*, 83.

61.   George, *Our Land and Land Policy*, 85, 97.

62.   Barker, *Henry George*, 146–54, 160; George, *Our Land and Land Policy*, 98–131; George Jr., *Life of Henry George*, 219–35.

63.   Barker, *Henry George*, 156–57; Henry George, "Bribery in Elections," *Overland Monthly* 7 (December 1871): 497–504.

64.   Barker, *Henry George*, 157–58, 161; George Jr., *Life of Henry George*, 236–37. Annie George's illness is described in her letters during the fall of 1871 through the summer of 1872.

65.   *San Francisco Daily Post*, December 4, 1871.

66.   Barker, *Henry George*, 161–63, 167.

67.   George's experiences at the convention are detailed in the *San Francisco Daily Post*, June 10, 11, and 12, 1872.

68.   Barker, *Henry George*, 170.

69.   Barker, *Henry George*, 165–67; George Jr., *Life of Henry George*, 237–40. For notices of *San Francisco Daily Post*'s success, see December 30, 1871; January 9, 1872; January 10, 1872; December 11, 1872; and November 29, 1873.

70.   Barker, *Henry George*, 174–75.

71.   Ibid., 197–202, 214.

72.   Ibid., 177–79.

73.   For examples of this coverage, see *San Francisco Daily Post*, December 6, 1781; December 16, 1871; June 3, 1875.

74.   Barker, *Henry George*, 183–84, 194–95. *San Francisco Daily Post*, January 2, 1873.

75.   George Jr., *Life of Henry George*, 252. For more on the intertwining of Christianity and reform, see Hugh McLeod, *Piety and Poverty: Working-Class Religion in Berlin, London, and New York, 1870–1914* (New York: Holmes & Meyer, 1996).

76.   *San Francisco Daily Post*, July 4, 1874; Barker, *Henry George*, 207–10.

77.   Throughout this book, I characterize George as a radical. By "radical," I mean one who advocates for dramatic social, economic, and political reforms that depart in fundamental ways from commonly

accepted norms. In George's case, his radicalism was centered on two such departures: his call for an end to the traditional definition of private property in land and for an empowered state to guarantee republican liberties. For more on the history of American radicalism, see Mari Jo Buhle, Paul Buhle, and Harvey J. Kaye, eds., *The American Radical* (New York: Routledge, 1994); and Michael Kazin, *American Dreamers: How the Left Changed a Nation* (New York: Knopf, 2011).

78. Sidney Fine, *Laissez-Faire and the General-Welfare State: A Study of Conflict in American Thought, 1865–1901* (Ann Arbor: University of Michigan Press, 1956), 3–25; Foner, *Story of American Freedom*, 54–55; Huston, *Securing the Fruits* 70, 79–80, 134, 150, 292–94.

2. "POVERTY ENSLAVES MEN WE BOAST ARE POLITICAL SOVEREIGNS": *PROGRESS AND POVERTY* AND HENRY GEORGE'S REPUBLICANISM

1. Barker, *Henry George*, 66, 72, 169–70; George Jr., *Life of Henry George*, 250–61; George Diary, February–March 1875, HGP.

2. Barker, *Henry George*, 223–27.

3. Samuel Bernstein, "American Labor in the Long Depression, 1873–1877," *Science and Society* 20 (Winter 1956): 60–82; Rendigs Fels, *American Business Cycles, 1865–1897* (Chapel Hill: University of North Carolina Press, 1959), 99–101; Klein, *Genesis of Industrial America*, 124; Samuel Rezneck, "Distress, Relief, and Discontent in the United States During the Depression of 1873–1877," *Journal of Political Economy* 58 (December 1950): 495–97.

4. Barker, *Henry George*, 223–27; George Jr., *Life of Henry George*, 247–49. HG to John Swinton, October 6, November 28, and December 27, 1875, HGP; HG to Charles Nordhoff, January 31, 1880, HGP.

5. Klein, *Genesis of Industrial America*, 124; Richard Schneirov, "Thoughts on Periodizing the Gilded Age: Capital Accumulation, Society, and Politics, 1873–1898," *JGAPE* 5 (July 2006): 189–224.

6. Huston, *Securing the Fruits*, 144–46, 348–49; Klein, *Genesis of Industrial America*, 48; Tomlins, *The State and the Unions*, 10–31; Trachtenberg, *Incorporation of America*, 54–56, 68–69; Voss, *Making of American Exceptionalism*, 53–56.

7. Philip S. Foner, *The Great Labor Uprising of 1877* (New York: Monad Press, 1977), 17; Foner, *History of the Labor Movement*, 1:440.

8. For the best account to date on the Molly Maguires, see Kevin Kenny, *Making Sense of the Molly Maguires* (New York: Oxford University Press, 1998).

9. Jerry M. Cooper, "The Army as Strikebreaker—The Railroad Strikes of 1877 and 1894," *Labor History* 18, no. 2 (Spring 1977): 181–96; Foner, *Great Labor Uprising*, 47–48, 63–64, 76, 90; David O. Stowell, *Streets, Railroads, and the Great Strike of 1877* (Chicago: University of Chicago Press, 1999), 70–115.

10. Douglas C. Rossinow, *Visions of Progress: The Left-Liberal Tradition in America* (Philadelphia: University of Pennsylvania Press, 2008), 16; Daniel Rodgers, *Atlantic Crossings: Social Politics in a Progressive Age* (Cambridge, Mass.: Harvard University Press, 1998), 35; Samuel P. Hays, *The Response to Industrialism, 1885–1914* (Chicago: University of Chicago Press, 1957), 107.

11. Burke, *Conundrum of Class*, 134; Alan Dawley, *Struggles for Justice: Social Responsibility and the Liberal State* (Cambridge, Mass.: Harvard University Press, 1991), 26; Huston, *Securing the Fruits*, 344–48; Christopher Lasch, *The True and Only Heaven: Progress and Its Critics* (New York: Norton, 1991), 64; Laurie, *Artisans into Workers*, 49–50; Rossinow, *Visions of Progress*, 16–17.

12. Lears, *Rebirth of a Nation*, 79; Rossinow, *Visions of Progress*, 17.

13. President James A. Garfield, *Inaugural Address*, (speech, Washington, D.C., March 4, 1881).

14. Foner, *Great Labor Uprising*, 82. Eugene E. Leach, "Chaining the Tiger: The Mob Stigma and the Working Class, 1863–1894," *Labor History* 35, no. 2 (1994): 187–215; Troy Rondinone, "'History Repeats Itself': The Civil War and the Meaning of Labor Conflict in the Late Nineteenth Century," *American Quarterly* 59, no. 2 (2007) 397–419. John Hay quoted in Lears, *Rebirth of a Nation*, 80–81.

15. Foner, *Story of American Freedom*, 119–20; Huston, *Securing the Fruits*, 295, 341–42; Klein, *Genesis of Industrial America*, 132; Trachtenberg, *Incorporation of America*, 87; Fine, *Laissez-Faire*, 96–125; Rodgers, *Atlantic Crossings*, 78–79.

16. Robert C. Bannister, *Social Darwinism: Science and Myth in Anglo-American Social Thought* (Philadelphia: Temple University Press, 1979), 57–136; Fine, *Laissez-Faire*, 43–46, 82–85, 97–102, 113–14; David Nasaw, "Gilded Age Gospels," in *Ruling America: A History of Wealth and Power in a Democracy*, eds. Steve Fraser and Gary Gerstle (Cambridge, Mass.: Harvard University Press, 2005), 127–33, 144–45. George condemns social Darwinism as a "comfortable theory" in *Social Problems*, 49.

17. Sven Beckert, *The Monied Metropolis: New York City and the Consolidation of the American Bourgeoisie, 1850–1896* (New York: Cambridge University Press, 2001), 215–19; Richardson, *West From Appomattox*, 194–95, 346–47; Nancy Cohen, *The Reconstruction of American Liberalism, 1865–1914* (Chapel Hill: University of North Carolina Press, 2002), 126–28.

18. Beckert, *Monied Metropolis*, 288; Richard Franklin Bensel, *Yankee Leviathan: The Origins of Central State Authority in America, 1859–1877* (New York: Cambridge University Press, 1990), 422; Nasaw, "Gilded Age Gospels," 124; William J. Novak, *The People's Welfare: Law and Regulation in Nineteenth-Century America* (Chapel Hill: University of North Carolina Press, 1996), 235–48; Richardson, *West From Appomattox*, 2; Rossinow, *Visions of Progress*, 16.

19. Beckert, *Monied Metropolis*, 232–36; Huston, *Securing the Fruits*, 148; Nasaw, "Gilded Age Gospels," 136; Rondinone, "'History Repeats Itself,'" 397–419. See also Larry Isaac, "To Counter 'The Very Devil' and More: The Making of Independent Capitalist Militia in the Gilded Age," *American Journal of Sociology* 108, no. 2 (September 2002): 353–405. The quote from the New York City-based *Independent* cited in Foner, *Great Labor Uprising*, 192.

20. Burke, *Conundrum of Class*, 133–39; Lears, *Rebirth of a Nation*, 81; Heather Cox Richardson, *The Death of Reconstruction: Race, Labor, and Politics in the Post–Civil War North, 1865–1901* (Cambridge, Mass.: Harvard University Press, 2001), 185–86; Allan Pinkerton quoted in Richardson, *West From Appomattox*, 164.

21. Roger R. Olmsted, "The Chinese Must Go!," *California Historical Quarterly* 50, no. 3 (1971): 285–94. For more on anti-Chinese sentiment, see Alexander Saxton, *The Indispensible Enemy: Labor and the Anti-Chinese Movement in California* (Berkeley: University of California Press, 1971).

22. Barker, *Henry George*, 223–27; George Jr., *Life of Henry George*, 247–49; HG to Charles Nordhoff, January 31, 1880, HGP.

23. George Diary, September 1877, HGP; George, *Progress and Poverty*, 557.

24. Barker, *Henry George*, 251–52.

25. Ibid., 268; Cohen, *Reconstruction of American Liberalism*, 143.

26. George, *Progress and Poverty*, 4.

27. Ibid., 5. For more on the republican faith in progress, see Lasch, *True and Only Heaven*, passim; Lustig, *Corporate Liberalism*, 232–40; Charles Postel, *The Populist Vision* (New York: Oxford University Press, 2007), 4–11. For more on the dawning awareness of a republican crisis, see Huston, *Securing the Fruits*, 344; Nell Irvin Painter, *Standing at Armageddon: The United States,*

1877–1919 (New York: Norton, 1987), 24; Richard Schneirov, *Labor and Urban Politics: Class Conflict and the Origins of Modern Liberalism in Chicago, 1864–97* (Urbana: University of Illinois Press, 1998), 69–70; Sheldon Stromquist, *Reinventing "The People": The Progressive Movement, The Class Problem, and the Origins of Modern Liberalism* (Urbana: University of Illinois Press, 2006), 17.

28. George, *Progress and Poverty*, 6–7.

29. Ibid., 8.

30. Ibid., 9–10; Sklansky, *Soul's Economy*, 116–17.

31. George, *Progress and Poverty*, 11–13; Burke, *Conundrum of Class*, 140–51; Lears, *Rebirth of a Nation*, 1; Lustig, *Corporate Liberalism*, 58.

32. For very useful short guides to *Progress and Poverty*, see Jacob Oser, *Henry George* (New York: Twayne Publishers, 1974), 32–50; and Edward J. Rose, *Henry George* (New York: Twayne Publishers, 1968), 64–82.

33. George, *Progress and Poverty*, 153; Lustig, *Corporate Liberalism*, 59–60; Mary O. Furner, "Republican Tradition and the New Liberalism: Social Investigation, State Building, and Social Learning in the Gilded Age," in *The State and Social Investigation in Britain and the United States*, eds. Michael James Lacey and Mary O. Furner (New York: Cambridge University Press, 1990), 177–79.

34. Barker, *Henry George*, 273; George, *Progress and Poverty*, 98–99, 123–25; Jim Horner, "Henry George on Thomas Robert Malthus: Abundance vs. Scarcity," *American Journal of Economics & Sociology* 56, no. 4 (October 1997): 595–607; John L. Thomas, *Alternative America: Henry George, Edward Bellamy, Henry Demarest Lloyd, and the Adversary Tradition* (Cambridge, Mass.: Harvard University Press, 1983), 110. George's firm rejection of fixed economic "laws" that justified inequality constituted a bold challenge to the prevailing discourse among Gilded Age elites. See Nasaw, "Gilded Age Gospels," 131; and Burke, *Conundrum of Class*, 140–51.

35. George, *Progress and Poverty*, 153–64, 219.

36. Barker, *Henry George*, 274; George, *Progress and Poverty*, 162–64; Sklansky, *Soul's Economy*, 122–28.

37. George, *Progress and Poverty*, 203. For a comparison between George's ideas and Marxist thought, see Hellman, *Henry George Reconsidered*, 94–102.

38. George, *Progress and Poverty*, 222–24; Lustig, *Corporate Liberalism*, 58–59.

39. Kazin, *Populist Persuasion*, 32

40. Burke, *Conundrum of Class*, 133–39; George, *Progress and Poverty*, 227; Huston, *Securing the Fruits*, 77; Lustig, *Corporate Liberalism*, 63; Thomas, *Alternative America*, 112.

41. George, *Progress and Poverty*, 242; Lustig, *Corporate Liberalism*, 63.

42. George, *Progress and Poverty*, 255, 259; Hays, *Response to Industrialism*, 122; Sklansky, *Soul's Economy*, 123–28.

43. George, *Progress and Poverty*, 38, 283.

44. Postel, *Populist Vision*, 4–5, 11; Lustig, *Corporate Liberalism*, 44. Karl Marx, writing from London, noted George's pro-capitalist radicalism. However, he dismissed *Progress and Poverty* as a "last attempt to save the capitalist regime." See Saul K. Padover, *The Genius of America* (New York: McGraw-Hill, 1960), 230. For an opposing view of George and other Gilded Age reformers as conservatives trying to fend off radicalism to preserve their way of life, see Lasch, *True and Only Heaven*, 213.

45. George, *Progress and Poverty*, 288, 294.

46. Ibid., 263, 272–74, 288, 294–95. For more on the traditionally American fear of land engrossment that led to the abolition of entail and primogeniture, see Huston, *Securing the Fruits*, 46–50. It

is also important to point out that George anticipated key elements of Frederick Jackson Turner's influential "frontier thesis" by more than a decade. See Barker, *Henry George*, 389–90; Ian Barron, "'Frontier' Realities: Frederick Jackson Turner's Debt to Henry George," *Land & Liberty* 97–98 (January–February 1991): 15; Alex Wagner Lough, "Henry George, Frederick Jackson Turner, and the 'Closing' of the American Frontier," *California History* 89, no. 2 (April 2012): 4–23; David M. Wrobel, *The End of American Exceptionalism: Frontier Anxiety from the Old West to the New Deal* (Lawrence: University Press of Kansas, 1996), 3, 9–10, 13–25.

47. George, *Progress and Poverty*, 299–327.

48. Roswell Dwight Hitchcock, *Socialism* (New York: A. D. F. Randolph, 1879), 24.

49. George, *Progress and Poverty*, 300–27; Rodgers, *Atlantic Crossings*, 29. For more on working-class interest in socialism and quasi-socialist ideas, see Moss, "Republican Socialism and the Making of the Working Class," 390–413; and Furner, "Republican Tradition," 171–241.

50. George, *Progress and Poverty*, 328.

51. Ibid., 370.

52. Ibid., 328.

53. Foner, *Story of American Freedom*, 9, 20–21, 32, 62, 113, 143; Huston, *Securing the Fruits*, 292–94.

54. George, *Progress and Poverty*, 405 (emphasis in original); Thomas, *Alternative America*, 118–19.

55. Lustig, *Corporate Liberalism*, 59, 67.

56. The term "single tax" never appears in *Progress and Poverty*. It was first used by George in print in an earlier article (Henry George and David Dudley Field, "Land and Taxation: A Conversation," *North American Review* [July 1885], 1–14) and was later popularized by his supporters in the late 1880s and 1890s in order to capture, in a single phrase, the essence of George's radical program. For the sake of simplicity, I will use the term from here on to describe land-value taxation.

57. Steven J. Ross, "The Culture of Political Economy," *Southern California Quarterly* 65, no. 2 (Summer 1983): 149–50.

58. George, *Progress and Poverty*, 403, 436.

59. Ibid., 406, 434, 438; Lustig, *Corporate Liberalism*, 44.

60. George, *Progress and Poverty*, 454–55.

61. Fine, *Laissez-Faire*, 3–25; Foner, *Story of American Freedom*, 54–55; Huston, *Securing the Fruits*, 70, 79–80, 134, 150, 292–94.

62. George, *Progress and Poverty*, 440–41, 455–57; Burke, *Conundrum of Class*, 108; Fine, *Laissez-Faire*, 293–94; Lustig, *Corporate Liberalism*, 74. For more on the trend toward taxing businesses to provide for public services, see R. Rudy Higgens-Evenson, *The Price of Progress: Public Services, Taxation, and the American Corporate State, 1877–1929* (Baltimore: Johns Hopkins University Press, 2003), especially pages 12–51.

63. George, *Progress and Poverty*, 458, 461–63; Furner, "Republican Tradition," 172; James T. Kloppenberg, *Uncertain Victory: Social Democracy and Progressivism in European and American Thought, 1870–1920* (New York: Oxford University Press, 1986), 170–71; Lasch, *True and Only Heaven*, 15; Lustig, *Corporate Liberalism*, 72; Rossinow, *Visions of Progress*, 19; Sklansky, *Soul's Economy*, 19. On the popularity of cooperation, see Steven Leiken, *The Practical Utopians: American Workers and the Cooperative Movement in the Gilded Age* (Detroit: Wayne State University Press, 2005).

64. George, *Progress and Poverty*, 475, 485, 537; J. G. A. Pocock, *The Machiavellian Moment: Florentine Republican Thought and the Atlantic Republican Tradition* (Princeton, N.J.: Princeton University Press, 1975), 545. For what he describes as George's "economic syllogism," see Barker, *Henry George*, 268–71.

65. George, *Progress and Poverty*, 508–17; Sklansky, *Soul's Economy*, 123–30
66. George, *Progress and Poverty*, 518–19.
67. Ibid., 528, 533, 535, 537.
68. Ibid., 530–34; Lustig, *Corporate Liberalism*, 61.
69. George, *Progress and Poverty*, 537–38. For more on apocalyptic reform literature, see Frederic Cople Jaher, *Doubters and Dissenters: Cataclysmic Thought in America, 1885–1918* (Glencoe, Ill.: Free Press, 1964), 19–32; Lears, *Rebirth of a Nation*, 6; Kenneth M. Roemer, *The Obsolete Necessity: America in Utopian Writings, 1888–1900* (Kent, Ohio: Kent State University Press, 1976), 22–24, 171–78.
70. George, *Progress and Poverty*, 240–41, 537–38; Josiah Strong, *Our Country: Its Possible Future and Its Present Crisis* (New York: American Home Missionary Society, 1885), 128–43; John D. Fairchild, *The Mysteries of the Great City: The Politics of Urban Design, 1877–1937* (Columbus: Ohio State University Press, 1997), 4–5, 16–17, 23; Postel, *Populist Vision*, 1–11.
71. George, *Progress and Poverty*, 522–24.
72. Ibid., 543, 546, 547, 548.
73. Ibid., 521–22.
74. Ibid., 527. See also Huston, *Securing the Fruits*, 58–59.
75. George, *Progress and Poverty*, 548–49.
76. Ibid., 552.
77. Cohen, *Reconstruction of American Liberalism*, 110–76; Currarino, *Labor Question*, 11–35; Rodgers, *Atlantic Crossings*, 33–111; Schneirov, *Labor and Urban Politics*, 70; Stromquist, *Reinventing "The People"*, 13–46.
78. Furner, "Republican Tradition," 172; Michael E. McGerr, *A Fierce Discontent: The Rise and Fall of the Progressive Movement in America, 1870–1920* (New York: Free Press, 2003), 59; Rossinow, *Visions of Progress*, 4.
79. Cohen, *Reconstruction of American Liberalism*, 160–65; William Forbath, "Caste, Class, and Equal Citizenship," in *Moral Problems in American Life: New Perspectives on Cultural History*, eds. Karen Halttunen and Lewis Perry (Ithaca, N.Y.: Cornell University Press, 1999), 180–83; Furner, "Republican Tradition," 172–76, 187; Lustig, *Corporate Liberalism*, 39; McGerr, *Fierce Discontent*, 59; Stromquist, *Reinventing "The People"*, 15, 34–38.
80. Fine, *Laissez-Faire*, 25; Rossinow, *Visions of Progress*, 15; Stromquist, *Reinventing "The People"*, 34. See also Robin Archer, "American Liberalism and Labour Politics: Labour Leaders and Liberty Language in Late Nineteenth Century Australia and the United States," *Labour History* 92 (May 2007): 1–15; Mary O. Furner, "Structure and Virtue in United States Political Economy," *Journal of the History of Economic Thought* 27, no. 1 (March 2005): 1–27.
81. Cohen, *Reconstruction of American Liberalism*, 156–57; Rodgers, *Atlantic Crossings*, 96–111; Dorothy Ross, *The Origins of American Social Science* (New York: Cambridge University Press, 1991), 53–138; Joseph Dorfman, *The Economic Mind in American Civilization, 1865–1918* (New York: Viking, 1949), 3:87–98, 160–64. See also Mary O. Furner, *Advocacy and Objectivity: A Crisis in the Professionalization of American Social Science, 1865–1905* (Lexington: University Press of Kentucky, 1975); Thomas Haskell, *The Emergence of Professional Social Science: The American Social Science Association and the Nineteenth-Century Crisis of Authority* (Urbana: University of Illinois Press, 1977).
82. Cohen, *Reconstruction of American Liberalism*, 158–61; Henry Clark Adams quoted in Rodgers, *Atlantic Crossings*, 96; Lears, *Rebirth of a Nation*, 87. See also John Bates Clark, "The Nature and Progress of True Socialism," *New Englander* 39 (July 1879).

83. Barker, *Henry George*, 299–300, 478–79, 556–58; Donald R. Stabile, "Henry George's Influence on John Bates Clark: The Concept of Rent Was Pivotal to Equating Wages with the Marginal Product of Labor," *American Journal of Economics & Sociology* 54 (July 1995): 373–82.

84. Cohen, *Reconstruction of American Liberalism*, 143–76; Rodgers, *Atlantic Crossings*, 100–102. McGerr, *Fierce Discontent*, 58–59.

85. Rossinow, *Visions of Progress*, 4–5; Fine, *Laissez-Faire*, 293–94.

86. D. Appleton to HG, April 9, 1879, HGP; Barker, *Henry George*, 312–13.

87. HG to Richard George, September 15, 1879, HGP.

88. Barker, *Henry George*, 314.

89. George, *Progress and Poverty*, 315–21.

3. "NEW YORK IS AN IMMENSE CITY":
THE EMPIRE CITY IN THE EARLY 1880S

1. HG to Richard George, September 2, 1880, HGP.

2. Gordon Atkins, *Health, Housing, and Poverty in New York City, 1865–1898* (Ann Arbor: Edwards Brothers, 1947) 209.

3. Seymour Mandelbaum, *Boss Tweed's New York* (New York: John Wiley, 1965), 19–26.

4. Statistics for New York's ethnic composition in 1880 are drawn from Ira Rosenwaike, *Population History of New York City* (Syracuse: Syracuse University Press, 1972), 67, 73, tables 23 and 26 respectively, and U.S. Census Bureau, *Tenth Census of the United States, 1880*, vol. 1 (Washington, D.C.: U.S. Government Printing Office, 1883).

5. John J. Appel, "From Shanties to Lace Curtains: The Irish Image in *Puck*, 1876–1910," *Comparative Studies in Society and History* 13 (1971): 365–75; Maureen Murphy, "Bridget and Biddy: Images of the Irish Servant Girl in *Puck* Cartoons, 1880–1890," in *New Perspectives on the Irish Diaspora*, ed. Charles Fanning (Carbondale: Southern Illinois University Press, 2000), 152–75; Edwin G. Burrows and Mike Wallace, *Gotham: A History of New York City to 1898* (New York: Oxford University Press, 1999), 1003–8.

6. For statistics on the occupational breakdown of Irish and Germans immigrants in the United States, see U.S. Census Bureau, *Tenth Census, 1880*, 1: 865–92. See also Ronald Bayor and Timothy Meagher, eds., *The New York Irish* (Baltimore: Johns Hopkins University Press, 1996), 217, 229–31, 301–4; Robert Ernst, *Immigrant Life in New York City, 1825–1863* (New York: Columbia University Press, 1949), 206–21; David Hammack, *Power and Society: Greater New York at the Turn of the Century* (New York: Columbia University Press, 1987), 67–68.

7. Stanley Nadel, *Little Germany: Ethnicity, Religion, and Class in New York City, 1845–80* (Urbana: University of Illinois Press, 1990), passim.

8. Marquis James, *Merchant Adventurer: The Story of William R. Grace* (New York: Scholarly Resources, 1993), 142–79.

9. Frederick Binder and David Reimers, *All Nations Under Heaven: An Ethnic and Racial History of New York City* (New York: Columbia University Press, 1996), 109–13; Rosenwaike, *Population History of New York*, 77. See also James Weldon Johnson, *Black Manhattan* (New York: Knopf, 1930); and Seth M. Scheiner, *Negro Mecca: A History of the Negro in New York City, 1865–1920* (New York: New York University Press, 1965).

10. George, *Progress and Poverty*, 9–10; Rodgers, *Atlantic Crossings*, 113–14.

11. Hammack, *Power and Society*, 46; Beckert, *Monied Metropolis*, 247–48, 257–58. See also Eric Homberger, *Mrs. Astor's New York: Money and Social Power in a Gilded Age* (New Haven:

Yale University Press, 2004). Edgar Saltus quoted in Ric Burns, James Sanders, and Lisa Ades, *New York: An Illustrated History* (New York: Knopf, 1999), 185.

12. Beckert, *Monied Metropolis*, 257; Burrows and Wallace, *Gotham*, 1071–72; Trachtenberg, *Incorporation of America*, 87. See also Rebecca Edwards, *New Spirits: Americans in the Gilded Age, 1865–1905* (New York: Oxford University Press, 2006), 97–98; *New York Times,* March 27, 1883, 1.

13. Walt Whitman quoted in Trachtenberg, *Incorporation of America*, 70. Whitman delivered this address several months before George published *Progress and Poverty*.

14. George, *Social Problems*, 34; Hays, *Response to Industrialism*, 122. Richard T. Ely quoted in Stromquist, *Reinventing "The People,"* 17.

15. Atkins, *Health, Housing, and Poverty*, 313; John F. McClymer, "Late-Nineteenth Century American Working-Class Living Standards," *Journal of Interdisciplinary History* 17 (Autumn 1986): 379–98; John F. McClymer, "The 'American Standard' of Living: Family Expectations and Strategies for Getting and Spending in Gilded Age America," *Hayes Historical Journal* 9 (September 1990): 20–43. See also Edith Abbott, *The Wages of Unskilled Labor in the United States, 1850–1900* (Chicago: University of Chicago, 1905).

16. Statistics on women's employment drawn from U.S. Department of the Interior, Census Office, *Compendium of the Tenth Census of the United States*, vol. 2 (Washington, D.C.: U.S. Government Printing Office, 1883), 1070–77; U.S. Department of the Interior (Census Office), *Report on Manufacturing Industries in the United States at the Eleventh Census*, part 2 (Washington, D.C.: U.S. Government Printing Office, 1895), 390–409. Quote referring to "strictest economy" from *JSP*, November, 18, 1883, 1.

17. Roy Lubove, *The Progressives and the Slums: Tenement House Reform in New York City, 1890–1917* (Pittsburgh: University of Pittsburgh Press, 1962), 25–48; Richard Plunz, *A History of Housing in New York City: Dwelling Type and Social Change in the American Metropolis* (New York: Columbia University Press, 1990), 21–49; David M. Scobey, *Empire City: The Making and Meaning of the New York City Landscape* (Philadelphia: Temple University Press, 2002), 71–73, 148.

18. Testimony of Charles F. Wingate, in the U.S. Senate Committee on Education and Labor, *Report of the Committee of the Senate upon the Relations Between Labor and Capital* (Washington, D.C.: U.S. Government Printing Office, 1885) [hereafter referred to as *RCSRLC*], 2:1044; George F. Waring, "Sanitary Drainage," *North American Review* 137 (July 1883): 57–67.

19. Lubove, *Progressives and the Slums*, 25–48; *JSP*, November 18, 1883, 1. For statistics on rents in 1889, see also Jacob A. Riis, *How the Other Half Lives: Studies Among the Tenements of New York*, ed. David Leviatin (Boston: Bedford, 1996), 158.

20. *New York Times*, July 4 and July 6, 1880. See also *Harper's Weekly*, August 15, 1868; August 9, 1879; and June 30, 1883.

21. Atkins, *Health, Housing, and Poverty*, 190.

22. Ibid., 46–52; Charlotte G. O'Brien, "The Emigrant in New York," *The Nineteenth Century* 16 (October 1884), 531–32; *Harper's Weekly*, March 1, 1884; July 12, 1884; Scobey, *Empire City*, 140; Testimony of Frederick Koezly, *RCSRLC*, 2:404; Testimony of William H. Morrell, *RCSRLC*, 2:1004–7; *New York Times*, May 20, 1881.

23. Riis, *How the Other Half Lives*, 257; George, *Social Problems*, 24, 73, 115.

24. Quoted in Riis, *How the Other Half Lives*, 67.

25. Testimony of Charles F. Wingate, *RCSRLC*, 2:1043–49. Other sources of information regarding death rates in the tenements are found in the following: Riis, *How the Other Half Lives*, 100–101;

JSP, January 6, 1884, 1; *Irish World*, April 8, 1882, 4; November 17, 1883, 4; February 28, 1885, 4; *New York Times*, July 23, 1882, 5.

26. George, *Social Problems*, 114–15; *Irish World*, May 6, 1882, 5; May 13, 1882, 3; William P. McLoughlin, "Evictions in New York's Tenement Houses," *Arena* 7, no. 54 (December 1892), 48–57; Riis, *How the Other Half Lives*, 174.

27. *New York Times*, May 16, 1880, 6.

28. Philip S. Foner, *History of the Labor Movement*, 2:12.

29. Henry Adams, *The Education of Henry Adams* (New York: Modern Library, 1931), 462–63.

30. Hammack, *Power and Society*, 31, 37–39, 40–41.

31. U.S. Department of the Interior, Census Office, *1870 Census of Manufactures* (Washington, D.C.: U.S. Government Printing Office, 1872), 703; U.S. Department of the Interior, Census Office, *1890 Census of Manufactures* (Washington, D.C.: U.S. Government Printing Office, 1894), 402–3; Hammack, *Power and Society*, 51–56; Trachtenberg, *Incorporation of America*, 122.

32. *1870 Census of Manufactures*, 702; *1890 Census of Manufactures*, 394–95.

33. Kenneth T. Jackson, ed., *The Encyclopedia of New York City* (New Haven, Conn.: Yale University Press, 1995), 166; Scobey, *Empire City*, 189–216, 258–65. Detailed budget statistics can be found in Edward Durand, *The Finances of New York City* (New York: MacMillan, 1898).

34. Hammack, *Power and Society*, 41.

35. Thomas Kessner, *Capital City: New York City and the Men Behind America's Rise to Economic Dominance, 1860–1900* (New York: Simon & Schuster, 2003), 33–34, 42–43, 48–49, 208–14. *Frank Leslie's Weekly* quote from Scobey, *Empire City*, 40.

36. Klein, *Genesis of Industrial America*, 106–9.

37. George, *Social Problems*, 42.

38. Tracy Campbell, *Deliver the Vote: A History of Election Fraud, An American Political Tradition, 1742–2004* (New York: Carroll & Graf, 2005), 18–22, 62–66; Jerome Mushkat, *Tammany: The Evolution of a Political Machine, 1789–1865* (Syracuse, N.Y.: Syracuse University Press, 1971).

39. Kenneth D. Ackerman, *Boss Tweed: The Rise and Fall of the Corrupt Pol Who Conceived the Soul of Modern New York* (New York: Carroll & Graf, 2005); Leo Hershkowitz, *Tweed's New York: Another Look* (Garden City, N.Y.: Anchor Press, 1978), 167–265.

40. New York City Council of Political Reform, *Report for the Years 1872, '73, '74* (New York, 1875), quoted in Mandelbaum, *Boss Tweed's New York*, 113.

41. Beckert, *Monied Metropolis*, 207–36. On the disenfranchisement effort, see also David Quigley, *Second Founding: New York City, Reconstruction, and the Making of American Democracy* (New York: Hill & Wang, 2004), 111–74.

42. Hammack, *Power and Society*, 55–58; Mandelbaum, *Boss Tweed's New York*, 75–102; Iver Bernstein, *The New York City Draft Riots: Their Significance for American Society and Politics in the Age of the Civil War* (New York: Oxford University Press, 1990), 201–7; Michael Gordon, "Studies in Irish and Irish-American Thought and Behavior in Gilded Age New York City" (Ph.D. diss., University of Rochester, 1977), 382–447.

43. Disenfranchisement estimates can be found in Beckert, *Monied Metropolis*, 221; *New York Times*, October 21, 1877; Michael E. McGerr, *The Decline of Popular Politics: The American North, 1865–1928* (New York: Oxford, 1986), 45–49; Quigley, *Second Founding*, 122–30, 145–59.

44. Adonica Y. Lui, "The Machine and Social Policies: Tammany Hall and the Politics of Public Outdoor Relief, New York City, 1874–1898," *Studies in American Political Development* 9, no. 2 (1995): 386–403.

45. Richard Oestreicher, "Urban Working-Class Political Behavior and Theories of American Electoral Politics, 1870–1940," *Journal of American History* 74, no. 4 (March 1988): 1257–86.

46. Steven P. Erie, *Rainbow's End: Irish-Americans and the Dilemmas of Urban Machine Politics, 1840–1985* (Berkeley: University of California Press, 1988), 53, 58.

47. Herbert J. Bass, "The Politics of Ballot Reform in New York State, 1888–1890," *New York History* 59 (1961): 253–72.

48. Ira Katznelson, *City Trenches: Urban Politics and the Patterning of Class in the United States* (New York: Pantheon, 1981), 1–72.

49. Hammack, *Power and Society*, 110, 120–21. For similar data on New York's Board of Aldermen, see Anthony Gronowicz, "Labor's Decline within New York City's Democratic Party from 1844 to 1884," in *Immigration to New York*, eds. William Pencak, Selma Berrol, and Randall M. Miller (Philadelphia: Balch Institute Press, 1991), 9–10, 15–17.

50. *New York Herald*, June 25, 1872, 8.

51. Bernstein, *New York City Draft Riots*, 238–39, 246–55; Lawrence Costello, "The New York City Labor Movement, 1861–1873" (Ph.D. diss., Columbia University, 1967), 357–76; David Montgomery, *Beyond Equality: Labor and the Radical Republicans, 1862–1872* (New York: Vintage Books, 1972), 326–34; Stanley Nadel, "Those Who Would Be Free: The Eight House Strikes of 1872," *Labor's Heritage* 2, no. 2 (April 1990): 70–77.

52. Foner, *History of the Labor Movement*, 1:439–40; Atkins, *Health, Housing, and Poverty*, 67–74.

53. Foner, *History of the Labor Movement*, 2:14.

54. Testimony of Charles Miller, *RCSRLC*, 1:748–50. See also the testimonies of Conrad Carl, Gabriel Edmonston, Joseph T. Finnerty, Samuel Gompers, Edward King, John S. McClelland, and John Morrison. For other specific references to the disruption wrought by mechanization, see the following issues of *JSP*: December 2, 1883, 4; October 5, 1884, 4; September 13, 1885, 1; January 24, 1886, 1; March 14, 1886, 4; May 16, 1886, 1; October 31, 1886, 4; and *Irish World*, October 22, 1881, 4.

55. Beckert, *Monied Metropolis*, 210–11, 289; *JSP*, December 9, 1883, 1, and January 31, 1886, 4 (boss tailors); January 6, 1884, 4 (boss book printers); June 29, 1884, 1, 2, and July 6, 1884, 1 (boss plumbers); July 27, August 3, August 10, and August 17, 1884, 1 (boss builders); September 14, 1884, 4 (boss stonecutters); November 2, 1884, 4 (boss framers); June 21, 1885, 4 (boss brewers); December 6, 1885, 4 (boss machinists); May 23, 1886, 4 (boss bakers); September 5, 1886, 4 (boss barbers). See also Clarence E. Bonnett, *History of Employers' Associations in the United States* (New York: Vantage Press, 1956), 102–321.

56. Foner, *History of the Labor Movement*, 2:18; Moses Rischin, *The Promised City: New York Jews, 1870–1914* (Cambridge, Mass.: Harvard University Press, 1962), 249. For more on the impact of immigration on unions, see A. T. Lane, *Solidarity or Survival: American Labor and European Immigrants, 1830–1924* (Westport, Conn.: Greenwood Press, 1987).

57. New York State Bureau of Labor Statistics (hereafter NYSBLS), *Annual Report for 1884* (Albany: Weed, Parsons, 1884), 2:145–81.

58. Beckert, *Monied Metropolis*, 192–97; Herbert Gutman, "The Workers' Search for Power: Labor in the Gilded Age," in *The Gilded Age: A Reappraisal*, ed. H. Wayne Morgan (Syracuse, N.Y.: Syracuse University Press, 1963), 38–68.

59. Beckert, *Monied Metropolis*, 207.

60. Ibid., 207–97; Robert M. Fogelson, *America's Armories: Architecture, Society, and Public Order* (Cambridge, Mass.: Harvard University Press, 1989), 51; Lisa Keller, *The Triumph of Order: Democracy and Public Space in New York and London* (New York: Columbia University Press, 2009), 190–201; Nasaw, "Gilded Age Gospels," 127–33. The dinner honoring Spencer is detailed in Barry Werth, *Banquet at Delmonico's: Great Minds, The Gilded Age, and the Triumph of Evolution in America* (New York: Random House, 2009). See also *New York Times*,

November 11, 1882. Quote from the Charities and Correction commissioner is cited in Beckert, *Monied Metropolis*, 216.

61. George, *Social Problems*, 46; Testimony of Thomas McGuire, *RCSRLC*, 1:779.

62. Foner, *History of the Labor Movement*, 1:448; Samuel Gompers, *Seventy Years of Life and Labor* (New York: E. P. Dutton, 1925), 1:96; Herbert Gutman, "The Tompkins Square 'Riot' in New York City on January 13, 1874: A Reexamination of Its Causes and Its Aftermath," *Labor History* 6 (Winter 1965): 48–65; Marilyn Johnson, *Street Justice: A History of Police Violence in New York City* (Boston: Beacon Press, 2003), 12–50; Keller, *Triumph of Order*, 173–78; John Swinton, *The Tompkins Square Outrage* (Albany, N.Y.: n.p., 1874); *New York Times*, January 14, 1874. See Schneirov, *Labor and Urban Politics*, 74–75, for a similar incident in Chicago.

63. Fink, *Workingmen's Democracy*, 4; Sender Garlin, *Three American Radicals: John Swinton, Crusading Editor; Charles P. Steinmetz, Scientist and Socialist; William Dean Howells and the Haymarket Era* (Boulder, Colo.: Westview Press, 1991), 11–13; David Nicholas Lyon, "The World of P. J. McGuire: A Study of the American Labor Movement, 1870–1890" (Ph.D. diss., University of Minnesota, 1972), 33–35; Eugene Debs was similarly radicalized by the violence meted out by the military during the Great Uprising of 1877; see Nick Salvatore, *Eugene Debs: Citizens and Socialist* (Urbana: University of Illinois Press, 1982), 31–38.

64. Keller, *Triumph of Order*, 183–90; Burrows and Wallace, *Gotham*, 1035–36. Schneirov details a similar consolidation of bourgeois solidarity in Chicago in the 1870s and 1880s in *Labor and Urban Politics*, 57–75, 87.

65. Burrows and Wallace, *Gotham*, 1095; Currarino, *Labor Question*, 86–145; Foner, *History of the Labor Movement*, 1:512–18.

66. Bruce Laurie, *Artisans into Workers*, 141–46.

67. Laurie, *Artisans into Workers*, 146–56; Craig Phelan, *Grand Master Workman: Terence Powderly and the Knights of Labor* (Westport, Conn.: Greenwood Press, 2000), 70–72; Robert E. Weir, *Beyond Labor's Veil: The Culture of the Knights of Labor* (University Park: Pennsylvania State University Press, 1996), 8–13. Text of the 1878 preamble in Terence Powderly, *Thirty Years of Labor, 1859–1889* (n.p.: Excelsior Publishing, 1889), 128–30.

68. Gordon, "Studies in Irish and Irish-American Thought and Behavior," 499–501.

69. HG to Dr. Edward Taylor, November 2, 1880; HG to James Coffey, December 15, 1880; George to [illegible], December 16, 1880, HGP.

70. HG to Dr. Edward Taylor, December 18, 1880, HGP.

4. "RADICALLY AND ESSENTIALLY THE SAME": IRISH AMERICAN NATIONALISM AND AMERICAN LABOR

1. HG to Dr. Edward Taylor, January 4, 1881, HGP.

2. HG to James McClatchy, February 22, 1881; HG to Dr. Edward Taylor, January 27 and May 21, 1881, HGP.

3. Barker, *Henry George*, 337; *Truth*, October 9, 1881, 2; Joan Waugh, *Unsentimental Reformer: The Life of Josephine Shaw Lowell* (Cambridge, Mass.: Harvard University Press, 1997), 179–90.

4. HG to [illegible], August 31, 1880, HGP; HG to Dr. Edward Taylor, March 26, 1881, HGP; *Irish World*, May 1, 1880, 6.

5. For the sake of clarity, I use "Fenians" here as a term meant to encompass members of militant Irish nationalist organizations such as Devoy's Clan na Gael in the United States and the Irish Republican Brotherhood in Ireland.

6. Kerby Miller, *Emigrants and Exiles: Ireland and the Irish Exodus to North America* (New

York: Oxford University Press, 1985), 441–42; R. F. Foster, *Modern Ireland, 1600–1972* (New York: Viking, 1988), 397–99; Thomas N. Brown, *Irish-American Nationalism, 1870–1890* (New York: J. B. Lippencott., 1966), 65–74.

7. Brown, *Irish-American Nationalism,* 94; Foster, *Modern Ireland,* 402–3; Miller, *Emigrants and Exiles,* 398–400.

8. Brown, *Irish-American Nationalism,* 80–83, 101–3; Foster, *Modern Ireland,* 403–5; Terry Golway, *Irish Rebel: John Devoy and America's Fight for Ireland's Freedom* (New York: St. Martins, 1998), 104–14; T. W. Moody, *Davitt and the Irish Revolution, 1846–1882* (New York: Oxford University Press, 1981), 271–281, 284–92.

9. Michael Davitt, *The Fall of Feudalism in Ireland, or The Story of the Land League Revolution* (London: Harper and Row, 1904), 160–61.

10. Brown, *Irish-American Nationalism,* 85–98; John Devoy, *Land of Eire: The Irish Land League, Its Origin, Progress and Consequences* (New York: Patterson & Neilson, 1882), 43–44; F. S. L. Lyons, *Charles Stewart Parnell* (New York: Oxford University Press, 1977), 79–83, 88–90; Owen McGee, *The IRB: The Irish Republican Brotherhood from the Land League to Sinn Fein* (Dublin: Four Courts, 2005), 58–65; Moody, *Davitt and the Irish Revolution,* 250–58, 261–66; William O'Brien and Desmond Ryan, eds., *Devoy's Post-Bag, 1871–1928* (Dublin: Fallon, 1948), 1:370–81.

11. Joyce Marlow, *Captain Boycott and The Irish* (London: Cox & Wyman, 1973).

12. James P. Rodechko, *Patrick Ford and His Search for America: A Case Study of Irish American Journalism, 1870–1913* (New York: Arno Press, 1976), 27–57.

13. Eric Foner, "Class, Ethnicity, and Radicalism in the Gilded Age: The Land League and Irish America," in *Politics and Ideology in the Age of the Civil War* (New York: Oxford, 1980).

14. Paul Gilje, *The Road to Mobocracy: Popular Disorder in New York City, 1763–1834* (Chapel Hill: University of North Carolina Press, 1987), 127–42, 229–31, 245–46; 255–57; Noel Ignatiev, *How the Irish Became White* (New York: Routledge, 1996), 125–30, 134–39, 155–56. Theodore Parker quote from Carl Wittke, *The Irish in America* (New York: Russell & Russell, 1970), 116.

15. David H. Bennett, *The Party of Fear: From Nativist Movements to the New Right in American History* (Chapel Hill: University of North Carolina Press, 1988), 105–55; Ray Allen Billington, *The Protestant Crusade* (Chicago: Quadrangle Books, 1964), 166–436.

16. Foner, "Class, Ethnicity, and Radicalism," 183; Brown, *Irish-American Nationalism,* 43–60.

17. *Irish World,* February 19, 1881, 4; May 20, 1882, 4.

18. Brown, *Irish-American Nationalism,* 49–54; Rodechko, *Patrick Ford,* 58–70.

19. Rodechko, *Patrick Ford,* 70–90; Brown, *Irish-American Nationalism,* 49–54.

20. *Irish World,* July 8, 1882, 4.

21. *Irish World,* December 31, 1881, 4; Foner, "Class, Ethnicity, and Radicalism," 157–61; Schneirov, *Labor and Urban Politics,* 119–35. See also *Irish World,* January 8, 1881; 4, December 4, 1880, 4; June 4, 1881, 1.

22. Testimony of P. J. McGuire, *RCSRLC,* 1:343–44. See also John R. Stobo, "Organized Labor, Housing Issues, and Politics: Another Look at the 1886 Henry George Campaign in New York City" (Masters thesis, Columbia University, 1993).

23. *Irish World,* December 11, 1880, 4; January, 8, 1881, 3; March 12, 1881, 4, 7.

24. HG to James McClatchy, January 27, 1881, HGP; *Irish World,* April 16, 1881; July 18, 1885, 8; November 4, 1882, 6; Barker, *Henry George,* 336.

25. For an explanation as to why most workers, especially Irish Americans, opposed free trade, see Robert E. Weir, "A Fragile Alliance: Henry George and the Knights of Labor," *American Journal of Economics & Sociology* 56 (October 1997): 421–39.

26. Barker, *Henry George*, 125–27, 320; Henry George, "The Land Question in Ireland," *Sacramento Bee*, December 25, 1879, reprinted in the *Irish World*, May 1, 1880. For examples of his *Monitor* editorials, see *San Francisco Monitor*, August 14 and 21, 1869.

27. Barker, *Henry George*, 53, 57–59, 435; See also George's correspondence with Rev. Thomas Dawson, a Catholic priest he met in Ireland.

28. Stephen Bell, *Rebel, Priest, and Prophet: A Biography of Dr. Edward McGlynn* (New York: Devin-Adair Company, 1937), 9–11; Alfred Isacsson, *The Determined Doctor: The Story of Edward McGlynn* (Tarrytown, NY: Vestigium Press, 1996), 65–71.

29. Bell, *Rebel, Priest, and Prophet*, 23.

30. Bell, *Rebel, Priest, and Prophet*, 23; Isacsson, *Determined Doctor*, 78–80. See also Manuel Scott Shanaberger, "Reverend Dr. Edward McGlynn: An Early Advocate of the Social Gospel in the American Catholic Church: An Intellectual History" (Ph.D. diss., University of Virginia, 1993).

31. HG to Dr. Edward Taylor, November 2, 1880, HGP; *Irish World*, February 19, 1881, 7; Brown, *Irish-American Nationalism*, 118.

32. James H. Murphy to HG, March 10, 1881, HGP.

33. *Irish World*, November 20, 1880, 1; April 23, 1881, 5; May 14, 1881, 5; May 21, 1881, 8; *New York Times*, April 13, 1881, 3; Schneirov, *Labor and Urban Politics*, 133.

34. HG to Poultney Bigelow, June 10, 1881; HG to Dr. Edward Taylor, June 13, 1881, HGP; *Irish World*, July 9, 1881, 8; Barker, *Henry George*, 320, 334–36, 339–40.

35. HG to Dr. Edward Taylor, September 12, 1881, HGP; Barker, *Henry George*, 339–40; *Irish World*, October 29, 1881, 1.

36. *Irish World*, December 3, 1881, 1. For other examples of George's dispatches published in the *Irish World*, see Kenneth C. Wenzer, ed., *Henry George, The Transatlantic Irish, and Their Times* (Bingley, UK: JAI Press, 2009), 41–131.

37. *Irish World*, November 19, 1881, 4, and August 19, 1882, 5; *Irish Nation*, August 19, 1882, 5; *Irish-American*, August 19, 1882, 1; *New York Times*, August 10, 1882, 4.

38. *Irish-American*, March 20, 1880, 1; August 7, 1880, 5; *Irish World*, January 17, 1880, 1; *New York Times*, January 3, 1880, 5; January 5, 1880, 8; Brown, *Irish-American Nationalism*, 103; Lyons, *Charles Stewart Parnell*, 107–15; Michael V. Hazel, "First Link: Parnell's American Tour, 1880," *Éire-Ireland* 15, no. 1 (1980): 6–24.

39. *New York Times*, March 12, 1880, 3. For more details on the founding of the Land League in America, see Edward T. O'Donnell, "Henry George and the 'New Political Forces': Ethnic Nationalism, Labor Radicalism, and Politics in Gilded Age New York City" (Ph.D. diss., Columbia University, 1995), 241–64.

40. *Irish-American*, May 1, 1880, 5; May 22, 1880, 2; May 29, 1880, 1; *Irish World*, May 29, 1880, 5; *New York Times*, March 12, 1880, 3; May 19, 1880, 8; May 20, 1880, 3.

41. *Irish World*, May 29, 1880, 5; *Irish-American*, May 29, 1880, 1.

42. *Irish-American*, March 20, 1880, 1, 7.

43. *Irish World*, March 20, 1880, 2, 8; *New York Times*, March 1, 1880, 8; March 12, 1880, 8.

44. *Irish World*, March 19, 1881, 8; *Irish-American*, March 12, 1881, 8, and June 4, 1881, 5; *Irish Nation*, April 15, 1882, 2. For information regarding the League's financial reports and the number of branches, see O'Donnell, "Henry George and the 'New Political Forces,'" 251–53.

45. *Irish World*, June 5, 1880, 1; November 20, 1880, 1; April 23, 1881, 5; April 1, 1882, 5; April 8, 1882, 5; *Irish-American*, November 20, 1880, 1; April 23, 1881, 8.

46. See the *Irish-American* editorial of March 13, 1880 for a discussion of the problems of Irish-American disunity.

47. *Irish World*, April 3, 1880, 8; Brown, *Irish-American Nationalism*, 24, 41, 46; Foner, "Class, Ethnicity, and Radicalism," 194–95; Oliver Rafferty, "Fenianism in North America in the 1860s: The Problems for Church and State," *History* 84, no. 274 (April 1999): 257–77.

48. *Irish World*, April 15, 1882, 1, 2, 7; *New York Times*, April 4, 1882, 2.

49. *Irish World*, March 12, 1881, 5, and February 25, 1882, 4, 6; Foner, "Class, Ethnicity, and Radicalism," 150–51; Schneirov, *Labor and Urban Politics*, 119–35.

50. Ford took no direct role in the local movement, choosing instead to lead through the pages of his paper. *Irish World*, June 5, 1880, 1.

51. Testimony of Robert Blissert, *RCSRLC*, 1:840–41.

52. *New York Times*, March 12, 1880, 3; *Irish-American*, March 13, 1880, 5; *New York Times*, March 1, 1880, 8. See also *Irish-American*, June 26, 1880, 1, regarding a large donation by the Journeymen Shoemakers Association.

53. Michael Gordon writes that Irish laborers established separate "industrial" branches of the League in New York City, but all branches, working-class and lace-curtain alike, existed under the auspices of the Irish National Land and Industrial League (with a separate wing called the Parnell Land League being the exception). See Gordon, "Studies in Irish and Irish-American Thought and Behavior," 452–61.

54. *Irish World*, June 5, 1880, 1.

55. *Irish-American*, November 6, 1880, 5.

56. *Truth*, May 1, 1882, 1.

57. *Irish Nation*, July 8, 1882, 8.

58. *Irish World*, April 23, 1881, 5; November 20, 1880, 1; May 14, 1881, 5.

59. David Brundage, "After the Land League: The Persistence of Irish-American Labor Radicalism in Denver, 1897–1905," *Journal of American Ethnic History* 11 (Spring 1992): 3–26; Schneirov, *Labor and Urban Politics*, 119–35.

60. Foner, "Class, Ethnicity, and Radicalism," 167–79; Schneirov, *Labor and Urban Politics*, 122–35; *Irish World*, October 28, 1882, 8. See also *Irish Nation*, June 10, 1882, 4, and *Irish-American*, October 14, 1882, 4, for editorials critical of Ford.

61. Phelan, *Grand Master Workman*, 21, 41n33, 92–93; Powderly, *Thirty Years of Labor*, 337–48; Knights of Labor, *Record of the Proceedings of the General Assembly* (New York, 1882), 282–83; Knights of Labor, *Record of the Proceedings of the General Assembly* (Cleveland, 1886), 40.

62. David Brundage, *The Making of Western Labor Radicalism: Denver's Organized Workers, 1878–1905* (Urbana: University of Illinois Press, 1994), 52.

63. Brown, *Irish-American Nationalism*, 109.

64. *Irish World*, February 16, 1884. This summary financial report of Land League funds states that the *Irish World* took in $343,000 up to October 1882.

65. *Irish-American*, January 10, 1880, 4.

66. *Irish-American*, July 1, 1882, 4. See also *Irish-American*, September 16, 1882, 4.

67. *Irish World*, October 2, 1880, 8. See Brundage, *Making of Western Labor Radicalism*, 45–52, regarding tensions between the Denver Land League's middle-class and working-class participants.

68. Brundage, *Making of Western Labor Radicalism*, 43–44.

69. Anna Parnell eventually wrote *The Land League: Tale of a Great Sham* (posthumously published in 1986), a critical account of the Ladies' Land League and its poor treatment at the hands of male nationalists.

70. Patricia Groves, *Petticoat Rebellion: The Anna Parnell Story* (Cork, Ireland: Mercier Press, 2009), 159–251; Ely M. Janis, "Petticoat Revolutionaries: Gender, Ethnic Nationalism, and the Irish

Ladies Land League in the United States," *Journal of American Ethnic History* 27 (Winter 2008): 5–27; Tara McCarthy, " 'Progress and Poverty': An Irish Catholic Woman in the American Reform Tradition," *The Recorder* 19 (Summer 2007): 172–84; Tara McCarthy, "True Women, Trade Unionists, and the Lessons of Tammany Hall: Ethnic Identity, Social Reform, and the Political Culture of Irish Women in America, 1880–1923" (Ph.D. diss., University of Rochester, 2005), 1–89; Margaret Ward, *Unmanageable Revolutionaries: Women and Irish Nationalism* (London: Pluto Press, 1983), 4–39; Fanny Parnell, "Ladies' Land League: A Permanent Organization to be in New York City," *Irish World*, September 25, 1880, 1.

71. *Irish World*, October 29, 1881, 4.

72. Brown, *Irish-American Nationalism*, 120–22; McGee, *The IRB*, 93–94; *Irish Nation*, December 17, 1881, 2; *Irish World*, December 17, 1881, 4; December 24, 1881, 4; February 25, 1882, 4; June 4, 1883, 4. Regarding nationalist attempts to give the *No Rent Manifesto* a conservative interpretation, see *Irish-American*, December 17, 1881, and January 14, 1882; as well as *Irish Nation*, March 11, 1882, 4.

73. *Truth*, October 29, 1881, 1; November 2, 1881, 1; November 11, 1881; November 18, 1881; December 12, 1881; December 19, 1881, 1; December 25, 1881, 4; January 9, 1882, 4; January 23, 1882, 3; *Irish World*, December 3, 1881, 1.

74. For detailed portrait of labor activism within New York's German community, see Dorothee Schneider, *Trade Unions and Community: The German Working Class in New York City, 1870–1900* (Urbana: University of Illinois Press, 1994). See Appendix II for the "No Rent" rally's declaration of principles.

75. *Irish Nation*, February 2, 1882, 7; *JSP*, February 28, 1886, 1. See Appendix I for the "No Rent" rally's proclamation to the workers of the world.

76. For the names and occupations of the founders, see O'Donnell, "Henry George and the 'New Political Forces,' " 272.

77. J. T. McKechnie, *JSP*, February 28, 1886, 1; *Irish World*, February 11, 1882, 7; Philip S. Foner, *History of the Labor Movement*, 2:33.

78. All references to working-class republicanism throughout this work rely upon Kim Voss's definition of the phrase. See Voss, *Making of American Exceptionalism*, 80–89. For the full text of the CLU Declaration of Principles, see Appendix II.

79. Testimony of P. J. McGuire, *RCSRLC*, 1:808–13. See also *Truth*, April 17, 1882, 4, for an earlier version of the platform, which differs only slightly in wording (refer to Appendix II).

80. *Irish World*, April 1, 1882, 5; *Truth*, March 20, 1882, 1.

81. Ward, *Unmanageable Revolutionaries*, 30–32.

82. McGee, *The IRB*, 99–102; Brown, *Irish-American Nationalism*, 124–25; Lyons, *Charles Stewart Parnell*, 207–14.

83. Brown, *Irish-American Nationalism*, 124, 126–27, 130; Lyons, *Charles Stewart Parnell*, 527–32, 537–40.

84. Brown, *Irish-American Nationalism*, 72–73, 117–27; Davitt, *Fall of Feudalism*, 330–44; *Irish Nation*, May 27, 1882, 2; June 3, 1882, 4; *Irish World*, June 10, 1882, 4; June 17, 1882, 4. *Irish-American*, June 17, 1882, 1, 4; *Truth*, June 9, 1882, 1; Moody, *Davitt and the Irish Revolution*, 519–25, 539–40.

85. *Irish Nation*, June 10, 1882, 4.

86. *Irish Nation*, June 10, 1882, 4. See also *Irish Nation*, June 17, 1882, 1, 2, 4, and June 17, 1882, 2; *Irish-American*, June 17, 1882, 4; July 1, 1882, 4. The original sign of a rift between Devoy and Ford appeared in 1881, when Ford accused Devoy of withholding funds raised for the cause (Golway, *Irish Rebel*, 138–139, and *Irish World*, April 16, 1881).

87. *Irish Nation*, June 10, 1882, 4; *Irish World*, June 17, 1882, 4.

88. *Irish-American*, June 24, 1882, 4; *Irish World*, July 1, 1882, 1–3; *Irish Nation*, June 17, 1882, 1; June 24, 1882, 1, 3, 5; July 1, 1882, 4; *New York Times*, June 19, 1882, 8, and June 20, 1882, 2; *Truth*, June 19, 1882, 1.

89. *Irish World*, July 1, 1882, 2.

90. *Irish World*, July 1, 1882, 3; James J. Green, "American Catholics and the Irish Land League," *Catholic Historical Review* 35 (1949): 19–42.

91. *Irish World*, July 29, 1882, 4.

92. George Jr., *Life of Henry George*, 387; Bell, *Rebel, Priest, and Prophet*, 29.

93. Bell, *Rebel, Priest, and Prophet*, 29.

94. Brown, *Irish-American Nationalism*, 129; Schneirov, *Labor and Urban Politics*, 132–33; *Truth*, June 19, 1882, 1.

95. *New York Times*, July 6, 1882, 2.

96. *Irish World*, July 15, 1882, 1.

97. *Irish World*, July 15, 1882, 1; George Jr., *Life of Henry George*, 384–85.

98. *Irish World*, July 15, 1882, 1; *New York Times*, July 6, 1882, 2.

99. Brown, *Irish-American Nationalism*, 122, 128; Foner, "Class, Ethnicity, and Radicalism," 157; *Irish-American*, July 22, 1882, 5; October 21, 1882, 4; *Irish Nation*, March 3, 1882, 2.

100. *Irish World*, October 14, 1882, 1, 4 (emphasis in original).

101. *Irish-American*, November 4, 1882, 4; See also *Irish-American*, October 14, 1882, 4; October 21, 1882, 1, 4, 5; October 28, 1882, 4; November 4, 1882, 4; *Irish Nation*, October 14, 1882, 1, 4; October 21, 1882, 6; November 4, 1882, 5.

102. Brown, *Irish-American Nationalism*, 129–30; Lyons, *Charles Stewart Parnell*, 215, 226–34.

103. It would be six months before the American body followed suit and eight months for the New York organization to do so.

104. Testimony of P.J. McGuire, *RCSRLC*, 1:808–9.

105. *Irish World*, July 15, 1882, 1; *Truth*, May 15, 1882; May 22, 1882, 1; Testimony of P. J. McGuire, *RCSRLC*, 1:808–9; Gordon, "Studies in Irish and Irish-American Thought and Behavior," 541–49.

106. *Irish World*, October 28, 1882, 8.

5. "LABOR BUILT THIS REPUBLIC, LABOR SHALL RULE IT"

1. *Truth*, September 18, 1882, 1; October 9, 1882, 1; October 16, 1882, 3; October 18, 1882, 3.

2. Among them were Theodore F. Cuno, James E. Quinn, Edward King, Patrick Doody, William McCabe, John Jay Joyce, and Edward J. Rowe, as well as Germans Samuel Schimkowitz and August Ernst.

3. *Irish World*, November 4, 1882, 1, 6; November 11, 1882, 1, 6, 8; *New York Times*, October 21, 1882, 5; *Truth*, October 21, 1882, 1.

4. *Irish World*, October 14, 1882, 5.

5. Voss, *Making of American Exceptionalism*, 80–89.

6. The full record of the committee's hearings is contained in a five volume collection: United States Senate, Committee on Education and Labor, *Report of the Committee of the Senate upon the Relations between Labor and Capital*, 5 vols. (Washington, D.C.: U.S. Government Printing Office, 1885), cited throughout as *RCSRLC*.

7. Furner, "Republican Tradition," 197.

8. *Truth*, October 10, 1882; February 12, 1883, 1; February 19, 1883, 3. Letter of Louis F. Post to *RCSRLC*, 1:501–2; Furner, "Republican Tradition," 201–2. See the Testimony of Edward King,

RCSRLC, 1:687, for an articulation of labor's concern over fraudulent individuals "appearing to speak for the workingmen."

9. Dawley, *Struggles for Justice*, 25; Huston, *Securing the Fruits*, 344; Kazin, *Populist Persuasion*, 16, 344–45; Lasch, *True and Only Heaven*, 64; Aileen S. Kraditor, *The Radical Persuasion, 1890–1917: Aspects of the Intellectual History of the Historiography of Three American Radical Organizations* (Baton Rouge: Louisiana State University Press, 1981), 75; Rossinow, *Visions of Progress*, 16; Trachtenberg, *Incorporation of America*, 54.

10. Testimony of Joseph Finnerty, *RCSRLC*, 1:740–46, and Testimony of James E. Smith, *RCSRLC*, 1:765–70.

11. Testimony of Thomas McGuire, *RCSRLC*, 1:771–83; Testimony of Jeremiah Murphy, *RCSRLC*, 2:678–87. See also Licht, *Industrializing America*, 184–85.

12. Testimony of Conrad Carl, *RCSRLC*, 1:413–16; Testimony of Joseph Finnerty, *RCSRLC*, 1:740–46; Testimony of John Morrison, *RCSRLC*, 1:756; Testimony of Charles L. Miller, *RCSRLC*, 1:746–54.

13. Testimony of Conrad Carl, *RCSRLC*, 1:416; Testimony of Joseph Finnerty, *RCSRLC*, 1:740–46; Testimony of Samuel Gompers, *RCSRLC*, 1:376; Testimony of John Morrison, *RCSRLC*, 1:760.

14. Testimony of P. J. McGuire, *RCSRLC*, 1:343–44.

15. Testimony of Robert Blissert, *RCSRLC*, 1:842, 859; Testimony of James E. Smith, *RCSRLC*, 1:765–70.

16. On the pervasiveness of the self-made man ideal in the Gilded Age, see Judy Hilkey, *Character Is Capital: Success Manuals and Manhood in Gilded Age America* (Chapel Hill: University of North Carolina Press, 1997), passim; Kilmer, *Fear of Sinking*, 1–21; Lears, *Rebirth of a Nation*, 55–57; Edwards, *New Spirits*, 88–89; Daniel T. Rodgers, *The Work Ethic in Industrial America, 1850–1920* (Chicago: University of Chicago Press, 1978), 125–52.

17. Testimony of Joseph Finnerty, *RCSRLC*, 1:740–46; Testimony of Thomas McGuire, *RCSRLC*, 1:771–72; Testimony of Charles L. Miller, *RCSRLC*, 1:746–54; Testimony of P. J. McGuire, *RCSRLC*, 1:358; Kazin, *Populist Persuasion*, 36; Trachtenberg, *Incorporation of America*, 74.

18. Testimony of Thomas McGuire, *RCSRLC*, 1:775.

19. Testimony of John Morrison, *RCSRLC*, 1:760.

20. Beckert, *Monied Metropolis*, 256–60; Huston, *Securing the Fruits*, 193–202; Testimony of Conrad Carl, *RCSRLC*, 1:419.

21. Testimony of Edward King, *RCSRLC*, 1:688–89, and *RCSRLC*, 2:869–70; Klein, *Genesis of Industrial America*, 132; Richardson, *Death of Reconstruction*, 190; Rossinow, *Visions of Progress*, 14; Tomlins, *State and the Unions*, 51. For other examples of worker criticism of labor as a "mere commodity," see the text of P. J. McGuire's speech, *Irish World*, November 4, 1882, 1, 6, and the letter of W. A. Millington, "Brooklyn Harness Makers," *JSP*, February 24, 1884, 4.

22. Testimony of Thomas McGuire, *RCSRLC*, 1:778.

23. Ibid., *RCSRLC*, 1:781; Testimony of John Morrison, *RCSRLC*, 1:760; Trachtenberg, *Incorporation of America*, 74–78.

24. Testimony of Edward King, *RCSRLC*, 2:888.

25. Burke, *Conundrum of Class*, 133–58; Kazin, *Populist Persuasion*, 34–35; Stromquist, *Reinventing "The People,"* 20; Kloppenberg, *Uncertain Victory*, 208; Testimony of P. J. McGuire, *RCSRLC*, 1:343–44. See also Terence Powderly, "A Few Practical Hints," *Journal of United Labor* 1 (1880): 21, for a typical condemnation of "class."

26. Testimony of Edward King, *RCSRLC*, 2:878–83.

27. Voss, *Making of American Exceptionalism*, 80–81; Stromquist, *Reinventing "The People,"* 20; Furner, "Republican Tradition," 172; Kloppenberg, *Uncertain Victory*, 170–95. Currarino, *Labor Question*, 14–15; Testimony of P. J. McGuire, *RCSRLC*, 1:326.

28. Testimony of Robert Blissert, *RCSRLC*, 1:860; Testimony of John Morrison, *RCSRLC*, 1:758. See also Richardson, *Death of Reconstruction*, 196–97; Jaher, *Doubters and Dissenters*, passim.

29. *Truth*, May 15, 1882; *JSP*, February 28, 1886, 1; Jonathan Grossman, "Who Is the Father of Labor Day?," *Labor History* 14, no. 4 (1973): 612–23; Michael Kazin and Steven J. Ross, "America's Labor Day: The Dilemma of a Workers' Celebration," *Journal of American History* 78, no. 4 (March 1992): 1125.

30. *Truth*, September 6, 1882, 1; *New York Times*, September 5, 1882, 1; September 6, 1882, 1; September 7, 1882, 2; *Irish World*, September 16, 1882, 1; *Irish Nation*, September 9, 1882, 8; *New York Herald*, September 6, 1882; Matthew Dennis, *Red, White, and Blue Letter Days: An American Calendar* (Ithaca, N.Y.: Cornell University Press, 2002), 243.

31. *Truth*, August 7, 1882, 1; August 21, 1882, 1; August 28, 1882, 1; September 4, 1882, 1; September 5, 1882, 1; September 6, 1882, 1; *New York Times*, September 5, 1882, 1; September 6, 1882, 1; September 7, 1882, 2; *Irish World*, September 16, 1882, 1; *Irish Nation*, September 9, 1882, 8; *New York Herald*, September 6, 1882.

32. *Truth*, August 20, 1883, 3; September 3, 1882, 1; September 6, 1883, 1; *Irish World*, September 15, 1883, 4, 5; *New York Times*, September 6, 1883, 4, 8.

33. *JSP*, August 10, 1884; August 17, 1884, 4; September 7, 1884, 2; *Boycotter*, August 2, 1884; August 16, 1884, 2; August 23, 1884, 1; August 30, 1884, 3; September 13, 1884, 1; *New York Times*, September 1, 1884, 1; September 2, 1884, 8; *Irish World*, September 13, 1884, 5.

34. Knights of Labor, *Record of the Proceedings of the General Assembly* (Philadelphia, 1884), 726; Federation of Organized Trades and Labor Unions, *Report of the Fourth Annual Session of the Federation of Organized Trades and Labor Unions of the United States and Canada* (Chicago, 1884), 16; *JSP*, September 6, 1885, 1; *New York Times*, September 8, 1885, 8; *Irish World*, September 12, 1885, 4, 5; *JSP*, September 12, 1886, 4; *Irish World*, September 11, 1886, 4.

35. See Dennis, *Red, White, and Blue Letter Days*, 243, for his observation about the dual quality of Labor Day celebrations.

36. Testimony of P. J. McGuire, *RCSRLC*, 1:808; *New York Herald*, September 6, 1882, quoted in Kazin and Ross, "America's Labor Day," 1302.

37. *JSP*, September 7, 1884, 2. See also *JSP*, February 28, 1886, 1.

38. Foner, *History of the Labor Movement*, 2:32–33; Julie Greene, *Pure and Simple Politics: The American Federation of Labor and Political Activism, 1881–1917* (New York: Cambridge University Press, 1998), 55–58; Fink, *Workingmen's Democracy*, 3–37.

39. Fink, *Workingmen's Democracy*, 24–25; Greene, *Pure and Simple Politics*, 58; Phelan, *Grand Master Workman*, 134–37; Testimony of Robert Blissert, *RCSRLC*, 1:860; Testimony of Thomas B. McGuire, *RCSRLC*, 1:783.

40. For more on the development of party loyalty, see David Brody, "Labor Movement," in *Encyclopedia of American Political History*, ed. Jack P. Greene (New York: Scribner's, 1984), 709–27; Voss, *Making of American Exceptionalism*, 120–22. For more on the many structural obstacles faced by third parties, see Greene, *Pure and Simple Politics*, 55; Katznelson, *City Trenches*, 45–72, and "Working-Class Formation and the State: Nineteenth-Century England in American Perspective," in *Bringing the State Back In*, eds. Peter Evans, Dietrich Rueschemeyer, and Theda Skocpol (Cambridge: Cambridge University Press, 1985), 257–84; Richard Oestreicher, "Urban Working-Class Political Behavior and Theories," 1282–84.

41. "Circular Letter, no. 3," *Truth*, March 27, 1882, 3; *Truth*, April 3, 1882, 3; April 17, 1882, 4; *New York Times*, April 17, 1882, 8.

42. *Truth*, June 26, 1882, 4.

43. *New York Times*, July 10, 1882, 10; *Truth*, July 17, 1882, 3.

44. *New York Times*, July 20, 1882, 2.

45. *Truth*, August 7, 1882, 1.

46. *New York Times*, July 20, 1882, 2; *Truth*, July 24, 1882, 1; August 7, 1882, 1; August 16, 1882, 1; September 23, 1882, 3. For a detailed discussion of this election and a list of the ULP's platform demands, see O'Donnell, "Henry George and the 'New Political Forces,'" 365–66.

47. *Truth*, August 7, 1882, 1; August 8, 1882, 1; September 4, 1882, 1; September 9, 1882; September 11, 1882, 3; September 18, 1882, 1; November 27, 1882, 2; December 4, 1882, 2; January 8, 1883, 3; *New York Times*, August 28, 1882, 8. On the fear of political meddling in labor's affairs by outsiders, see Testimony of P. J. McGuire, *RCSRLC*, 1:809.

48. *Truth*, October 2, 1882, 1.

49. *Truth*, August 9, 1882, 2.

50. *Truth*, November 9, 1882, 1; November 13, 1882, 3; December 25, 1882, 3; and January 8, 1883, 2. For a comparison with the views and strategies of workers in Chicago, see Schneirov, *Labor and Urban Politics*, 82, 89, 139, 145, 152, 162, 172.

51. *Truth*, November 13, 1882, 3; July 9, 1883, 3; *Irish World*, July 28, 1883, 7.

52. *Truth*, October 8, 1883, 3; October 15, 1883, 2; October 22, 1883, 4; October 29, 1883, 3; November 5, 1883, 1; November 12, 1883, 3; *New York Times*, October 22, 1883, 5; November 5, 1883, 5.

53. William Forbath, "The Ambiguities of Free Labor: Labor and Law in the Gilded Age," *Wisconsin Law Review* 4 (July–August 1985): 816.

54. *Boycotter*, February 21, 1885, 1; November 14, 1885, 3; December 5, 1885; December 19, 1885, 2; January 9, 1886, 2; January 16, 1886, 3; January 23, 1886, 1; *JSP*, January 18, 1885, 4; February 1, 1885, 4; February 8, 1885, 4; Fink, *Workingmen's Democracy*, 18–37; Greene, *Pure and Simple Politics*, 55–58; Gerald N. Grob, *Workers and Utopia: A Study of Ideological Conflict in the American Labor Movement, 1865–1900* (Chicago: Quadrangle Books, 1969), 34–59; Montgomery, *Beyond Equality*, 195–96, 249–60; Norman Ware, *The Labor Movement in the United States, 1860–1895: A Study in Democracy* (New York: D. Appleton, 1929), 350–70. For more details on continued efforts by labor activists to promote an independent labor party, see O'Donnell, "Henry George and the 'New Political Forces,'" 379–84.

55. Testimony of Edward King, *RCSRLC*, 1:691.

56. *JSP*, November 29, 1885, 4; December 6, 1885, 4; June 13, 1886, 4; September 12, 1886, 4; *Truth*, May 8, 1882, 1.

57. *JSP*, December 6, 1885, 4; February 7, 1886, 4; May 16, 1886, 4; *Boycotter*, January 23, 1886, 3.

58. *Boycotter*, December 19, 1885, 2; *Irish Nation*, June 24, 1882, 1, 3, 5; July 8, 1882, 8; *Irish World*, July 1, 1882, 1–2; July 15, 1882, 1; April 26, 1884, 1; *JSP*, April 6, 1884; April 13, 1884, 4; May 4, 1884, 4; September 14, 1884, 4; October 19, 1884, 4; June 7, 1885, 1; December 27, 1885, 4; January 31, 1886, 4; February 7, 1886, 4; May 2, 1886, 1; *New York Times*, June 20, 1882, 2, and October 21, 1882, 5; *Truth*, May 15, 1882, 1; May 22, 1882, 1; October 20, 1882, 3; Gordon, "Studies in Irish and Irish-American Thought and Behavior," 498.

59. George, *Social Problems*, 46.

60. *Truth*, July 17, 1882, 3. See also *Truth*, November 13, 1882, 3.

61. For biographical information on Swinton, see Garlin, *Three American Radicals*, 3–46; Marc Ross, "John Swinton, Journalist and Reformer: The Active Years, 1857–1887" (Ph.D. diss., New York University, 1969); Frank T. Reuter, "John Swinton's Paper," *Labor History* 1 (Fall 1960): 298–307; *JSP*, June 1, 1884.

62. Letter of CLU Secretary J. T. McKechnie, *JSP*, November 15, 1885, 2.

63. Testimony of George G. Block, *RCSRLC*, 1:437–42; *Irish World*, July 28, 1883, 7; *JSP*, August 10, 1884, 4; March 1, 1885, 4; March 28, 1886, 1; Semi-Annual Report of CLU Secretary Charles Miller, *JSP*, July 13, 1884, 4; *JSP*, November 1, 1885, 4; January 17, 1886, 4; *New York Times*, April 25, 1881,

8; May 3, 1881, 8; May 4, 1881, 5; *Truth*, July 9, 1883, 3; Samuel Gompers, *Seventy Years of Life and Labor*, 1:143–55; Schneider, *Trade Unions and Community*, 89–118.

64. Estimates on the number of women workers and their earnings come from *JSP*, November 25, 1883. For additional articles regarding the effort to organize women workers, see *JSP*, February 10, 1885, 4; February 24, 1885, 1; February 22, 1885, 4; March 1, 1885, 4; March 15, 1885, 4; April 19, 1885, 4; April 26, 1885, 4; May 3, 1885, 2; June 7, 1885, 4; June 14, 1885, 4; July 5, 1885, 4; July 19, 1885, 4; August 9, 1885, 4; August 16, 1885, 4; September 6, 1885, 1; October 11, 1885, 4; November 1, 1885, 1; December 13, 1885, 4; January 24, 1886, 4; January 31, 1886, 4; March 14, 1886, 1, 4; May 16, 1886, 4; May 30, 1886, 4; July 18, 1886, 4.

65. *JSP*, August 2, 1885, 4; August 16, 1885, 4; August 23, 1885, 4; September 6, 1885, 4.

66. Testimony of P. J. McGuire, *RCSRLC*, 1:820–21; Testimony of John S. McClelland, *RCSRLC*, 1:152, 209. See also Edwin Gabler, *The American Telegrapher: A Social History, 1860–1900* (New Brunswick, N.J.: Rutgers University Press, 1988), 5–29, and Edward Renehan, *The Dark Genius of Wall Street: The Misunderstood Life of Jay Gould* (New York: Basic Books, 2005), 279–80.

67. *JSP*, April 11, 1884, 4; Semi-Annual Report of CLU Secretary Charles Miller, *JSP*, July 13, 1884, 4; *Irish World*, June 28, 1884, 8. See Licht, *Industrializing America*. 173–74, for statistics on Gilded Age strikes that show a 47 percent success rate nationally between 1880 and 1900.

68. Testimony of P. J. McGuire, *RCSRLC*, 1:808–9; *JSP*, February 17, 1884; March 2, 1884, 4; August 10, 1884; August 2, 1885; October 11, 1885; November 8, 1885; May 2, 1886; May 9, 1886, 4; May 16, 1886, 4; September 26, 1886; October 10, 1886; October 17, 1886, 4.

69. *JSP*, November 30, 1884, 1; December 7, 1884, 1; June 7, 1885, 4; August 2, 1885, 4; February 14, 1886, 4; May 9, 1886, 4.

70. Gordon, "Studies in Irish and Irish-American Thought and Behavior," 541–600. For more on the history of American workers' use of the boycott, see Lawrence B. Glickman, *Buying Power: A History of Consumer Activism in America* (Chicago: University of Chicago Press, 2009); Harry W. Laidler, *Boycotts and the Labor Struggle Economic and Legal Aspects* (New York: John Lane, 1914); and Leo Wolman, *The Boycott in American Trade Unions* (Baltimore: Johns Hopkins University Press, 1916).

71. Gordon, "Studies in Irish and Irish-American Thought and Behavior," 541–600; Ware, *Labor Movement*, 334–45; Gutman, "The Workers' Search for Power," 38–68.

72. NYSBLS, *Third Annual Report*, Senate Documents 3, no. 23 (1886), 343; *JSP*, September 13, 1885, 4; November 2, 1885, 4; January 17, 1886, 4; September 26, 1886, 4; April 25, 1886, 4; *Boycotter*, January 9, 1886, 2, and Jan 16, 1886, 3. For a discussion of similar efforts by Chicago workers to organize and manage boycotts, see Schneirov, *Labor and Urban Politics*, 123–28, 192.

73. *Bradstreet's*, December 19, 1885, 394–97; NYSBLS, *Third Annual Report*, 333–62; NYSBLS, *Fourth Annual Report*, Assembly Documents 5, no. 27 (1887), 738–43; NYSBLS, *Fifth Annual Report*, Assembly Documents 5, no. 74 (1888), 521–23. See also William A. Hammond, "The Evolution of the Boycott," *Forum* (June 1886), 369–76.

74. *JSP*, February 10, 1884, 4; *Irish World*, March 1, 1884, 7; Burrows and Wallace, *Gotham*, 1013, 1036, 1095–98, 1192, 1201–2; Johnson, *Street Justice*, 12–86; Keller, *Triumph of Order*, 49–60, 173–78; 189–90.

75. *JSP*, April 13, 1884, 2; February 8, 1885, 1; *Truth*, May 1, 1882, 1; *Irish World*, July 15, 1882, 1; *Irish Nation*, July 8, 1882, 8; *Truth*, July 3, 1882, 1; Keller, *Triumph of Order*, 22, 29–31. Schneirov cites a similar incident in Chicago in *Labor and Urban Politics*, 75.

76. *JSP*, May 4, 1884, 4; Dawley, *Struggles for Justice*, 200–9. *Boycotter*, May 17, 1884, 2.

77. *JSP*, March 16, 1884, 1, 4; *Truth*, July 24, 1882, 1.

78. *JSP*, February 17, 1884, 4; February 24, 1884; March 16, 1884, 1.

79. *JSP*, October 19, 1884, 1; Eileen Boris, "'A Man's Dwelling House Is His Castle': Tenement House Cigarmaking and the Judicial Imperative," in *Work Engendered: Toward a New History of American Labor*, ed. Ava Baron (Ithaca, N.Y.: Cornell University Press, 1991), 114–44; William E. Forbath, *Law and the Shaping of the American Labor Movement* (Cambridge, Mass.: Harvard University Press, 1991), 38–39; Gompers, *Seventy Years of Life and Labor*, 1:183–198.

80. Daniel R. Ernst, *Lawyers Against Labor: From Individual Rights to Corporate Liberalism* (Urbana: University of Illinois Press, 1995), 70–76; Forbath, *Law and the Shaping*, 61–62, 88–89, 131; Hays, *Response to Industrialism*, 177; Tomlins, *State and the Unions*, 36–52.

81. Voss, *Making of American Exceptionalism*, 33; Wilentz, *Chants Democratic*, 286–94; Beckert, *Monied Metropolis* 302–4; Hays, *Response to Industrialism*, 175–79; Tomlins, *State and the Unions*, 44–49; Montgomery, *Beyond Equality*, 146–47; John R. Commons et al., *History of Labour in the United States* (New York: Macmillan, 1936), 2:404–12. For a detailed, line-by-line critique of the New York State Penal Code, see *Truth*, May 29, 1882, 1.

82. *Truth*, May 22, 1882, 1; David Montgomery, *Citizen Worker: The Experience of Workers in the United States with Democracy and the Free Market during the Nineteenth Century* (New York: Cambridge University Press, 1993), 47–50, 151; Laurie, *Artisans into Workers*, 137–38; Victoria Hattam, "Economic Visions and Political Strategies: American Labor and the State, 1865–1896," in *Studies in American Political Development*, eds. Karen Orren and Stephen Skowronek (New York: Cambridge University Press, 1990), 4:82–129; *New York Times*, April 16, 1883, 4; *Truth*, April 16, 1883, 3. For a useful overview of the penal code and the effort to amend it in 1882, see Peter Speek, "The Singletax and the Labor Movement" (Ph.D. diss., University of Wisconsin, 1915), printed in the *Bulletin of the University of Wisconsin*, no. 878, Economic and Political Science Series 8, no. 3 (Madison: University of Wisconsin, 1917), 53–56.

83. Phelan, *Grand Master Workman*, 134–37.

84. *JSP*, March 9, 1884, 4; March 30, 1884, 4; April 13, 1884, 2, 4; April 20, 1884, 4; April 27, 1884, 4; May 11, 1884, 4.

85. *JSP*, February 3, 1884, 4 (ironclad oath); February 24, 1884, 4 (the penal code); March 2, 1884, 4 (tenement manufacturing); March 2, 1884, 4 (foreign contract labor); April 20, 1884, 4 (eight-hour workday); June 1, 1884, and July 13, 1884, 4 (CLU condemnation); February 22, 1885, 4 (child labor); April 5, 1885, 4 (contract convict labor). For an examination of the struggle between progressives, including labor activists, and the courts, see William G. Ross, *A Muted Fury: Populists, Progressives, and Labor Unions Confront the Courts, 1890–1937* (Princeton, N.J.: Princeton University Press, 1994).

86. Knights of Labor membership statistics drawn from Leo Wolman, *The Growth of American Trade Unions, 1880–1923* (New York: National Bureau of Economic Research, 1924), 31–33.

87. Phelan, *Grand Master Workman*, 70–72, 77–79; Gordon, "Studies in Irish and Irish-American Thought and Behavior," 503–16. See also Weir, *Beyond Labor's Veil*, regarding the centrality of rituals in the culture of Knights members.

88. Henry J. Browne, *The Catholic Church and the Knights of Labor* (Washington, D.C.: Catholic University Press, 1949), passim; Robert Emmett Curran, *Michael Augustine Corrigan and the Shaping of Conservative Catholicism in America, 1878–1902* (New York: Arno Press, 1978), 189–94.

89. Phelan, *Grand Master Workman*, 47–80.

90. Speek, "The Singletax and the Labor Movement," 41; Knights of Labor, *Record of the Proceedings of the General Assembly of the Knights of Labor of America* (Richmond, Va., 1886), 326–28.

91. Letter of Matthew Maguire, William Horan, Theodore F. Cuno, et al. to HG, April 17, 1881, HGP. For more on the role of DA 49 in the rise of the Knights in New York and the subsequent contro-

versies associated with its "Home Club" faction, see Craig Phelan, "The Warp of Fancy: The Knights of Labor and the Home Club Takeover Myth," *Labor History* 40, no. 3 (August 1999): 283–99; Robert E. Weir, "'Here's to the Men Who Lose': The Hidden Career of Victor Drury," *Labor History* 36, no. 4 (Fall 1995): 530–56; Robert E. Weir, "Powderly and the Home Club: The Knights of Labor Joust Among Themselves," *Labor History* 34, no. 1 (Winter 1993): 84–113; Robert E. Weir, *Knights Unhorsed: Internal Conflict in a Gilded Age Social Movement* (Detroit: Wayne State University Press, 2000), 23–46.

92.   Patricia A. Cooper, *Once a Cigar Maker: Men, Women, and Work Culture in American Cigar Factories, 1900–1919* (Urbana: University of Illinois Press, 1987), 21–25; Foner, *History of the Labor Movement*, 2:133; Gordon, "Studies in Irish and Irish-American Thought and Behavior," 561.

93.   Foner, *History of the Labor Movement*, 1:517–18.

94.   Burrows and Wallace, *Gotham*, 1091.

95.   Phelan, *Grand Master Workman*, 33; Barker, *Henry George*, 433–35. For details on George and Powderly's meeting, see Terence Powderly, *The Path I Trod* (New York: Columbia University Press, 1940), 182–83; HG to Terence Powderly, April 19, 1883, and July 25, 1883 in Terence Powderly Papers, Catholic University, Washington, D.C.; and *Baltimore Sun*, August 2, 1883.

96.   Powderly, *Thirty Years of Labor*, 335–51; Ware, *Labor Movement*, 88–89, 364–67.

97.   Brundage, *Making of Western Labor Radicalism*, 33–34; Gompers, *Seventy Years of Life and Labor*, 1:82; Schneirov, *Labor and Urban Politics*, 133; George, *Social Problems*, 60–61; Testimony of Edward King, *RCSRLC*, 2:76. See also the letter of W. A. Millington, "Brooklyn Harness Makers," in *JSP*, February 24, 1884, 4, and the Testimony of Robert Blissert, *RCSRLC*, 1:854, for representative expressions of worker admiration for George's *Progress and Poverty*.

98.   George, *Progress and Poverty*, 11; Stromquist, *Reinventing "The People,"* 41–44.

99.   George, *Progress and Poverty*, 537.

100. Ely, *Recent American Socialism*, 18; Steve Fraser and Gary Gerstle, introduction to *Ruling America: A History of Wealth and Power in a Democracy*, eds. Steve Fraser and Gary Gerstle (Cambridge, Mass.: Harvard University Press, 2005), 10; Huston, *Securing the Fruits*, 345.

101. Cohen, *Reconstruction of American Liberalism*, 160–65.

102. Huston, *Securing the Fruits*, 342.

103. George, *Progress and Poverty*, 453.

104. Ross, "Culture of Political Economy," 151; Kazin, *Populist Persuasion*, 33; Lears, *Rebirth of a Nation*, 10; Rossinow, *Visions of Progress*, 13; Kenneth Fones-Wolf, *Trade Union Gospel: Christianity and Labor in Industrial Philadelphia, 1865–1915* (Philadelphia: Temple University Press, 1989), xv, 64–94. See also McLeod, *Piety and Poverty*.

105. Oser, *Henry George*, 32–50, and Rose, *Henry George*, 29, quoted in Ross, "Culture of Political Economy," 152; Burke, *Conundrum of Class*, 140–51.

106. George, *Progress and Poverty*, 559.

107. Ely, *Recent American Socialism*, 19; *Irish World*, November 4, 1882, 4; Ross, "Culture of Political Economy," 151–52.

108. Foner, "Class, Ethnicity, and Radicalism," 184, Huston, *Securing the Fruits*, 130–32, 189–91; Kloppenberg, *Uncertain Victory*, 208; Laurie, *Artisans into Workers*, 150–58; Richard Oestreicher, "Terence Powderly, the Knights of Labor, and Artisanal Republicanism," in *Labor Leaders in America*, eds. Melvin Dubofsky and Warren Van Tine (Urbana: University of Illinois Press, 1987), 34–36; Ross, "Culture of Political Economy," 148, 157–58; Rossinow, *Visions of Progress*, 16–17; Stromquist, *Reinventing "The People,"* 42–43.

109. George, *Progress and Poverty*, 543; Huston, *Securing the Fruits*, 345; Ross, "Culture of Political Economy," 151, 154; Rossinow, *Visions of Progress*, 18. See the CLU's Declaration of Principles (Appendix II) for an assertion nearly identical to George's.

110. Huston, *Securing the Fruits*, 375.

111. For examples of reports sounding the alarm regarding the sharp increase in wealth inequality in late nineteenth-century America, see W. M. Dickson, "The Apotheosis of the Plutocrat," *Magazine of American History* 18 (1887), 497–509; Eltweed Pomeroy, "The Concentration of Wealth," *Arena* 17 (December 1896), 82–96; Robert N. Reeves, "Has Wealth a Limitation?" *Arena* 18 (August 1897), 160–67; Thomas G. Shearman, "The Owners of the United States," *Forum* 8 (November 1889), 262–73; Charles B. Spahr, *An Essay on the Present Distribution of Wealth in the United States* (New York: T. Y. Crowell, 1896).

112. Burrows and Wallace, *Gotham*, 766–73; Currarino, *Labor Question*, 23–24; Foner, "Class, Ethnicity, and Radicalism," 184, Huston, *Securing the Fruits*, 259–95; Lustig, *Corporate Liberalism*, 60–68; Schneirov, *Labor and Urban Politics*, 176; Thomas, *Alternative America*, 3, 50–53, 64–65; Wrobel, *End of American Exceptionalism*, 3–25. For more on the appeal of land reform in the antebellum period, see Jamie L. Bronstein, *Land Reform and Working-Class Experience in Britain and the United States, 1800–1862* (Palo Alto, Calif.: Stanford University Press, 1999), passim, and Norman Ware, *The Industrial Worker, 1840–1860: The Reaction of American Industrial Society to the Advance of the Industrial Revolution* (New York: Quadrangle Books, 1974), 181–84.

113. W. M. Dick, "Two Views of the Knights of Labor: Centennial Symposium, Chicago, May 1979," *Labour/Le Travail* 5 (May 1980): 185–92; Jason Kaufman, "Rise and Fall of a Nation of Joiners: The Knights of Labor Revisited," *Journal of Interdisciplinary History* 31, no. 4 (March 2001): 553–79.

114. Postel, *Populist Vision*, 4–5, 11; Stromquist, *Reinventing "The People,"* 41.

115. Hays, *Response to Industrialism*, 93; Voss, *Making of American Exceptionalism*, 81–89; Furner, "Republican Tradition," 194–95. For more on the emergence of an economic dimension of citizenship, see Eric Foner, *Story of American Freedom*, 139–62.

116. Huston, *Securing the Fruits*, 150; Voss, *Making of American Exceptionalism*, 83.

117. Currarino, *Labor Question*, 60–85; George, *Progress and Poverty*, 319–21; Kloppenberg, *Uncertain Victory*, 170–95; Rodgers, *Atlantic Crossing*, 140; Schneirov, *Labor and Urban Politics*, 176; Stromquist, *Reinventing "The People,"* 42. For a discussion of George's popularity among telegraph operators due in part to his call for state ownership of telegraph lines, see Gabler, *American Telegrapher*, 133–34, 206–8.

118. Weir, *Beyond Labor's Veil*, 68; Fones-Wolf, *Trade Union Gospel*, 64–94; Lears, *Rebirth of a Nation*, 10; McLeod, *Piety and Poverty*, 103–26. For examples of worker antipathy toward organized religion, see Testimony of Edward King, *RCSRLC*, 2:80–85, and Testimony of P. J. McGuire, *RCSRLC*, 1:358. An examination of the linkage between Christianity and labor reform can be found in David A. Zonderman, *Uneasy Allies: Working for Labor Reform in Nineteenth-Century Boston* (Amherst: University of Massachusetts Press, 2011), 174–81. For an analysis of George's impact on the social gospel movement, see Kazin, *American Dreamers*, 77–79; Eileen W. Lindner, "The Redemptive Politic of Henry George: Legacy to the Social Gospel" (Ph.D. diss., Union Theological Seminary, New York, 1985); and Fred Nicklason, "Henry George: Social Gospeller," *American Quarterly* 22, no. 3 (Autumn 1970): 649–64.

119. Letter of C. P. Atkinson, *JSP*, October 24, 1886, 2.

120. George Jr., *Life of Henry George*, 425; Barker, *Henry George*, 431–48.

121. George Jr., *Life of Henry George*, 408.

122. According to Henry George Jr. (*Life of Henry George*, 408, 425), Sumner had *Progress and Poverty* in mind when writing his essays. George's series ran from April 14–October 20, 1883; Sumner's ran from February 24–May 5, 1883. Sumner, like George, later published his essay in book form under the title, *What Social Classes Owe Each Other* (New York: Harper's, 1883); Barker, *Henry*

George, 425–27; Joshua Brown, *Beyond the Lines: Pictorial Reporting, Everyday Life, and the Crisis of Gilded Age America* (Berkeley: University of California Press, 2002), 183–84. For a comparative analysis of George and Sumner, see Jeff Sklansky, "Pauperism and Poverty: Henry George, William Graham Sumner, and the Ideological Origins of Modern American Social Science," *Journal of the History of the Behavioral Sciences* 35, no. 2 (Spring 1999): 111–38.

123. Henry George, "Problems of the Time: The Necessity of Giving Greater Attention to Social Questions," *Frank Leslie's Illustrated Newspaper*, April 14, 1883, 119.

124. Trachtenberg (*Incorporation of America*, 42) posits that George's warnings about mechanization appeared to be in direct response to an essay a few months earlier by Carroll Wright ("The Factory System as an Element of Civilization," *Journal of Social Science* 16, no.1 (1882), 101–26).

125. George, *Social Problems*, 6, 9, 15, 16, 47, 49, 140, 150–60.

126. Ibid., 181.

127. Ibid., 160.

128. Ibid., 84.

129. Ibid., 129.

130. Ibid., 78.

131. Ibid., 176.

132. Ibid., 15. See also pages 97–98 for a similar statement.

133. Ibid., 40–48.

134. Ibid., 34, 57, 177, 191. For more on George's views on socialism, see Charles R. McCann, "Apprehending the Social Philosophy of Henry George," in *Henry George: Political Ideologue, Social Philosopher and Economic Theorist*, ed. Lawrence S. Moss (New York: Blackwell, 2008), 74–80.

135. Ely, *Recent American Socialism*, 16–21.

136. For more on the widespread popularity of a loosely defined socialism in the 1880s, see Greene, *Pure and Simple Politics*, 55; B. H. Moss, "Republican Socialism and the Making of the Working Class in Britain, France, and the United States," *Comparative Studies in Society and History* 35, no. 2 (April 1993), 390–413; Phelan, *Grand Master Workman*, 66–68, 101–2, 146–47; Rodgers, *Work Ethic in Industrial America*, 117–18; Schneirov, *Labor and Urban Politics*, 54, 145, 173–76.

137. Some of these works include: Richard T. Ely, *Recent American Socialism* (1885); Laurence Gronlund, *The Cooperative Commonwealth* (1884); and Josiah Strong, *Our Country: Its Possible Future and Its Present Crisis* (1885). In addition to these works of nonfiction, many novels also appeared, such as: Stewart Denison, *An Iron Crown: A Tale of the Great Republic* (1885); George T. Dowling, *The Wreckers: A Social Study* (1886); Martin Foran, *The Other Side: A Social Study Based on Fact* (1886); and John Hay, *The Bread Winners* (1884).

138. Strong includes in his 1885 book a quotation from one of George's essays in *Social Problems* (67).

139. George, *Social Problems*, 9, 63.

140. Barker, *Henry George*, 427–31; Steven B. Cord, "Walker: The General Leads the Charge," in *Critics of Henry George: A Centenary Appraisal of Their Strictures on Progress and Poverty*, ed. Robert V. Andelson (Cranbury, N.J.: Associated University Presses, 1979), 178–86; John K. Whitaker, "Enemies or Allies? Henry George and Francis Amasa Walker One Century Later," *Journal of Economic Literature* 35, no. 4 (December 1997): 1891–1915.

141. Brown, *Beyond the Lines*, 183–84.

142. George Jr., *Life of Henry George*, 410.

143. Testimony of Henry George, *RCSRLC*, 1:466–524.

144. *New York Times*, September 6, 1883, 8.

145. Ely, *Recent American Socialism*, 20; *New York Times*, September 6, 1883.

146. Browne, *Catholic Church*, 228–30, 317–19; Curran, *Michael Augustine Corrigan*, 214–15.

147. George Jr., *Life of Henry George*, 395.

148. Barker, *Henry George*, 395; Rodgers, *Atlantic Crossings*, 5, 31.

149. George Jr., *Life of Henry George*, 444–47; Barker, *Henry George*, 395–410; His Grace the Duke of Argyll [George Douglas Campbell], "The Prophet of San Francisco," *Nineteenth Century* 86 (April 1884), 537–58. George responded to the duke with an essay that appeared in the journal's July issue: Henry George, "The 'Reduction to Iniquity,'" *Nineteenth Century* 89 (July 1884), 134–55. See also J. A. Hobson, "The Influence of Henry George in England," *Fortnightly Review* 68 (December 1897); and John Plowright, "Political Economy and Christian Polity: The Influence of Henry George in England Reassessed," *Victorian Studies* 30, no. 2 (Winter 1987): 235–52.

150. *New York Times*, April 30, 1884, 2.

151. Barker, *Henry George*, 444.

6. "THE COUNTRY IS DRIFTING INTO DANGER"

1. Edward T. O'Donnell, "Striking Scenes: Robert Koehler, *The Strike* (1886), and Competing Visions of Labor-Capital Conflict in the Gilded Age," *Common-Place* 11, no. 1 (October 2010), http://www.common-place.org/vol-11/no-01/lessons/; *New York Times*, April 4, 1886, 4.

2. Licht, *Industrializing America*, 173.

3. Richard T. Ely, *The Labor Movement in America* (New York: T. Y. Crowell, 1886), 113.

4. Painter, *Standing at Armageddon*, 40–45; Phelan, *Grand Master Workman*, 158–61, 178–83; Renehan, *Dark Genius of Wall Street*, 280–81. For a full treatment of the strike, see Theresa A. Case, *The Great Southwest Railroad Strike and Free Labor* (College Station: Texas A&M University Press, 2010).

5. President Grover Cleveland, Special Message to the U.S. House of Representatives and the U.S. Senate, April 22, 1886, in full-text at http://www.presidency.ucsb.edu/ws/index.php?pid=71895#ixzz1r73tSCJn. See also Gerald Friedman, "Worker Militancy and Its Consequences: Political Responses to Labor Unrest in the United States, 1877–1914," *International Labor and Working-Class History* 40 (Fall 1991): 5–17.

6. Burrows and Wallace, *Gotham*, 1098; Donna T. Haverty-Stack, *America's Forgotten Holiday: May Day and Nationalism, 1867–1960* (New York: New York University Press, 2008), 24–32; Montgomery, *Beyond Equality*, 176–85; David R. Roediger and Philip S. Foner, *Our Own Time: A History of American Labor and the Working Day* (Westport, Conn.: Greenwood Press, 1989), 123–44.

7. *New York Times*, May 6, 1886, 1.

8. James Green, *Death in the Haymarket: A Story of Chicago, the First Labor Movement, and the Bombing That Divided Gilded Age America* (New York: Anchor Books, 2006), 3–11, 174–208; Painter, *Standing at Armageddon*, 48–50; Haverty-Stack, *America's Forgotten Holiday*, 32–37.

9. *Forum* (August 1886).

10. *Irish World*, April 24, 1886, 7; HG to Richard McGhee, April 14, 1886, and June 4, 1886, HGP.

11. Sidney L. Harring, "Car Wars: Strikes, Arbitration, and Class Struggle in the Making of Labor Law," *Review of Law and Social Change* 14 (1986): 849–72; Sarah M. Henry, "The Strikers and Their Sympathizers: Brooklyn in the Trolley Strike of 1895," *Labor History* 32 (Summer 1991): 329–53; Schneirov, *Labor and Urban Politics*, 168–73.

12. NYSBLS, *Annual Report for 1886* (1886), 4:744, 809.

13. Testimony of Samuel Gompers, *RCSRLC*, 1:270–85; *JSP*, February 24, 1884, 1; NYSBLS, *Annual Report for 1886*, 4:809–39; *Boycotter*, March 6, 1886, 2.

14. *New York Times*, January 26, 1886, 3; February 2, 1886, 8; February 4, 1886, 8; February 5, 1886, 4; February 17, 1886, 2; February 18, 1886; February 19, 1886, 4, 5; February 20, 1886, 2; *JSP*, January 31, 1886, 4; February 21, 1886, 4; *Boycotter*, January 16, 1886, 2; January 30, 1886, 2; February 20, 1886, 2.

15. For details on the Dry Dock Company, see *Harper's Weekly* 30, no. 1525, March 13, 1886, 172; and *Irish World*, March 13, 1886, 7.

16. NYSBLS, *Annual Report for 1886*, 4:823–26; *JSP*, March 7, 1886, 4; *Irish World*, March 13, 1886, 7.

17. *Irish World*, March 13, 1886, 7; *Boycotter*, March 6, 1886, March 13, 1886, 2. For details on the Dry Dock Company's financial health, see *Irish World*, March 13, 1886, 7.

18. *Harper's Weekly* 30, no. 1525, March 13, 1886, 172; *New York Sun*, March 5, 1886, 1; *New York Times*, March 5, 1886, 1; *New York Tribune*, March 5, 1886, 1.

19. *Harper's Weekly* 30, no. 1525, March 13, 1886, 172; *New York Sun*, March 5, 1886, 1; *New York Times*, March 5, 1886, 1; *New York Tribune*, March 5, 1886, 1.

20. *New York Sun*, March 5, 1886, 1; *New York Times*, March 5, 1886, 1; *JSP*, March 14, 1886, 1. For more on the role of women in community protests, see Elizabeth Ewen, *Immigrant Women in the Land of Dollars: Life and Culture on the Lower East Side, 1890–1925* (New York: Monthly Review Press, 1985).

21. *New York Times*, March 5, 1886, 1.

22. Ibid.

23. Beckert, *Monied Metropolis*, 292–301; Nasaw, "Gilded Age Gospels," 136; Novak, *People's Welfare*, 235–48; Richardson, *West From Appomattox*, 2–3. Richard Schneirov notes that in the early 1880s Chicago's police practiced a conscious neutrality when it came to labor disputes, but that they shifted dramatically to a pro-business stance in the wake of a major 1885 streetcar strike (*Labor and Urban Politics*, 111–14, 151, 168–73, 192).

24. *Boycotter*, October 23, 1886, 2; July 17, 1886, 2.

25. *Irish World*, March 13, 1886, 7.

26. *New York Times*, March 6, 1886, 1; *New York Sun*, March 6, 1886, 1; *Irish World*, March 13, 1886, 4.

27. *New York Times*, March 6, 1886, 1; March 11, 1886, 3; *New York Sun*, March 6, 1886, 1; *New York Tribune*, March 6, 1886, 1; *Irish World*, March 13, 1886, 7; *JSP*, March 14, 1886, 1, *Boycotter*, March 6, 1886, 2.

28. *New York Times*, March 11, 1886, 3.

29. *New York Times*, April 18, 1886, 1.

30. *New York Times*, March 20, 1886, 2; April 30, 1886, 1. For another example of a denunciation of unions as tyrannical organizations, see Henry Clews, "The Labor Crisis," *North American Review* 142 (June 1886), 598–602.

31. *New York Times*, April 16, 1886, 1; *Boycotter*, April 24, 1886, 2; Cohen, *Reconstruction of American Liberalism*, 128; Kraditor, *Radical Persuasion*, 81; Tomlins, *State and the Unions*, 6. For a vivid cartoon depicting labor unions as tyrannical, see "The New Slavery and the New Slave-Driver," *Puck*, March 9, 1887.

32. *New York Times*, April 17, 1886, 1. For a similar expression invoking "the public" by Jay Gould, see *New York Times*, March 16, 1886, 1.

33. *New York Times*, April 19, 1886; April 20, 1886, 1.

34. *New York Times*, April 19, 1886, 1; April 21, 1886, 1; April 30, 1886, 5.

35. *New York Times*, April 19, 1886, 1; Phelan, *Grand Master Workman*, 178–83.

36. *New York Times*, April 30, 1886, 3.

37. *New York Times*, April 21, 1886, 1; April 23, 1886, 5; April 26, 1886, 1; May 3, 1886, 8; May 4, 1886, 2; May 15, 1886, 3; *Irish World*, May 1, 1886, 7.

38. *JSP*, May 2, 1886, 4; May 16, 1886, 4; June 6, 1886, 4; June 13, 1886, 4; June 20, 1886, 4; *New York Times*, April 24, 1886, 1; April 26, 1886, 1; April 29, 1886, 1; April 30, 1886, 5; May 1, 1886, 5; May 3, 1886, 8; May 9, 1886, 7; *Irish World*, May 8, 1886, 7.

39. *New York Times*, April 20, 1886, 1. For an example of bourgeois interests heaping praise on the New York City Police Department for maintaining law and order (including suppressing labor radicals), see Richard Wheatley, "The New York Police," *Harper's New Monthly Magazine* 74 (March 1887), 7–30.

40. *New York Times*, May 2, 1886, 7; *JSP*, May 9, 1886, 2; May 23, 1886, 4.

41. *New York Times*, April 17, 1886; April 20, 1886; April 22, 1886, 1.

42. *JSP*, May 2, 1886, 1. For more commentary by labor on police abuse, see *Boycotter*, May 1, 1886, 1; May 22, 1886, 2–3; July 10, 1886, 2; *New York Star*, April 26, 1886; *JSP*, March 28, 1886, 1.

43. *JSP*, June 20, 1886, 2; July 11, 1886, 2; *New York Times*, April 30, 1886, 4; April 30, 1886, 5.

44. Shortly after the Dry Dock strike, the streetcar lines formed the Surface Railroad Association of the State of New York, the charter of which legally bound all member companies to pay for the losses of any company suffering from a strike (*New York Times*, March 11, 1886, 3). Lyons did meet with representatives of other streetcar lines, but vehemently denied any pooling of money or collusion (*New York Times*, May 9, 1886, 7).

45. *Boycotter*, May 1, 1886, 1; *New York Times*, April 29, 1886, 1; May 1, 1886, 5. See Hays, *Response to Industrialism*, 174–79, regarding the predisposition of courts in the Gilded Age to render decisions favorable to business.

46. *New York Times*, April 30, 1886, 2; *JSP*, January 10, 1886; May 23, 1886, 1; *Boycotter*, May 1, 1886, 2; June 26, 1886, 1. David Nasaw ("Gilded Age Gospels," 138–39) notes that business leaders in the 1880s recognized that it was more beneficial to defang and control regulatory agencies rather than fight their outright establishment.

47. On the gradual weakening of the EPA, see *Boycotter*, May 8, 1886, 1; May 15, 1886, 1; May 22, 1886, 1; June 5, 1886, 3; June 12, 1886, 3; *JSP*, May 9, 1886, 4; May 30, 1886, 1; June 13, 1886, 4; *Irish World*, June 12, 1886, 7; *New York Times*, April 28, 1886, 1; May 6, 1886, 5; May 7, 1886, 1; May 26, 1886, 2; June 6, 1886, 1–2; June 7, 1886, 1, 4. On the third tie-up and the subsequent indictment of EPA officials, see NYSBLS, *Annual Report for 1886*, 4:744. *New York Sun*, June 6, 1886, 1–2; *New York Times*, June 6, 1886, 1–2; June 7, 1886, 1; *JSP*, June 13, 1886, 1; *Irish World*, June 12, 1886, 7.

48. *JSP*, April 25, 1886, 4. See also *JSP*, May 16, 1886, 1, for Swinton's call for police superintendents, inspectors, and captains to be directly elected by the people.

49. For a compelling analysis of how strike waves gain momentum through "positive feedback," see Michael Biggs, "Positive Feedback in Collective Mobilization: The American Strike Wave of 1886," *Theory and Society* 32 (April 2003): 217–54.

50. Burrows and Wallace, *Gotham*, 1055–77. See also Jacob Sharp's obituary in *New York Times*, April 6, 1888, 5. For more on the awarding of streetcar franchises in New York in this period, see Henry J. Carman, *The Street Surface Railway Franchises of New York City* (New York: Columbia University Press, 1919), 148–203.

51. "The Broadway Railroad," *Harper's Weekly* 30, no. 1525, March 13, 1886, 174. For a summary of the Broadway Railroad financing, see *Boycotter*, March 6, 1886, 3.

52. *New York Times*, March 19, 1886, 1.

53. *New York Times*, April 14, 1886, 1.

54. *New York Times*, May 16, 1886, 1; May 21, 1886, 1. For more details on the scandal and how the cases were resolved, see O'Donnell, "Henry George and the 'New Political Forces,'" 429–42.

55. *New York Times*, February 4, 1886, 8; February 5, 1886, 4; March 11, 1886, 3; April 20, 1886, 1; *JSP*, February 7, 1886, 4.

56. *JSP*, May 16, 1886, 1.

57. "Henry George on Strikes," *Irish World*, April 24, 1886, 7. For other examples of the Sharp-Gould connection and streetcar companies exploiting public property, see *Boycotter*, March 6, 1886, 3; *Irish World*, March 6, 1886, 4; *JSP*, May 2, 1886; May 30, 1886, 2; June 6, 1886, 3.

58. *New York Times*, May 8, 1886, 2; *JSP*, May 16, 1886, 3.

59. *JSP*, April 11, 1886, 2; May 2, 1886, 2; May 9, 1886, 2; May 16, 1886, 2; May 23, 1886, 2; July 11, 1886; July 18, 1886, 2.

60. *New York Times*, April 14, 1886, 1.

61. Gordon, "Studies in Irish and Irish-American Thought and Behavior," 387–88.

62. The ULP platform is outlined in Post and Leubuscher, *Henry George's 1886 Campaign*, 14.

63. *Boycotter*, June 14, 1884, 1, December 12, 1885, 1; December 19, 1885, 2; January 2, 1886, 1; January 31, 1886, 2; March 21, 1886, 1; Gordon, "Studies in Irish and Irish-American Thought and Behavior," 554–61; *JSP*, March 22, 1885, 4; May 24, 1885, 4; May 31, 1885, 4; August 23, 1885, 4; October 11, 1885, 4; November 1, 1885, 1, 4; November 22, 1885, 4; November 29, 1885, 3; December 6, 1885, 2; December 13, 1885, 4; December 20, 1885, 4; December 27, 1885, 4; January 3, 1886, 4; February 7, 1886, 4; February 14, 1886, 4; February 21, 1886, 4; March 14, 1886, 4; April 18, 1886, 4; May 30, 1886, 4; June 20, 1886, 1.

64. For earlier hints that authorities intended to suppress the boycott, see *Boycotter*, October 24, 1885, 2; *New York Daily Telegraph*, December 16, 1885; and *New York Morning Journal*, December 17, 1885 (the latter two cited by Adam Rothman, "'Freedom's Cause,' Boycott, and Conspiracy in 1886 New York" [Masters thesis, Columbia University, 1994], 24).

65. NYSBLS, *Annual Report for 1886*, 4:745–47; Gordon, "Studies in Irish and Irish-American Thought and Behavior," 571–73.

66. NYSBLS, *Annual Report for 1886*, 4:764–65.

67. Gordon, "Studies in Irish and Irish-American Thought and Behavior," 571–72; *JSP*, December 21, 1884; December 28, 1884, 4; January 18, 1885, 4; *New York Times*, April 30, 1886, 8; NYSBLS, *Annual Report for 1886*, 4:746–47.

68. *JSP*, March 28, 1886, 4; Gordon, "Studies in Irish and Irish-American Thought and Behavior," 572; NYSBLS, *Annual Report for 1886*, 4:745–48, 767. For other examples of unions imposing "fines" on boycotted businesses, see *Truth*, May 22, 1882, 1; *New York Times*, December 7, 1885, 8, and December 26, 1885, 4; *JSP*, January 3, 1886, 4.

69. NYSBLS, *Annual Report for 1886*, 4:748–50; Gordon, "Studies in Irish and Irish-American Thought and Behavior," 567–68.

70. On the importance of expanding a boycott to include a network of related interests beyond the offending business, see Glickman, *Buying Power*, 131–39.

71. *New York Times*, April 9, 1886, 8; April 10, 1886, 3; April 13, 1886, 8; April 15, 1886, 8; April 16, 1886, 8; April 17, 1886, 5. NYSBLS, *Annual Report for 1886*, 4:748–50.

72. NYSBLS, *Annual Report for 1886*, 4:749; Glickman, *Buying Power*, 139–42; Gordon, "Studies in Irish and Irish-American Thought and Behavior," 568–69.

73. *New York Times*, April 11, 1886, 2; April 13, 1886, 8; Beckert, *Monied Metropolis*, 273–86; Glickman, *Buying Power*, 140–43, 149, 163.

74. *New York Times*, April 9, 1886, 8; April 11, 1886, 2; April 17, 1886, 5; April 18, 1886, 3.

75. Beckert, *Monied Metropolis*, 286; Richardson, *West From Appomattox*, 164, 207.

76. NYSBLS, *Annual Report for 1886*, 4:750–51; Gordon, "Studies in Irish and Irish-American Thought and Behavior," 573; *New York Times*, April 18, 1886, 2; April 20, 1886, 8.

77. *New York Times*, April 18, 1886, 2; April 20, 1886, 8; April 21, 1886, 8; Gordon, "Studies in Irish and Irish-American Thought and Behavior," 574.

78. NYSBLS, *Annual Report for 1886*, 4:750–51; *New York Times*, April 23, 1886, 2.

79. *New York Times*, April 23, 1886, 2; April 24, 1886, 8; April 25, 1886, 9.

80. *New York Times*, April 22, 1886, 5; April 23, 1886, 2; April 24, 1886, 8; April 25, 1886, 9; April 28, 1886, 8; April 30, 1886, 1; May 4, 1886, 4; May 6, 1886, 5; May 13, 1886, 9; June 4, 1886, 2; June 5, 1886, 8; June 29, 1886, 2; July 1, 1886, 4; July 10, 1886, 5.

81. *JSP*, April 25, 1886, 4.

82. David Scobey, "Boycotting the Politics Factory: Labor Radicalism and the New York City Mayoral Election of 1884 [*sic*]," *Radical History Review* (September 1984): 301–2. Scobey writes that the Haymarket bombing raised the specter of "class revolt," which then prompted the "wave of repression." For a full treatment on the boycott as a subversive assault on established authority, see Forbath, *Law and the Shaping*, 81–97, and Rothman, "'Freedom's Cause,'" passim.

83. *New York Times*, April 22, 1886, 5; *JSP*, May 2, 1886, 1. See Ernst, *Lawyers Against Labor*, 70–76, for background on the theory of conspiracy and its application to labor disputes in the Gilded Age.

84. Ware, *Labor Movement*, 302–3, 312–13.

85. *JSP*, May 2, 1886, 1; *New York Times*, May 2, 1886, 2; *New York Tribune*, May 2, 1886; *New York Sun*, May 2, 1886; Gordon, "Studies in Irish and Irish-American Thought and Behavior," 575–77; Burrows and Wallace, *Gotham*, 1098.

86. *JSP*, May 9, 1886, 1.

87. Barrett was a long-time Tammany judge (Hammack, *Power and Society*, 353n49).

88. NYSBLS, *Annual Report for 1886*, 4:754 (emphasis in original).

89. *New York Times*, June 23, 1886, 3; June 24, 1886, 1; *JSP*, June 27, 1886, 1; NYSBLS, *Annual Report for 1886*, 4:753–55; Gordon, "Studies in Irish and Irish-American Thought and Behavior," 578–80.

90. NYSBLS, *Annual Report for 1886*, 4:756–760; Gordon, "Studies in Irish and Irish-American Thought and Behavior," 580–81; *New York Times*, June 29, 1886, 1; June 30, 1886, 8.

91. *New York Times*, July 1, 1886, 8; NYSBLS, *Annual Report for 1886*, 4:760–61; Gordon, "Studies in Irish and Irish-American Thought and Behavior," 581–82.

92. *New York Times*, July 3, 1886, 8.

93. Beckert, *Monied Metropolis*, 285; Cohen, *Reconstruction of American Liberalism*, 126; Glickman, *Buying Power*, 146–51; Richardson, *West From Appomattox*, 194–95, 346–47; Trachtenberg, *Incorporation of America*, 88.

94. *JSP*, July 11, 1886, 1; *New York Times*, July 3, 1886, 8.

95. NYSBLS, *Annual Report for 1886*, 4:770.

96. *Boycotter*, July 10, 1886, 2. The law required that a juror possess a minimum of $250 in personal or real property. New York Session Laws, 1882, Chapter 410, "An Act to consolidate into one act and to declare the special and local laws affecting the public interests in the City of New York," Chapter XIX, Title 3, Section 1652. Cited in Rothman, "'Freedom's Cause,'" 31.

97. Appeal by CLU Law Committee to Governor David B. Hill, printed in NYSBLS, *Annual Report for 1886*, 4:762. For details on the occupations of the jurors, see *New York Times*, June 23, 1886, 3; June 29, 1886, 1; *JSP*, June 27, 1886, 1. For Swinton's editorial on the jury composition, see *JSP*, July 11, 1886, 1.

98. *JSP*, July 11, 1886, 1–2; Robin Archer, "Unions, Courts, and Parties: Judicial Repression and Labor Politics in Late-Nineteenth Century America," *Politics and Society* 26 (September 1998): 391–422.

99. Henry George, "Labor in Pennsylvania, Part 1," *North American Review* 143, no. 357 (August 1886), 165–82; Henry George, "Labor in Pennsylvania, Part 2," *North American Review* 143, no. 358 (September 1886), 268–77; Henry George, "Labor in Pennsylvania, Part 3," *North American Review* 143, no. 359 (October 1886), 360–70.

100. *New York Sun*, July 8, 1886, 1; *Boycotter*, July 10, 1886, 1.

101. *New York Sun*, July 8, 1886, 1.
102. Ibid.
103. NYSBLS, *Annual Report for 1886*, 4:744, 786; *New York Times*, July 9, 1886, 8; July 8, 1886, 8.
104. *JSP*, July 25, 1886, 1.
105. George, *Progress and Poverty*, 530; Stromquist, *Reinventing "The People*," 18.
106. Post and Leubuscher, *Henry George's 1886 Campaign*, 5–6.

7. "TO SAVE OURSELVES FROM RUIN"

1. *New York Sun*, July 26, 1886; *Irish World*, July 31, 1886, 7; *JSP*, August 1, 1886, 1.
2. No one seemed care that George had once run for office back in California.
3. Letter of James Smith, *Boycotter*, September 4, 1886, 1.
4. *Boycotter*, August 7, 1886, 1; *New York Times*, August 6, 1886, 2. The resolution to reform the ULP passed by an overwhelming margin of 362 to 40.
5. HG to Thomas F. Walker, August 3, 1886, HGP; Barker, *Henry George*, 460–62.
6. George Jr., *Life of Henry George*, 463. George related this story in 1897 when running for mayor a second time. Ivins confirmed that they had met, but denied offering George a deal.
7. Post and Leubuscher, *Henry George's 1886 Campaign*, 7–10.
8. Barker, *Henry George*, 461–62; George Jr., *Life of Henry George*, 459–61; *Standard*, January 8, 1887, 1; *New York Times*, August 27, 1886, 2; Post and Leubuscher, *Henry George's 1886 Campaign*, 7–11.
9. *New York Times*, August 27, 1886, 2; Post and Leubuscher, *Henry George's 1886 Campaign*, 10–11; *New York Daily News*, September 21, 1886, HGSB, 17:11; *Public*, November 3, 1911, 1130.
10. *New York World*, September 7, 1886; *New York Times*, September 7, 1886, 8; *Boycotter*, September 11, 1886, 1.
11. *New York Daily News*, September 25, 1886; HGSB, 17:11; Marguerite Moore, "My Experiences in a New York Campaign," *Woman's Journal*, November 19, 1887, 376.
12. *Boycotter*, September 4, 1886; September 11, 1886, 1.
13. *New York Morning Journal*, September 24, 1886; *New York Star*, September 24, 1886, HGSB, 17:2–3. *New York Times*, September 24, 1886, HGSB, 17:5–6; *New York Tribune*, September 24, 1886, HGSB, 17:6–7; *New York World*, September 24, 1886.
14. *New York Times*, September 3, 1886, 5. Weeks later another "labor" candidate, most likely a Tammany puppet intended to split the labor vote, emerged. See *Boycotter*, October 2, 1886, 2; *Commercial Advertiser*, September 30, 1886, HGSB, 17:41; *New York Daily News*, September 24, 1886, HGSB, 17:11.
15. *New York Herald*, September 24, 1886, HGSB, 17:1.
16. Post and Leubuscher, *Henry George's 1886 Campaign*, 13.
17. *New York Star*, September 24, 1886; *New York Times*, September 24, 1886, HGSB, 17:5–6.
18. *New York Sun*, September 24, 1886, HGSB, 17:1–2.
19. *New York Herald*, September 24, 1886; *New York Times*, September 24, 1886, HGSB, 17:5–6.
20. *New York Herald*, September 24, 1886; *New York Star*, September 24, 1886, HGSB, 17:2–3; *Boycotter*, September 25, 1886, 1.
21. *New York Sun*, September 25, 1886; *New York Morning Journal*, September 25, 1886, HGSB, 17:12–13; *New York World*, September 28, 1886, HGSB, 17:29. *New York World*, October 2, 1886, HGSB, 17:51. McGlynn's speech, printed in *Irish World*, October 9, 1886.
22. See Barker, *Henry George*, 470, for a discussion of support for George's campaign expressed in private by ex-president Rutherford B. Hayes and other powerful public figures.

23. See Rossinow, *Visions of Progress*, 3–4, on the limits of the middle-class reformers' willingness to share power with working-class interests. See also Stromquist, *Reinventing "The People,"* 41–44, for more on the appeal of George's emphasis on class harmony among middle-class Americans.

24. Post and Leubuscher, *Henry George's 1886 Campaign*, 19.

25. Ibid., 20.

26. Ibid., 29.

27. *New York Star*, September 24, 1886, HGSB, 17:3.

28. Fink, "The Uses of Political Power," 133; Fink, *Workingmen's Democracy*, 26. For a detailed discussion of the ULP campaign in Chicago, see Schneirov, *Labor and Urban Politics*, 211–32. For analysis of the ULP effort in Boston, see Friedman, "Success and Failure in Third-Party Politics."

29. Letter from "Enud," *JSP*, September 19, 1886, 1; Letter from "Abolitionist," *JSP*, October 24, 1886, 2; *Boycotter*, October 9, 1886, 1; *JSP*, October 10, 1886, 4.

30. HG to Dr. Edward Taylor, September 10, 1886, HGP.

31. HG to C. D. F. Gutschow, October 8, 1886. For other examples of George's belief that he could win, see HG to Dr. Edward Taylor, September 28, 1886, and October 11, 1886.

32. Beckert, *Monied Metropolis*, 286; *New York Tribune*, September 26, 1886, HGSB, 17:16.

33. Alan Nevins, *Abram S. Hewitt: With Some Account of Peter Cooper* (New York: Harper, 1935), 409–19; U.S. House of Representatives, "Investigation by a Select Committee of the House of Representatives Relative to the Causes of the General Depression in Labor and Business," in *Miscellaneous Documents of the House of Representatives for the Third Session, Forty-Fifth Congress, 1878–1879* (Washington, D.C.: U.S. Government Printing Office, 1879).

34. *New York Times,* September 27, 1886; September 28, 1886.

35. *New York Sun*, September 26, 1886, HGSB, 17:18. See Post and Leubuscher, *Henry George's 1886 Campaign*, 124, on how Irving Hall, the smallest of the three Democratic Party factions, came to endorse George.

36. *New York Sun,* September 26, 1886, HGSB, 17:18–19.

37. Kathleen Dalton, *Theodore Roosevelt: A Strenuous Life* (New York: Knopf, 2002), 107–8.

38. Post and Leubuscher, *Henry George's 1886 Campaign*, 33–34.

39. Ibid., 46–48. See also Kazin, *Populist Persuasion*, 34, on the utility of populist phrases like "the masses vs. the classes."

40. Post and Leubuscher, *Henry George's 1886 Campaign*, 51–55.

41. Ibid., 55–57.

42. Ibid., 61–67.

43. Beckert, *Monied Metropolis*, 279; Cohen, *Reconstruction of American Liberalism*, 159; *New York News*, September 23, 1886; *New York World*, September 26, 1886, HGSB, 17:10, 49.

44. *New York Daily Graphic*, September 30, 1886.

45. For other examples, see *Brooklyn Daily Eagle*, September 24, 1886, HGSB, 17:10, 43; *New York Daily Graphic*, September 30, 1886.

46. Post and Leubuscher, *Henry George's 1886 Campaign*, 65.

47. For an examination of *Puck* magazine's coverage of George during the campaign, see Samuel J. Thomas, "Maligning Poverty's Prophet: *Puck*, Henry George and the New York Mayoral Campaign of 1886," *Journal of American Culture* 21, no. 4 (Winter 1998): 21–40.

48. *New York Times*, October 21, 1886, 1; Beckert, *Monied Metropolis*, 277–79. Samuel Barlow quoted in Beckert, *Monied Metropolis*, 278.

49. Bell, *Rebel, Priest, and Prophet*, 29.

50. Fr. Edward McGlynn to Michael Augustine Corrigan, September 29, 1886, in ibid., 34.

51. Bell, *Rebel, Priest, and Prophet*, 32–40.

52. Ibid., 35; Curran, *Michael Augustine Corrigan*, 196–97. The names of the men reputed to have spoken to the archbishop against McGlynn include Bourke Cochran, John O'Donohue, Judge Joseph Daly, Eugene Kelly, John Crimmins, and George Bliss.

53. Letter of "Printer," *Boycotter*, July 31, 1886, 1; Letter of James Smith to *Boycotter*, September 4, 1886, 1.

54. Letter of "W. A. L.," *Boycotter*, October 9, 1886, 2. Stromquist argues that George, "deliberately fused the language of class with that of citizenship" (*Reinventing "The People*,*"* 43).

55. Letter of "W. A. L.," *Boycotter*, October 9, 1886, 2; Speech of Henry George, *JSP*, October 31, 1886, 2. See also Beckert, *Monied Metropolis*, 292; Kazin, *Populist Persuasion*, 36–37; James J. Connolly, *An Elusive Unity: Urban Democracy and Machine Politics in Industrializing America* (Ithaca, N.Y.: Cornell University Press, 2010), 96–102, 106–8.

56. Post and Leubuscher, *Henry George's 1886 Campaign*, 23–24; Burke, *Conundrum of Class*, 134–39; Kazin, *Populist Persuasion*, 34–35.

57. Post and Leubuscher, *Henry George's 1886 Campaign*, 23; *Boycotter*, October 23, 1886, 2. For an expression of voting as an act of boycotting, see *Boycotter*, October 2, 1886, 2.

58. *New York Times*, September 30, 1886, 4.

59. For an analysis of the George campaign as a class-conscious movement, see Scobey, "Boycotting the Politics Factory." For a depiction of it as a watered-down (by George and his land-value taxation panacea) form of protest, see Thomas, *Alternative America*, 220–32. The complete text to the 1882–1883 and the 1886 platforms can be found in Appendix II and Appendix III.

60. Greene, *Pure and Simple Politics*, 57.

61. Edward Aveling and Eleanor Marx Aveling, *The Working-Class Movement in America* (London: Swan Sonnenschein, 1891), 183–90; Foner, *History of the Labor Movement in the United States*, 2:148; Samuel Gompers, *Samuel Gompers Papers*, ed. Stuart B. Kaufman (Chicago: University of Illinois Press, 1986), 1:446–47.

62. The state's constitution required a vote in 1886 on whether to authorize such a convention.

63. *Boycotter*, October 2, 1886, 1. See also *Boycotter*, October 23, 1886, 2; *New York Journal*, September 26, 1886, HGSB, 17:20; and especially the letter of J. T. McKechnie, *JSP*, October 17, 1886, 2, which parodies the reaction of the police, landlords, rumsellers, placemen, and aldermen, to the George campaign.

64. Letter of "Jack Plane," *JSP*, September 19, 1886, 1.

65. Currarino, *Labor Question*, 14–15; Furner, "Republican Tradition," 172; Kloppenberg, *Uncertain Victory*, 170–95; Stromquist, *Reinventing "The People*,*"* 20; Voss, *Making of American Exceptionalism*, 80–81.

66. *Boycotter*, July 17, 1886, 2; *New York World*, September 28, 1886, HGSB, 17:29; *New York Herald*, September 29, 1886, HGSB, 17:30.

67. *Boycotter*, October 2, 1886, 1; October 16, 1886, 2; *JSP*, October 31, 1886, 1.

68. For examples of the popularity of the issue of land monopoly among workers during the election, see *New York Sun*, August 1, 1886, 2; *Boycotter*, July 31, 1886, 1; September 11, 1886, 1; and October 16, 1886, 2. See also Stobo, "Organized Labor, Housing Issues, and Politics: Another Look at the 1886 Henry George Campaign in New York City."

69. Post and Leubuscher, *Henry George's 1886 Campaign*, 26.

70. Gabler, *American Telegrapher*, 206–7. Gabler notes that George was very popular among telegraph workers because of his call for public ownership of the telegraph system.

71. Fairchild, *Mysteries of the Great City*, 4–5, 33–41, 77–82; Post and Leubuscher, *Henry George's 1886 Campaign*, 27; Rodgers, *Atlantic Crossings*, 114–40. See also Testimony of Conrad Carl, *RCSRLC*, 2:77, for a statement on the popularity of applying George's single tax to cities.

72. *New York Sun*, September 25, 1886, HGSB, 17:12; September 26, 1886, HGSB, 17:18; September 29, 1886, HGSB, 17:29; *New York Morning Journal*, September 29, 1886, HGSB, 17:29; *New York World*, September 30, 1886, HGSB, 17:37.

73. HG to C. D. F. Gutschow, October 8, 1886, HGP.

74. HG to Dr. Edward Taylor, October 11, 1886, HGP.

75. *New York Daily News*, September 25, 1886; HGSB, 17:11; September 26, HGSB, 17:17; *New York Sun*, September 29, 1886; HGSB, 17:29; September 30, 1886, HGSB, 17:35.

76. These intentionally flawed ballots would be cast by unknowing voters and then subsequently disqualified during the count. In 1886, Tammany secretly distributed ballots identical to those handed out by the ULP—except that they read "George Henry" and were thus not valid.

77. *New York Tribune*, September 26, 1886, HGSB, 17:16; Campbell, *Deliver the Vote*, 62–66; William Ivins, *Machine Politics and Money in Elections in New York City* (New York: Harper, 1887), 58, cited in James F. Donnelly, "Catholic New Yorkers and New York Socialists, 1870–1920" (Ph.D. diss., New York University, 1982), 103.

78. *New York Daily News*, September 21, 1886, HGSB, 17:11.

79. *New York Times*, September 26, 1886, HGSB, 17:14; *Boycotter*, October 9, 1886, 3; Gompers, *Samuel Gompers Papers*, 1:431.

80. George Jr., *Life of Henry George*, 474.

81. Post and Leubuscher, *Henry George's 1886 Campaign*, 106–12.

82. *New York Star*, October 17, 1886, in Gompers, *Samuel Gompers Papers*, 1:434; Kazin, *American Dreamers*, 71.

83. Moore, "My Experiences in a New York Campaign," 376; McCarthy, "True Women, Trade Unionists, and the Lessons of Tammany Hall," 86–87; David Montgomery, "Racism, Immigrants, and Political Reform," *Journal of American History* 87 (March 2001): 1266; Louis F. Post, *The Prophet of San Francisco: Personal Memories and Interpretations of Henry George* (New York: Vanguard, 1930), 73, 86. For a biographical profile of Marguerite Moore, see Frances Willard and Mary Livermore, eds., *American Women* (1897; repr., New York: Mast, Vrowell, & Kirkpatrick, 1973), 517.

84. Post and Leubuscher, *Henry George's 1886 Campaign*, 91–104.

85. Speech of Henry George, printed in *JSP*, October 17, 1886, 2.

86. Letter of "H. W.," *JSP*, August 15, 1886, 2; Letter of "Printer," *Boycotter*, July 31, 1886, 1; Testimony of P. J. McGuire, *RCSRLC*, 1:344–45.

87. Ross, "Culture of Political Economy," 145, 151; Rossinow, *Visions of Progress*, 18. Words of Gordon Clark quoted in editorial, *JSP*, October 31, 1886, 1.

88. *JSP*, October 31, 1886, 3; Post and Leubuscher, *Henry George's 1886 Campaign*, 150–54.

89. *New York Times*, October 29, 1886, 2.

90. *New York Times*, October 29, 1886, 2; Scobey, *Empire City*, 281.

91. Post and Leubuscher, *Henry George's 1886 Campaign*, 132–33.

92. George Jr., *Life of Henry George*, 477; Post and Leubuscher, *Henry George's 1886 Campaign*, 132–34.

93. Post and Leubuscher, *Henry George's 1886 Campaign*, 118–20.

94. Ibid., 155.

95. *Standard*, January 8, 1887, 2; Powderly, *The Path I Trod*, 150; *New York Star*, November 3, 1886, HGSB, 17.

96. Post and Leubuscher, *Henry George's 1886 Campaign*, 169–70.

97. George Jr., *Life of Henry George*, 481; Agnes de Mille, *Henry George: Citizen of the World* (Chapel Hill: University of North Carolina Press, 1950), 152, Post, *Prophet of San Francisco*, 79; Charles Edward Russell, *Bare Hands and Stone Walls: Some Recollections of a Side-Line*

Reformer (New York: C. Scribner's Sons, 1933), 46–48, 50–51; Gustavus Myers, *The History of Tammany Hall* (New York: Boni & Liveright, 1917), 270; Lothrop Stoddard, *Master of Manhattan: The Life of Richard Croker* (New York: Longmans, Green, 1931), 86; Barker, *Henry George*, 479–81.

98. *Leader*, November 4, 1886, and November 6, 1886; Post and Leubuscher, *Henry George's 1886 Campaign*, 172.

99. Barker, *Henry George*, 479.

100. See the *Irish American*, November 13, 1886, for an editorial confirming that many Irish did vote for George but predicting they would soon return to the Democratic Party.

101. George won the 17th district (20.0) and came in second in the 1st (18.6), 5th (17.95), 16th (18.76), 20th (19.15), and 22nd (19.65). Donnelly, "Catholic New Yorkers and New York Socialists," Appendix III.2.

102. Roosevelt won the 7th (13.54), 11th (15.75), 13th (15.18), and 21th (12.71) districts. Hewitt won the 9th (15.30), 23rd (16.18), and 24th (8.64). PPD's shown in parentheses. Donnelly, "Catholic New Yorkers and New York Socialists," Appendix III.2.

103. The 2nd, 3rd, 6th, 12th, and 18th A.D.'s.

104. Donnelly, "Catholic New Yorkers and New York Socialists," 108–12, Appendix III.2.

105. Martin Shefter, "The Electoral Foundations of the Political Machine: New York City, 1884–1897," in *The History of American Electoral Behavior*, eds. Joel Silbey, Allan G. Bogue, and William H. Flanigan (Princeton, N.J.: Princeton University Press, 1978), 282, 288; Hammack, *Power and Society*, 175–77; Oestreicher, "Urban Working-Class Political Behavior and Theories," 1274–75; Schneider, *Trade Unions and Community*, 123–25; *JSP*, July 25, 1886, 1. For more on political boycotting, see also *Boycotter*, October 2, 1886, 2.

106. Poultney Bigelow, *Seventy Summers* (New York: Longmans, Green), 2:12.

107. James Donnelly, for example, argues that blaming the Catholic Church for George's loss started not in 1886 but in 1887, in the wake of McGlynn's excommunication and George's falling out with the socialists ("Catholic New Yorkers and New York Socialists," 120–21).

108. Shefter, "Electoral Foundations of the Political Machine," 282.

109. Emmett Larkin, "The Devotional Revolution in Ireland, 1850–1875," *American Historical Review* 77 (June 1972): 625–52.

110. Donnelly, "Catholic New Yorkers and New York Socialists," 106–7. According to the census data, 336,137 men were twenty-one years of age or older in 1880; in 1890, 446,798.

8. "YOUR PARTY WILL GO INTO PIECES"

1. *JSP*, November 7, 1886, 1. For another optimistic view of the election, see Aveling and Marx Aveling, *Working-Class Movement in America*, 148–53.

2. George Jr., *Life of Henry George*, 483; Edwin L. Godkin quoted in Hammack, *Power and Society*, 176. Godkin's nervous assessment of the election was shared by the former New York mayor William R. Grace, who wrote to Hewitt: "This whole business brings up a new force in politics which will not be easy to handle in the future" (quoted in Beckert, *Monied Metropolis*, 278).

3. For more details of the labor vote in 1886, see Ware, *Labor Movement*, 362–63, and Foner, *History of the Labor Movement*, 2:128–31.

4. Marx and Engels, *Letters to Americans*, 162–63; Oser, *Henry George*, 32–50; Rose, *Henry George*, 82–84. For a comparative analysis of the Great Upheaval in the United States, and similar labor activism in Britain, see: J. H. M. Laslett, "Haymarket, Henry George, and the Labor Upsurge in Britain and America during the Late 1880s," *International Labor and Working-Class History* 29 (Spring 1986): 68–82.

5. Post and Leubuscher, *Henry George's 1886 Campaign*, 171–74; *Irish World*, November 13, 1886, 7; Speek, "Singletax and the Labor Movement," 90–91; *Public*, November 3, 1911, 1130; *Leader*, November 8, 1886. For another expression of the plans to form a national labor party, see Fr. Edward McGlynn, "The Labor Party View," *North American Review* 143, no. 6 (December 1886), 576.

6. *New York Times*, December 3, 1886, 2; *Irish World*, November 13, 1886, 7; *Standard*, January 8, 1887, 7; *JSP*, December 12, 1886, 1; Post and Leubuscher, *Henry George's 1886 Campaign*, 174–77; Speek, "Singletax and the Labor Movement," 90–92. See also Speek, "Singletax and the Labor Movement," Appendix II (ULP constitution) and Appendix III (a list of acts desired to be addressed at upcoming state constitutional convention).

7. *JSP*, November 14, 1886, 2, and November 21, 1886, 2

8. George Jr., *Life of Henry George*, 484–85, 489; Barker, *Henry George*, 486, 491; *Standard*, January 8, 1887, 4.

9. *JSP*, November 21, 1886, 2.

10. *Leader*, May 6, 1887, 1; Speek, "Singletax and the Labor Movement," 96.

11. *JSP*, November 21, 1886, 1.

12. Foner, *History of the Labor Movement*, 2:145; NYSBLS, *Fifth Annual Report* (1887), 736–76; Howard L. Hurwitz, *Theodore Roosevelt and Labor in New York State, 1880–1900* (New York: Columbia University Press, 1943), 143; Mark Wahlgren Summers, *Party Games: Getting, Keeping, and Using Power in Gilded Age Politics* (Chapel Hill: University of North Carolina Press, 2004), 221–27. For an examination of prolabor legislation passed in Massachusetts after 1886, see Zonderman, *Uneasy Allies*, 240–63.

13. Barker, *Henry George*, 487; Curran, *Michael Augustine Corrigan*, 203–10; George Jr., *Life of Henry George*, 486; Isacsson, *Determined Doctor*, 111–18; Post and Leubuscher, *Henry George's 1886 Campaign*, 134–39; *New York Tribune*, November 26, 1886.

14. *Standard*, January 8, 1887, 1–2; January 15, 1887, 1; February 5, 1887, 1; Curran, *Michael Augustine Corrigan*, 216–17; George Jr., *Life of Henry George*, 486–87.

15. Barker, *Henry George*, 487–90; Curran, *Michael Augustine Corrigan*, 215. For a representative counterattack against George in the Catholic press, see Rev. Henry A. Brann, "Henry George and His Land Theories," *Catholic World* 44 (March 1887): 810–28.

16. *Standard*, January 15, 1887, 1.

17. Curran, *Michael Augustine Corrigan*, 220–21; *New York Tribune*, January 17, 1887.

18. *Standard*, January 22, 1887, 1; Curran, *Michael Augustine Corrigan*, 221–23.

19. *Irish World*, November 13, 1886, 7.

20. *Standard*, January 22, 1887, 1–2; Barker, *Henry George*, 490.

21. Bell, *Rebel, Priest, and Prophet*, 79–83; Curran, *Michael Augustine Corrigan*, 231; George Jr., *Life of Henry George*, 491; Isacsson, *Determined Doctor*, 162–66, *Standard*, April 2, 1887. See also Shanaberger, "Reverend Dr. Edward McGlynn."

22. Curran, *Michael Augustine Corrigan*, 231; George Jr., *Life of Henry George*, 492; *Standard*, May 7, 1887, 4. For examples of George's talks, see Henry George, *An Anthology of Henry George's Thought: Volume 1 of the Henry George Centennial Trilogy*, ed. Kenneth C. Wenzer (Rochester, N.Y.: University of Rochester Press, 1997), 27–29.

23. George Jr., *Life of Henry George*, 492n.

24. *Standard*, May 7, 1887, 4.

25. *New York Times*, April 15, 1887, 5; May 19, 1887, 8; *Standard*, May 28, 1887, 8; June 11, 1887, 4. McCarthy, "'Progress and Poverty,'" 172–84. Women appear prominently in the many anti-McGlynn political cartoons generated by the controversy. See Samuel J. Thomas, "Portraits of a Rebel Priest: Edward McGlynn in Caricature, 1886–1893," *Journal of American Culture* 7, no. 4 (1984): 23, 27.

26. George Jr., *Life of Henry George*, 495; Bell, *Rebel, Priest, and Prophet*, 178–82.

27. Cooper, *Once a Cigar Maker*, 21–25; Foner, *History of the Labor Movement*, 2:135–36; Phelan, *Grand Master Workman*, 116–22, 140–49, 192–96, 203–9; *New York Sun*, July 26, 1886, 1; *Boycotter*, July 31, 1886, 2; August 7, 1886, 1, 2; August 9, 1886, 2; August 14, 1886, 2. For details on DA 49's attempt to stymie the CLU reorganization and stop the annual Labor Day parade, see O'Donnell, "Henry George and the 'New Political Forces,'" 514–20.

28. Foner, *History of the Labor Movement*, 2:140–41; Phelan, *Grand Master Workman*, 206–8; Phelan, "The Warp of Fancy," 283–99. Weir, *Knights Unhorsed*, 23–46; Weir, "Powderly and the Home Club," 84–113; *New York Sun*, October 4, 1886, 1; October 5, 1886, 1; October 6, 1886, 3; October 7, 1886, 5; October 9, 1886, 1; October 10, 1886, 2; *Boycotter*, October 23, 1886, 2.

29. Foner, *History of the Labor Movement*, 2:141–44; Gompers, *Seventy Years of Life and Labor*, 1:264–69; Gompers, *Samuel Gompers Papers*, 1:450–54; *JSP*, November 28, 1886, 4; December 5, 1886, 1; December 12, 1886, 4.

30. Commons et al., *History of Labour*, 2:420.

31. Kaufman, "Rise and Fall of a Nation of Joiners," 553–79; Commons et al., *History of Labour*, 2:420–23; NYSBLS, *Annual Report for 1887* (1887), 327–85; Weir, *Knights Unhorsed*, passim; *JSP*, February 20, 1887; Knights of Labor, *Record of the Proceedings of the General Assembly* (Cleveland, 1886), 326–28, and *Record of the Proceedings of the General Assembly* (Minneapolis, 1887), 1847–50.

32. *JSP*, December 26, 1886, 4; *New York Sun*, December 18, 1886, and January 10, 1887; *New York Times*, January 3, 1887; Gompers, *Seventy Years of Life and Labor*, 1:274–78; Greene, *Pure and Simple Politics*, 57.

33. Laurie, *Artisans into Workers*, 165.

34. Greene, *Pure and Simple Politics*, 57; Oestreicher, "Terence Powderly, The Knights of Labor, and Artisanal Republicanism," 58–59; *Leader*, December 21, 1886; *Union Printer* (formerly the *Boycotter*), December 11, 1886, 1.

35. Knights of Labor, *Record of the Proceedings* (1886), 326–28, and *Record of the Proceedings* (1887), 1847–50; Paul Avrich, *The Haymarket Tragedy* (Princeton, N.J.: Princeton University Press, 1986), 309, 348–49; Foner, *History of the Labor Movement*, 2:158–65; Phelan, *Grand Master Workman*, 203–4, 208; Schneirov, *Labor and Urban Politics*, 223, 244–46; Commons et al., *History of Labour*, 2:420.

36. *New York Herald*, July 4, 1887. Jose Marti quoted in Montgomery, "Racism, Immigrants, and Political Reform," 1267.

37. Curran, *Michael Augustine Corrigan*, 250–55.

38. George Jr., *Life of Henry George*, 494; McLeod, *Piety and Poverty*, 120–24; *New York Herald*, June 19, 1887, and July 4, 1887, cited in Curran, *Michael Augustine Corrigan*, 250–55; Elizabeth Gurley Flynn, *The Rebel Girl: An Autobiography, My First Life, 1906–1926* (New York: International Publishers, 1973, originally published in 1955 as *I Speak My Own Piece: Autobiography of "The Rebel Girl"*), 43. For another memoir chronicling defections from the Catholic Church after McGlynn's excommunication, see Thomas Sugrue, *An American Catholic Speaks His Mind on America's Religious Conflict* (New York: Harper, 1952), 44.

39. McLeod, *Piety and Poverty*, 122–23; Rodechko, *Patrick Ford*, 92–121; *Irish World*, October 29, 1887. A similar retreat from radicalism by Irish nationalists is discussed in Mimi Cowan, "Ducking for Cover: Chicago's Irish Nationalists in the Haymarket Era," *Labor: Studies in Working-Class History of the Americas* 9, no. 1 (2012): 53–76.

40. Redpath edited the *North American Review* and Barnes was a commercial publisher.

41. *Standard*, May 7, 1887, 1.

42. *Leader*, October 30, 1887, 6.
43. *Standard*, January 8, 1887, 7; January 15, 1887, 3; January 22, 1887, 6; May 7, 1887, 3; *Leader*, January 7, 1887, 1, January 22, 1887, 3; May 6, 1887, 1; October 30, 1887, 6; Speek, "Singletax and the Labor Movement," 91–95; *JSP*, November 21, 1886, 2.
44. *Leader*, October 30, 1887, 6.
45. Henry George, "The New Party," *North American Review* 368 (July 1887), 1–7.
46. *JSP*, November 28, 1886; December 19, 1886, 1.
47. *Cigar Makers' Official Journal*, April 1887, and May 1887 quoted in Foner, *History of the Labor Movement*, 2:148
48. George, "The New Party," 1–7; *Leader*, July, 30, 1887, 2; Speek, "Singletax and the Labor Movement," 104–5.
49. *Leader*, June 28, 1887, 2. For other editorials critical of George, see *Leader*, June 23, 1887; June 24, 1887; July 14, 1887, 2.
50. *Standard*, August 13, 1887, 1; Barker, *Henry George*, 496.
51. *Standard*, August 13, 1887, 1; Speek, "Singletax and the Labor Movement," 112.
52. See Michael Hudson, "Henry George's Political Critics," in *Henry George: Political Ideologue, Social Philosopher and Economic Theorist*, ed. Lawrence S. Moss (New York: Blackwell, 2008), 1–47.
53. Ely, *Recent American Socialism*, 18, 20.
54. George, *Progress and Poverty*, 456; George, *Social Problems*, 191.
55. Phelan, *Grand Master Workman*, 147, 203–4, 208.
56. Cohen, *Reconstruction of American Liberalism*, 140; Stromquist, *Reinventing "The People*," 23.
57. The ULP in Chicago experienced a similar struggle between radicals and moderates. See Schneirov, *Labor and Urban Politics*, 212–28.
58. *Standard*, August 13, 1887, 4; *Leader*, August 17, 1887, 1.
59. George Jr., *Life of Henry George*, 497; *Standard*, August 13, 1887, 1; *Leader*, August 6, 1887, 1.
60. Speek, "Singletax and the Labor Movement," 107.
61. *Standard*, August 27, 1887, 1; Speek, "Singletax and the Labor Movement," 121.
62. *Leader*, August 6, 1887, 1. For Frederick Engels's positive interpretation of the socialist purge, see Marx and Engels, *Letters to Americans*, 191. For a similarly optimistic view, see Aveling and Marx Aveling, *Working-Class Movement in America*, 148–53, 183–90.
63. *Leader*, August 18, 1887, 1; *Standard*, August 27, 1887, 6; Barker, *Henry George*, 498; Speek, "Singletax and the Labor Movement," 121–23.
64. For details on the other candidates, see *Standard*, August 27, 1887, 7; Barker, *Henry George*, 499.
65. *Standard*, August 27, 1887, 7.
66. Speek, "Singletax and the Labor Movement," 131–38; *Standard*, August 27, 1887, 4.
67. *Leader*, August 22, 1887, 2; *New York Sun*, September 19, 1887, 1.
68. The last issue of the paper was August 14, 1887. Reuter, "John Swinton's Paper," 298–307.
69. *JSP*, August 1, 1886, 1; Barker, *Henry George*, 500.
70. *Standard*, January 15, 1887, 4.
71. *Standard*, October 8, 1887, 4; George Jr. *Life of Henry George*, 498; Barker, *Henry George*, 503–5; Green, *Death in the Haymarket*, 257–58; Thomas, *Alternative America*, 225–26, 230–31.
72. Barker, *Henry George*, 504–5; Emma Goldman quote from *Chicago Labor Enquirer*, October 29, 1887, in Barker, *Henry George*, 504.
73. George Jr., *Life of Henry George*, 502,
74. See, for example, Kevin Boyle, *Organized Labor and American Politics, 1894–1994: The Labor-Liberal Alliance* (Albany: State University of New York Press, 1998); Lizabeth Cohen,

Making a New Deal: Industrial Workers in Chicago, 1919–1939 (New York: Cambridge University Press, 1990); Julie Greene, *Pure and Simple Politics: The American Federation of Labor and Political Activism, 1881–1917* (New York: Cambridge University Press, 1998); Gary Marks, *Unions in Politics: Britain, Germany, and the United States in the Nineteenth and Early Twentieth Centuries* (Princeton, N.J.: Princeton University Press, 1989); Gwendolyn Mink, *Old Labor and New Immigrants in American Political Development: Union, Party, and State, 1875–1920* (Ithaca, N.Y.: Cornell University Press, 1986); and Clayton Sinyai, *Schools of Democracy: A Political History of the American Labor Movement* (Ithaca, N.Y.: ILR Press, 2006).

75. For more on the New York City labor movement circa 1890–1920, see Melvin Dubofsky, *When Workers Organize: New York City in the Progressive Era* (Amherst: University of Massachusetts Press, 1968).

76. For an examination of the continued centrality of Catholicism among the New York City Irish after 1886, see Hugh McLeod, "Catholicism and the New York Irish, 1880–1910," in *Disciplines of Faith: Studies in Religion, Politics, and Patriarchy*, eds. Jim Obelkevich, Lyndal Roper, and Raphael Samuel (New York: Routledge, 1987), 337–50.

77. Philip S. Foner, Marc Karson, and others have argued that Catholic conservatism played a determining role in thwarting the development of an American socialist tradition. See Foner, *History of the Labor Movement*, 4:333–34; Marc Karson, "Catholic Anti-Socialism," in *Failure of a Dream? Essays in the History of American Socialism*, eds. John H. M. Laslett and Seymour Martin Lipset (Garden City, N.Y.: Doubleday, 1974), 82–117. For a contrary interpretation, see Henry J. Browne, *Catholic Church and the Knights of Labor*, 357; Grob, *Workers and Utopia*, 166; and Donnelly, "Catholic New Yorkers and New York Socialists," 172–270.

78. *Irish American*, November 13, 1886.

79. Beckert, *Monied Metropolis*, 316–20; Connolly, *An Elusive Unity*, 89–114, 165–216; Hammack, *Power and Society*, 179–81, 316–19; Kenneth Finegold, *Experts and Politicians: Reform Challenges to Machine Politics in New York, Cleveland, and Chicago* (Princeton, N.J.: Princeton University Press, 1995), 3–67; Lui, "Machine and Social Policies," 386–403; Kevin P. Murphy, *Political Manhood: Red Bloods, Mollycoddles, and the Politics of Progressive Era Reform* (New York: Columbia University Press, 2008), 38–67; Shefter, "Electoral Foundations of the Political Machine," 281–98.

80. Archer, "Unions, Courts, and Parties," 391–422; Beckert, *Monied Metropolis*, 285–315; Ernst, *Lawyers Against Labor*, 77–213; Forbath, *Law and the Shaping*, 59–97; Friedman, "Worker Militancy and Its Consequences," 11–14; Hattam, "Economic Visions and Political Strategies," 4:82–129; David Brian Robertson, *Capital, Labor, and State: The Battle for American Labor Markets from the Civil War to the New Deal* (Lanham: Rowman & Littlefield, 2000), 37–151; Ross, *A Muted Fury*, 23–109; Voss, *Making of American Exceptionalism*, 185–228.

81. Fink, *Workingmen's Democracy*, 6.

82. Nick Salvatore, "Response to Sean Wilentz, 'Against Exceptionalism: Class Consciousness and the American Labor Movement, 1790–1920,'" *International Labor and Working Class History*, no. 26 (Fall 1984): 28.

83. John H. M. Laslett and Seymour Martin Lipset, eds., *Failure of a Dream? Essays in the History of American Socialism* (Garden City, N.Y.: Doubleday, 1974); Eric Foner, *Who Owns History? Rethinking the Past in a Changing World* (New York: Hill & Wang, 2003), 110–48; Sean Wilentz, "Against Exceptionalism: Class Consciousness and the American Labor Movement, 1790–1920," *International Labor and Working Class History*, no. 26 (Fall 1984): 1–24.

84. Burrows and Wallace, *Gotham*, 1170–84; Fine, *Laissez-Faire*, 25; Huston, *Securing the Fruits*, 339–78; Kazin, *American Dreamers*, 73–76; Kloppenberg, *Uncertain Victory*, 170–95; Lustig,

Corporate Liberalism, 71; Schneirov, *Labor and Urban Politics*, 330–31; Stromquist, *Reinventing "The People*," 34–38.

85. Annie L. Diggs, *The Story of the Jerry Simpson* (Wichita, Kan.: Jane Simpson, 1908), 55, 80, 148.

86. Barker, *Henry George*, 600–601, 604–7, Martin Ridge, *Ignatius Donnelly: The Portrait of a Politician* (Chicago: University of Chicago Press, 1962), 256, 297, 342–43.

87. Salvatore, *Eugene Debs*, 62, 103.

88. Gronlund was inspired by George's ideas, but ultimately found them insufficiently radical. See his book, *The Insufficiency of Henry George's Theory* (New York: New York Labor News, 1887). See also Fred Harrison, "Gronlund and Other Marxists," in *Critics of Henry George*, ed. Robert V. Andelson (Madison, N.J.: Fairleigh Dickinson University Press, 1979), 196–221.

89. Carlotta R. Anderson, *All-American Anarchist: Joseph A. Labadie and the Labor Movement* (Detroit: Wayne State University Press, 1998), 63–65, 155.

90. Barker, *Henry George*, 466, 485, 492.

91. Richard B. Dressner, "William Dwight Porter Bliss's Christian Socialism," *Church History* 47, no. 1 (March 1978): 66–82.

92. Rodgers, *Atlantic Crossings*, 140.

93. Sinclair lived for a time in the Georgist colonies Arden, Delaware, and Fairhope, Alabama.

94. Steve Weinberg, *Taking on the Trust: How Ida Tarbell Brought Down John D. Rockefeller and Standard Oil* (New York: Norton, 2008), 200.

95. Emma Lou Thornbrough, *T. Thomas Fortune: Militant Journalist* (Chicago: University of Chicago Press, 1972), 54–55, 70–71, 78, 89.

96. Tom Buk-Swienty, *The Other Half: The Life of Jacob Riis and the World of Immigrant America* (New York: Norton, 2008), 194–95, 241; Bonnie Yochelson and Daniel J. Czitrom, *Rediscovering Jacob Riis: Exposure Journalism and Photography in Turn-of-the-Century New York* (New York: New Press, 2008), 77–81. Riis may very well have found inspiration for the famous title of his book by reading George's *Leslie's* essays, one of which included the passage: "That 'one-half the world does not know how the other half lives,' is much more true of the upper than the lower half" (*Social Problems*, 64). According to Burrows and Wallace (*Gotham*, 1181–83), Riis admired George and wrote articles for his 1886 campaign that appeared in the *Leader*.

97. Postel, *Populist Vision*, 228–33; Russell B. Nye, "Hamlin Garland and Henry George," *Freeman* (May 1943), accessed at http://www.cooperativeindividualism.org/nye-russel_hamlin-garland-and-henry-george-1943.html.

98. Burrows and Wallace, *Gotham*, 1179; William Dean Howells, *My Literary Passions* (New York: Harper, 1895), and introduction to *A Hazard of New Fortunes* (1890; repr., New York: Harper, 1909).

99. Barker, *Henry George*, 631.

100. George Jr., *Life of Henry George*, 457–58; Barker, *Henry George*, 446, 455, 471, 623–25; Tom L. Johnson, *My Story: The Autobiography of Tom L. Johnson* (New York: B. W. Huebsch, 1911), 48–58, 66–67.

101. Rodgers, *Atlantic Crossings*, 140; Barker, *Henry George*, 626; Kenneth E. Miller, *From Progressive to New Dealer: Frederic C. Howe and American Liberalism* (State Park, Penn.: Penn State University Press, 2010).

102. Barker, *Henry George*, 631; C. H. Cramer, *Newton D. Baker: A Biography* (Cleveland: World Publishing, 1961), 41.

103. Robert H. Bremner, "George and Ohio's Civic Revival," *Georgist Journal* (September 14, 2012), http://www.georgistjournal.org/2012/09/14/george-and-ohios-civic-revival/.

104. Bremner, "George and Ohio's Civic Revival"; Barker, *Henry George*, 626.

105. Robert D. Johnston, *The Radical Middle Class: Populist Democracy and the Question of Capitalism in Progressive Era Portland, Oregon* (Princeton, N.J.: Princeton University Press, 2006), 129, 159–78; Thomas C. McClintock, "Seth Lewelling, William S. U'Ren, and the Birth of the Oregon Progressive Movement," *Oregon Historical Quarterly* 68, no. 3 (Fall 1967).

106. Fine, *Laissez-Faire*, 295.

107. Peter Witt, *Cleveland Before St. Peter: A Handful of Hot Stuff* (Cleveland: C. Lezius, 1899); "Witt, Peter," *Encyclopedia of Cleveland History*, http://ech.case.edu/ech-cgi/article.pl?id=WP4.

108. Fairfield, *Mysteries of the Great City*, 29; Daniel Aaron, *Men of Good Hope: A Story of American Progressives* (New York: Oxford University Press, 1951), 79–80, 113–14.

109. Kathryn Kish Sklar, *Florence Kelley and the Nation's Work: The Rise of Women's Political Culture, 1830–1900* (New Haven, Conn.: Yale University Press, 1995), 115, 123–24.

110. Burrows and Wallace, *Gotham*, 1176–79; Waugh, *Unsentimental Reformer*, 186–90.

111. Barker, *Henry George*, 629–30.

112. Francis L. Broderick, *Right Reverend New Dealer: John A. Ryan* (New York: Macmillan, 1963), 22–23, 60–61, 68–69. While influenced by his broad critique of laissez-faire industrialism, Ryan ultimately opposed George's land and tax theory. See Robert V. Andelson, "Msgr. John A. Ryan's Critique of Henry George," *American Journal of Economics and Sociology* 33, no. 3 (July 1974): 273–86.

113. Barker, *Henry George*, 493.

114. Donovan Ebersole Smucker, *The Origins of Walter Rauschenbusch's Social Ethics* (Montreal: McGill-Queen's University Press, 1994), 103–9.

115. Barker, *Henry George*, 590; Hellman, *Henry George Reconsidered*, 85.

116. John Dewey, introduction to *Significant Paragraphs from Henry George's "Progress and Poverty,"* ed. Harry Gunnison Brown (Garden City, N.Y.: Doubleday, Doran, 1928), 1–3.

117. Barron, "'Frontier' Realities," 15; Lough, "Henry George, Frederick Jackson Turner, and the 'Closing' of the American Frontier," 4–23.

118. Adler was a eulogist at Henry George's funeral. Horace Leland Friess, *Felix Adler and Ethical Culture: Memories and Studies* (New York: Columbia University Press, 1981); Robert S. Guttchen, *Felix Adler* (New York: Twayne Publishers, 1974); Benny Kraut, *From Reform Judaism to Ethical Culture: The Religious Evolution of Felix Adler* (Cincinnati: Hebrew Union College Press, 1979).

119. John R. Commons, *Myself* (1934; repr., Madison: University of Wisconsin Press, 1963), 39.

120. Postel, *Populist Vision*, 229–31; Clarence Darrow, *Argument of Clarence Darrow in the Case of the Communist Labor Party in the Criminal Court, Chicago* (Chicago: C. H. Kerr, 1920).

121. Magie, a Henry George devotee, originally called it the "Landlord's Game" (patented in 1904). She designed it to concretely demonstrate George's theory on how land monopoly and rent lead to inequality. http://www.henrygeorge.org/dodson_on_monopoly.htm.

122. Robert Knowles, "Tolstoy's Henry George: 'A Step on the First Rung of the Ladder …'," in *Henry George's Legacy in Economic Thought*, ed. John Laurent (Northampton, Mass.: Edward Elgar Publishing, 2005), 51–72; Kenneth C. Wenzer, "The Influence of Henry George on Lev Nikolaevich Tolstoy: The Period of Developing Economic Thought (1881–1897)," *Pennsylvania History* 63, no. 2 (Spring 1996): 232–52.

123. George Raymond Geiger, *The Philosophy of Henry George* (New York: Macmillan, 1933), 461–62; Sein Lin, "Sun Yat-Sen and Henry George: The Essential Role of Land Policy in Their Doctrines," *American Journal of Economics and Sociology* 33, no. 2 (April 1974): 201–20; Paul B. Trescott, "Henry George, Sun Yat-sen, and China: More Than Land Policy Was Involved," *American Journal of Economics and Sociology* 53, no. 3 (July 1994): 363–75.

124. Shaw wrote, "When I was swept into the great Socialist revival of 1883, I found that five-sixths of those who were swept in with me had been converted by Henry George" (Kazin, *American Dreamers*, 81).

125. Kazin, *American Dreamers*, 83.

126. Eric Goldman to Robert Clancy, May 12, 1954, quoted in Steven Cord, "A New Look at Henry George," *American Journal of Economics and Sociology* 27, no. 4 (October 1968): 393–404.

127. John Dewey, introduction in *Significant Paragraphs from Henry George's "Progress and Poverty,"* 1–3.

EPILOGUE

1. Henry George, "Socialism vs. the Single Tax," *Standard*, December 31, 1887, 1.

2. The ULP did survive and participate in the 1888 elections, nominating two single taxers for president and vice president. They received less than two thousand votes, mostly in Brooklyn and Manhattan. See George Jr., *Life of Henry George*, 512–13. For details on the schism between George and McGlynn, see Bell, *Rebel, Priest, and Prophet*, 183–90.

3. George Jr., *Life of Henry George*, 505–8, 511–13; Barker, *Henry George*, 513–16

4. Barker, *Henry George*, 523–33, 521; George Jr., *Life of Henry George*, 513–21.

5. Barker, *Henry George*, 548–51; George Jr., *Life of Henry George*, 522–41, *New York Times*, September 2, 1890; September 3, 1890; September 4, 1890.

6. Barker, *Henry George*, 572–77; George Jr., *Life of Henry George*, 563–68; Henry George, *The Condition of Labor: An Open Letter to Pope Leo XIII* (New York: United States Book Company, 1891).

7. Barker, *Henry George*, 578–80; Oser, *Henry George*, 32–50; Rose, *Henry George*, 73–75.

8. Barker, *Henry George*, 576–80; George Jr., *Life of Henry George*, 559–62, 569–71; Bell, *Rebel, Priest, and Prophet*, 206–52.

9. Barker, *Henry George*, 588–89; Bell, *Rebel, Priest, and Prophet*, 251–52.

10. George Jr., *Life of Henry George*, 541.

11. Burrows and Wallace, *Gotham*, 1191–94, 1200–1203; Richard Zacks, *Island of Vice: Theodore Roosevelt's Quest to Clean Up Sin-Loving New York* (New York: Anchor, 2012).

12. George Jr., *Life of Henry George*, 593–97.

13. Ibid., 599–600; *New York Times*, October 6, 1897, 1.

14. George Jr., *Life of Henry George*, 601–7; *New York Times*, October 30, 1897, 1–2.

15. George Jr., *Life of Henry George*, 608–11; Bell, *Rebel, Priest, and Prophet*, 265–69; *New York Times*, November 1, 1897, 1–2; November 2, 1897, 16.

16. *New York Times*, November 3, 1897, 1.

17. George Jr., *Life of Henry George*, 611.

Index

George, Henry, 1887 campaign of: election results, 265–66; encouraging signs, 245–46, 251; George's dominance over ULP, 256–63; George seen as ideal candidate, 244–45; middle class courted, 261–62; Powderly and the Knights' withdrawal of support, 254; retreat from radicalism, 258–65, 266

George, Henry, influences on: Christianity, 8–9, 27, 31–32 (*see also* Christianity); early influences, xxii, 3–4, 6–10, 155, 269–70; McClatchy, 16, 18, 21, 106

George, Henry, Jr. (son of Henry George), 16, 22, 24, 26, 28, 98, 234

George, Henry, writings of, 96; after 1887, 279; on the boycotters' sentences, 197; on Chinese immigrants, 24–25; on the Church's suppression of McGlynn, 247; on the dangers of concentrated wealth/power, 20; determination to overcome faults (journal entries), 16–18; on the difficulty of establishing a labor newspaper, 141; emerging reformers and radicals influenced by, 163; on the failure of the 1887 campaign, 265; for *Frank Leslie's Weekly*, 160–63 (see also *Social Problems*); ghostwriting for Hewitt, 96, 98, 212; "The Great Work of Reform," 28; on his mission to fight for social justice, 23–24, 42; on Ireland, 108–9; on land and land policy (*see* land, in George's thought); on Manhattan Island's land monopoly, 77; on McGlynn's support, 124; on the need for high wages, 18–20; New York described (1880), 69–70; on the pre-industrial system, 4–5; on progress and poverty, 44–45; on *Progress and Poverty*'s success, 65, 66, 97–98; on public acceptance of his work, 281; on railroads, 22, 26; revisionist view of 1886 campaign, 258–59; rhetorical style, 154–56, 159,

161; on the rise of service industries, 84; on running for mayor, 203, 204–5, 211, 225, 234–35 (*see also* George, Henry, 1886 mayoral campaign of); sea journal (1855–56), 10–11; social Darwinism condemned, 39; on the *Standard*, 245; on the ULP's purge of socialists, 262; on the universality of the land question, 112; "We, the workers of mankind" essay (1865), 18; on wealth inequity, xx. See also *Progress and Poverty*; *and specific topics and works*

George, James (cousin of Henry George), 13

George, Richard Samuel Henry (father of Henry George): career, 3, 7; Henry George's wife and children sent to live with, 22, 24, 28; jobs secured for son, 10, 11; *Progress and Poverty* sent to, 65

George, Richard (son of Henry George), 17, 22, 24, 26, 28, 98

George, Thomas (brother of Henry George), 65

German Americans, 119, 120, 235

German immigrants, 71–72

Gibbons, James, Bishop, 150

Gilded Age, The: A Tale of Today (Twain and Warner), 43

Goldman, Emma, 265

Goldman, Eric F., 275

Gompers, Samuel: and the AFL, 253; and the Cigar Makers International Union, 152; and the George campaign, 226; and the Land League, 227; on police brutality in the Tompkins Square protest, 93; practical unionism of, 119; and the State Workingmen's Association, 220, 253; on Tammany politics, 137–38; Tompkins Square incident a turning point for, 93–94

Gould, Jay, 132, 143, 171, 178, 185. *See also* railroads

Grace, William R., 72, 111